THEORY AND METHOD

SKILLS-BASED SOCIOLOGY

Series Editors: Tony Lawson and Tim Heaton

The *Skills-based Sociology* series is designed to cover all the key concepts, issues and debates in Sociology. The books take a critical look at contemporary developments in sociological knowledge as well as essential social theories. Each title examines a key topic area within sociology, offering relevant examples and student-focused pedagogical features to aid learning and develop essential study skills.

Published

THEORY AND METHOD (*second edition*)
Mel Churton and Anne Brown

RELIGION AND BELIEF
Joan Garrod and Marsha Jones

CULTURE AND IDENTITY
Warren Kidd

POLITICS AND POWER
Warren Kidd, Philippe Harari and Karen Legge

STRATIFICATION AND DIFFERENCE
Mark Kirby

CRIME AND DEVIANCE (*second edition*)
Tony Lawson and Tim Heaton

EDUCATION AND TRAINING (*second edition*)
Tony Lawson, Tim Heaton and Anne Brown

HEALTH AND ILLNESS
Michael Senior and Bruce Viveash

Forthcoming

THE MEDIA (*second edition*)
Marsha Jones, Emma Jones and Andy Jones

THE FAMILY (*second edition*)
Liz Steel, Warren Kidd and Anne Brown

Skills-based Sociology
Series Standing Order ISBN 0–333–69350–7
(*outside North America only*)

You can receive future titles in this series as they are published. To place a standing order please contact your bookseller or, in the case of difficulty, write to us at the address below with your name and address, the title of the series and the ISBN quoted above.

Customer Service Department, Macmillan Distribution Ltd, Houndmills, Basingstoke, Hampshire RG21 6XS, England

Theory and Method

Second Edition

Mel Churton

and

Anne Brown

First edition 1999
Second edition 2010

Published by
PALGRAVE MACMILLAN

Palgrave Macmillan in the UK is an imprint of Macmillan Publishers Limited, registered in England, company number 785998, of Houndmills, Basingstoke, Hampshire RG21 6XS.

Palgrave Macmillan in the US is a division of St Martin's Press LLC, 175 Fifth Avenue, New York, NY 10010.

Palgrave Macmillan is the global academic imprint of the above companies and has companies and representatives throughout the world.

Palgrave® and Macmillan® are registered trademarks in the United States, the United Kingdom, Europe and other countries.

ISBN 978–0–230–21781–2

This book is printed on paper suitable for recycling and made from fully managed and sustained forest sources. Logging, pulping and manufacturing processes are expected to conform to the environmental regulations of the country of origin.

A catalogue record for this book is available from the British Library.

A catalog record for this book is available from the Library of Congress.

10   9   8   7   6   5   4   3   2   1
19   18   17   16   15   14   13   12   11   10

Printed and bound in Great Britain by
CPI Antony Rowe, Chippenham and Eastbourne

To Phil Brown

Contents

Acknowledgements   x

1 **Introduction**   1
   The philosophy behind the book   1
   Content of the book   2
   What is society?   3
   What is theory?   4
   What is methodology?   5

2 **Traditional Theory**   7
   A society based on conflict   7
   A society based on consensus   34
   A society based on social action, interpretation and meaning   44
   A society based upon male domination: feminist theory   61

3 **Theoretical Debates**   84
   Introduction   84
   Modernism versus postmodernism – the status of evidence   85
   Structuralism versus social action   87
   Social action   96
   The evolutionary view versus here-and-now analysis   104
   Positivism versus antipositivism   110

4 **Contemporary Theory**   118
   Introduction   118
   The Contemporary Left   119
   Realism   123

The New Right 127

Postmodernism 132

Postfeminism 141

Critical race theory 151

Theories of sexuality and queer theory 152

Disability theory 156

5 **Contemporary Debates** **160**

Introduction 160

Poststructuralism 161

Structuration 165

Actor–network theory (ANT) 174

Modernity versus postmodernity 175

Globalization: one world or a society of states? 188

Sociology of society or sociology of self? 199

The risk society 204

6 **Research Concepts** **208**

Introduction 208

Key research concerns 209

Types of data 218

Triangulation or methodological pluralism 223

Selecting research participants 223

The nature of social facts 228

7 **Research Techniques** **236**

Introduction 236

The scientific method 237

Non-experimental methods: quantitative methods 244

Non-experimental methods: qualitative methods 253

Evaluation of quantitative versus qualitative methods 267

8 **Contemporary Trends in the Use of Research Techniques** **269**

Introduction 269

Quantitative and qualitative methods 270

Ethnographic research 281

Comparative and longitudinal research   288

Quantitative and qualitative methods – an evaluation   295

The forward march of less-known
     techniques   296

Visual methodologies as research techniques   300

The impact of information technology on sociological
     research   305

9   Choosing a Research Method   **322**

Introduction   322

Theoretical considerations   323

Practical considerations   329

10   Sociology and Science   **359**

Introduction   359

What is science?   360

The reality of science   365

Sociology as a science   370

The future of sociology and science   379

References   388

Index   403

Acknowledgements

Thanks to Phil Brown for his contributions to Chapters 3, 4, 5 and 10, and especially the material for the PASW exercises in Chapter 8. Also thanks to Tony Lawson for his support with editing the new material, Anna-Marie Reeves for her skilful general guidance, advice and support during the rewriting process, and Keith Povey for copy-editing.

The authors and the publishers would like to thank SPSS Inc. for giving kind permission to reproduce images from the PASW Statistics software (formerly SPSS Statistics). Every effort has been made to contact all the copyright-holders, but if any have been inadvertently omitted the publishers will be pleased to make the necessary arrangement at the earliest opportunity.

Chapter 1

Introduction

THE PHILOSOPHY BEHIND THE BOOK

The aim of this book is threefold. Firstly, we wish to encourage you to take an active part in your education. *Interpretation, application, analysis* and *evaluation* are the central skills that candidates must demonstrate in any sociology examination. These are also the central skills that any sociologist should demonstrate at all levels.

- *Interpretation* means you should be able to look at different types of text, such as tables or newspapers, and be able to communicate your understanding of them.
- *Application* is the ability to take sociological material and use it in relevant ways to answer the questions set.
- *Analysis* means being able to show you can dissect arguments and theories, accounts, evidence, as well as understand the debates about particular issues.
- *Evaluation* means being able to assess sociological debates and arguments by considering the evidence.

The best way of developing these skills is to practise them yourself. Therefore a series of exercises have been designed that are tied to the three skills, and if you carry them out you should be able to improve your performance in these areas. The skills each exercise is designed to develop are indicated by the following symbols: *I* for interpretation, *A* for application, *AN* for analysis and *E* for evaluation. It is also important that you understand the interconnections between the separate pieces of information in this book, so there are also link exercises for you to do. These will not only help you to perform skilfully, but will also increase your understanding of sociological theory and research methods.

The second aim of the book is to present you with sociological knowledge that is appropriate to and useful for your examination performance, as the ability to convey *knowledge k* and *understanding u* is another skill that every level of sociology examination includes. This book does not present knowledge you could glean easily from other textbooks as it would be pointless to try to cover ground that is more than adequately covered elsewhere. But it does attempt to revise familiar material by focusing on developments in sociology during the 1980s, 1990s and 2000s, so that you can apply up-to-date information in your examinations.

This book does not aim to tell you all there is all to know about sociology in this period, because to develop your sociological skills you should be finding out for yourself what has been happening in society and sociology during this time. It does, however, try to give an overview of the debates that have been going on and the sociologists who have been writing about theoretical perspectives and research methods. You will find that much of the material concerns the theories and ideas of the New Right and of the postmodernists, and how other sociologists have responded to these developments during this period.

A third aim is to help you develop the common assessment skills required to pass examinations successfully in sociology. A series of exam-type questions are included with associated tasks for you to do by yourself. Use these activities to supplement the work you do in class, lectures or seminars as you progress through your course and as a revision aid as you approach your assessment points.

The important thing to remember is that you will gain most from this book if you approach it in an active way and are prepared to apply the information and skills in your examinations and assessments. If you just read the text and miss out the exercises, you will be doing only half of what is necessary to pass.

CONTENT OF THE BOOK

Although this book is concerned with theory and method in sociology it is usually the theoretical understanding that challenges students the most. This is because it is often viewed as abstract and difficult to relate to the 'real world'. We would encourage you to develop the skill of theorizing rather than seeing theory as just something to learn. The key point about social theory is that it does tell us about the world around us and about our place within that world. So you should actively use and apply theory in your everyday life in the questions about society that you may have or in issues that emerge from your experience in the 'real world'. As Ian Craib so aptly put it:

> The power of theory is its ability to transform consciousness, to change people not necessarily by intellectual conviction but by enabling them to grasp their own world and their own experience in a radically new way and to become aware of ways of changing the world. If . . . theory is to do this, then it must be able to live inside everyday representations of the world, to take them as the starting point of its argument, and it must be able to transform those representations into an adequate understanding of the world. (Craib, 1984)

WHAT IS SOCIETY?

Before we begin to look at the importance of social theory, we should ask the question: 'What are we theorizing about?' Sociologists often take 'society' for granted, assuming that the object of their study is obvious. However, we should draw your attention to some features of society that are important when looking at social theory. Society consists of the social institutions and social relationships that we inhabit in a dense and intense way. However, these institutions and relationships are both concrete and abstract at the same time.

For example, consider the institution of the monarchy. Some people will have met the monarch of their country personally and some courtiers may have an ongoing relationship with the king or queen on a daily basis. Others will have only an abstract relationship with their monarch – that is, they are subjects of the monarch but have had no direct interaction with him or her. The relationship, though abstract, is nonetheless real in its effects – for example the taxes given by the subjects support the monarch in his or her duties.

The monarchy is also an institution and not just a person. While individual kings and queens come and go, the institution of the monarchy persists in the form of the functions it performs and its focus for identity for the subjects of the monarch. Note, however, that a monarchy is not necessarily a permanent feature of society – the institution can be overthrown and lose its role as a locus of loyalty. Thus, the institution of the monarchy exists as an abstract concept, fulfilling constitutional and emotional elements of society. It is the abstract nature of much of society and our experiences of it that leads to the need for social theory.

A second feature of society that is important for theorizing is that it is patterned. That is, society and our lives within it demonstrate regularities and routines that are open to theorizing by sociologists. These patterns vary from the simple and individual, such as the ebb and flow of activity between day and night, so that there is a more dense web of interactions during daylight hours. However, regularities also appear beyond the surface level of human activity. For example, it can be shown that educational attainment demonstrates enduring patterns, such that certain social groups (the working class and some ethnic minorities) persistently underperform in examinations. Sociological theory seeks to explain both the surface and the deep patterns of social behavior.

WHAT IS THEORY?

The idea of a theoretical sociology is drawn from the natural sciences, which acts as a model for many sociologists (see Chapter 10 for a full discussion of this issue). For purposes of introduction to theory, we are concerned with three aspects of this model. Theory is first defined as a *generalized* statement about a social phenomenon. What this means is that sociologists seek to go beyond the simple description of single events to a different level of analysis. Theoretical statements therefore cover a number of similar events and describe the similarities between them and why any differences might occur. To use our example of educational attainment, sociologists might look to the statistics of achievement over a number of years and produce theoretical statements about the persistence of group differences and also why the differences might change over time.

This leads to a second feature of theory that is important, namely that theory seeks to *explain* social phenomena, producing supported reasons why such differences exist and why changes might be occurring. The purpose of explaining social phenomena is to be able to predict future patterns and influence social policies that might effect beneficial changes to the patterns. In terms of educational underachievement, if we know why some groups perform less well, then we might be able to produce circumstances in which they are supported to perform better. It is worth noting at this point that this is not necessarily an easy thing to do, and this is because society differs from natural circumstances in two important respects. First, human beings have free will and change their behaviour according to their preferences, ideologies or even whims. Second, societies do not remain static, but change over time and in unpredictable ways, so that establishing universal laws that would hold true for all societies and for all time is impossible.

A third aspect of theory is that theoretical statements should be able to be checked by others who are not responsible for developing them. This is because sociologists, as human beings, are affected by their own presuppositions and biases. In developing their theories, sociologists exhibit systematic ways of thinking that constitute perspectives, which inform and shape their theoretical work. Therefore it is important that the evidence that sociologists use to support their theoretical statements can be checked independently, and this is where methodology comes into play.

WHAT IS METHODOLOGY?

At its simplest, methodology is the strategies that sociologists develop to gather evidence from the real world about specific social phenomena. Methodology is more than just choosing a particular tool, such as a questionnaire, to collect information about something. It also involves observing a particular social issue, asking questions about it, developing researchable ideas about it and then choosing a particular tool or tools to investigate it. There are a huge range of particular methods that sociologists can use and these are constantly being refined and new ones added, as, for example, information technology improves (see later chapters for specific methods). Once the data has been gathered it has to be analysed and applied to hypotheses developed in an earlier stage of research to support the generation of theoretical statements.

The relationship between theoretical positions and choice of particular methods has been much discussed and this will be covered in Chapter 9. At this point it is worth noting that there is often a disjunction between sociologists who are concerned primarily with developing grand theories of society and those who are more interested in specific issues and who empirically investigate their chosen area. While the former refer to evidence collected by others in formulating their theories and the latter are influenced by theoretical positions in designing their empirical studies, it is comparatively rare that a sociologist covers both ends of the spectrum. Bearing these aspects in mind, we will now detail how these will be covered in the rest of the book.

The subject content is broken down into nine areas. Chapter 2 considers the main theoretical perspectives associated with traditional sociology. Chapter 3 looks at traditional theoretical debates. Chapter 4 moves on to consider recent developments in sociology, focusing on contemporary theoretical debates. Chapter 5 addresses contemporary debates that have captured the sociological imagination. Key research concepts are explored in Chapter 6, while

Chapter 2

Traditional Theory

By the end of this chapter you should be able to:

- identify the four main interpretations of society offered by traditional theories:

  1. society based on conflict
  2. society based on consensus
  3. society based on social action; interpretation and meaning
  4. society based upon male domination: feminist theory

- recognize the main writers associated with each approach and understand the impact they have had on sociological thinking
- recognize the basic assumptions of each approach
- provide examples of sociological research to demonstrate the applications of each approach
- identify the relative merits and criticisms of each approach and evaluate the contribution each has made

A SOCIETY BASED ON CONFLICT

Theories of society which are based on the notion of conflict take as their starting-point the divisions and differences which exist between groups of people in society. There is a belief that power relations lead to the creation of a particular structure of society which serves the interests of dominant groups against the interests of subordinate groups which can then lead to conflict between them. Differences in power could be between men and women, the old and young, different ethnic groups and, in the case of Marxist and neo-Marxists, social class. However, there can also be complex interplay between these categories which is dynamic and changing as society continues to evolve.

Marxism

Marxism evolved from the work of Karl Marx (1818–83), some of which was in collaboration with Friedrich Engels. Despite the fact that his name is widely associated with the development of sociology, Marx's work has been controversial and has had a mixed reception. In the East, Marxism was regarded as highly significant whereas in the West its impact was less apparent until relatively recently.

Some anti-Marxism can be attributed to a lack of understanding of Marx's work. For example, the most commonly cited critiques of Marx focus on:

- his prediction of a revolution that has yet to occur;
- his overemphasis on social structure, particularly the structures of capitalist society, at the expense of social relationships.

Such criticisms do little justice to the complexity of Marxist theory and display a limited perception of Marx's contribution to an understanding of social life.

Central to Marx's work (1867/1967) was the concept of 'dialectics', defined as the art of discussing, or that branch of logic which teaches the rules and modes of reasoning. Marx attempted a dialectical analysis of the material world – that is, capitalism. He rejected the search for simple cause-and-effect relationships between parts of the social world, in favour of analysis of complex, interdependent, reciprocal social relationships. He also rejected the popular assumption of his time that social values are separable from social facts.

Dialectics influenced the way in which Marx viewed the social world. Rather than seeing its components as distinct and separate, he saw them as interrelated and defined by social relationships between individuals and groups of people and organizations. Thus analysis should focus both on these interconnections and on the units in isolation and their place within the overall social structure.

Marx's (1852/1970) historical analysis of society was characterized by dialectical thinking. In seeking to understand the contemporary world, he looked to the past and the future. This led him to explore both the roots of capitalism and to speculate about the future of society. Marx viewed people as being both shaped by and having the potential to shape their own destiny. The impact of the past on people is indisputable, but Marx believed that people can have a bearing on the future by making changes. People are able to develop an understanding of social change by exploring the impact of the past on contemporary society. This provides useful information to help them to understand how their actions may affect their future. Marx did however recognize that external constraints exist to limit individuals' recognition of the role they can play in shaping their destiny and the future of the social world.

The basic assumptions of Marxism

A point often overlooked by critics is that Marx sought to understand both the natural state of individuals and the social structure. In his early work (Marx, 1845/1956) his main interest was to explore humanity, but in his later work (1867/1967) this was overshadowed by his desire to provide a scientific analysis of capitalist society. However he did not lose sight of the individual, rather he intended his critique of the inherent contradictions of capitalism to provide the downtrodden and disadvantaged with the necessary inspiration and insight to engage in revolutionary change.

Individual potential

Marx, with Engels (1845/1956), was interested in what he saw as the potential of humanity. He viewed people as inherently creative, but their creativity as having been suppressed by the harsh conditions of pre-capitalism, when people's efforts were bound up in the production and consumption of goods for their own survival.

For Marx and Engels, creativity would not come to fruition under capitalism because people's existence is defined by mass production. People have little control over the products of their labour, nor over their relationships with other workers. Hence their potential for creativity is stunted.

Marx and Engels (1845/1956) were also interested in consciousness because this differentiates humans from animals. Consciousness is an internal mental process that gives people the capacity for creative intelligence and abstract thinking. Marx and Engels regarded consciousness as crucial to the expression of human potential – for only truly conscious individuals will be able to free themselves from the constraints of capitalism.

Marx (1857–1858/1964) presented a historical analysis of the development of human potential, arguing that individuals have not yet reached creative fulfilment. In primitive society, people's capacity to be creative was stunted by lack of resources and lack of opportunity: 'In the lowest stages of production...few human needs have yet been produced and thus few are to be satisfied' (Marx, 1857-8/1974, p. 398).

In capitalist society, while the potential exists for appropriation, human creativity is stifled by mass production and consumption. Productivity is characterized by fragmentation and specialization, and workers are alienated (distanced/detached) from the products of their labour and the labour process. Since labour is the defining identity of capitalist workers, they also become alienated from themselves.

Marx (1857-8/1964) predicted that it will take the demise of capitalism for humanity to fulfil its potential. Then people will be able to apply the technological and organizational knowledge of capitalism in innovative and creative ways and ultimately reach the pinnacle of their potential.

The structure of society

Marx's early works explore the impact that capitalism has upon man, while his later works are very much preoccupied with the structures of capitalist society. Marx's work can be broadly divided into separate discussions of the economy, relationships and culture, and each will be briefly discussed in turn.

The economy

Marx's (1867/1967) consideration of the capitalist economy focuses largely on commodities. He argued that in pre-capitalist society commodities were simply objects produced by people in order to survive. Hence they had a 'use value' only. By this he meant that the objects were products of human labour and could not achieve an independent existence because they were used only by their producer (Ritzer, 2008). However in capitalist society commodities are not produced to be used directly by the producer. Instead they are produced in order to be exchanged on the open market for money. Thus they have acquired 'exchange value' and their status in society has become more complex. Marx suggested that objects are initially consumed for their utility, but as capitalism takes hold the objects themselves are coveted. This causes them to become independent phenomena beyond the control of those who produce them. Marx largely attributed this to the process of 'fetishism', whereby those who produce the objects reject the idea that it is their labour that gives them value and instead come to believe that value arises from the natural properties of the things themselves, or that the market gives them value. The fetishism of commodities forces up their market value until workers become alienated from the products of their labour – that is, they have insufficient resources to buy them. This idea has been developed by contemporary writers and is explored further in Chapter 4 (see pages **107–9**, postmodernism and popular culture).

For Marx (1867/1967) the exchange of commodities creates capital (revenue) to sustain the capitalist economy. By manipulating the production process so as to ensure that the demand for goods always outstrips the supply, capitalists perpetuate commodity fetishism and maintain the high market value of goods. The price of goods is far higher than the cost of the raw materials and labour power. Thus a surplus of capital is generated – that is, profit. To ensure the survival of capitalism, profit is reinvested to increase productivity and further reduce production costs. This generates surplus capital, which can be reinvested to strengthen capital's control over the production process. In this way, capital also takes on an independent existence as an exploitative structure, oppressing the workers who are responsible for its creation.

Marx's term for the process whereby aspects of capitalism (for example, capital, commodities, social relationships) take on an independent existence is 'reification'. He regarded this as crucial to capitalism, as it is the process whereby workers cease to recognize their influence over aspects of the social system. Instead they believe that such aspects are inevitable and central features of the capitalist system that cannot be altered.

For Marx, capitalist economies would always be subject to periods of boom and recession. The periods of economic boom would be characterized by high rates of employment, business confidence, profitability, rising standards of living. Periods of economic recession would be characterized by crises in profitability, poor business confidence, high rates of unemployment, business bankruptcy and declining standards of living. The essential contradiction of capitalism is between the drive to increase profits and accumulate capital on the part of the capitalist class – the owners of business – and those who work for the bourgeoisie, the proletariat, who demand higher living standards through increased wages, salaries and benefits. Periods of 'bust' are a delayed reaction to this essential contradiction of the system. Hence economic recessions are crises of profitability, not of confidence as they are often portrayed. The Great Depression of the 1930s and the so-called 'credit crunch' of 2008 could be described as examples of economic instability or capitalism going 'bust' in Marxist terms.

Hence, these recurrent financial crises are systemic. In 2008 the economic recession can be explained in Marxist terms as follows:

The expansion of capital, gross domestic product and the crisis of 2008

As discussed above, the history of capitalism is a history of the self-expansion of capital. This is because capital must grow in size progressively in order for profits to be made. This is the point of the production cycle – to make a profit at the end. A measure of the expansion of capital across the economy is the gross domestic product (GDP). As Marx indicated, periodically there is a profits crisis under capitalism that results in downward pressure on incomes. Prior to the 2008 crisis, however capital *continued to expand*, on average at a rate of 2.1 per cent during 2006 and 2007. Yet during these two years the increase in average incomes declined from 2.1 per cent in the period 1997 to 2005 to just 0.8 per cent, with average earnings increasing less than 0.5 per cent. So, unusually, the conditions for recession were evident yet at the same time there was a continued growth of capital.

Marx argued that a profits crisis experienced by capitalists leads to downward pressure on the incomes of workers, which results in falling demand, a decline in production (capitalists will not produce goods they cannot sell) and a downturn in the whole economy. Jobs are lost, GDP falls and recession occurs. Incomes fell from 2006, as we have seen, yet the recession did not occur until 2008. Why was this? Marxists would argue that financial institutions fuelled a credit boom. This allowed consumer demand to be maintained – as income declined, so credit expanded to fill the gap. People could borrow money to buy goods, housing and so on. In the UK total personal debt at the end of October 2007 stood at £1.391 billion; by the end of December 2007 it was increasing by £1 million every four minutes (www.creditaction.org.uk/dec.html). For this reason, capital continued to expand. However the situation eventually became unsustainable. As Marx comments, 'In a system of production where the continuity of the reproduction process rests upon credit, a crisis must obviously occur' (Marx, 1894/1974, p.190).

The recession of 2008 arose in the US sub-prime market where people simply could not afford to pay their mortgages. Banks found themselves with billions of pounds' and/or dollars' worth of bad debts. The supply of credit dried up. As a result businesses that relied upon the banking system rapidly got into difficulties as consumer demand weakened. The credit bubble burst and the recession (delayed for two or three years) came about. Hence according to Marx the financial crisis occurred because of the inherent nature of the capitalist system itself.

Relationships

According to Marx (1867/1967), in capitalist society people not only produce economic objects (commodities) but also social relationships. It is these social relationships that affirm the social structures of capitalist society. Two sets of relationships are identified as important. The first concerns workers' relationships with their fellow workers, the second concerns workers' relationships with capitalists.

As discussed earlier, the production process is seen as beyond the control of individual workers in capitalist society. Instead of being producers of the goods they need to survive, workers are forced to sell their labour power, their energies, to capitalists. Their workplace is characterized by automation and specialization. Instead of workers engaging in communal activities to produce goods, they engage in repetitive limited tasks that form only a small part of the production process. Hence they are 'alienated' from their fellow workers because they have little need to communicate or cooperate with others. They are also alienated from their work because they are denied the opportunity to engage in all aspects of the productive process and instead are responsible for a fragmented and meaningless aspect of production.

Marx (1867/1967) termed this fragmentation of the productive process the 'division of labour'. He identified a number of negative effects of this. First, the individual becomes artificially separated from the community as a whole. People become inward-looking and lose sight of the interests of the whole community. Second, work becomes less fulfilling because human potential is stunted. Workers seek enjoyment outside work and consumption becomes a means to escape from the dehumanizing work of capitalism. Finally, workers lose control of both the objects of their labour and the market in which the objects are sold. Their power is diminished and they lose sight of their role in perpetuating capitalism.

Second, Marx (1859/1967) conceptualized the relationship between the workers and the capitalists in terms of social class. Marx gave limited consideration to social class as a concept, but did make it clear that he viewed social classes as structures that are external to and coercive of people. Marx identified two primary social classes in capitalist society: the bourgeoisie (those who own the means of production) and the proletariat (those who sell their labour power). The relationship between the two groups is an exploitative one. The bourgeoisie control the production process and the proletariat exchange their productive rights for wages. By carefully controlling the productive process to keep costs low and profits high, the bourgeoisie are able to exploit the proletariat. The proletariat are unable to withdraw their labour because they depend on the capitalist wage to support their families in a consumer society where goods are exchanged for capital. Hence, the interests of the two groups are always opposed – the bourgeoisie have a vested interest in capitalism and the production of profit which leads to the accumulation of wealth, while the proletariat who exchange their productive rights for wages have an interest in the fight for higher wages to improve their living standards. At some point the two worlds collide into a crisis of profitability whereby the economy goes into recession.

Marx (1932/1964) did not see capitalism as continuing indefinitely. Instead he believed that the contradictions within the capitalist system would eventually lead to its destruction. Marx predicted that as capitalism took hold, the number of workers exploited and the degree of exploitation would increase. The escalation in exploitation would generate resistance in the proletariat, who would become aware of their common experience of oppression. They would join together, united by the desire to overthrow their bourgeois oppressors and rise up in 'final' revolution. Capitalism would be replaced by a communist society where all workers would be equal and human potential could be realized.

Culture

Although Marx's interest was primarily in the economic structure of capitalism, he gave some attention to culture because it provided some insight into why capitalism was proving successful. Marx looked at culture at the individual and structural levels, and linked the two by suggesting how they could influence each other. When considering the individual, Marx (1857–8/1964) wrote about class consciousness and false consciousness. Consciousness is defined as 'the totality of mental states and processes (perception, feelings, thoughts), mind at its widest sense, awareness'. Marx saw consciousness as pivotal to the capitalist structure.

Item A

A Marxist approach to understanding US foreign policy, 9/11 and the 'War on Terror'

According to writers such a David Harvey (2005) the wars in Iraq and Afghanistan are best understood in terms of part of a longer-term strategy by the USA to create and maintain its position of power on the world stage. Economic and military superiority is dependent upon making sure there is a reliable source of oil most of which lies in the Middle East. Furthermore the American domestic economy is heavily dependent upon the consumption of oil. The attack by al-Qaeda on the twin towers of the World Trade Center in New York on 9 September 2001 could be seen as a justification for the increased influence of the USA in Iraq and beyond under the guise of a 'war on terror'. This also deflects the attention of the public away from economic and social problems being experienced in the US economy such as unemployment, debt, corporate scandals and increasing inequality between rich and poor (see Exercise 2.1).

According to Jason Burke (2004), a journalist working in the Middle East, al-Qaeda see the USA as an imperialist power which ruthlessly pursues its own interests in the world, often through the use of force, spreading anti-Islamic views and creating pro-Western culture and values. This is also part of the role of US transnational corporations such as McDonald's and Coca-Cola. Terrorism is seen to be a legitimate military weapon to use to resist American power and imperialism.

(Adapted from Karl Thompson, 'Radical Theory and 9/11', *Sociology Review* 16(3), 2007)

Exercise 2.1

(A) 1. According to Harvey what is the longer-term economic strategy of the USA?
(An) 2. How might the USA – that is, government, business and media – be creating a 'false consciousness' in the people of the USA?
(E) 3. Explain how the behaviour of the USA could be used to understand the beliefs of al-Qaeda.
(A) 4. Define what is meant by 'anti-Islamic views' and 'pro-Western culture and
(E)   values'.

Structure and ideology

At the structural level, Marx considered the importance of the cultural super-structure and 'ideological forms', that is – the law, politics, religion, art, philosophy and so on: the sources of thinking and reasoning, and values and beliefs in society. Ideology forms an important part of Marx's explanations of why such a revolution is yet to occur, in that capitalism to some extent creates ways of thinking that favour the maintenance of the system. Lefebvre (1968) defines an ideology as an integrated system of ideas that is external to and coercive of people. In Marx's analysis (1857–8/1964), the dominant ideology in capitalist society is based on the ideas of the ruling class. These ideas are inherent in the legal, political and religious systems of society and serve to affirm and legitimate bourgeois power. The consciousness of all members of society is infused with ruling-class ideology, which proclaims the essential rightness, normality and inevitability of the *status quo*.

Perhaps the most interesting aspect of the cultural superstructure for Marx was the political structure. He devoted much effort to criticizing what he termed 'bourgeois democracy', rejecting the values of political pluralism in favour of decentralized political organization. For Marx, the ultimate system of political government would be direct democracy, facilitated through workers' councils, which would make political decisions that would be enacted without being processed by any other organization or form of government. As Mouzelis (1992) notes, Marx was reluctant to recognize the potential of Western democracy and regarded it as yet another form of bourgeois oppression.

Marx (1867/1967) presented an economic analysis of politics, regarding party as inextricably linked to economic power. Politics mirrors the inequalities of capitalist society and democracy simply creates the illusion of political representation.

Item B

Marx and Democracy

Marx believed that economic power was the most important facet of power in any society and that as long as there was economic inequality, there could be no political equality. In this sense, he did not believe there could be a real democracy until a level economic playing field was established. Why then did political democracy come into being? Parliamentary representation evolved in Marx's view as one of the many ways in which the bourgeoisie attempted to control the proletariat. While conceding formal democracy, their grip on economic power ensured that the bourgeoisie could manipulate politics and society to suit their interests. For example, economic power ensured that the mass media were under the control of the agents of the bourgeoisie and could present a view of the world that coincided with their interests. This was achieved largely by removing controversial economic ideas from the public arena. Nor did the existence of competing political parties convince him of the value of democracy. Rather they were organized elites (oligarchies) who inevitably betrayed the interests of the people they were supposed to be representing. This led the mass of the population towards political apathy, as they were frustrated by their leaders' inability to change things for the better. Marx therefore looked not to the widening of parliamentary structures in a communist society but to a withering away of the state itself as a direct democracy was established.

Exercise 2.2

This exercise will enable you to explore Marx's views of politics in more detail. Read Item B and answer the following questions.

1. According to Item B, what is a democracy?

2. What is the name of the group of people who own the means of production?

3. How does control of the media benefit capitalists?

4. What is meant by 'political apathy'?

5. How do you think that political apathy might benefit the dominant group in society?

6. What is an oligarchy?

7. Why does the existence of oligarchies pose a threat to democracy?

8. What do you think Marx meant when he referred to the withering away of the state?

9. To what extent do you agree with Marx's view that political pluralism does not benefit the working class? Justify your answer.

Marxism – an evaluation

Strengths

1. Marx drew attention to the plight of the disadvantaged in capitalist society and demonstrated how various aspects of the social structure function to perpetuate large-scale social inequality.

2. In providing a critique of capitalism, Marx demonstrated that it is neither inevitable nor indestructible. In doing so he challenged the widely held assumption that capitalism has an independent existence and therefore he demystified the power of the capitalist.

3. Marx reaffirmed that it is the labour of the worker that sustains capitalism and without it capitalism cannot survive. He suggested that worker unity and a common desire to overthrow the bourgeoisie and halt oppression can be a powerful force for social change. This gives workers the knowledge and means by which to liberate themselves.

4. Marx's concern with human emancipation is worthy of credit. Prior to his work, sociologists had been largely interested in developing an understanding of the *status quo* rather than engaging in critical analysis motivated by a desire to improve the lot of individual members of society. Little attention had been given to issues such as human potential and creativity.

5. In adopting a dialectical approach, Marx provided an alternative to previous theories that had failed to recognize the subtle relationships between aspects of the social world and the way in which interconnections influence that world. He demonstrated how social relationships can be as powerful as social structures.

6. Marx generated a number of concepts (for example, the free market economy, commodity fetishism, reification, ideology, alienation) that captured the imagination of later sociologists, providing them with new ways to interpret and explore the world. Many of these concepts are still of interest and in use today.

Limitations

1. Perhaps the most common criticism levelled at Marx is that he predicted a revolution, but this has yet to occur. Some regard this as sufficient grounds for entirely dismissing his contribution to sociology. Societies that did adopt and implement broadly Marxist principles to run their economies and infrastructures such as the former Soviet Union, Yugoslavia, Hungary, the Czech Republic, East Germany were regarded as authoritarian and repressive. These countries eventually adopted a pro-capitalist stance and became subdivided along quasi-ethnic/religious lines, often after military conflict which still continues today. China, Cuba and North Korea are three remaining overtly Marxist-based societies.

2. Linked to the above, some have argued that Marx underestimated the flexibility of capitalism – that is, that the bourgeoisie can make concessions to the proletariat – for example, offering higher wages and voting rights, allowing the private ownership of commodities/property and so on – without relinquishing their power.

3. Marx is also criticized for being too radical. His revolutionary leanings have led conservative and liberal thinkers to depict him as 'a blood-crazed fanatic' (Ritzer, 2008). Much of the 'revolutionary' fervour was written in political pamphlets of his day for propaganda purposes. A full and scholarly account of the development of the revolution was never contained in his academic work such as *Das Kapital*.

4. Another common criticism of Marx is that he was ideologically biased. In particular, critics suggest that Marx placed too much emphasis on the economy at the expense of other influential aspects of the social structure. Further criticism is directed at Marx's political stance. It has been argued that his enthusiasm for political decentralization led him to dismiss the value of political pluralism in protecting individual rights (Mouzelis, 1992).

5. Marxist theory has also been criticized in the light of the collapse of socialist and communist societies, which have been replaced by capitalist-orientated economies. Communism was Marx's utopia, providing the

ultimate conditions for the fulfilment of human potential and creativity. It would emerge from the contradictions of capitalism and provide a stable social structure based on mutual cooperation and consent. Marxist theory cannot explain the collapse of communism and return to capitalism because it is something that Marx never envisaged.

Neo-Marxism

A number of writers have sought to build upon Marx's theory. Those who have worked within the guidelines set down by his original works are termed neo-Marxists. Those who have gone beyond the traditional boundaries of Marxian theory are termed Post-Marxists. The work of neo-Marxists will be discussed in this section. Neo-Marxists have sought to develop Marxist theory in the light of increasing criticism of economic determinism. The discussion here will focus on the work of one neo-Marxist, Antonio Gramsci, to demonstrate the scope of neo-Marxist analysis.

Gramsci (1891–1937), perhaps the most influential writer in the neo-Marxist tradition, rejected the overarching role of the economy in bringing about a communist revolution. For Gramsci (1917/1977), while the effect of the economy cannot be denied, the economic inequalities of capitalism alone are not sufficient to generate class consciousness among the proletariat. The proletariat do not have the capacity to generate revolutionary ideas from within; instead revolutionary ideology will be generated by revolutionary intellectuals and put into practice by the proletariat.

Gramsci saw collective ideas rather than social structures such as the economy as the key to understanding social life and social change. He sought to analyse the source of ideas in society, giving particular attention to the source of dominant ideas and how such ideas are transmitted to the masses. For Gramsci, the key to bourgeois domination is the control of ideas. Thus for a revolution to be successful, the proletariat will not only need to seize control of the means of production but also provide moral and cultural leadership.

Central to Gramsci's (1932/1995) analysis is the concept of 'hegemony', which he defined as 'moral and philosophical leadership which manages to win the active consent of those over whom it rules – leadership designed to create a popular, collective will' (Slattery, 1991). The consent of the governed is achieved simply by leading them to believe that the ruling class are the most suitable group to wield power in society.

For Gramsci, the mass media are an important tool for achieving ideological control of the masses. They can be used to present a particular world view that is assimilated into the collective consciousness of the masses and becomes their view. The following exercise will enable you to explore how the media can be used to shape people's ideas about social events and how this may be used to the advantage of powerful groups in society at the expense of the powerless.

Item C

News Production: The Hegemonic Model

Hegemonic theorists admit that the media in Britain are not, as a rule, directly commanded and organized by the state, neither do they directly speak for the ruling class. The reason for the bias in the media lies in the media professionals themselves. Media personnel are middle-class, affluent people (usually men) who tend to take a 'reasonable', consensus-orientated view on most issues . . .

Hegemonic theorists argue that those involved in the media unconsciously encode the dominant ideology when they create output for the media. This process involves selecting codes which put suitable meanings into events and stories. The codes embody 'natural' explanations which most members of society would accept (that is, which appear naturally to embody the 'rationality' of a particular society). This process of encoding the dominant ideology, for giving weight to the views of the wealthy and powerful, is sometimes masked by professional values (news values, news sense, lively presentation, exciting pictures, good stories, hot news, good jokes). However, these values themselves incorporate the dominant ideology.

An example of this is the way in which policing is portrayed in the media as a highly successful activity. From the forensic specialists of *Crime Scene Investigation* to *A Touch of Frost* and *Inspector Morse*, fictional police officers solve their cases. In the news, too, cases where serious crimes are detected are given more air time and coverage. However, Reiner (2000) suggests that police work is not a particularly effective form of crime control. Perhaps the police are contributing to the maintenance of order in urban industrial society and their portrayal in the media as 'mythical' helps to maintain the dominant ideology that we are all protected by the police.

(Adapted from P. Trowler, *Sociology in Focus: Investigating the Media.* London: Collins, 1991; Sean O'Sullivan, 'Cops on the Box: The Media and Policing', *Sociology Review* 16(1), 2006)

Exercise 2.3

Item C outlines how Gramsci's concept of hegemony can be applied to the process of news production and the portrayal of the police. Read the text carefully and answer the following questions.

1. According to Item C, how do the media homogenize (that is, make similar) people's views?
2. What role do the media Establishment play in reinforcing the *status quo?*
3. To what extent do you agree with the hegemonic view that the responsibility for media bias lies with media professionals themselves?
4. Marx would have disagreed with the view that the media *unconsciously* encode the dominant ideology when they create output for the media. How?
5. According to Item C, what factors influence the way a story/event is treated, particularly in relation to the police?
6. To what extent do you agree that individuals' views are shaped by the way in which the news is presented to them?

Item D

TWO WORLDS COLLIDE

An ordinary couple, a carload of hippies and a Sunday drive that ended in tragedy

Special report by John Hamshire

THE driver responsible for an horrific car crash in which five people died was a 14-year-old hippy girl who may have been high on drugs, police revealed yesterday.

Four New Age travellers, including the girl, Kierra Loughlin, were killed in the three-car pile-up, along with a married businessman.

Police examining the wreckage of the hippies' untaxed and uninsured Renault Fuego discovered a 'substantial' quantity of cannabis inside.

A four-year-old boy, Leroy Graham, the only survivor from the hippies' car, was fighting for his life last night. The businessman who died was 39-year-old Glen Carroll. His wife Susan, a secretary who was also 39, was seriously injured.

Police believe Kierra, who celebrated her birthday last week, could have been smoking cannabis when she pulled out in front of Mr Carroll's Rover 216 saloon at a notorious crossroads on the A39 at Green Ore, Somerset, on Mother's Day.

A third car, a Peugeot 605, smashed into the wreckage but the male driver escaped injury.

Kierra died instantly, together with Michaela Storer, 15, and Chandra Thomas, 16, and Jason McLoughlin, 25-year-old father of little Leroy.

They lived with around 80 others in a filthy commune of ramshackle caravans and broken-down lorries near Weston-super-Mare.

Leroy, who suffered serious spinal injuries, was in a serious condition last night in the intensive care unit of Bristol Children's Hospital.

Mrs Carroll was in the city's Royal Infirmary with leg and neck injuries.

Her condition, though serious, was not thought to be life-threatening.

Her distraught father Mr John Norgrove, 74, who lived with the couple at Croscombe, near Wells, said last night: 'How can a 14-year-old girl come to be driving a car on a busy road? It just doesn't make sense. Some young people have no regard for the law or what is right or wrong. What a terrible waste of life.'

Below, the Daily Mail looks at the very different people who fate brought together during that Sunday drive. . .

(*Source*: John Hamshire, 'Two worlds collide', *Daily Mail* 16 March 1994.)

Exercise 2.4

The previous exercise enabled you to familiarize yourself with the way that Gramsci's concept of hegemony can be applied to the mass media. This exercise will enable you to apply Gramsci's ideas yourself by analysing a newspaper article.

1. Read Item D, which reports a fatal road accident on Mother's Day.
2. Discuss the following questions as a small group of students:

    (a) How might the layout of the article affect its impact?
    (b) How might the description of the people in the article influence the reader's impression of the accident?
    (c) What use was made of language/discourse in the article?
    (d) Why was this story considered newsworthy?

3. Refer to the ideas presented in Exercise 2.3 and answer the following questions:

    (a) To what extent does the article reflect ideas embodied in the hegemonic model?
    (b) What other explanations could be offered for the way in which the story was reported?

Neo-Marxism – an evaluation

Strengths

1. Gramsci's focus on hegemony provides an alternative to the economic determinism of traditional Marxism. Economic Marxists tend to emphasize the economic and coercive aspects of state determinism. In contrast Gramsci suggests that domination stems from acceptance of the ideology that perpetuates ruling-class power.
2. Gramsci provides an alternative route to revolution – implying that seizing control of the means of production is not enough. Revolutionaries will only achieve total domination if they gain cultural leadership over the rest of society.
3. Gramsci pinpoints the significant role of education in revolution. In his view, class consciousness will not simply emerge as workers become aware of their common experience of oppression. Instead, intellectual enlightenment is vital to provide momentum to revolutionary action. Gramsci highlights that the communist party has a vital role to play here – drawing public attention to those who can provide the inspiration for revolutionary change.
4. Perhaps Gramsci more aptly demonstrates the value of dialectical analysis than Marx. His meshing of cultural awareness, moral and philosophical leadership and political and economic control provide a more sophisticated and probable analysis of state and societal control than Marx's more one-dimensional material analysis.
5. Gramsci's acknowledgement that complete ideological dominance is rare and that society is characterized by interest groups with conflicting philosophies seeking ideological dominance can be more easily aligned with Western democracy than the totalitarian picture painted by Marx. In Gramsci's work there is acknowledgement not just of the sources of power of the dominant group, but also the existence and scope of potential successors.

Limitations

1. Gramsci's more humane, open and gradualistic analysis of socialist strategy has been subject to severe criticism by more orthodox Marxists for being too liberal and for denying the historical importance of

the laws of historical materialism – the process whereby social change happened through the clash between material interests in society (Slattery, 1991).

2. Communist parties have been critical of Gramsci's assertion that the proletariat are dependent upon education to become revolutionary. This denies their power to bring about change in their own right.

3. The limited impact of the communist parties in the West could be seen as eroding the power of Gramsci's analysis. He speculated that radical intellectuals would become increasingly involved with the working classes to spread revolutionary fervour. If anything the working class have become more conservative and accepting of the *status quo*, and more resistant to communist politics. Far from appealing to the masses in society, the communist parties and their direct successors today appear to attract only minority groups (for example, students, women, blacks) who are marginalized from the working class and thus could be construed as non-proletarian.

Critical theory

Critical theory is associated with the work of the Frankfurt School, a group of German neo-Marxists who sought to address what they perceived to be the weakness of Marxism: its tendency towards economic determinism. Theodor Adorno, Max Horkheimer and Herbert Marcuse argued for a more sophisticated interpretation of the social structure, with emphasis on aspects of society that could contribute to 'domination' – that is, the way the system dominates, forces and blinkers people so as to ensure the reproduction of the prevailing social and economic situation.

Critical theorists provide a critique of modern society. Central to this is the analysis of culture and its role in perpetuating the masses. Marcuse (1964) devotes much of his writing to what he terms 'one-dimensional culture', which he sees as pervasive in contemporary society (see Exercise 2.5 to develop your understanding of this idea). He identifies a powerful role for the culture industry in creating and disseminating a false culture to stupefy the masses and create false needs. This serves to prevent thoughts of revolutionary acts against dominant groups. By spreading a pre-packaged set of ideas, the culture industry is able to subjugate the masses. People become obsessed with trivia and gossip, fashion and fad, and wish to keep abreast of popular culture rather than develop revolutionary insight into their social circumstances and routes to liberation.

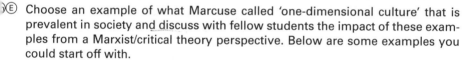

Exercise 2.5

Choose an example of what Marcuse called 'one-dimensional culture' that is prevalent in society and discuss with fellow students the impact of these examples from a Marxist/critical theory perspective. Below are some examples you could start off with.

- Reality TV shows such as Big Brother.
- The fixation with 'designer' labels in clothing and footwear.
- The cult of celebrity – the desire to be famous for its own sake.

Critical theorists consider that modern society is irrational, oppressive and takes away the basic features of human life, particularly the ability to transform the environment and make collective rational choices about life. However, modern society is also characterized by rationalization – a process whereby knowledge and objects become means to ends rather than ends in themselves. This is associated with the emergence of technocratic thinking, which emphasizes domination at the expense of emancipation.

The proponents of the Frankfurt School call the rationalized, bureaucratized structures that control modern culture the 'culture industry'. The culture industry is seen as responsible for producing a phoney culture that dupes and pacifies the masses. If those in the Frankfurt School are right, it should be possible to find evidence that the media draw attention to trivia, presenting it as important and diverting attention away from 'real' issues that might lead the masses to be critical of the current social system and structures. The following exercise is designed to help you assess how well these ideas stand up to investigation.

Exercise 2.6

As a class, collect newspapers for one week. Try to gather together a broad range: tabloids, broadsheets; dailies, weeklies.

1. In small groups, perform a rough content analysis using the questions below as a guide. Formulate a content analysis grid which helps you count and code the number of examples you are looking at. A content analysis grid is a tick chart or tally chart that has important characteristics down the first column (football, celebrity item, soap opera and so on) and the names of the newspapers spread along the top row. By indicating in some way in each cell how much of a newspaper is devoted to each type of item (in column inches

for example) you can carry out a semiological analysis of the signs/symbols being displayed.

NB Semiology means to study the signs or signifiers in all forms of communication. A signifier is the visible, face-value image, word or picture. What is signified by the signifier, what is under the surface, is based on the context within which the signifier exists. For example an advertisement for a car is the superficial, visible message but under the surface is the selling of a life-style, set of values and attitudes associated with the ownership of a particular car (see Chapter 8). A semiological analysis of a celebrity's photo for example would look at what the image suggested about income, lifestyle, attitudes towards politics and so on.

(a) Look for items that relate to mass culture, for example, celebrities, pop stars, royalty, TV stars, football, soap operas and so on, and answer these questions:

- o What proportion of each page do such items take up, compared with what could be viewed as 'serious' news?
- o How are such articles set out? That is, what use is made of pictures, and what slant do the articles take?
- o How balanced are the articles?

(b) Look for 'serious' items, for example, on politics, crime, war and peace, the economy and so on, and answer these questions:

- o What proportion of these take a mass culture slant – that is, focus on trivial issues at the expense of the facts?
- o What explanations might be offered for this?

(c) Compare the contents of two different newspapers and answer these questions:

- o Which newspaper appears to favour trivia over 'serious' news?
- o Does either allow trivia to 'creep in through the back door' – that is, focus on trivial issues within 'serious' items?
- o Look at the editorials: to what extent does each encourage critical thinking?

2. Compare the ideas generated from exploring the questions above with another group. Discuss:

(E)   (a) The extent to which your ideas are compatible.
(E)   (b) The extent to which you were surprised by your findings.
(E)   (c) The extent to which your findings support the Frankfurt School's arguments.

Critical theory – an evaluation

Strengths

1. Critical theory gives further credence to the argument that social structure cannot be understood in economic terms alone.
2. By focusing attention on the role of culture in perpetuating ruling-class power, critical theorists alert the masses to the potential threat posed by cultural influences.
3. Critical theorists provide much food for thought in their critiques. They demonstrate that everything is open to criticism. This could be a source of new knowledge that leads to social change, in contrast with unquestioning acceptance of the *status quo*.
4. By linking the economic, social and cultural worlds, critical theorists provide a useful working example of the potential of dialectical analysis.

Limitations

1. Critics argue that critical theorists contribute little to sociology, except a range of empty criticisms.
2. Critical theory has been condemned for paying insufficient attention to the historical and comparative context in which events occur.
3. Critical theory has been seen as overemphasizing the influence of culture at the expense of economic factors.
4. Critical theory implies that cultural forces have eroded the revolutionary potential of the working classes. Traditional Marxists would disagree.

Jürgen Habermas

Habermas's theory is an interesting development of critical theory. Habermas (1979) suggests that 'communication' holds the key to understanding relationships and structures in the modern world. He sees communication as the key to emancipation and argues that contemporary society is oppressive because communication is distorted. Communication is not an expression of truth but the spreading of ideology designed to promote the interests of the powerful. For the masses to be liberated, the two main causes of distorted communication – that is, 'legitimations' and 'ideology', need to be eliminated.

In contrast to earlier critical theorists, who were pessimistic about the future of society, Habermas presents an optimistic view based upon his idea of utopia. For Habermas (1970), utopia is a 'rational' society where barriers that distort communication are removed and ideas can be openly presented and defended against criticism. He does, however, see a place for critical thinking in his ideal society. For Habermas, when distorted communication has been overcome, knowledge will emerge from society itself. Critical appraisal of competing arguments will ensure that what emerges as truth will stem from a consensus of opinion. Habermas calls this state the 'ideal speech situation', ideal because it is not force or power that determines which arguments win out, but the quality of the arguments themselves.

Habermas (1984) provides an innovative interpretation of oppression to those who condemn critical theory as offering more criticisms than positive contributions. In outlining his utopia, he also provides the masses with something to aspire to and some indication of the barriers that stand in the way. However he fails to address the question of how these barriers could and should be removed. This pitfall was identified much earlier by Marx, who refused to provide an example of his utopia for fear of diverting attention away from the need to use criticisms of current society as a basis for promoting the necessary conditions for social change.

Conflict theory

Conflict theory has developed Marx's ideas on the dominance of social groups. The theory first emerged in response to the work of the structural functionalists, who proposed that social life can best be understood through consensus theories. Consensus theories see shared norms and values as fundamental to society, focus on social order based on tacit agreements, and suggest that social change occurs in a slow and orderly way (see pages 34–43). In contrast, conflict theory emphasizes the dominance of some social groups by others, sees social groups as based on manipulation and control by dominant groups, and suggests that social change occurs rapidly and in a disorderly fashion as subordinate groups overthrow dominant groups (Ritzer, 2008).

Perhaps the most famous work in the tradition of conflict theory is that by Ralph Dahrendorf (1959), who produced an innovative theory of social conflict and change. Dahrendorf's theory is more sophisticated than those that preceded it. Simple conflict theories picture society as a confused battleground, with a variety of groups fighting each other, constantly forming and reforming, making and breaking alliances (Craib, 1984). Dahrendorf, however, sees conflict in terms of a kaleidoscope of overlapping interest groups competing for power and authority. His interpretation of power and authority is informed by Weber's idea that power involves reliance on force or coercion whereas authority involves legitimatized control.

Dahrendorf sees authority as crucial, for the mere existence of authority is enough to create conflict. He looks at sources of authority and the impact that such authorities have upon individuals and the social structure, and finds that power and authority are divisive as those in power seek to maintain their position and those without power seek to gain it.

Dahrendorf regards authority as arising from the occupation of certain social positions, rather than stemming from individuals themselves. Thus authority is transient and is defined in each social situation by the positions that are occupied. Potentially, an individual could wield authority in one social situation but not in another. However, the position and the individual cannot be separated and it is quite possible for an individual to experience conflict between the interests inherent in their role and their personal interests.

In Dahrendorf's (1959) view, interests unite groups at the top and at the bottom of the social structure. Interests are construed as 'structurally generated orientations' because they emerge from the actions of people in defined social positions. There is conflict between the interests of those in power and those without power. This is because those in power seek to maintain the *status quo* and those without power seek to change it. Thus the legitimation of authority is always precarious.

Dahrendorf (1959) proposed an analysis of three groups in society whose presence can be used to explain conflict: (1) quasi-groups – that is, groups of people who share similar social positions and thus similar role interests; (2) interest groups – that is, groups within quasi-groups with common modes of behaviour, structure, form of organization and goal(s); and (3) conflict groups – that is, interest groups that engage in group conflict. Such an analysis explores why small pockets of conflict occur within larger expanses of social cohesion.

Dahrendorf (1959) provides a link between conflict groups and social change. He argues that intense conflict leads to radical change. If violence is involved, this change will be sudden. The potential for social change is omnipresent because the legitimacy of authority is precarious. If sociologists are fully to understand social life, they must focus on whether the conditions are right for social change as well as the relationship between conflict and the *status quo*.

Item E

New Social Movements

The emergence of the concept of new social movements is hard to pinpoint exactly. They are often associated with 'protest politics' and it is seen as a term devised by left-wingers. The key defining characteristic of NSMs is that they stand outside the institutional politics of the old social movements, such as the trade unions. NSMs are therefore seen as confronting the settled established way of doing things and as vehicles for expressing the interests of traditionally outsider groups. They also represent a 'cultural' turn in politics, in the sense that they agitate not just for new laws on issues, but also campaign to change people's conceptions and practices towards the groups that they represent. NSMs cover a large number of different fields and it is sometimes difficult to distinguish between new and old social movements, if defined only by being outsiders. Within the definition of 'new' would come feminist and gay groups who have challenged existing social arrangements and been relatively successful in establishing a 'cultural turn'. Perhaps less successful have been various environmental campaign groups, though their time might be arriving with the issue of global warming taking centre stage. Animal rights groups are usually counted as NSMs, though there are powerful animal lobbies represented in old social movements such as the RSPCA. More difficult to categorize are groups such as anti-abortion organizations. While they may be conceived as 'conservative' in their objectives, they do stand in opposition to a settled legal situation and therefore could also be seen as outsiders.

Exercise 2.7

This exercise will enable you to consider the extent to which Dahrendorf's ideas about groups and conflict are applicable to contemporary Britain. Read Item E and answer the following questions.

Ⓐ 1. Who developed the concept of new social movements (NSMs)?

ⒾⒶ 2. To what does the term 'new social movements' refer?

ⒾⒶ 3. What common purpose do NSMs share?

ⒾⒶ 4. In terms of Dahrendorf's analysis, which type of group would NSMs fit into (that is, quasi, interest or conflict)?

5. Why might new religious movements, for example, the Moonies or Krishna consciousness, be considered as NSMs?

6. Why is the term NSM rarely applied to groups that defend existing values?

7. Which of Dahrendorf's groups (that is, quasi, interest or conflict) could be described as old social movements (OSMs)?

Globalization

Marx referred to globalization in the *Communist Manifesto* (1848) and described a process whereby industrial capitalism would be transported to every corner of the world in the push for developing world markets and employing cheap labour. We must suppose that Marx thought the 'transportation' would involve conflict of some description. Globalization in its early form of imperialism and colonialism is characterized as Western countries literally plundering the resources and labour of other countries. More recent examples include what Ritzer (2008) has called the 'McDonaldization' of the world – developed and undeveloped – whereby the US in particular has transported and transplanted its brand of culture from Mickey Mouse to Coca-Cola to Intel Pentium processors. Global Americanization has both an economic and military force. The use of military means to overthrow governments seen as a threat to America has been a feature of the twentieth century and the early years of the twenty-first century and had earlier legacies in Latin America. Undercover American activities conducted by the US Central Intelligence Agency (CIA) are now known to have brought about the overthrow of democratically elected governments in Guatemala, Chile and Nicaragua in the 1950s, 1970s and 1980s. In more recent examples such as Afghanistan and Iraq the use of military force has been overt and largely accepted by other powerful industrial nations in the West. The Marxist writer David Harvey (2005) has argued that the continuing superiority of America – militarily and economically – is mainly about making sure of a long-term and secure supply of oil, sources of which lie in the Middle East. Thus the linking of Iraq (described by George Bush as part of the axis of evil) with the 9/11 attack on America by al-Qaeda and the global treat of terrorism has had a two-fold effect – justifying the war in the Middle East and diverting attention away from problems at home such as economic recession, social inequality and poverty. Hence the 'new imperialism' can be viewed from a conflict perspective as a more sophisticated version of the period of colonialist expansion which can integrate economic, military–political and ideological control into activities beyond national borders.

Other examples of globalization take the form of companies relocating their operations to areas of world where labour is cheaper and more compliant and legal protection of working practices and conditions less strict than in the West. The expansion of call centres to third-world locations has been a feature of the banking, insurance and ICT sectors of many Western economies. Companies like Dyson vacuum cleaners have relocated their entire business operation abroad to take advantage of cheaper production processes and labour.

However, writers such as Fukuyama (1992) and Giddens (2003) have characterized globalization as a two-way process. Globalization, they say, can have a positive impact upon local cultures and identities; for example, some call centre jobs in India are viewed as high-status, sought-after posts, paying above the local wage and with excellent working conditions. Also, some large Indian companies such as Tata Motors have a significant foothold in the British economy and can compete with the traditional Western industries in the development and production of cars. Hence Spybey (1998) has argued that although globalization had its origins in the West, non-Western societies are an integral part of the process now and multiple centres have emerged, particularly in India, which have challenged leading businesses in the West (see Chapter 5 for a more detailed discussion and Exercise 2.8 to evaluate competing views of globalization).

Exercise 2.8

 Divide sheet of paper into two columns. At the top of the first column write the heading 'A Conflict View of Globalization' and at the top of the second column write the title 'An Anti-Conflict View of Globalization'. Now, using the material you have read and other sources of information, compile a list of as many arguments as you can think of and put them under the appropriate heading.

Look at some internet sites of some international companies (such as ib.tatamotors.com and www.dyson.co.uk). How is the international nature of one of these companies represented on the website?

Evaluation of conflict theory

Strengths

1. Conflict theory provides a radical contrast to consensus theory and draws attention to the sources of conflict in society.

2. In seeking to build upon existing theories, conflict theory demonstrates the value of an eclectic approach to understanding social life.
3. Conflict theory can account for social stability and social change, and recognizes that change is an inevitable feature of social life.
4. Conflict theory attempts to integrate macro-level and micro-level analysis to provide a more rounded analysis of social conflict and change.

Limitations

1. Critics of conflict theory argue that too little attention is given to order and stability.
2. Conflict theory has been attacked as ideologically radical.
3. It is argued that conflict theory is not a theory in its own right – it is simply a polar opposite of structural functionalism (see pages 38–41). Ironically, although it claims to be informed by Marxism, some critics believed that conflict theory is closer to structural functionalism than to Marxism.
4. Dahrendorf's work has been criticized on a number of counts. For example, it has been described as macroscopic: focusing on social structures at the expense of the way people interpret the world. Also, he provides little explanation of how conflict escalates into social change.

Exercise 2.9

Copy and complete the table here, using the information you have read so far in this chapter.

A society based on conflict?

Main theories	Marxist	Neo-Marxist	Critical theory	Conflict theory
Key writers				
Basic assumptions of theory				
Strengths				
Limitations				

Post-Marxism

Since the collapse of the former USSR and the Eastern Bloc communist regimes and the introduction of free-market policies in these countries Marxist theories could be seen as somewhat redundant (Best et al. 2000). The move to introduce Western-style democratic governments in these countries and some in the Middle East has added weight to this general demise of Marxist thought. Furthermore there seems to have been a decline in the working class, especially manual workers, as the class system generally has become more fragmented and class positions have become increasingly difficult to locate within a Marxist class structure.

Socialism as a political force also seems to have been abandoned by left-wing parties in European countries in an attempt to address the modern social and political changes taking place in relation to the position of the individual and their place in society. Commentators have pointed to the policies of Labour governments in the 1990s and 2000s in the UK largely continuing in the same mould as the former Conservative policies, as a case in point.

A SOCIETY BASED ON CONSENSUS

Sociologists who base their theories of society on the notion of consensus take their starting-point as what appears to be the obvious agreement that must exist in society if it runs smoothly and people generally obey rules, have similar attitudes and values. At least superficially it would appear that the foundations of society are built upon the common and accepted ways of going about organizing the way we live. People carry out their roles and responsibilities in a consensual way because they actively agree with the ways things are done. This leads to a general consensus in society and there being no need for coercion.

Functionalism

Early functionalism is embodied in the work of Emile Durkheim (1858–1917), a French sociologist who contributed much to the theory that later became known as structural functionalism. Durkheim was motivated by concern about the impact that large-scale social structures have upon individuals within society. He saw it as important to try to explore this systematically, through empirical research.

Durkheim (1895/1964) developed a number of concepts to structure his research and enable him to analyse his research findings coherently. The most influential of these was the concept of a 'social fact', which determined the way he approached the study of society. Durkheim used the term 'social facts' to refer to the social structures and cultural norms that, although existing independently of the individual, affect social action.

Durkheim distinguished between two types of social facts – material social facts and non-material social facts. Material social facts relate to the structural components of society (church, state and so on) and the 'morphological' components of society, for example, population distribution, channels of communication and housing arrangements. Non-material social facts relate to the moral and cultural components of society, for example, morality, collective conscience, collective representation and social currents.

Durkheim (1893/1964) analysed various aspects of social change with reference to his two types of social facts. He explored the transition from primitive to modern society by conceptualizing an 'ideal type' (that is, a theoretical model) for each type of society and analysing the processes of change involved in moving from one to the other. He did not limit his analysis to the structural components of change (for example, working practices, working relations and economic factors) but also sought to understand the changes that occur at the moral and cultural levels.

The two ideal types of society Durkheim (1893/1894) conceptualized were (1) mechanistic (primitive) society and (2) organic (modern) society. Not only are the types of society structurally different; in Durkheim's view these structural differences affect the prevailing moral and cultural conditions where relationships are essentially face-to-face (or mechanical) and the division of labour is very simple, with most people involved in essentially the same occupation. There is a common lifestyle, a common set of beliefs, rituals and so on. There is an underlying consensus, or common morality ('collective conscience') upon which social solidarity is based and which guides individual behaviour (Slattery, 1991). Thus mechanistic society has a largely homogeneous social structure with little division of labour. This contributes to the development of mechanistic solidarity by enabling people to identify with others because they are similar to them.

Durkheim (1893/1894) recognized that as societies develop and industrialize, divisions of labour become increasingly complex. Individuals perform increasingly narrower tasks and their work becomes ever more specialized. They are dependent on other people for their survival. This mutual dependence holds society together, and organic solidarity emerges, where people cooperate to ensure they are all supported by the same resource base. This involves a balance being struck between individual freedom and social order. Social order is no longer promoted by a common set of values, but instead is enshrined in law.

Other aspects of Durkheim's work demonstrate a similar commitment. For example, his famous study of suicide (1897/1951) (discussed in Chapter 3) explores the connection between structural changes in society (material social facts) and the prevailing social and moral conditions (non-material social facts). By conducting large-scale, cross-cultural, historical research, Durkheim found that the structure of society at any given time affects the degree of social solidarity present in that society. This aids the conceptualization and understanding of suicide.

Another large piece of research conducted by Durkheim was his study of religion – *The Elementary Forms of Religious Life* (1912/1965). Religion was of interest to Durkheim because he regarded it as the ultimate non-material social fact. He considered that religion in primitive society was a direct expression of collective morality, and as such, the primary force for social regulation. However as society modernized, social relationships developed and social structures became more complex. This means that religion has become only one force for social regulation in society and only one means of expressing collective sentiments. Others have emerged, for example, law and science, and some would now argue that religion has little influence on secular society. However, Durkheim advocated the continued importance of religion, arguing that most non-religious structures in society involve values rooted in religion.

Durkheim's (1893/1964) analysis of society was primarily optimistic. He regarded social stability as of paramount importance and was confident that problems in society could be solved through social reform rather than radical action. He referred to the problems of society as pathologies, implying that they could be overcome or 'cured'. He construed the sociologist as a social physician whose job was to alleviate difficulties through structural reform. He even proposed that the difficulties in the workplace (which so concerned Marx) could be overcome if workers were encouraged to develop a common morality. He felt that this could be achieved through the establishment of 'occupational associations', which would encompass 'all the agents of the same industry united and organized into a single group' (Durkheim, 1893/1964, p. 5). These would be superior to worker unions, which Durkheim felt only served to intensify the differences between owners and workers.

In his later work, Durkheim (1973) also gave consideration to the way that collective morality was being enforced in society. His attention turned to how social morals are internalized, a process known as socialization. Durkheim saw various aspects of society as influential in aiding the socialization process, although his maintain interest was the education of children. He saw the education system as vital to the prevention of a further decline in morality, by teaching discipline, promoting autonomy and engendering a sense of devotion to society. These ideas formed the foundation for later work by functionalists (see pp. 41–3).

Durkheim's work – an evaluation

Strengths

1. Durkheim's work is straightforward and offers a more coherent theory than those put forward by other classical sociological theorists. His writings clearly state his concepts and ideas and demonstrate how they can be applied in a variety of specific situations.
2. In developing the concept of social facts, Durkheim was able to impose a systematic framework on the study of social life. His distinction between material and non-material social facts enables consideration to be given to the importance of both structures and collective beliefs in determining the nature of society.
3. Although regarded as a structuralist because of his concern with the impact of large-scale societal structures on society's members, Durkheim did seek to explore the more individual aspects of human nature. His later work constituted an attempt to examine the micro aspects of society.

Limitations

1. Durkheim's concept of social facts has attracted criticism. It is alleged to reify phenomena – that is, give them an independent existence they do not have. Critics argue that this is wrong because all phenomena are the product of the labours or interactions of society's members.
2. Durkheim's work on suicide attracted heavy criticism. It was argued that he was wrong to assume that the 'most individual of human acts' (suicide) could be studied with the use of structuralist methods. He was also condemned for using objective methodology (the scientific method) to study a subjective phenomenon (suicide).
3. Durkheim devoted little attention to micro-level phenomena, treating them as mere by-products of the social structure. Interpretive sociologists would refute Durkheim's assumption that society can be understood best in terms of large-scale forces and their causal impact on the individual.

Structural functionalism

From the 1930s to the 1960s structural functionalism, which was developed from the writings of Emile Durkheim, was the dominant sociological theory. Structural functionalism is regarded as a consensus theory in that its proponents see shared norms and values as fundamental to society, focus on social order based on tacit agreements and view social change as occurring in a slow and orderly way (Bernard, 1983).

To understand structural functionalism it is helpful to consider the meaning of the terms 'structure' and 'function'. The term 'structure' is generally used to refer to the fabric of society – that is, the social institutions and systems that combine to make it up – whereas 'function' refers to the role played by each social institution in the maintenance of society as a whole. Hence structural functionalists are interested both in the infrastructure of society and in the roles that must be fulfilled and the needs that must be met to ensure its survival.

Structural functionalism involves a macroscopic approach to the study of social phenomena, a focus on the social system as a whole and interest in the subsystems that comprise it. Structural functionalists regard the subsystems as interdependent, and all make a contribution to the wellbeing of society as a whole. Social relationships are harmonious as opposed to conflictual. The natural state of society is stability, and equilibrium is maintained by various aspects of society changing together to complement each other. Structural functionalists do recognize that social change occurs, but regard this as orderly rather than radical and revolutionary.

According to structural functionalists, we need to understand how the various aspects of the social system contribute to society as a whole. Of particular interest is the role that those aspects play in promoting social order and cohesion. Inspired by Durkheim, Parsons (1951) took as the starting-point for his work the question of how social order is maintained. Central to his work is a four-part model, developed to represent the basic features that all social systems must possess if they are to ensure their survival. The features that Parsons identified were as follows.

1. *Adaptation* – The ability to harness environmental and economic resources to feed, clothe and safeguard the welfare of the people who make up a given society.
2. *Goal attainment* – Strategic planning and decision-making to structure and organize social life.

3. *Integration* – The creation and dissemination of a set of core values to promote cooperation and social cohesion and minimize the risk of conflict.
4. *Latency* – Ensuring the continuation of society through procreation and the transfer of rituals, customs, traditions and cultural practices.

For society to function properly, all subsystems within the broader social structure must contribute in some way to meeting its basic needs. The subsystems can have complementary influences and there is considerable overlap between the contributions. Parsons highlights the place of collective values in uniting the various subsystems and ensuring that their contributions are cohesive. Three processes are seen as central to the synchronization (harmonious bringing together) of society: (1) socialization (2) social control and (3) role performance. Slattery provides a concise summary of how these processes combine:

> Every individual has to perform a wide variety of social roles – as a parent, worker, citizen – and although other people's expectations pressure the individual into effective role performance and the system can force him/her to carry out these duties, real efficiency comes from people being committed to the social system. Such 'internal' motivation comes from effective socializing, from parents bringing up their children properly, teaching them the prevailing norms and moral values of society to the point where they are externalized and become part of the child's own consciousness, even conscience. (Slattery, 1991, p. 242)

Exercise 2.10

In small groups, and drawing on the quotation above, discuss the extent to which you agree with the view that the best force for social control is individual commitment to society's values. Think about how social conformity is expected and accepted in places like Singapore. Singapore is a tiny former British colony of 3 million people most of whom are ethnic Chinese with a small proportion of Malay and Indian people. It is an industrialized, urban, affluent society with per capita income roughly equivalent to that of the USA. However, socially and politically Singapore is referred to as 'softly authoritarian' because of the ways in which the government controls people's personal behaviour. The government has powers to ensure there is no political dissent, can detain people without trial and demand public confessions from those arrested. The government restricts any behaviour which may cause racial or religious tension; it owns and controls the media and press. Well-educated people are encouraged to have more children by receiving tax incentives in the belief that they will create superior people.

Littering, failing to flush a public toilet, smoking in public and chewing gum (which is illegal) are considered to be antisocial. In the past males with long hair have been detained and had their hair cut. Do individuals realize the 'greater good' to be gained from having such rules in a heavily populated society or are they controlled through coercion?

Individuals, roles and society

Parsons used his model as a basis for exploring the nature of the social system, which he defines as:

> a plurality of individual actors interacting with each other in a situation which has at least a physical or environmental aspect, actors who are moti-vated in terms of a tendency to the 'optimization of gratification' and whose relation to their situations, including each other, is defined as mediated in terms of a system of culturally structured and shared symbols. (Parsons, 1951, pp. 5–6)

Parsons considers that the roles played by the family and the education system are vital to social order and maintenance of the *status quo*. In his analysis of the family in modern American society, Parsons (1959) argues that the fam-ily retains two 'basic and irreducible functions' that are common to families in all societies: the 'primary socialization of children' and the 'stabilization of adult personalities' (quoted in Haralambos and Holborn, 2004). He goes on to analyse in detail how the family performs these functions and why they are so important to society as a whole. To summarize his argument, the social-ization function ensures that social values are inculcated and become part of individuals' consciousness, thus contributing to value consensus in society. The stabilization function relates to the emotional security provided within the family, which serves to counteract the pressures of life that cause individuals to become stressed and sometimes unstable.

He also recognizes the purpose that the education system serves in society. School acts as a bridge between the family and society as a whole, preparing children for their adult roles. It does so by teaching the basic values of soci-ety, which are essential if society is to operate effectively. American schools instil two major values: the value of achievement and the value of equality of opportunity. Finally, the education system 'functions to allocate these human resources within the role-structure of adult society' (quoted in Haralambos and Holborn, 2004). Thus schools, by testing and evaluating students, match their talents, skills and capacities to the jobs for which they are best suited. The school is therefore seen as the major mechanism for role allocation.

An E Parsons suggests that education performs a vital selection function, fitting people to their appropriate place in society. Tests presumably form a part of this. Discuss in groups and write a report on the following:

1. The advantages of school tests/public examinations as a means of assessing potential/selecting people for their place in society.
2. The disadvantages of school tests/public examinations as a means of assessing potential/selecting people for their place in society.
3. What are the implications of this for Parsons's argument that schools promote equality of opportunity?

Neofunctionalism

Historically, functionalism declined during the 1960s when other theories such as Marxism and interactionism began to address its fundamental weaknesses on power, conflict and action. There was a tide of change in sociology which attacked the theoretical consensus basis of Parsonian functionalism. However in the 1980s and 1990s the work of Alexander (1988, 1990) brought about a revival in the form of what has become known as 'neofunctionalism' (Swingewood 2000).

Alexander sought to re-establish a major macro sociology within the functionalist paradigm. Moving away from the focus on factors in society which bring about and maintain social stability and cohesion, Alexander introduced concepts and issues of power, struggle and conflict to the processes within the functionalist model of society. Alexander also sought to link the actions of individuals at the micro level of society, particularly the internationalization of culture, to wider structural forces at the macro level. Parsonian functionalism is perceived to be limited in its consideration of how social action, or what Alexander calls 'contingency', is theorized in relation to adherence to the social order. Because Parsons was writing before the development of interactionism he defined the individual in terms of their roles and patterns of behaviour brought about through the socialization process and therefore failed to adequately conceptualize social interaction. Alexander seeks to explain how 'environments' – the social system, the cultural system and the personality system – develop, generate and condition action. Environments are created through action, and action results from environments in a reflexive process where there is the possibility of free will.

Where Parsons linked values to the institutional regulation of society, the neofunctionalists allow for a voluntaristic concept of action – that is, that action can stem from an individual personality or culture. Alexander is arguing that internalizing of culture through socialization can lead to a variety of different meanings, not just a single dominant value system (Swingewood, 2000). However, this does not overcome the problem of where culture begins, and its relationship to wider economic and political structures. Hence while neofunctionalism goes some way to overcoming the lack of an adequate theory of action there are still fundamental weaknesses. As a result, Alexander has indicated that neofunctionalism cannot be a fully developed theory, and he has therefore moved beyond it into a 'new theoretical movement', which draws upon a number of other theoretical traditions such as symbolic interactionism to plug the gaps that neofunctionalism left behind (see Seidman and Alexander, 2001).

Structural functionalism – an evaluation

Strengths

1. Structural functionalism is regarded by some as 'without any doubt, the single most significant body of theory in the social sciences in the present century' (Nisbet, cited in Turner and Maryanski, 1979, p. xi).
2. Its concepts are attractive because of their simplicity and because they can be applied easily to contemporary society. Although many of the ideas were developed through the analysis of American society, they are seen as applicable to modern Britain.
3. The theory is accessible to the layperson because it is structured with reference to the social system and the subsystems that make up that system, and seeks explicitly to identify the functions that the latter perform in maintaining the former. It is relatively easy to understand that each section of society has a job to do to keep society as a whole ticking over, and to hazard a reasonable guess as to what that job is. The layperson is helped further by examples of how the analysis can be applied to the family and the education system.

4. Neofunctionalism has attempted to address the lack of attention in structural functionalist theory as to how action can be explained and understood in relation to the social system.

Limitations

1. The most common criticism levelled at structural functionalism concerns its naivity – that is, its apparent inability or reluctance to acknowledge that far from being a harmonious place based upon consensus, society is characterized by groups with conflicting interests seeking to gain power over others.
2. Critics argue that functionalism is misguided in its assertion that stratification is functional for society and its members. They argue that stratification is functional for those in the most powerful and financially lucrative positions, but dysfunctional for the majority.
3. Structural functionalists could be criticized for failing to give consideration to the issue of whose ideas form the basis of the value consensus and whose interests they serve. Marxists argue that far from being the expression of morals and common interests to promote unity and cohesion, ideas that form the 'value consensus' are the expression of dominant ideology used to justify and perpetuate ruling-class power.
4. Functionalism as a theory of the social system fails to give an adequate account of action or contingency.

Exercise 2.12

Ⓐ Using the knowledge you have gained from reading this section on a society based on consensus, complete a copy of the summary table below.

A society based on consensus

Main theories	Functionalism	Structural functionalism	Neofunctionalism
Key writers			
Basic assumptions			
Strengths			
Limitations			

A SOCIETY BASED ON SOCIAL ACTION, INTERPRETATION AND MEANING

Sociologists who adopt the social action perspective reject the idea that any theory of society can be based on the notion that society can be viewed as a whole entity. For social action theorists it is precisely this social action which creates, maintains and recreates society. The dynamic structure of society is created through social action and interaction in the everyday lives we are involved in. The practical nature of social interaction and the ways we create meanings to help us understand our lives is what sociology should be about. Hence these theorists focus their attention on the micro aspects of societal interaction.

Weberianism

Weberianism arose from the contribution that Max Weber (1864–1930) made to sociology. This contribution was twofold: he presented a view of what sociology should be and offered a number of insights into various aspects of the social world. Weber's approach to the study of the social world represented an attempt to reconcile the differences between those who advocated large-scale research at the macro level and those who advocated small-scale research at the micro level. Weber (1921/1968) believed that it was possible to make use of both general principles and individual inquiry. He saw this combination as working best when general concepts were developed and used to enhance the understanding of individual empirical events.

Thus Weber (1903–1917/1949) favoured both individuality and generality, and claimed that his primary interest was in the individual component of general analysis. By analysing historical data, Weber aimed to arrive at an understanding of individual experiences and events through the use of concepts that could be applied universally to all social phenomena. The four most influential of these concepts were *Verstehen*, causality, ideal type and values. Each will be considered in turn.

Verstehen is probably the most widely known but most misinterpreted of Weber's concepts. *Verstehen*, which translates as understanding, was used by Weber (1921/1968) to refer to the sociologist's ability to understand the phenomena under study. Weber's application of the concept has led to some confusion. It is uncertain whether *Verstehen* is aimed at the individual level (that is, understanding the meanings individuals give to social phenomena and the influence of these meanings on their actions) or whether it is a technique to understand culture, particularly 'the socially constructed rules which define the meaning of action in a given society' (Hekman, 1983). The former would be akin to symbolic interactionism and the latter to the macro sociology of structural functionalism. It is now considered that both interpretations of the term could be equally valid.

The second concept of central interest to Weber was causality – that is, the relationship between cause and effect. Weber's (1921/1968) research was dominated by the desire to explore not just the meaning behind social change, but also the reason behind it. Perhaps his most famous analysis in this vein was *The Protestant Ethic and the Spirit of Capitalism* (1904/1958).

Weber's (1903–17/1949) third concept, the 'ideal type', referred to a pure picture of a phenomenon developed by sociologists immersing themselves in historical data. Ideal types were construed as heuristic tools (aids to understanding), designed to provide templates for sociological inquiry by giving exaggerated, one-sided examples of social phenomena. Weber felt that such templates could be compared with actual phenomena in order to identify deviations. Sociologists could then study the possible reasons for these deviations.

Weber (1903–17/1949) also gave consideration to the place of values in teaching and research. He felt strongly that values had no place in academic teaching and suggested that it was possible to conduct value-free research in sociology. It wasn't that Weber sought totally to exclude values from the research process, just from the process of data collection. Ideally, values should be expressed before the research begins, but thereafter sociologists should seek to maintain objectivity to ensure that their findings are value-free.

Although it is difficult to do justice to the complexity of Weber's work in a few paragraphs, there is value in briefly exploring some of his ideas to demonstrate the breadth of his interests and the diverse contribution he made to sociological thinking. Starting with his view of what sociology should be, Weber (1921/1968) argued that sociology should be scientific, concerned with causality and utilize interpretive understanding (*Verstehen*). When proposing his theory of social action, Weber considered it important to make a distinction between voluntary (considered) action and involuntary (reactive and instinctive) action. He saw the study of the former as offering the best means to develop an understanding of human behaviour.

Despite this early commitment to micro-level sociology, Weber's work drifted further and further away from this over the years. His work on social structure demonstrated his intention to focus on the individual, but he also gave consideration to the role that social action played in the formation and life of groups. Weber's (1921/1981) analysis was popular because it rejected an economic interpretation of social stratification and instead focused on social groupings. Weber conceptualized social stratification in terms of class (the economic order of society), status (social honour assigned to individuals/groups in society) and party (group organization designed to attain power – see Exercise 2.13).

Recognition of party as a dimension of power was the most evident example of Weber's desire to understand society in terms of the actions of its members. The term 'party' can be used to refer to the way groups organize themselves to achieve a goal or an objective. They may be formed on the basis of class, status or a combination of the two. Weber considered the actions of party members to be important in determining how successful a given party will be in meeting its objectives. However, he also emphasized the structural aspect of parties. As noted by Gerth and Mills (1958): 'parties are always structures struggling for domination'. Even here it appears that Weber is seduced by structure at the expense of the individual, as the following comment demonstrates:

> Thus parties are the most organized elements of Weber's stratification system. Weber thinks of parties very broadly as including not only those that exist in The State but also those that may exist in a social club. Parties usually, but not always, represent class and/or status groups. Whatever they represent, parties are orientated towards the attainment of power. (Gerth and Mills, 1958)

Item F

Changes in the social composition of left- and right-wing political parties and the changing characteristics of the activities of trade unions have been cited as illustrations of a 'new' style of politics in Western democracies. Political analysts claim that the 'old-style' pressure groups such as trade unions have less influence today. It is argued that a 'new' style of political participation is emerging where individuals pick and choose which issues to support. The 'new' style involves class dealignment, partisan dealignment and loosely linked campaigns for social and political change with greater emphasis on wider moral concerns. Media coverage of political debates and issues also forms part of the wider awareness people have of how policies will affect or benefit them and therefore they behave more like consumers in the approach they adopt. New social movements have also increased in number and can be issue-based such as anti-fox-hunting or longer-term such as Greenpeace. This may indicate a dissatisfaction with the political system and show that people want to influence the formation of policies by taking direct action.

(Adapted from I. Marsh, 'Making Sense of Society', *Sociology Review* 16(2), 2006)

Exercise 2.13

Ⓐ Discuss with a group of fellow students how material in Item F could be seen
Ⓔ as both a challenge to and support for Weber's concept of the party. Make
sure you understand the key terms 'partisan dealignment' and 'class dealignment'. Try to give other examples of new social movements. Might the role of
NSM differ according to different groups based on age, gender, social class,
disability?

Weber (1921/1968) also presented an analysis of the structures of authority,
distinguishing between traditional authority (that is, authority based upon historical factors), charismatic authority (authority based upon the charm or
personality of a charismatic leader) and rational–legal authority (authority
based upon reason or law). He traced the emergence of the different forms
of authority through history, regarding rational–legal authority as the most
prevalent form of authority in the contemporary Western world. This led him
to conduct a comprehensive analysis of the rational structures in society. His
most famous work here is his detailed study of bureaucracy, where his 'ideal
type' concept is applied to maximum effect.

In his work on bureaucracy, Weber (1921/1968) acknowledged the potential
of bureaucratic organizations and structures, but expressed reservations about
the impact such organizations could have upon individuals. As well as regarding them as dehumanizing for the worker, Weber considered bureaucracies as
potentially damaging to society, owing to the increased emphasis on rationalization as a process for ensuring greater efficiency. Weber was concerned that
this process would spread beyond bureaucracy and that rationalization would
pervade social structures and relationships.

Weber – an evaluation

Strengths

1. Weber's work demonstrates that structural analysis alone is insufficient to
    understand society. He bridges the gap between macro-level and micro-
    level sociology by presenting a theory of society that combines the
    value of causal analysis with the importance of individual motives in
    behaviour.

2. The breadth of his work is impressive. He sought to apply his ideas to a number of spheres of social life, with notable success. These studies have provided the inspiration for much subsequent sociological inquiry from a variety of perspectives.

Limitations

1. Despite Weber's assertion that meaning was his central interest, the majority of his work focuses on large-scale structures. This juxtaposition of intention and structure is at best confusing and at worst incomprehensible.
2. Weber's oscillation between macro and micro approaches renders his work vulnerable to criticism from both camps. Structuralists would condemn his assertions about *Verstehen* as lacking empirical credibility, and interpretive sociologists would criticize the structural aspects of his work for overlooking the role of individuals in influencing their environment.

Marxism, functionalism and Weberian sociology as modernist theories

Marxism, functionalism and Weberian sociology have been seen as products of a particular period of history that has become know as modernism. Modernism has its origins in the Enlightenment of the sixteenth and seventeenth centuries and is characterized by the belief that it is possible to obtain empirically valid and demonstrable knowledge of the world through rigorous scientific inquiry. Marxism, functionalism and Weberianism are characterized as 'grand stories' – that is, perspectives that view society as a whole and can therefore be explained and understood as whole entities with patterns and trends in their overall development and progress. Postmodernists argue that we have moved beyond the time when there can be such knowledge, as the world has become more diverse and fragmented. No overarching theory or body of thought such as Marxism, functionalism or Weberianism is any longer capable of providing explanations for the whole of a society. Postmodernists refer to such 'grand theories' as 'metanarratives', and see them as now inadmissible and redundant in attempting to provide explanations about the workings of whole societies. These issues will be further discussed in Chapters 4 and 5.

Interpretive sociology

Symbolic interactionism

'Symbolic interactionism' is commonly associated with work of G. H. Mead, although the term was used first by Blumer in 1937. Symbolic interaction developed in response to the theories of social structure that dominated sociology from the turn of the century. The interests of symbolic interactionists are widely documented as being (1) a focus on the interaction between actor and society, (2) a focus on the actor and social world as dynamic processes and (3) the importance of actors' interpretations of that world.

Mind, Self and Society (1934) provided a forum for Mead's ideas to be expressed. The inspiration for his theory came from two areas. The first was pragmatism – that is, the broad assumption that truth is created through the actions of individuals and their interactions with others – and Mead believed that any attempt to understand society should be based on the study of social action and interaction. The second was behaviourism – that is, a psychological perspective involving the systematic study of human behaviour.

Mead developed a number of key concepts to aid our understanding of the social world. First, he identified the existence of a phenomenon known as the 'act'. This was the term he used to describe the behaviour in which individuals engage. Mead recognized that the 'act' does not occur in isolation, so proposed another concept – 'gestures' – to accommodate the social aspect of the act. Mead used the term gestures to refer to the interplay between the individual (the social actor) and another/others. He recognized that another's response could influence subsequent acts of the individual, construing this as a 'conversation of gestures'. This process of mutual influence is described as a 'dance' between interacting individuals by Christopher (2001). This was the starting-point for Mead's analysis of the relationship between individual and society.

Mead also formulated a theory of mental processes. Mead viewed intelligence not in terms of cognitive ability, but in terms of the ability of individuals to adapt to the environment. Not only can individuals adapt physically to the environment; they can also adapt symbolically. It is this feature that marks them out as distinct from animals. For example, just as individuals can alter their conversation in response to the actions and reactions of the listener, so they can alter their behaviour in response to social feedback. According to Mead, human beings are unique because they can have internal conversations with themselves to consider possible interpretations of events or courses of action.

This formed the basis of Mead's theory of self. His idea that feedback from others shapes the meaning individuals assign to events was developed a stage further. He identified the existence of 'self' within each individual, a kind of coherent impression or identity formed through action and interaction with society. Mead regarded the self as both a mental and a social process, because it is formed by the synthesis (coming together) of ideas and insights developed from social experiences and personal reflection. The self develops through a process known as 'reflexivity', where individuals use others' reactions and their own life experiences to modify their subsequent thinking and behaviour.

Mead identified the self as comprising two aspects – the 'I' and the 'Me'. The 'I' is the most personal component of the self, the source of dynamism and creativity. The 'Me' relates to the prevailing attitudes of society, which are internalized by individuals and serve to shape their behaviour. It is these social expectations and beliefs that create the conventional, habitual individual identified in Mead's work. Mead saw the two aspects as contributing different features to the self –the 'I' providing the necessary creativity and dynamism to inspire the individual to change, and the 'Me' tempering this with conscious responsibility.

Mead's work inspired a number of writers, the most famous being Cooley, who sought to explore and expand Mead's analysis of self (see Gross, 1992, for a review), and Goffman (1961), who developed dramaturgy, a theatrical analogy that construes the self as a product of dramatic interaction between the actor and the audience. Others, such as Blumer (1954/1969), used Mead's ideas as the basis for a critique of macro-level sociology and scientific method, and advocated the use of more empathetic methods – that is 'sympathetic introspection' in the study of social world.

Erving Goffman was an influential sociological figure writing and researching extensively within the interactionist tradition, adding to the work of the early theorists and developing a distinctive qualitative methodology using observation and ethnography. One of his earliest contributions to interactionist theory was his development of the dramaturgical analogy which presented the world as a drama or stage in which we are all reflexively acting out our various roles in society depending upon the circumstances in which we find ourselves and who we are interacting with; family roles – mother, father, brother, cousin; work roles – teacher, office/shop worker, waitress, doctor; social roles – friend, neighbour, acquaintance, confidant. All these could be aspects of one personality. Goffman showed the complexity of how we 'present' ourselves to the outside world through negotiation, impression management and manipulation. His study of the day-to-day minutiae of social interaction developed from a summer job he undertook as a student studying for his PhD working in a hotel on Shetland in his younger years where he observed the complex cultural meanings behind our action and interaction with others. He became aware of the tensions between 'locals' and visitors in the ways surreptitious communication was developed through nuances, gestures, intonation and demeanour when Shetlanders wanted to be cryptic or coded when visitors were about. Much of this research from his Shetland experience went into *Presentation of the Self in Everyday Life* (1959, 1999) but also continued to appear in other publications throughout his career. In later work, he stressed the ways in which individuals draw upon 'frames of understanding' to make sense of what would be otherwise chaotic and unrelated events (see Chambliss 2005). While these frames were pre-existing schema of interpretation, the individual still has to choose which frame to employ in any situation to articulate a meaning to an event (Snow, 2007).

According to Goffman we actively create and recreate the social world in which we live through our experiences and reflexivity. In his study of mental illness Goffmann showed how the 'self' is systematically annihilated through the process of labelling and incarceration. He worked in a mental hospital to gather the material for his now famous work *Asylums* (1961), which formed the basis for a general theory of total institutions. Goffman also studied the ways stigmas are attached to particular forms of behaviour and people through his study of labelling in crime called *Outsiders,* and also gender and advertising and the role teachers play in labelling pupils.

Symbolic interactionism – an evaluation

Symbolic interactionism commonly attracts criticism for focusing on action at the expense of social structure, thus overlooking the overarching forces – for example, power, conflict, change and so on – that can help to explain the nature of social life. In an exploration of the value of symbolic interactionism, Craib (1984) suggests that to accept this view is to oversimplify the contribution made by the perspective. For Craib, part of the value of a theory is its ability to encompass abstract theorizing and flexibility of thought. By making individual interpretation and action its starting-point for understanding society, symbolic interactionism provides a means to develop an understanding of social life free from structural constraints.

Despite defending symbolic interactionism against unfair criticism, Craib (1984, p. 74) highlights limitations of the theory that undermine its ability to add to our understanding of social life:

Interactionists see people as purely cognitive beings, as if we understand people when we understand what they think they know about the world, their meanings and self conceptions. Yet people also have emotions and it is arguable that unconscious processes occur as well...A theory of persons must also deal with different levels of the personality and relationships between them...We act, but we are more than actors...the way people form and develop their view of the world can be seen as subjected to certain rules and that there are general processes of meaning formation that are not investigated by interactionism...Meanings and symbols themselves might be seen as possessing an organized structure, even comprising yet another type of reality in the social world.

So, for Craib, symbolic interactionism's value is as a theory of persons, albeit an incomplete one. It does not attempt to be a theory of society, although it is often criticized for not being one. Craib's analysis suggests that if symbolic interactionism is to contribute more to our understanding of society, it should endeavour to explore the relationship between formation in the individual and the organized structure of rules and symbols external to the individual. It is this that may define reality in the social world.

Exercise 2.14

Using the ideas expressed by Craib above and information provided earlier in the section, identify two strengths and two limitations of symbolic interactionism. Record this information in a two-column summary chart.

Phenomenology

Phenomenologists construe the social world as largely dependent upon the meaning and interpretations of social actors. Husserl made the point that the world is based upon and understood in terms of the 'sense-experiences' we give to it. In other words, what we have previously gained from an experience is applied to other similar experiences to make them meaningful. The work most relevant to sociology is that of Schutz (Schutz and Luckman, 1973), who applies phenomenology to the study of the social world. Like that of Mead, Schutz's work stemmed from an interest in social life, but instead of focusing on meaning, for Schutz the central concept is 'intersubjectivity'. Schutz used this term to refer to a network of common influences and understandings that characterize the social world and individual experiences.

He saw analysis of this intersubjective social world as the key to understanding society.

Schutz developed a number of concepts. He coined the term 'typifications' to explain the way in which individuals' behaviour is structured or organized. Typifications are prestructured constructs (schemas or patterns of ideas) that are used to communicate and to make sense of the world. Schutz saw language as potentially the most versatile mechanism for typifying: 'the typifying medium par excellence' (Schutz and Luckman, 1973). Typifications exist in all aspects of social life and are generally derived from and approved by society. People develop and use typifications in daily life to help them to understand their experiences. For example, when people meet others for the first time they may compare them with similar people they have met before and use this to guide their behaviour. People may also use typifications to make sense of a particular individual's behaviour – for example, 'that's typical of him – always late!' Typifications can also be used to group similar individuals into conceptual clusters. All individuals who fit a particular 'type' become members of that group.

As typifications refer to people, Schutz coined the term 'recipes' to refer to situations. These are the unnoticed rules that determine our response to routine social situations. It is these rules that prevent us from making social *faux pas*. For example, when someone asks you how you are, your response is determined by who is asking the question. If it is a friend or a colleague you may say 'OK thanks – and you?', but if a doctor asks you during a consultation you will provide her or him with details about your condition and probably will not enquire about the health of the doctor. It is these social conventions (recipes) that shape the way we respond in social situations.

Although typifications and recipes are presented as mechanisms that define individuals' relationships and responses to social situations, they are flexible rather than fixed. The individual interprets relationships and situations and modifies the typifications accordingly. This ability, or 'practical intelligence', identified by Schutz is similar to that highlighted by Mead (1934) in his discussion of the uniqueness of human beings.

Further work in the phenomenological tradition was conducted by Husserl (1931), whose aim was to establish a philosophy free from all preconceptions to discover the very heart of each individual's 'life-world' (see Slattery, 1991). 'Life-world' is the term Husserl used to refer to the social world from an intersubjective point of view. He identified a number of basic features that he claimed characterize this life-world, including tension of consciousness, purposeful physical action, suspension of disbelief, intersubjective communication and a specific time perspective.

Item G

The Life-World

What does Schutz mean by the 'life-world'? It is seen as a specific form of consciousness in which the social actor is alert to all the possibilities in the real world and in particular to the world of work. The world of work is the specific locus of the life-world, as it is here that the social actor can bring about their intentions and produce a desired effect. Work allows our bodies to act upon the material objects that are within our reach, and by carrying out routine activities that have been tested again and again we can shape those objects in a planned and conscious way to produce things that are useful to us.

It is in work then that we experience ourselves as full human beings and engage in communication and interaction with others to constitute the life-world. However, even when we are acting in this intersubjective life-world, we inhabit a life-world that is essentially our own, though we may share many characteristics with others in the same work-space In our life-world there are many other individuals and we inhabit many others' life-worlds.

Exercise 2.15

This exercise will enable you to explore Schutz's analysis in more detail. Read Item G and answer the following questions.

1. According to Item G, what is meant by 'alert to all the possibilities'?
2. What do you think Schutz means by 'we experience ourselves as full human beings'?
3. Why is work seen to lie at the heart of the life-world?
4. To what extent do you agree with the view that *in the world of work* 'we experience ourselves as full human beings'? (Hint: How far does our role as worker dominate other facets of self in the workplace?)
5. Drawing on Item G, explain how it is possible for others to belong to our life-world and for us to belong to the life-world of others.

Husserl also devoted attention to the nature of knowledge and the structure of social reality. The two concepts were seen as related because in Husserl's view it is knowledge that gives society coherence and effectively structures social reality. Husserl identified two types of knowledge: shared knowledge – that is, commonly held beliefs about truth; and private knowledge – that is, knowledge based on personal experience, but influenced by society. Central to his analysis of interpersonal relationships were the concepts of 'we' and 'they' relations, the former being associated with intimacy and friendship and the latter with impersonal associations. He saw the prevalence of each as significant in defining the nature of social reality.

The theme of social reality was developed further by Berger and Luckmann (1967), who applied the approach to an understanding of social structures and institutions. The essence of their argument was that there is no objective social reality. Instead, society and all the components that go to make it up are socially constructed – that is, produced by society's members. For Berger and Luckmann the social structure was simply composed of typifications.

Berger and Luckmann went on to consider how social structures appear to have an objective reality or are assigned an objective existence. They identified two distinct processes of significance here – reification and legitimation. Reification is the process whereby social phenomena (the products of individual actions and interactions) are assigned an independent existence – that is, they have status in their own right (as we have seen, this was also an element in Marx's thought); legitimation is the process whereby the institutional structures of society are explained and justified.

Item H

Modernization, Moral Panics and the Gypsies

At either end of Europe different moral panics are sweeping gypsies into the biggest crisis of a generation. In different ways Europeans suffering from global recession have seized onto this most powerless of minorities to blame them for the ills of the age. National governments do little to defend their Romani citizens and expel non-citizens. Each claims the situation is a local problem that foreigners cannot understand. This pattern has been recurring for five centuries since the nation-state first emerged; but in the last 35 years something has changed, organizations of gypsies have come together to resist; and international organizations such as the European Union have begun to take their side against national governments...

On 10 July 1992 in Helsinki the Conference on Security and Cooperation in Europe (CSCE) adopted its strongest ever condemnation of racial, ethnic and religious discrimination and violence. European governments, including that of the UK, affirmed (OSCE, 1992):

> the need to develop appropriate programmes addressing problems of their respective nationals belonging to Roma and other groups traditionally identified as Gypsies and to create conditions for them to have equal opportunities to participate fully in

the life of society and will consider how to co-operate to this end.

In London, on 18 August 1992, just 39 days after John Major signed the Helsinki Document, the government published a consultative paper proposing to end the public provision of Gypsy caravan sites and encourage all Travellers to settle, with ferocious penalties for any still left on the road.

(Adapted from T. A. Acton, 'Modernisation, Moral Panics and the Gypsies', *Sociology Review* 4(1), 1994)

Exercise 2.16

This exercise encourages you to explore the ideas of phenomenology in more detail. It focuses on the way that a particular social phenomenon (Gypsies) is assigned an objective reality – that of 'social problem' – through the process of moral panic. Item H suggests that this has become the Gypsies' defining identity in the eyes of the community, obscuring all sense of their unique history and culture. Read the item and answer the following questions.

(K) 1. What do you think is meant by the term 'moral panic'? (Hint: If you are
(U)   unsure, look up Cohen's work in Lawson and Heaton, 2009.)

2. What do you think are the 'ills of the age' to which the article
(I)   refers?

(A) 3. According to the item, what impact has the CSCE had on the Gypsies'
      situation?

(I)(A) 4. What 'problems' do you suppose the Gypsies face that currently prevent
(An)   them from participating fully in the life of society?

(I)(A) 5. According to the item, why was John Major's action out of step with the
      Helsinki Document?

(An) 6. What do you think may have motivated this action? (Hint: At the
(E)   time the media were giving a lot of negative publicity to New Age
      travellers.)

(An) 7. To what extent do you agree with the view that Gypsies are powerless
(E)   to resist scapegoating and persecution in Europe? (Hints: what weakens
      their social position? What mechanisms exist to promote their rights, and

how successful are these likely to be in the light of the prevailing social conditions, for example, global recession, social attitudes – for example, prejudice and discrimination – and social processes – for example, stereotyping, marginalization?)

Phenomenology – an evaluation

Strengths

1. Phenomenology attempts to develop symbolic interactionism in an innovative way – that is, moving away from consciousness towards analysis of the micro structures that influence human behaviour.
2. It draws upon concepts from a number of theoretical perspectives, including Weber (social action), Marxism (reification, legitimations) and symbolic interactionism (reflexivity/adaptation) and seeks to unite them in a single eclectic approach to the study of social life.
3. Phenomenologists seek to conduct both micro-level and macro-level analyses, undertaking structural analysis from the perspective of the individual.

Limitations

1. Work is seen by critics as nothing more than a subjective characterization of the social world. The theory and its various interpretations lack empirical validity. It is more a collection of abstract concepts than a coherent theory.
2. Denying the existence of social reality has generated controversy. By failing to explain the pervasive existence of structures, Berger and Luckmann (1967) in particular lose credibility, which weakens the significance of their work, and more broadly the credibility of phenomenology as a perspective.

Ethnomethodology

Ethnomethodologists are interested in the methods people use in their daily lives. Their emphasis is on doing, not thinking – that is, they choose to study human action rather than interpreting meaning, but recognize that action is essentially social because it is influenced by the social world. They do not go as far as to adopt the structuralist beliefs of structural functionalists, but they do give more credence than symbolic interactionists to the influence that social norms and conventions have on behaviour.

Ethnomethodologists see social action as largely a response to the pre-structured routines of the prevailing society. Thus they reject the interactionist notion that behaviour is reflexive, conscious and/or calculated. Instead of exploring the meaning behind action, ethnomethodologists study the 'existing but unnoticed' rules that govern human behaviour. It is these rules, in their view, that bring organization to everyday life.

The most high-profile ethnomethodologist is Garfinkel, whose work inspired others to expand and diversify the theory. The majority of studies conducted in the ethnomethodological tradition have sought to challenge or debunk many of the taken-for-granted practices and procedures of the social world, seeing this as a means towards greater understanding and the development of knowledge. Because the subject matter of ethnomethodology is everyday life, anyone can conduct research.

To demonstrate the accessibility of some aspects of ethnomethodology, brief consideration will be given to examples of research. Almost anything is a potential object for study, as long as it involves the existing but unnoticed rules that underlie human behaviour. Thus queuing at the cinema, going to a cashpoint, ordering a drink at a bar and even using a urinal are all rich areas of inquiry. Although none of these topics has yet to attract the attention of ethnomethodologists, this does not mean it will not in the future. The examples outlined below show that the topics chosen for research are often mundane.

The most famous studies are the breaching experiments conducted by Garfinkel in the 1960s. The basic objective of these studies was to breach (go against) the commonly expected patterns of behaviour in a given social setting. The most often quoted example of this research documents what happened when Garfinkel (1967) got his students to go home and spend 15 minutes to an hour pretending to be boarders (house guests). The purpose was to explore the impact that an individual's behaviour can have upon others when commonsense assumptions about behaviour are overturned. Garfinkel showed that breaching conventions can cause great personal distress and discomfort, which individuals try to cope with by seeking rational explanations for the change in behaviour. Examples from the boarders study included parents assuming the student was sick, in some kind of trouble or going crazy. Ironically all of these seemed more comfortable alternatives than accepting the breach of convention.

Not surprisingly, the world of business has been quick to capitalize on research exploring the nuances of job interviews and negotiations between business executives. Furthermore the potential of such research is being recognized by public as well as commercial enterprises. For example, in 1996 Birmingham City Council Education Department commissioned a study (Bozic, 1997) to explore conversations between special-needs coordinators in schools and educational psychologists. It was hoped that this would lead to more productive working relationships. The research was regarded as successful in that it highlighted potential areas for improvement in practice.

Item I

Sincere and Cynical Performances

You might be surprised that teachers and lecturers can feel very nervous about 'performing' in front of a group of students. Ken Plummer has said that as a young lecturer who had received no training in how to lecture he used to get so nervous he would stutter. Goffman (1959) argued that when we see a person portraying a character we tend to take the 'performance' at face value and therefore believe that this is the person's real self. Generally students perceive their lecturers to be 'sincerely wise and knowledgeable' and therefore prefer them to maintain this status difference, according to research by Goffman. This makes it easier both for the students and their educators in being able to predict and anticipate how the performance will unfold – a degree of formality even in a friendly context goes a long way to ensuring the situation works well for participants.

However, Goffman also says that performers like lecturers and teachers can feel a discrepancy between their performance and who they really are. Hence, they work really hard to create impressions and manage the presentation of themselves. This means they might have a 'cynical' approach to their own performance seeing it as a form of 'roleplay'. 'Stage-fright' may occur if the lecturer suffers a crisis of confidence and fears their performance may not live up to the expectations of their students – it is almost like a fear of being unmasked.

(Adapted from Susie Scott, 'Symbolic Interactionism in the Classroom',
Sociology Review 16(4), 2007)

Exercise 2.17

1. Engage in some ethnomethodological research (see Link Exercise 2.1 below) in your next classroom or lecture experience. Try to uncover systematically

the rules governing the situation. Look for the signs that might indicate your teacher/lecturer adopting a 'sincere' or 'cynical' approach. Is their dress an indication of an attempt to look professional – that is fulfil their role appropriately? Does improvisation occur when the control of the 'performance' is relaxed? Is the language used in interaction with students of a particular 'type'? Is there any evidence of 'stage-fright'?

2. In small groups, select one topic from the following list and write down the rules that govern behaviour in that situation. Compare your ideas:

   (a) Starting a new job.
   (b) Trying on clothes in a communal changing room.
   (c) New Year's Eve party.
   (d) Family celebration at Auntie Flo's.
   (e) Accepting an unwelcome gift.
   (f) Buying something embarrassing from the chemist.
   (g) Someone you *think* you know calling out your name across a crowded room.

Link Exercise 2.1

Try to conduct your own piece of ethnomethodological research following the steps outlined below. Before making a start, it may be helpful to read about ethnographic studies in Chapter 8 (pp. 282–4).

1. Select an aspect of human behaviour or a social phenomenon that you consider is underpinned by subtle rules.
2. Note down any 'existing but unnoticed' rules you think may be relevant.
3. Conduct an observation of your chosen topic. Record the subtle rules that shape the behaviour/action. If you have enough time you may wish to conduct more than one observation of the same phenomenon in order to clarify your thinking/interpretation.
4. Analyse your data and list the rules you have identified as relevant.
5. Compare the rules you have identified with your initial thoughts (recorded in step 2). How accurate were your initial thoughts? Did your research reveal anything unexpected/unusual? What? Why?

Ethnomethodologists also offer a critique of structuralist sociology. They argue that any sociology that goes beyond the level of the individual is fundamentally flawed. This is because it involves sociologists imposing their own sense of social reality on the world. For this reason they also reject the scientific study of society, arguing that it is impossible to study objectively what is essentially a collection of subjective phenomena.

Ethnomethodology – an evaluation

Strengths

1. There is little doubt that the ideas and research are innovative, interesting and accessible to all.
2. The research appears to have a number of practical applications. Businesses and other institutions can use ethnomethodological techniques to improve the quality of relationships and working practices.

Limitations

1. Critics argue that the work is small-scale and lacks a historical and social setting. It lacks the sweeping power of a grand theory and offers little explanation of society at large.
2. It has been criticized as being highly unscientific, being nothing more than the subjective interpretation of individual sociologists studying a particular social situation.

Exercise 2.18

Now you have read the section on a society based on interpretation of meaning, devise a table in which to summarize the main theories (see earlier in the chapter for an example). Using the completed table to help structure your thoughts, write a summary of the main arguments presented in this section (no more than 250 words). Attempt to strike a balance between the basic assumptions of each theory, plus its strengths and limitations.

A SOCIETY BASED UPON MALE DOMINATION: FEMINIST THEORY

Feminist theory has a long history both in terms of trying to understand the position of men and women in society theoretically and also in terms of practical action to gain equality and justice for women in society. The basis of all feminist accounts is the same – the notion that men have more power, privilege, freedom and rights in society than women and can dominate women in many spheres – work, leisure, home and education. The variations in the perspectives are related to the belief in the different extents of the divisions and differences between the genders and the means by which to address them. Feminists believe that women should have equal rights in society and any aspect of society which oppresses women should be changed.

Feminist theorists seek to understand society from the perspective of women and to use this knowledge pro-actively to try to overcome the oppression and disadvantage that women face in daily life. As Pilcher (1993) notes, the word 'feminism' is French in origin and dates from the 1890s, when *feminisme* began to be used as a synonym for the emancipation of women. Feminist theory is women-centred in three ways:

- It focuses on women's position and experience in society.
- It applies a woman's perspective to the study of the social world.
- It criticizes the *status quo* and works to improve the position of women.

Although feminists are assumed to share a common purpose with regard to their work, feminism is not a unified theory, and although feminist research has developed its own approach there are also variations in the ways feminists go about their work. This is because feminists do not agree about the ways we can explain women's subordination or about how women can be emancipated (Abbott and Wallace, 1990). Instead a range of feminisms exist. Pilcher (1993) offers a reason for this 'theoretical plurality', arguing that increased awareness has developed of the differences between women. These differences are based on class, ethnicity, age and sexuality, and could have more bearing than gender on an individual's life experience. Therefore it no longer seems appropriate to speak of a single feminism. Feminism gave rise to gender studies in sociology which highlighted the many areas of women's lives and experiences which had been previously ignored or considered unimportant by traditional sociologists. More recently there has been a focus on men and masculinities with the rise of the 'laddism', 'chavs' and 'metrosexuals' (Parker and Lyle, 2005; Simpson, 2007), which we will explore later in Chapter 4.

What are the features of feminist theory that mark it out as distinct from most sociological theories? First, feminism has developed from a range of disciplines – anthropology, law, religion, politics, biology, economics, history, social science, psychology. Second, feminism seeks not just to understand the world but to use that knowledge to promote the emancipation of women and equality for women. Third, its basis is political rather than social – interested more in activism than enlightenment. Fourth, feminist theory and research bridges the micro–macro sociology gap, providing insights into each domain.

The theories considered in this section explore two basic issues: (1) the sources or causes of women's oppression and (2) the routes to emancipation. Each theory has its own views on how research should be conducted. We shall consider the impact of feminism on society and academia later in this chapter, after focusing on the five main forms of contemporary feminism: Marxist feminism, radical feminism, socialist feminism, liberal feminism and black feminism.

Marxist feminism

Marxist feminists draw inspiration from the writings of Marx and Engels, and seek to apply Marx's model of the capitalist structure to the experiences of women. The concepts of subordination and exploitation are of great interest to feminists, for in their view it is these that hold the key to gender inequality in contemporary society. Although inspired by Marx, Marxist feminists are also critical of him. This discontent stems from Marx's apparent lack of interest in and lack of concern for women as a social group. As Abbott and Wallace (1990, p. 214) note:

> Marx himself was not concerned with the position of women in capitalist society. Marx rejected notions of morality, justice and equal rights as bourgeois ideas. He was concerned not with reform, but with developing a scientific account of the exploitation of the working class under capitalism with a view to overthrowing that system.
>
> The concepts Marx uses appear to be neutral, but they are in fact sex-blind; he fails to recognize that women are subject to a special form of oppression within capitalist societies and does not analyse gender differences and gender ideologies.

Although dissatisfied with Marx, Marxist feminists use his work as the basis for their theory, focusing on the idea that women's disadvantaged position stems directly from the capitalist economy. Capitalism leads to the accumulation of wealth, and hence men need to have legitimate heirs to inherit that wealth. Historically, women were required to produce heirs, but to guarantee the legitimacy of the latter the family structure had to be 'tightened up'. The family that arose was characterized by a system of dominant and subordinate roles. It was both patrilineal, with descent and property passing through the male line, and patriarchal, with authority vested in the male household head. Sexual relations became monogamous – that is, a woman could only have sexual relations with her husband. Men had greater freedom owing to double standards and the existence of opportunity – whereas women's lives became increasingly home-centred, men became increasingly responsible for the family income, working outside the home.

Marxists feminists have used Marx and Engels's work as the basis of their argument that the oppression of women is inextricably linked to the capitalist order. For example, Barrett (1980) rejects the argument that women's oppression can be explained by the rise of capitalism alone. Instead she presents an analysis that focuses on ideology as well as class. Barrett uses the term 'familial ideology' to refer to the process whereby society legitimizes the family structure by claiming it is a fundamental universal institution.

Barrett argues that familial ideology succeeded because it fitted with the way bourgeois family relations developed. As Abbott and Wallace (1990, p. 216) note:

> It was not inevitable, but emerged through a historical process in which an ideology that maintained a women's natural role as a domestic labourer – that is, as wife and mother – became incorporated into the capitalist relations of production. This ideology came in part from pre-capitalist views of a woman's place ... and became accepted by the organized working class in the early 19th century. The family/household system became established in the mid nineteenth century as a result of an alliance of craft unions and capitalists, both arguing that women should be excluded from the workforce and men should earn a family wage.

This was significant not just because it condemned women to domestic labour and economic dependence on men, but also because it divided the working class into the waged and the unwaged. This reduced the revolutionary potential of the working class because they were split into different interest groups. It also benefited capitalism by ensuring that a ready supply of low cost workers was always available. Not only did these women form a reserve army of labour, they also reproduced the future labour force at little cost to the capitalist. Production costs were borne by the family wage, thus limiting a worker's ability to withdraw his labour in return for higher pay and better working conditions. Marxist feminists also recognize the economic role that women continue to play in providing unpaid healthcare (Graham, 1984) and 'emotion work' (Duncombe and Marsden, 1995) to benefit the capitalist system.

Because society can change rapidly at times, researchers have been keen to study the implications of these changes. Research by Morris (1993) provided a useful test of how applicable the ideas outlined above were to women in 1990s Britain. Morris's study of forty married or cohabiting couples in

Hartlepool, selected from the electoral register, revealed that despite significant changes in the economic structure in the past fifty years, gender roles have not changed greatly. This is partly because structural factors such as employment opportunities, the welfare system and culture have all inhibited reform.

Item J

Morris's Findings

In exploring the ways married couples interact, Morris argued that there were important contexts to be established. These were economic, ideological and social. In looking at how economic conditions affected conjugal relations, Morris noted that female employment opportunities were constrained by two main factors. First, a wife's decisions about a job were influenced by her husband's position in the labour market – where he worked, what income was brought into the household or, with changes in the labour market, whether he had a job at all,. Second, the labour market of women was largely of a part-time nature, which made it particularly hard if the husband was unemployed for any length of time. Moreover, the way the unemployment benefit rules operated at the time of her research acted as a disincentive to the wife to find full-time employment.

In ideological terms, there were still strong forces that reinforced traditional views of the role of women in relation to their family and to employment, such that, even when the husband was unemployed and the wife was working, prime responsibility for running the household remained with the women. In addition, even the provision of support from kinship networks to the working wife did not diminish this responsibility. Morris's conclusion was that changing economic conditions (male unemployment) do not provide a sufficient context for an alteration of the power balance between husband and wife for any substantial change in domestic responsibilities.

Exercise 2.19

This exercise allows you to explore Morris's ideas in more detail. Read Item J and answer the following questions.

1. Why do you think it might have been advantageous to dissuade women from seeking full-time employment?

①Ⓐ 2. Why does the pattern of child care while women are working support the view that inequality is not simply related to economic factors?

①Ⓐ 3. According to the item, why are gender roles impervious (totally resistant) to
Ⓐⁿ changes in the economic structure?

ⒶⁿⒺ 4. To what extent does Morris's research weaken the arguments upon which Marxist feminist theory is based? Justify your answer.

Marxist feminism – an evaluation

Strengths

1. Marxist feminism brings together Marxian class analysis and feminist social protest. In doing so, it draws attention to the marginal economic position of women. It alerts women to potential exploitation.

2. It provides a structuralist interpretation of oppression that can be applied to all areas of social life. It is a macro-level theory that demonstrates how the primary structure of society – the economy – shapes social relationships and life experiences.

Limitations

1. Marxist feminists reduce women's exploitation to the economy. They place little emphasis on the ways men exploit women in society and the home. Although they recognize a link between patriarchal relationships and capitalism, they do not explain why it is women and not men who are exploited.

2. Like other feminist theories, Marxist feminism gives the impression that women are a cohesive group sharing similar experiences of exploitation. Critics argue that this is an oversimplification: working-class or black women probably have more in common with working class or black men than they do with women from other social groups.

Radical feminism

The basic thesis of radical feminists is that the subordination of women is the result of patriarchy (a universal power system whereby men dominate women). Under patriarchy, women are categorized as an inferior 'class' to that of men because of their gender, and relations between men and women are therefore political (Pilcher, 1993). As Abbot and Wallace (1990) note, women have shared class interests because they are dominated by men.

Radical feminists see all society as characterized by oppression. Every institution is a system in which some people dominate others, and in society's most basic structures, in the associational patterns between broad groups or categories of people, there exists a continuous pattern of domination and submission. The most important of these, according to radical feminists, is patriarchy. Under patriarchy men learn to see women as non-human and seek to control them. Control can manifest itself in a number of ways, but all contribute to women's oppression by men. Central to an understanding of control is the concept of violence. Radical feminists have diverse and extreme views on what constitutes violence, but they are clear that it is inextricably linked to patriarchy. They consider that violence can be covert (hidden in complex patterns of exploitation and control) or overt, for example, in the form of physical cruelty, rape, sexual abuse and pornography.

Item K

Doctor Knows Best

Consultation 1

> DOCTOR: First baby?
> PATIENT: Second.
> DOCTOR: (laughing) So you're an expert?

Consultation 2

> DOCTOR: You're looking rather serious.
> PATIENT: Well, I am rather worried about it all. It feels like a small baby – I feel much smaller with this one than I did with my first, and she weighed under six pounds. Ultrasound last week said the baby was very small, as well.
> DOCTOR: Weighed it, did they?
> SECOND DOCTOR: (entering cubicle): They go round the flower shows and weigh cakes, you know.
> FIRST DOCTOR: Yes, it's a piece of cake, really.

Consultation 3

> PATIENT: I've got a pain in my shoulder.
> DOCTOR: Well, that's your shopping bag hand, isn't it?

Consultation 4

> DOCTOR: I think what we have to do is assess you – see how near you are to having it. (Does internal examination) Right – you'll go like a bomb, and I've given you a good stirring up. So what I think you should do is, I think you should come in.
> PATIENT: Is it possible to wait another week, and see what happens?
> DOCTOR: You've been reading the *Sunday Times*.
> PATIENT: No, I haven't. I'm married to a doctor.
> DOCTOR: Well, you've ripened up since last week and I've given the membranes a good sweep over.
> PATIENT: What does that mean?
> DOCTOR: I've swept them – not with a brush, with my finger. (Writes in notes 'Give date for induction.')
> PATIENT: I'd still rather wait a bit.
> DOCTOR: Well, we know the baby's mature now, and there's no sense in waiting. The perinatal morbidity and mortality increase rapidly after forty-two weeks. They didn't say that in the *Sunday Times,* did they?

> (*Source*: Ann Oakley, *Women Confined*. Oxford: Martin Robertson, 1984)

Radical feminism is primarily a revolutionary movement for the emancipation of women. Its exponents argue that no area of society is free from male domination. They seek to explore the reasons behind this and to use this knowledge as a route to women's emancipation. Firestone (1974) argues that the division between men and women has a biological base, because women have to take responsibility for the early care of babies. However she recognizes that social and ideological forces have sought to extend the women's role as carers beyond the realms of biological necessity.

Later research rejected biological explanations of gender inequality and instead highlighted the importance of structural factors. Men systematically dominate women in all spheres of social life. This is possible because all relationships between men and women are institutionalized relationships of power and are therefore political in nature (Abbott and Wallace, 1990). Men benefit as a class from the domination of women. Gender inequality is also construed by radical feminists as ideological. They argue that all knowledge valued in society is that which men have defined as important. They cite the status of science in society as a supreme example of this. They also recognize that sociology is equally responsible for promoting male-defined, male-distorted culture.

For radical feminists the solution to the problems that women face in society is sexual revolution, whereby women would develop a common consciousness, reject patriarchal pressures, establish a 'sisterhood' and unite in critical condemnation of patriarchal domination. This would give them the strength to attack male domination at source, or provide the necessary resources and mutual support to withdraw from the world of male domination and create their own economy, family and community structures based on a common appreciation of women's special worth. A small number of radical feminists advocate 'separatism' for men and women so that women can live by themselves to discover their true nature without the interference of men.

Exercise 2.20

This exercise requires you to explore some of the issues raised by radical feminists. Item K is taken from Oakley's (1980) book *Women Confined*. It documents transcripts from doctor–patient encounters observed for her 'Transition to Motherhood' study; the doctors were all males. Read the extracts carefully, and as part of a small group of students answer the following questions.

- (A) 1. What techniques were used by the doctors to erode the patients' status?
- (E) 2. Were any of the doctors' comments justified? If yes, which one(s) and why?
- (E) 3. Which exchange do you find the most offensive? Why?
- (An) 4. If you were to debrief (give feedback to) each doctor, what changes would you recommend they make when faced with a similar situation in the future?
- (E) 5. How could the transcripts be used to support the arguments of radical feminists?

Radical feminism – an evaluation

Strengths

1. Radical feminism is a powerful force for reaffirming women's worth and demonstrating the nature of the oppression and exploitation that threaten to devalue them.
2. The theory has been admired for the sheer force and venom with which the arguments are presented. Radical feminists appeal for and on behalf of women, and clearly state their position on social organization, gender oppression and strategies for change.

Limitations

1. A number of criticisms have been levelled at radical feminists. It has been argued they have failed to explain adequately the ways in which women are subordinated and exploited by men. They also take little account of

different patriarchal relationships in different societies. Furthermore they tend to assume that women from different social classes and backgrounds share the same experiences, whereas because of racism in society black women, for example, may share more experiences with black men than white women.

2. The radical aspect of the theory has made it a source of concern in certain circles and an object of ridicule in others. Some critics argue that radical theorists have gone too far in advocating a world free of men. It threatens social life as we know it and overlooks the fact that many women appear to enjoy reciprocal and satisfactory relationships with men.

Socialist feminism

Socialist feminists have sought to bring together the two broadest and most valuable feminist traditions: Marxian and radical feminist thought. This has led to the development of two types of socialist feminism. The first focuses exclusively on women's oppression and understanding it in a way that brings together knowledge (from Marxism) of class oppression and (from radical feminism) gender oppression. The second sets out to describe and explain all forms of social oppression, using knowledge on class and gender hierarchies as a base from which to explore systems of oppression centring not only on class and gender but also on race, ethnicity, age, sexual preference and location within the global hierarchy of nations.

Socialist feminism attempts to develop an understanding of the relationship between patriarchy and capitalism, arguing that patriarchy takes a specific form in capitalist societies (Abbott and Wallace, 1990). Socialist feminists argue that patriarchy predates and is thus independent of capitalism. In pre-industrial times women were gradually marginalized to the domestic realm as men became more dominant in the production realm. Capitalism continued this process, progressively excluding women from all areas of social life. Men's role in the public sphere was affirmed and women's defining identity stemmed from their domestic role.

Walby (1988) argues that the patriarchy that exists under capitalism has a different form from that in pre-industrial times. Before capitalism, patriarchy benefited the male head of the household; under capitalism it benefits capitalists, sometimes to the detriment of men. As Abbott and Wallace (1990) note, the interests of capitalism and patriarchy are not the same. Capitalists regard women as a good cheap source of labour. They can exploit their low status by paying them low wages and 'laying them off' in times of economic downturn. This does little to benefit the male head of the household, or men generally. Capitalists release women from their domestic duties and allow them to enter the public sphere. This can lead to women enjoying a degree of financial independence, albeit limited. This reduces the power that can be exercised over them in the home. Also, this readily available and cheap source of labour means men's jobs are permanently under threat.

This leads to a division in society between capitalists and men. Men take steps to exclude women from the labour market or to restrict their employment to 'women's work'. Capitalists collude with this until there is a labour shortage, but then actively seek to recruit women. This was demonstrated by the mass drive to employ women during the two world wars. Women's lives changed rapidly, as Item L shows, but when the men returned from war, patriarchal domination ensured that women were catapulted back into the private world of the home or into work that was considered more appropriate.

Item L

From Fashion to the Factory

The Second World War for Bunty was not so much a matter of getting a husband as getting a personality.

At the outbreak of war Bunty was working in a shop called 'Modelia – Quality Ladies' Fashions'. She'd been there since leaving school two years before and quite liked the unchallenging nature of each day, although she daydreamed furiously about all the exciting things that were going to happen to her in the future – like the charming, unbelievably handsome man who would appear from nowhere and sweep her away to a life of cocktails, cruises and fur coats.

The shop was deserted. It was a Sunday and Bunty had offered to come in and help with the stock-taking. They sat around listening to a programme called 'How to Make the Most of Tinned Food' while they waited for the Prime Minister to make his 'statement of national importance'. When Mr Chamberlain said *I have to tell you that no such undertaking has been received and Britain is at war with Germany* a little shiver ran down the back of Bunty's neck...

Bunty had great hopes for the war; there was something attractive about the way it took away certainty and created new possibilities. Bunty said it was like tossing coins in the air and wondering where they would land – and it made it likely that something exciting would happen to Bunty and it didn't really matter whether it was the unbelievably handsome man or a bomb – it would mean a change in one way or another...

1942 was the most eventful year of Bunty's war. She had left Modelia by now – Mrs Carter and Mr Simon gave her a very emotional farewell and they said they didn't know what they'd do without their little Bunty.... Like Babs, who was stuffing explosive into shell cases on the Rowntree's floor that had previously produced unlethal fruit gums, Bunty had also moved into war work. Her new job was in a technical instruments factory; before the war they'd made things like microscopes but now they were making things like gun sights. Bunty's job was to check the focus once everything was assembled, and in the beginning she used to pretend she was shooting the Germans, bang bang bang, but after a while the novelty wore off and she had to struggle to stop herself going cross-eyed by the end of the day. By the beginning of 1942 Bunty was pretty much fed up with the war.

(*Source*: K. Atkinson, *Behind the Scenes at the Museum*. London: Black Swan, 1995, pp. 92–3)

Exercise 2.21

Item L is taken from Kate Atkinson's book *Behind the Scenes at the Museum* (1995), which recounts the story of a family from the nineteenth century to the present day. Although a work of fiction, it realistically portrays the experiences endured as society industrialized and social life became more complex, particularly the experiences of women. Read the extract and answer the following questions.

 1. What evidence is there in the extract to validate the socialist feminists' interpretation of women's experience of work?

 2. Why does Bunty's view of employment challenge the ideas of socialist feminists?

Link Exercise 2.2

 Try to find a female family member or friend who worked before/during the Second World War. Conduct an interview to explore the following questions:

1. To what extent did their experience and perception of work mirror Bunty's?
2. To what extent did their experiences of work fit the socialist feminist interpretation of women in the labour market?

Hint: To conduct a successful interview it is important first to plan what format your interview will take and what questions you should ask in order to obtain the information you need. Before deciding the format and devising questions, read the section in Chapter 7 – interviews – pages **254–61**. This will introduce you to the various types of interview and provide points to consider when framing questions.

Socialist feminists therefore suggest that the position of women can be fully understood only if attempts are made to bridge the gap between macro-level institutional domination and the situationally specific, private, mundane experiences of oppressed women. They see this as the key to liberation, for it is this insight which will lead to a shared understanding of the sources of exploitation, which will become the force for collective emancipation.

Socialist feminism – an evaluation

Strengths

1. Socialist feminists attempt to blend the most influential forms of feminism into one coherent theory. In doing so they present a more sophisticated analysis of inequality than economic determinism allows and give credence to the importance of ideological as well as economic domination.
2. They attempt to bridge the gap between structuralist and interpretive perspectives of inequality. Their 'multifaceted system of domination' concept is a coherent attempt to unify personal experience and institutional influences.

Limitations

1. Critics argue that socialist feminism represents the aspirations of white, middle-class women, rather than those of all women. For some women, females too may be oppressors, and thus their route to liberation is social equality *per se* rather than women's emancipation.
2. The approach fails to recognize that women have broken into the labour market and become successful. In fact, in today's Britain women are increasingly becoming the main wage earner in the family as male unemployment rises (see the section in Chapter 4 on post-feminism).

Liberal feminism

Liberal feminism is a minority branch of feminist theory whose ideas are less radical and less controversial than those of the other branches. Liberal feminists consider that gender inequality is the result of the sexual division of labour. They argue that society promotes the attitude that separate public and private spheres should exist, with men being located primarily in the former and women in the latter. These ideas are reinforced by the socialization process, so that children grow up to accept unquestioningly their place in the gendered labour market. An increasingly important agent of socialization is the mass media. Liberal feminists argue that individuals are trained by the mass media and other social institutions to conform to patterns of behaviour that are performed unconsciously. Media images are resistant to change because they reflect the prevailing social attitudes (Trowler, 1991). Thus women are still ignored or trivialized in the media and their symbolic annihilation continues thirty years after the birth of feminism.

Liberal feminism reduces the source of gender inequality to a social process: sexism, which is similar to racism and consists partly of prejudices and discriminatory practices against women and partly taken-for-granted beliefs about the 'natural' differences between women and men that equip them for their different social destinies. Bernard (1982) has explored the impact of sexism upon women. Her research on marriage led her to conclude that marriage is culturally and structurally sexist, with women being assigned inferior roles and asymmetrical chores. She was the first to draw attention to the fact that within marriage there are two marriages – the man's marriage and the woman's marriage:

> in which he holds to the belief of being constrained and burdened, while experiencing what the norms dictate – authority, independence, and a right to domestic, emotional, and sexual service by the wife; and ... in which she affirms the cultural belief of fulfilment, while experiencing normatively mandated powerlessness and dependence, an obligation to provide domestic, emotional and sexual services, and a gradual 'dwindling away' of the independent young person she was before marriage.

Marriage then is good for men and bad for women and will cease to be so unequal in its impact only when couples feel free enough from the prevailing institutional constraints to negotiate the kind of marriage that best suits their individual needs and personalities (Bernard, 1982).

More recent research has revisited marriage as an institution in order to explore whether gender inequality still prevails or whether changes in society have led to the types of relationship advocated above. Duncombe and Marsden (1995) explore the impact that increased female employment has had upon their experience within the home. They consider that pre-existing inequalities have altered little and, worryingly, that women are increasingly labouring under a triple burden. This is because their 'emotion work' has increased to keep pace with the stresses generated by complex industrial society. Duncombe and Marsden note that this gender asymmetry in emotional behaviour has been regarded by feminists as a further dimension of their exploitation by men. Research by the Equal Opportunities Commission (2005) also outlines how gender inequality becomes firmly entrenched when children are born and men and women revert to traditional roles both inside and outside the home.

Item M

Women's Triple Shift

Giddens (1991) explored the issue of intimate relationships in the context of late modernity. In particular he focused on the relationships between men and women in marriage and the way women were confronted with a triple burden of engaging in paid employment, taking prime responsibility for domestic labour, as well as performing 'emotion' work – that is shoring up the emotional and sexual needs of family members. Female engagement in the world of work leads them to turn towards their partners for the emotional and sexual intimacy unobtainable in the public realm. They are encouraged in this by media that put forward an ideal of marriage in which sexual and emotional openness is the bedrock, However, many men do not respond to the move towards an increase in intimacy, but resist it in an attempt to maintain the sexual dominance associated with traditional views of intimacy.

Exercise 2.22

This exercise requires you to consider the emotional side of relationships and whether the feminist interpretations are reasonable. Read Item M and answer the following questions.

1. To what extent do you agree with Giddens's view that women's dissatisfaction with the emotional side of marriage can be attributed to the media rather than to men?

2. What is your understanding of the term 'emotional and sexual openness'?

Ⓘ Ⓐ 3. Identify two benefits and two drawbacks of a relationship based on 'emotional and sexual openness'.

Ⓔ 4. To what extent do you agree that men's desire for dominance threatens emotional intimacy in relationships?

Ⓔ 5. To what extent do you agree with the view expressed in the item that the media have the power to define the ideal marriage?

Ⓐⁿ Ⓔ 6. What implications does the Item have for feminist concerns about asymmetry in 'emotion work'?

Liberal feminists argue for equal rights for women. This implies equality of access (the right to enter professions and occupations that are currently denied them) and equality of opportunity (equal treatment). As Abbott and Wallace (1990) note, liberal feminists fought against laws and practices that give rights to men and not to women, or are designed to 'protect' women, while pressuring governments to uphold legislation that outlaws sexual discrimination and ensures that women enjoy parity of esteem and financial reward in the workplace.

The goal of liberal feminists is not to develop a sophisticated understanding of the structural reasons behind women's exploitation, but to bring about equality. Thus little attention is given to the history of women's oppression or the overthrow of patriarchal or capitalist regimes. Liberal feminists consider that gender inequality will be eliminated only through political, economic and legal channels. The only direct attack they advocate is on sexism, which must be challenged at all levels. The liberal feminist utopia involves freedom of choice, where all individuals are free to select the lifestyle that suits them best, safe in the knowledge that their gender will not act as a barrier to opportunity.

Liberal feminism – an evaluation

Strengths

1. Liberal feminism presents the most pragmatic approach to addressing women's inequality in society, and possibly the most realistic route to change. This makes it more endearing to non-feminists than the extreme and radical theories.

2. Liberal feminism has done much to promote equality of opportunity and has provided social policy with a welcome direction. It has presented a number of key perspectives which have been compatible with mainstream

political beliefs, including careers for women, equal parenting, the need for gender-free schooling and so on.

Limitations

1. Liberal feminist theory displays little interest in the historical subjugation of women. Hard-core feminists would regard this as blatant disregard for the context that led to the current patterns of gender inequality.
2. Liberal feminists have not developed a theory to explore women's experiences or challenge 'malestream' knowledge. Rather than forcing social change from a position of strength, liberal feminists appear to be content with the concessions being made by those who dominate them.

Black feminism

The development of black feminism can be associated with the rise of 'third-wave feminism', a collection of critical and theoretical statements, formulated by the women's movement in the 1980s, that build on the theme of difference. This approach highlights that the majority of feminist contributions before 1980 tended to view women as a single category. This overlooks the differences that exist among women and the differing degrees of domination and exploitation faced by different groups of women.

Black feminists maintain that a feminism that fails to examine and theorize racism is flawed (Pilcher, 1993). They seek to explore sources of racism as well as sexism and to present the experience of some black women in terms of a 'triad of disadvantage' – that is, their disadvantages are compounded three-fold if they are working class, female and black. This view was presented by Bryan *et al.* in their book *The Heart of the Race: Women's Working Lives in Britain* (1985), in which the authors argue, 'if you're a black woman you've got to begin with race'. To support this view they draw attention to a range of racial disadvantages that women experience in contemporary Britain. More recently, Lawson *et al.* (2009) have drawn attention to the triple disadvantage, or 'nesting', that affects black girls' chance of success in the education system.

Hence it is not surprising that black feminists seek to challenge not only sexual ideology and the unequal status of women but all systems of domination. These include sexism, racism, classism, heterosexism and imperialism. They also give attention to the particular false consciousness that has let middle-class, white, heterosexual women use the term woman as a monolithic category in opposing male domination while ignoring their own acts of domination over women who do not share their class, their race or their affectional preferences.

Black feminists believe that the way to challenge domination is through research. By examining the specific experiences of black women within families, the education system and the labour market, they believe that they can arrive at an understanding of the sources of oppression. Recent examples of such work include Pnina Werbner's (1992) analysis of Pakistani social networks and the gift economy, and Butler's (1995) research on the experiences of young Muslim women in Britain. In citing these studies another difficulty is brought to light – just as black feminists are keen to stress that 'woman' should not be used as a generic concept, nor should 'black'. This raises the question of whether the term 'black feminism' should be modified to accommodate ethnic diversity. However, at present, it is probably reasonable to argue that the differences between women from ethnic minorities are less than those between ethnic minority women and the indigenous population.

Black feminism – an evaluation

Strengths

1. Black feminism draws attention to the fact that not all women experience similar disadvantages in society.
2. It has created an academic movement whereby black sociologists can apply their skills to the benefit of their cultural group and quantify the extent of ethnic exploitation.

Limitations

1. There is a danger that stressing difference rather than similarity may lead to fragmentation of the feminist movement and threaten coalitions aimed at bringing about women's emancipation.
2. In using the collective term 'black', black feminists may be as guilty of ignoring the distinct/diverse experiences of particular ethnic groups as those they criticize.

A feminist attack on 'malestream' sociology

Despite their differences, the main feminist perspectives are united about the male-dominated nature of sociology. Abbott and Wallace (1990) coined the term 'malestream' to define this phenomenon and quoted Ann Oakley to draw attention to the difficulties this poses:

Male orientation may so colour the organisation of sociology as a discipline that the invisibility of women is a structured male view, rather than a superficial flaw. The male focus, incorporated into the definitions of subject areas, reduces women to a side issue from the start. (Oakley, 1974, p. 4)

In her reader Oakley (2005) underlines her argument about the sexist nature of universities, research and sociology; despite the great advances made by women over the thirty or more years since she began writing and researching there is still male domination in many spheres of social life.

Although there has been some movement in the last twenty years towards the greater incorporation of women's issues into research and books, Abbott and Wallace (1997) argue that there is still considerable generalization from research on men to conclusions about men and women, and that textbooks still tend to incorporate gender issues as an incidental extra rather than an integral theme. If women are to achieve equality, Abbott and Wallace argue, the gaps in existing knowledge will have to be filled. They offer three possible options for overcoming the problems of malestream sociology:

- Integration – Remove the existing bias in sociology and centralize the place of women.
- Separatism – Seek to develop a separate discipline – 'a sociology for women by women' (ibid., p. 9).
- Reconceptualization – Recognize the mutual benefit that malestream and feminist research may generate and attempt to synthesize the two approaches in a coherent way.

Despite likely resistance on the part of malestream sociologists, Abbott and Wallace (1997) regard the last option as offering the most promise for feminists and women in general.

Feminism and sociological research

Sociology has been in its modes of thinking, methodologies, conceptual organization and subjects of inquiry, one of the most sexist of academic disciplines...the male's social world has constituted the world of male sociology. (Oakley, 1980, p. 71)

Feminist researchers like Abbot and Wallace (1990) and Oakley (1979–2005) have argued strongly against the traditional scientific, empirical model of enquiry adopted by male researchers in sociology. Their critique of traditional sociological research methods strikes at the heart of how sociological knowledge is produced, arguing that women have been excluded from both producing knowledge and being the subjects of it. The traditional view of the sociological world is from a male perspective – 'malestream'. Oakley (1979) also took issue with the uncritical application of the 'scientific method' to the study of society. She argued that the image of the white-coated, male researcher needed to be challenged, especially as part of the power relationship between the researcher and respondent. She argued that particularly when the subject of study was female this relegated her as the respondent to a secondary or subordinate position. In much of her own research into childbearing, domesticity, motherhood and housework, Oakley treated her research respondents as equal to her in status, sharing experiences and empathizing with feelings of the women, and she advocated qualitative methodologies. In her research on the transition to motherhood she had to reassess the nature of interviewing as a traditional research tool. She found that the textbook guidance on being detached, objective and neutral in interviews, and the hierarchical nature of the process, would undermine her research, which often involved discussion of highly personal and intimate issues. Oakley herself was asked for her opinions during interviews she conducted and concluded that the interview must be a two-way process if it is to truly reveal sociological knowledge about women. She found she developed close relationships with the women she interviewed and indeed she often became friends with her respondents and maintained contact for a number of years.

However, she also had a word of caution about such qualitative techniques:

[T]he automatically laudatory designation of qualitative methods within feminist social science and other 'anti-positivist' sociologies is a cause for concern, since such methods are no guarantee of equal power relations between the researcher and the researched. (*The Ann Oakley Reader*, 2005, p. 187)

It would be difficult to pinpoint a feminist methodology, as not all feminists subscribe to a common view. Nevertheless there are what Kelly (1988) calls a set of principles which have emerged from feminist 'practice' – first drawing on women's experience, second doing research that will be of benefit to women, third treating women as active participants in research who can express their opinions and views, and finally a rejection of the notion of objectivity by ensuring that the researcher is on the same 'critical plane' as those being studied (this is known as 'critical reflexivity').

Angela McRobbie is somewhat critical of earlier feminist researchers for failing to acknowledge that they too are the representatives of powerful academic establishments which use the relative powerlessness of some women to further their own careers (see for example McRobbie, 2008). She also points out that there are major differences and divisions between 'women' as a group: ethnicity, social class, and age account for a wide variety of experience and understanding of the world. As postmodernists would argue, it is naive to assume that what binds women together is their gender.

Exercise 2.23

Copy and complete a larger version of the following summary table, using the information you have read in this section on a society based on male domination.

A society based on male domination

Main theories	Marxist feminism	Radical feminism	Socialist feminism	Liberal feminism	Black feminism
Key writers					
Basic assumptions					
Strengths					
Limitations					

Exam focus: writing an essay

First, revise the summary charts you produced earlier on conflict and consensus theories. You may also wish to skim through the relevant sections of this chapter.

Second, attempt an essay on the following, using the hints on writing an essay below to help you:

1. Compare and contrast conflict and consensus theories. (33 marks)
2. Evaluate the contribution made by each to an understanding of social life. (33 marks)

Hints on writing an essay

General hints

1. Read and *think carefully* about the question.
2. *Answer the question set* – don't just write down great chunks of information from textbooks. Make the information fit the question.
3. Prepare and plan your answer carefully *before* you write.

4. Pay attention to *structure*:

   - Your answer should follow a logical pattern.
   - Start boldly – make reference to the question in the first line if possible.
   - Use clear, linking sentences to help structure your answer.
   - Conclude boldly – make a judgement and justify it.

5. Pay attention to *content*:

   - Make sure every paragraph is *relevant*.
   - Use enough *range* to demonstrate *knowledge*.
   - Do not describe evidence/studies – apply them to the question set.
   - *Evaluate* the evidence as you present it.

How do I go about answering a question?

Follow this simple five-point plan. Let it become second nature and it will help you to approach the question in a systematic way.

1. *Read* the question carefully.
2. *Think* – What exactly is the question asking? How can you best use the information/knowledge that you have to answer it?
3. *Brainstorm* – Write down all the information/evidence that you think might be relevant. You can always cross things out later.
4. *Plan* – construct an answer:

   - Put your brainstorm jottings into a logical series of ideas.
   - Decide on points for your introductory paragraph.
   - Decide on points for the conclusion.

5. *Write* – but only when you have followed steps 1 to 4. By then you will know the shape your answer will take and you should feel confident about approaching the question.

That's a lot to remember: can you remind me what to do?

- Use the five-point plan: read, think, brainstorm, plan, write.
- Make a bold start: demonstrate that you *understand* and are responding to the question set, with relevant *knowledge*.
- Use clear *linking* sentences to give your essay a logical framework.
- *Structure paragraphs*: linking sentences, evidence (clear and concise), *interpretation* (what does it show?), *application* (how relevant is it to the question?), *evaluation* (how useful is it, and how does it influence the argument?); link back to the question.
- Conclude boldly, giving a *reasoned/justified* answer that flows logically from the arguments presented in the essay.

Important concepts

ideology • hegemony • conflict • consensus • protestant ethic • interpretivism • patriarchy • malestream

Critical thinking

- Do traditional theories such as Marxism and functionalism still have a place in modern sociology and can they help us to explain and understand the modern social world?
- Do the theories which look at action and rules in society such as interactionism and ethnomethodology undermine or complement the structural theories?
- How relevant is feminism to the position of women in society today?

Chapter 3

Theoretical Debates

By the end of this chapter you should be able to:

- identify the four main debates that have captured the attention of traditional sociologists:
    1. modernism versus postmodernism – the status of evidence
    2. structuralism versus social action
    3. evolutionary view versus 'here-and-now' analysis
    4. positivism versus antipositivism

- be familiar with the arguments behind the two sides of each of the theoretical debates
- understand the implications of these arguments for the way society is understood and studied
- recognize the position each theoretical perspective adopts in each of the debates
- consider the relative merits of each debate and evaluate its contribution to our understanding of social life

INTRODUCTION

Chapter 2 familiarized you with the four main perspectives on the study of the social world. Although each was presented as a distinct approach, you may have noted some overlap between some of the approaches. One such overlap lies in the fact that all of the perspectives are 'modernist' in nature. By modernist we mean that each of these approaches, in their own way, claims to be able to represent the truth about the nature of society and to demonstrate that truth through the production of evidence. A more recent version of sociology – known as postmodernism – denies this possibility, arguing that there is no such thing as truth or falsity, only different versions of events. This debate is known as modernism versus postmodernism and centres on the status of 'evidence'.

Some theorists seem to be in favour of looking at the structural aspects of society and appear to see this as the key to understanding social life. Others prefer to take the individual as their starting-point for understanding society and focus on meaning, social action and interaction between the members of society. These different positions relate to the second debate to be considered in this chapter – structuralism versus social action.

You may also have noticed that some theorists appear to place particular emphasis on historical analysis, implying that earlier periods of social life can help us to understand why society has ended up as it has. Others appear more interested in looking at present-day phenomena and considering contemporary influences. These two positions will be considered in our discussion of the evolutionary view versus episodic characterization ('here-and-now') analysis.

Another theme touched upon in Chapter 2 provides the basis of the fourth debate: positivism versus antipositivism. This debate concerns the question of whether it is possible to adopt the methods used in the natural sciences to study the social world. Positivists would argue that it is, and that sociology would benefit greatly from doing so. Anti-positivists would strongly disagree with this, seeing a scientific approach in sociology as neither workable nor beneficial.

Each of these debates – modernism versus postmodernism; structure versus action; evolutionary versus episodic; positivism versus antipositivism – will be considered in turn. The main assumptions behind each position will be outlined, and links will be made between theorists featured in Chapter 2 and the positions they have adopted in each debate. Implications for the conduct of research will be discussed and a research example will be given. Finally, the relative merits of each side of each debate will be presented and brief consideration will be given to the usefulness of the debates to sociology as a discipline.

MODERNISM VERSUS POSTMODERNISM – THE STATUS OF EVIDENCE

For more detailed accounts of modernism and postmodernism you should consult Chapter 4 (pages **132–40**). The debate here concerns the nature of evidence and whether or not evidence can prove sociological knowledge to be true. Each of the four perspectives discussed in Chapter 2 claims to be able to represent the truth about social life – what it is actually like – and attempts to justify this claim through the production of empirical evidence.

Of course, the perspectives tend to differ regarding the nature and appropriateness of the evidence – some prefer more statistical, quantitative versions while others might generate more descriptive, qualitative forms. However, the proposition that, in principle, sociologists can offer evidence of proof is common to all four. This proposition is central to modernism and therefore we may say that the four perspectives in Chapter 2 are all modernist in nature.

Epistemology

Epistemology is a branch of philosophy and theory of knowledge that is very important to this debate. Epistemology is concerned with what counts as proof – that is, what conditions need to be met in order to establish the truth (or falsity) of sociological knowledge. The epistemological position of most modern perspectives like functionalism is that empirical evidence is the key criterion of proof. Empirical evidence is generated through the use of sociological methods which focus on *observable factors* that exist in society and can be studied. Hence these sociologists will conduct research using key primary methods such as interviews, questionnaires, observation and/or secondary data such as official statistics, documents and diaries to generate empirical evidence for/against their hypothesis. Postmodernists, however, argue that this criterion (empirical evidence) is not acceptable because it is self-justifying. Postmodernists ask: 'What evidence can we deploy in order to prove that any evidence is based on truth?' There is no sensible answer to this question of course – it is a tautology – that is, saying the same thing twice in different words. We would need to assume what we are trying to prove in order to prove it! Indeed postmodernists argue that *all* criteria of proof (empirical evidence, quantitative and qualitative; logical consistency; practical application – does it work?) are by their *nature* always self-justifying and therefore unacceptable precisely because the criteria are themselves beyond proof. On the basis of this argument, postmodernism rejects epistemology, and therefore truth and falsity and in its place proposes relativism.

Relativism is the position that, in the absence of proof, it is not possible to decide which sociological explanation is better or worse than others. As a result, society or social reality must be regarded as a construction. For postmodernists, all knowledge or so-called truth is related to the context or social situation from which it derives. There is no such thing as objective, neutral or value-free knowledge. Each of the four perspectives in Chapter 2 simply constructs the nature of society in its own image and there is no objective means of choosing between them.

Exercise 3.1

Think about different types of knowledge – scientific, religious, artistic, commonsense. How can we say we 'know' something? Write down a list of five things you think you 'know' to be true or false. Then try to apply a postmodernist approach to that statement. Here is one example to get you started.

The world is round – Scientific experiments and travel in space have provided us with incontrovertible proof that the Earth is round.

Postmodernists would suggest there are other interpretations of the evidence. The view of a round Earth fits with general views about the nature of the universe, science and belief systems much as the flat Earth view did during the middle ages when the church decided what was true or false. (See the Flat Earth Society website www.theflatearthsociety.org). Have we actually seen evidence for a round Earth from experiments or space travel with our own eyes?

STRUCTURALISM VERSUS SOCIAL ACTION

As Haralambos and Holborn (2004, p. 969) note:

> Structural approaches, such as functionalism and some versions of Marxism, emphasize the way that the structure of society directs human behaviour. Social action or interpretive approaches such as those advocated by Weber, symbolic interactionists and ethnomethodologists argue that humans create society through their own actions. This distinction is not neat and clear-cut; most perspectives in sociology show some concern for both social structure and social action, but most perspectives emphasize one aspect of social life at the expense of another.

This provides an ideal starting-point for our discussion of structuralism versus social action. During the course of the discussion it will become clear why 'the distinction is not clear-cut' and why most sociologists are forced to concede that their favoured theoretical position may be unable to accommodate all social phenomena. The discussion will also demonstrate that each position is more complex in its own right than we are generally led to believe.

Structuralism

Although the popular view of structuralism is that it emphasizes social structure at the expense of the way people interpret the world, the foundations of the approach are much more complex than this. Craib (1984) provides a useful insight into the historical development of structuralism and demonstrates that the approach is not unique to sociology but reflects thinking in a range of other academic disciplines, including philosophy, linguistics, cultural analysis, history and anthropology. Although structuralism gained cult status in the 1960s and 1970s, Craib traces its roots to the work of the French sociologists Auguste Comte and Emile Durkheim in the nineteenth century and to Ferdinand de Saussure and the Russian formalist school of literary criticism.

Structuralism developed in response to the need to understand society at a time of rapid social change. It was hoped that intellectuals could provide an insight into the functioning of society so that people would be better equipped to cope with the transition from one form of society (pre-industrial) to another (industrial). Structuralists took as the starting-point for their analysis of society a number of basic assumptions. These were drawn from a number of disciplines and were brought together to provide a cohesive framework for understanding social life.

Central to the approach was the assumption that human beings possess rational faculties that enable them to impose order on the world. Society is shaped by the existence of general meanings, which have an underlying logical structure. This structure is not generated by the individuals themselves (that is, from within), rather it is imposed by society (that is, from without) and reflects the structures of the world. Structuralists concede that the mind gives life to ideas, but the mind is a product of the society in which it exists. So individuals may think they are thinking their own thoughts, but in fact they are constrained by structures imposed by society.

How is this possible? Structuralists give considerable credence to the role of language in structuring thought. This has long been a matter of debate among those psychologists (see Whorf, 1941; Bruner, 1966; Vygotsky, 1962; Piaget, 1973) who have sought to answer the question, 'Does language determine thought or does thought determine language?' Structuralists have seized upon the former aspect of this debate, arguing that if we accept that thinking is a linguistic process, then we are captives of society, for it is society that has determined the structure and nature of language. We can only think what we can represent in language, and therefore our thinking is constrained by vocabulary and semantics (distinctions between meanings).

As Gross (1992) notes, much of the impetus behind the 'language and thought' debate was provided by Edward Sapir, a linguist and anthropologist (someone who studies and compares different societies and cultures), in the 1920s and Benjamin Lee Whorf, an amateur linguist, in the 1940s. The following quotes give a flavour of their work:

We see and hear and otherwise experience very largely as we do because the language habits of our community predispose certain choices of interpretation. Philosophically, this is very radical, it undermines the possibility of man's access to the real world. (Sapir, quoted in Gross, 1992)

The categories and types that we isolate in the world of phenomena we don't find there because they stare every observer in the face; we cut nature up, organize it into concepts and describe significance as we do, largely because we are party to an agreement which holds in the pattern of our language. (Whorf, quoted in ibid.)

These ideas have been the subject of much debate and research, with important implications for the credibility of structuralism as a theory. The following exercise will enable you to explore the language versus thought debate in greater detail.

Exercise 3.2

This exercise encourages you to explore the empirical evidence that has been collected to support/refute the views of Sapir and Whorf and to consider the validity of structuralism in the light of this.

1. Undertake your own research into Sapir and Whorf's ideas. Find and read a review of the language versus thought debate on the internet. You will have to think about the correct search terms to find what you are looking for. (Hint: Use Google Scholar rather than just Google to carry out a more focused search.)
2. Make a note of evidence in support of and against the views of Sapir and Whorf, using a summary chart like the one here to help structure your thoughts. Some information has been included to help you get started.

Language and thought debate – a summary

	Sapir	Whorf
Main ideas	The language habits of our community shape our ability to interpret our experiences	
Supporting evidence		
Refuting evidence		Eysenck and Keane (1990) use research on the ability to describe colours to argue that thought affects language.

3. Discuss with at least one other sociology student whether the information you have collected affects the credibility of the structuralist idea that the mind is a product of the society in which it exists.

Structuralism and ideas

Structuralists propose that the world we see around us is the product of our ideas (Craib, 1984). However these ideas are not randomly generated, but manifestations of the structure of society. Because of this they have an underlying logic. Structuralists believe that studying this underlying logic could provide important information about the way our ideas produce the world we know. Craib (1984, p. 108) provides an applied example to demonstrate this:

> [W]hen Levi-Strauss...claims to have discovered the underlying structure of kinship systems in tribal society, he is claiming to have discovered the underlying structure of kinship terminology, the ideas with which these societies talk about kinship.

Presumably structuralists would apply this assumption to any piece of sociological research. Thus in any research that draws attention to the structural components of any aspect of social life (education, religion, politics, law and so on), structuralists would use this information as a means of exploring the language and discourse (reasoning) that underlies it. In adopting such an approach, they would appear to be making the assumption that the structures or systems of society consistently and reliably reflect the coherent ideas of society's members.

Herein lies a weakness of the structuralist approach. There is a tendency to overlook the fact that structures are unlikely to be the physical manifestation (that is, tangible form) of all ideas because there will be conflicts of interest between people's ideas in society. Thus what exists in physical form may reflect the dominant or most popular discourse rather than an expression of a cohesive set of ideas. Also, in making the assumption that what exists is a reflection of what is thought and communicated, there is a tendency to overlook the fact that rhetoric (theory) and reality (practice) can differ. Craib demonstrates this with reference to the Levi-Strauss example, highlighting that it is possible for kinship behaviour to differ from what the underlying ideas expressed in kinship terminology would lead us to believe. Structuralism does not acknowledge this.

Structural functionalism (see Chapter 2) provides one example of a structuralist approach. In seeking to understand society, attention is given to the various subsystems of the social structure and the way in which these subsystems relate to each other to contribute to society as whole. The subsystems perceived as central are the economy, the family, the education system, the political system, the legal system and the cultural system. All these combine to create society – that is, the social system. All work cohesively to meet the basic needs (or 'functional prerequisites') of society, and each subsystem has a complementary role in performing functions for the benefit of other aspects of the social system.

Exercise 3.3

This exercise helps you to develop an understanding of the interrelationship between the subsystems and the social structure. Copy out the summary table here, and using the completed boxes as a guide, fill in the empty boxes to demonstrate the way each subsystem affects, and is affected by, the social system.

Structural functionalism's interpretation of the role of subsystems in the social system

Name of subsystem	What contribution does it make to society as a whole?	In what way is it affected by the social structure?	What other subsystems is it linked with? Nature of relationship?
Economy			The economy affects all aspects of social life and is affected by the way subsystems fulfil their roles.
Legal system	Ensures common standards of behaviour and sanctions against wrong-doing.		
Religion		Dominant attitudes and values can be inculcated into religious doctrine.	
Education system			
Culture			Culture is generated by and contributes to the values systems and beliefs in society.
Family	Socializing, nurturing society's members and giving people a place from which to relate to wider society.		
Political system			

Structural Marxism provides another example of the structuralist approach. Structural Marxists argue that underlying structures determine our actions, and our actions serve to maintain and reproduce social structures. Human beings become the puppets of social structures, which in turn become a sort of machine in permanent motion (Craib, 1984). For Marxists, the primary influence within the social structure is the economy. This has an overarching influence on the other subsystems, which are seen as performing a supportive role in reproducing the economic structure of society and, more broadly, the social system, which is seen primarily in economic terms.

The Marxist interpretation of the social structure differs from the functionalist interpretation in the following ways:

- Each subsystem is perceived to perform a role in reproducing the economic structure.
- Each subsystem is perceived to be influenced by the economy.
- Links between subsystems help to perpetuate and strengthen the economic structure.

Exercise 3.4

This exercise will enable you to explore the Marxist interpretation of the social structure in more detail.

1. Copy and complete the summary table shown here, using the completed boxes as a guide.

Marxism's interpretation of the role of subsystems in the social system

Name of subsystem	What contribution does it make to reproducing the economic structure?	In what way is it affected by the economy?	What other subsystems is it linked with? How do links strengthen the economic structure?
Legal system	Social order is needed for economic stability/ cohesive management of economic resources.		Religion and education serve to reinforce the law via socialization, which promotes social cohesion/ stability.
Religion			
Education system		Education is generally seen to reflect the needs of	

		the economy, and quality of education is influenced by financial resources available.
Culture		
Family		The family produces and rears the future workforce at little direct cost to the capitalist.
Political system		

2. You may have noticed that the table differs from the one completed previously for structural functionalism, because one box has been omitted:

  (a) Which aspect of the social structure is not treated as a discrete entity by Marxists?
  (b) Why?

As well as advocating an understanding of the social world that focuses on structures and systems, structuralists adopt this approach when undertaking research. They conduct large-scale, macro-level research to develop an understanding of the systems or logic behind their chosen research area. Their aim is to use this understanding as the basis for making generalizations and developing social laws.

Item A

A Three-Way Split

Will Hutton is an economist who writes in newspapers like *The Observer*. His influential book, *The State We're In* (Jonathon Cape, 1995), looked at contemporary social, political and economic change in Britain.

Hutton's analysis is strongly empirical – that is, he tends to base his approach on hard data or 'facts' rather than on any particular theoretical approach...

British society has become polarized, argues Hutton; the gap between the rich and poor is growing, opening up unacceptable and damaging levels of inequality between those in secure, well-paid work and those at the 'margins', who have low pay or who must rely on an increasingly stretched benefits system. This polarization was caused by Conservative monetary policies, especially since the late 1980s, which assert that the free market (rather than public bodies) is best placed to decide the 'price' of wages and goods and on how to deliver the most efficient services, e.g. for water, gas and electricity.

Hutton argues the demands of the free market have produced a segmented or segregated workforce – the 30–30–40 society. The first 30 per cent are at the bottom of the social and economic pile, unemployed or in low-paid, insecure work; the middle 30 per cent have at least some job security and quality of life; and the top 40 per cent are in secure, regular work and at least some of these are doing pretty well.

In 2003, according to the research published by the Joseph Rowntree Foundation, 12.5 million people were living in relative poverty. This comprises 3.8 million children, 6.6 million adults of working age and over 2 million pensioners. This is despite ambitious plans to eradicate poverty put in place by the Labour government.

(Adapted from Terry Ward, 'A Three-Way Split? The 30–30–40 Thesis', Research Roundup, *Sociology Review*, 6(3), 1997; and Denscombe, M., *Sociology Update*. Leicester: Olympus, 2004)

Exercise 3.5

This exercise will enable you to explore the form that structuralist analysis might take. Read Item A and answer the following questions.

1. What is the focus of Will Hutton's book?
2. According to Item A, what does the term 'empirical' mean?
3. What observation does Hutton make about the state of British society?
4. In your view, which social groups may find themselves at the 'margins' – that is, poorly paid and reliant upon benefits?
5. According to Hutton, what has caused polarization?
6. In Hutton's view, what impact has polarization had upon the British class structure?
7. Identify two features of structuralist analysis that are evident in Hutton's work.
8. To what extent do you agree with Hutton's view that polarization has occurred in British society?
9. What does the number of people in poverty indicate about society from a structuralist perspective?
10. Why might social policies fail to achieve their targets to eradicate poverty?

(Hint: Before answering, you may like to look at Kirby, *Stratification and Differentiation,* 1999, to gain an idea of what various sociologists have said about the composition of the British class structure.)

Structuralism – an evaluation

Strengths

1. The assumption that an underlying logic or structure exists and can be inferred from objective study of social systems provides a useful focus for research.
2. It is a cohesive attempt to understand society. Rather than being studied in isolation, social phenomena are studied in terms of their relationship with other aspects of the social system. It is context that gives meaning to certain phenomena, and if this is not studied valuable insight is lost (try Exercise 3.6 for an application of structural approaches to real events).

Limitations

1. Structuralism does not adequately explain how and why social change occurs. Instead of recognizing the role of individuals in shaping their own destiny, structuralists regard individuals as being affected by transformations within the social structure. However, the sources of these 'transformations' are left vague and little attention is paid to the way they manifest themselves in the minds and actions of society's members.
2. Action theorists and humanists are very critical of the structuralist puppet analogy, arguing that it is wrong to present human beings as products of society. Instead, they argue that humankind produces society through action and interactions, and society cannot exist independently of humankind. It does not have an independent existence – without people there would be no society.

(E)

Exercise 3.6

2008 saw the global economy go into crisis. Owing initially to massive losses in the sub-prime banking sector in America, large, previously profitable international banks went bankrupt. The stock markets suffered their largest falls in decades and the situation was likened to the Great Depression of the 1930s. The major governments in Europe and America stepped in to support their economies and banks were nationalized with debts being underwritten by the government. Newspaper headlines described the situation as a 'utter carnage', with Western economies on the edge of an 'abyss'.

Using your knowledge and understanding of functionalism and Marxism as structural perspectives apply them to the 2008 economic crisis. How would each perspective explain the role of the economy and its effect upon subsystems of society?

SOCIAL ACTION

This approach is associated primarily with the work of symbolic interactionists, phenomenologists and ethnomethodologists, although aspects of the approach can also be found in the work of Max Weber.

Both structural functionalists and conflict theorists give some credence to the role that individuals play in structuring society. Parsons (1937) emphasizes individual choice and mutual benefit in shaping social action. This action is given a structural emphasis because it is assumed to provide the basis for future social action: the way we behave as individuals is shaped by the larger society in which we live so that actions can be seen to have benefits for everyone. We therefore carry on behaving in a particular way.

Similarly Dahrendorf (1959) identifies the influence that human behaviour has upon the structure of society. He recognizes the importance of shared and conflicting interests in explaining the nature of society, and sees these as stemming from the roles people occupy in society and the way these affect their behaviour. Dahrendorf explores how and why conflict groups arise by considering the shared interests of individuals, which act as a basis of social action. He seeks to understand this in a systemic context, by giving consideration to the impact that the prevailing social conditions have upon the incidence of conflict and the form that conflict might take. For Craib (1984), it is this common ground that makes structural functionalism and conflict theory different from interpretive sociology.

Social action theorists reject the structuralist interpretations of social life. They strongly refute the structuralist assumption that people are the puppets of their ideas, and that their actions are not determined by choice or decision but are the outcome of the underlying structure or logic of ideas. Social action theorists argue that human action is based on the interpretations of the social actor. This interpretation is informed by social experience and shared meaning systems developed over time through the interaction process. Craib (1984, p. 72) uses the analogy of a conversation to capture the essence of this approach:

> The social world shows the same qualities of flow, development, creativity and change as we would experience in a conversation around a dinner table or in a bar. In fact the world is made of conversations, internal and external.

A number of key assumptions form the basis of the social action approach. Human beings are seen as unique owing to their capacity to think. Thinking is both influenced by and influences social interaction. It is through contact with other people and social experiences that people formulate and reformulate their ideas, attitudes and beliefs. A crucial part of this process is reflection, whereby individuals examine possible courses of action and their consequences through internal monitoring mechanisms. This is an integral part of human functioning, occurring internally at the subconscious level, but simultaneously affecting social interaction in the external or 'social' world.

Social action theorists explore the meanings behind human behaviour in a variety of social settings. Their work is generally small-scale and focuses on the way individuals interact with their environment. They see this as important because they believe that the social world is nothing more than a network of social interactions. If individuals did not assign meaning, act and interact there would be no social world.

The social action approach has been increasingly adopted by sociological researchers in recent times. Although many researchers have focused on new areas of study, some have revisited previous topics but applied an original perspective to the research evidence.

Item B

Language and Social Identity

Since 1987 Robin Wooffitt has been collaborating with Dr Sue Widdicombe (Department of Psychology, University of Edinburgh) on a series of projects concerning adolescent subcultures and social identity. In social psychology, social identity and group affiliation are treated largely as outcomes of mental or cognitive processes; sociologists, however, have tended to view subcultural membership as a collective symbolic response to class inequalities. As an alternative to these traditional approaches, they are investigating how identities are constructed in language and used as resources in social interaction.

Their methodology draws upon conversation analysis in sociology and discourse analysis in social psychology. The data for these studies comes from recorded interviews with members of youth subcultures, such as punks, skinheads, goths, rockers. These interviews were conducted in a variety of natural settings, such as London streets where members of particular subcultures are known to gather, and local and national music festivals. The results of the research were published as *The Language of Youth Subcultures: Social Identity In Action* (Harvester Wheatsheaf, 1994).

(*Source*: Research Initiative, Department of Sociology, University of Surrey, Project Director Robin Wooffitt)

This exercise will enable you to explore in more depth research conducted from a social action perspective. Item B describes how the social action approach can offer new insights into a well-documented topic: social identity. Read the item and answer the following questions.

(I)(A)   1.   How does Wooffitt and Widdicombe's research differ from the approach adopted by traditional sociologists?

(K)(U)   2.   What theoretical perspective appears to be reflected in their work?
(I)(A)

(An)(E)   3.   What pitfalls might come from their chosen methodology?

(An)(E)   4.   What insight does this research offer that would not have emerged if a structuralist study had been conducted?

Social action – an evaluation

Strengths

1. By focusing on the way individuals construct the world, there is no danger of society being 'reified' – that is, being attributed with an independent existence. Instead it is seen as produced by the actions and interactions of individuals. This gives importance to the influence that individuals can exert by their very existence.

2. The social action approach does not attempt to be a theory of society. Instead it remains true to its basic assumption that the starting-point for understanding society is human beings, and that it should remain at that level. It does not cause confusion by trying to bridge the gap between individuals and structures.

Limitations

1. The work is small-scale and lacks a historical setting. Critics would argue that it is inappropriate not to give consideration to social structures and institutions and the influence they have upon individuals' lives.

2. Structuralists would argue that the underlying meanings that shape social action and interaction are produced by society, and that what appears as common sense in the minds of individuals is structured by society, not created by them.

The acknowledgement of meaning: Weber's *Verstehen*

When reviewing the structuralism versus social action debate it has become clear that it is difficult to link some perspectives firmly with one side of the debate as opposed to the other. This is because work conducted in one tradition appears to show features of both. Although theorists may start their analysis from a particular perspective, be it structuralist or social action, they end up showing some concern for both social structure and social action. Therefore it is not surprising that sociologists have recently sought to develop a social theory that combines an understanding of both social structure and social action (Haralambos and Holborn, 2006).

Giddens's structuration theory (see Chapter 5) is widely regarded as the most recent attempt to do this, but it was started by Weber more than a hundred years earlier (see Chapter 2). Weber's approach to the study of the social world is somewhat unique, for he sought to reconcile the differences between those who advocated research of large-scale structures at a macro level and those who advocated small-scale research at a micro level.

Central to Weber's research process was his concept of '*Verstehen*', a philosophy emphasizing the need to understand the meanings individuals give to social phenomena and the need to explore the socially constructed rules that define the meaning of social action. Herein lies his way of addressing both sides of the structure/action debate – meshing meaning assigned by individuals with rules ascribed by society.

Weber's work has inspired a number of sociologists to adopt his ideas when developing their own theories. His influence can be detected in conflict theory, structural functionalism, critical theory and interactionism. It has also undoubtedly led others to bridge the gap between structuralism and social action by devising approaches to accommodate both aspects simultaneously in an analysis of social life.

For example, Evans (1997) details her involvement in research to explore the use of space in cities and perceptions of personal safety. This research, funded by the Economic and Social Research Council, sought to answer a number of questions:

- Who uses the public space in our cities and for what purposes?
- How do people experience different public spaces at different times?
- What feelings do different places generate for different people?
- What strategies do people employ to help them manage feelings of unease, fear and anxiety when they are using public spaces?

This list demonstrates that the researcher's interest was in both structural issues (patterns of city usage) and action issues (experiences of public space and feelings generated by it). The data that Evans and her team obtained from short interviews (based upon these questions) in the city centres of Sheffield and Manchester enabled them to build up a picture of how the streets were used during the month of August 1992. This enabled them to develop a series of supplementary questions in order further to explore city usage. Their aim was to develop an understanding of gender difference in the use of public spaces (see Exercise 3.8).

Item C

Sex and the City

Research presented to a Royal Geographical Society conference in 2008 found that cities and urban spaces are still being designed largely for the benefit of men. The Women's Design Service (WDS) has launched a database on gender and the built environment and celebrates the achievement of work by women architects. Nevertheless, their director Wendy Davis argues that 'most things in the built environment are designed on a male model' according to their height, strength, weight as well as their movement around the city. For example seats on trains that have been replaced by sloping shelves are only easily accessible to people of above average height. Male and female public toilets have the same number of allocated square metres, meaning that women have half as many toilets when compared to the urinals that are put into men's toilets. Crucially planning doesn't take account of the fact that women often have children with them, may need to breastfeed or feed toddlers, may be pregnant or menstruating – all aspects of women's lives that may require them to have some private space. Other areas which have been seen to disadvantage women in the urban environment are housing design, crèches, public transport, pavements and parks. According to Dr Gemma Burgess of Cambridge University town planners are ignoring equality planning regulations that were brought in during 2007.

However, in local authorities in East London and South Yorkshire architects have actively sought to include women in new initiatives and written their views into planning briefs. This may help to prevent women from having to restrict their access to physical and geographical spaces as they have had to do in the past.

(Adapted from Viv Groskop, 'Sex and the City', *The Guardian*, 19 September 2008)

Ⓐ
Ⓔ

Exercise 3.8

Think about the local built environment where you live. When you are next walking or travelling around your area take a note of where bus stops are, the lighting in the streets and shopping areas, the pavements, the public spaces such as parks and green spaces. Does the argument that design is based on the male model hold true for your area?

Visit the Women's Design Service website www.wds.org.uk or www.gender-site.org.uk to find out about projects and activities which reflect the needs and aspirations of women.

Item D

Men's Towns: Women and the Urban Environment

Over the month of August 1992, we placed interviewers in city-centre and out-of-town shopping centres, on all days of the week and from 9 o'clock in the morning until 8.30 at night. Interviewers were instructed to stop every fifth adult (defined as over the age of 16) who passed and to conduct a short interview with them. We also asked the interviewers to record some basic details of those who were approached but refused to participate in the research. From this we were able to build up a picture of use of the streets during that month.

We found that more men than women were using these city spaces at all times of the day and early evening and that the proportion of men and women was remarkably similar in both cities. For every 100 men that we encountered on the streets we met only 76 women. We were more likely to meet women during the daytime (from 9 a.m. to 6 p.m.) and less likely to meet them in the early evening (from 6 p.m. to 8.30 p.m.). During the early evening hours we met only 31 women for every 100 men. It is worth remembering, too, that the research was conducted during the month of August when the long daytime hours would mean more women might be expected to be using public space than in the dark winter months.

These findings can lead us as sociologists to ask many questions concerning male domination and women's place in society.

(Adapted from Karen Evans, 'Men's Towns – Women and the Urban Environment', *Sociology Review*, 6(3), 1997)

Read Item D, which summarizes Evans's initial research findings, and complete the following tasks.

(I)(A) 1. Identify and make a note of three supplementary questions you would like
(U)   answered to increase your understanding of gender differences in the use of
         public space. In each case, jot down why the information might be useful –
         that is, what precisely could it contribute?
(A)(E) 2. Compare your supplementary questions with the ones Evans actually asked
         (as noted in the first paragraph below). To what extent do they agree?

Evans's commitment to exploring both the structural and action aspects of city usage was reflected in the secondary questions she developed. Emphasis was placed on exploring (1) why fewer women than men frequent the public spaces of cities; (2) why women stay away from public spaces; and (3) who uses public spaces and why. Inevitably this involved exploring patterns of city usage and the meaning behind such patterns. Her analysis touched upon the historical context behind space usage (that is, increased male domination of public spaces with the onset of industrialization and confinement of women to the private sphere), popular thinking about women's right or otherwise to mobility, institutional influences on urban design (for example, male domination in town planning, architecture and civil engineering) and perceptions of danger.

The sheer range of dimensions Evans explored when conducting her research demonstrates the value of incorporating both structuralist and action-orientated interests into a single study. Her report is well structured and relayed with clarity, and it demonstrates the mutual influence of structural and interpersonal factors in determining use of public spaces:

> Although the popular view in society may be that men and women enjoy equal access to city streets and places, the findings which I have outlined ... tell a different story. The design of public spaces, women's fears and anxiety in public areas and the gendering of certain activities and places as masculine and feminine all militate against women's use of the city. (Evans, 1997, p. 17)

Summary of structuralism versus social action

(A)

Exercise 3.10

Complete the following summary of the structuralism versus social action debate by selecting words from the list provided to fill in the gaps.

Structuralism emphasizes the _____ or structures that shape individuals' lives. Structuralists claim that individuals do not own their _____ , instead they are structured by society. Individual _____ is constrained by the _____ of society. Thus individuals are seen as _____ rather than _____ of their ideas. This argument is extended to the analysis of _____ . Structuralists argue that the _____ should be upon understanding _____ as it is these that influence how individuals live their lives _____ provides an example of this approach, seeing the _____ as the dominant structure that _____ all aspects of social life and _____ . Action theory rejects this view, arguing that individuals _____ the _____ by their actions and _____ with others and the _____ they assign to _____ . Individuals are the authors of their _____ , thus the starting point for understanding society should be the individual. Emphasis should be given to how _____ meanings develop and how these _____ the way individuals _____ , act and _____ to their _____ provides an example of such an approach, arguing that the _____ of _____ and interaction makes up _____ and _____ . Although two _____ can be identified, in reality much of sociology is influenced by _____ and _____ action, although sociological _____ tend to emphasize one approach at the expense of the other. In recent times _____ theorists, for example, _____ , have sought to _____ the structure/action _____ , although the _____ for this were laid over 100 years earlier by _____ , who emphasized the need for '_____ ' in sociological theory and research.

Missing words

- shape • debate • social world • interpret • language system
- puppets • social life • underlying logic • structuralism
- emphasis • social structures • influence
- economy • intertwined patterns • groups • societies • opposing viewpoints • patterns • Symbolic • interactionism • action
- Giddens • foundations • Structural Marxism
- defines • social phenomena • interactions • experiences
- authors • life experiences • shared • meaning
- contemporary • social • react • Verstehen • reconcile
- Weber • ideas • thought • perspectives

THE EVOLUTIONARY VIEW VERSUS HERE-AND-NOW ANALYSIS

This debate concerns the value of studying society over time as opposed to studying it at a fixed point in time. The grand theorists who contributed to the development of sociology – Marx, Engels and Weber – appeared to favour analysing the evolution of society in the belief that studying the past and the transition to the present day would enable social processes to be understood and predictions made about what might happen in the future. Theorists adopting the evolutionary view advocated the use of historical analysis in the study of social life.

In contrast, more recent developments in sociology have reflected a move away from the past to the 'here and now' – that is, to studying social events in the present context and regarding the past as largely irrelevant to contemporary events and phenomena. Some branches of feminism typify this approach. For example, liberal feminism is said to display little interest in the historical subjugation of women; it considers how the existing legal, economic and political systems contribute to gender inequality rather than exploring how such systems have evolved over time.

The evolutionary view

Researchers who adopt an evolutionary view and give consideration to historical context in their research accept a number of basic assumptions. First, a continuum exists from the past to the present and social change does not alter the structure of society – it simply redefines its nature, marking the transition from one historical period (or 'epoch') to another.

Second, we can learn much about society by studying what contributed to this transition – that is: What were the prevailing social conditions at the time? What were the contributing factors encouraging change? What were the constraining factors inhibiting change? Was there an identifiable catalyst or precipitant of change? What impact did the change have on social institutions and social life? By studying the features of change it is possible to develop an insight into cause and consequence. This is seen as vital in informing our understanding of how contemporary society came into being.

Third, by studying the past and the present we can speculate about what the future might hold. Advocates of social engineering take this a stage further, arguing that we can use knowledge of cause and consequence to manipulate the present day in order to determine the future. Although this appears sinister, the process could have social benefits. For example, if we study the factors that contributed to the two world wars and how these interacted with those in power at the time to bring about a course of action (that is, the behaviour), and consider the outcome of this course of action (that is, the consequences), we can speculate about how war could be prevented. Alternatively, we can consider how mechanisms could be put in place to find a peaceful solution to conflict. This has obvious benefits.

The evolutionary view is generally adopted by structuralists – that is, those interested in arriving at an understanding of social life by analysing the social structure and its component systems. Social institutions are considered to have evolved and become more complex over time. Hence there is value in looking into the past in order to understand how such structures have come about. An assumption is made that the current structures have developed from previous structures – that is, they are refined versions of earlier ones. Alternatively, they have replaced previous structures that are no longer necessary or no longer able to meet the demands of a complex society – that is, they are alternatives.

Item E

The Quality of Service Initiative in the British Police

Recent years have seen a succession of Home Office and Inspectorate of Constabulary initiatives aimed at enhanced financial management, 'civilianization' and quality of service. Much of the inspiration for these initiatives has come from industry and commerce, as it is thought that current management practices have a lot to teach the police. Nevertheless, it is recognized that such approaches need to be adapted to suit the public sector environment and the particular nature of the services offered by the police.

The project takes one key initiative, namely quality of service, and examines its conception, emergence and application in a sample of four major police forces. Based on questionnaire surveys and interviews with officers of various ranks, an assessment is being made of the nature and extent of any changes in service delivery, force commitments and priorities, and local and central government relations that have resulted from the quality of service initiative.

(*Source*: Research Initiatives, Department of Sociology, University of Surrey, Project Director Nigel Fielding)

Exercise 3.11

This exercise enables you to explore a more recent example of work associated with the evolutionary view. Read Item E, which contextualizes project work undertaken by a sociologist at the University of Surrey, and undertake the following tasks in small groups.

(An)(E) 1. Discuss why the project appears to provide an applied example of the evolutionary view.

(I)(A) 2. Use recent journals/textbooks to identify *at least one* more example of work that has adopted an evolutionary approach. Take full reference details and make brief notes on:

(a) the research aim;
(b) the research methodology adopted;
(c) the key research findings;
(d) criticisms levelled at the research.

Evolutionary view – an evaluation

(I)(A)
(An)(E)

Exercise 3.12

Using the research example outlined above and the ones you collected for Exercise 3.8, identify two strengths and two limitations of the evolutionary view. Record them in a two-column summary chart.

Here-and-now analysis

Giddens (1984) coined the term 'episodic characterization' to refer to research conducted in the here-and-now, where interest lies in exploring specific episodes rather than ongoing phenomena. A number of basic assumptions underlie here-and-now analysis: social phenomena should be studied in the immediate social context; emphasis should be given to the meanings that individuals assign to this context because it is this that shapes their behaviour; and studying what happened in the past is of little value because each aspect of the social world is constantly being formulated and reformulated by individuals as they interact with it. To develop an understanding of this process, the most fruitful approach is to explore the underlying meanings and the processes by which meanings are assigned to objects and phenomena. This will give an insight into how the social world is constructed through social action and interaction (see Exercise 3.13).

An example of research conducted in this genre is that by Paterson (1984; cited in Black *et al.* 1984), who explored the meanings that kitchen maids assigned to their work at a large teaching hospital. Paterson chose participant observation (see Chapter 7 for a definition) as her research method because she saw this as offering an opportunity to 'examine the setting in a manner which contrasted with many traditional organisational analyses, which often neglected the purposes and definitions of the actors concerned' (cited in Black *et al.*, 1984, p. 242).

Paterson provides an ethnographic account of how the maids in her study did 'food-work' – that is, how they approached the tasks of preparing food for the patients and staff. She outlines the meanings they assigned to the types of food they were required to prepare and the implications this had for the work they did and the way they were viewed by fellow kitchen maids:

> Washing lettuce for salad was a job which maids tried to avoid. It was a long, boring task and also a back-breaking one, because it necessitated bending over a low sink while holding each leaf under the tap...Hence, 'doing lettuce' elicited sympathy from colleagues, a maid was considered brave to tackle it on her own and therefore it was a tactic which led to being classed as a 'good worker'. (Cited in Black *et al.*, 1984, p. 243)

Paterson also describes the maids' perception of the various recipients of the food they prepared and the effect this had upon the standards they adopted when preparing food:

> Standards differed for doctors and sisters, who were considered of high social worth, for nurses and technical staff who were lower in the hierarchy, for private patients who were considered almost as worthy as staff and for 'ordinary' patients, whose status was considered lowest of all. (Cited in Black *et al.*, 1984, p. 245)

Finally, Paterson demonstrates how engaging in 'food-work' impinged upon the maids' concept of self:

> Behaviour in the role of bulk food-producer often conflicted with that of food-producer in the home, and this 'role strain' was felt particularly acutely among newcomers or those whose relatives or friends were also patients. A further element of the maids' problem was that since their products seldom reached the consumer direct, there was no one to praise them...Furthermore maids were subordinate to all others in the kitchen hierarchy, low in power and status. (Cited in Black *et al.*, 1984, p. 245)

Although at first it might be hard to appreciate the practical value of research such as this, Paterson's analysis of the construct systems of maids and the way they approached their tasks does have implications for those dealing with healthcare provision and wider structural concerns:

> What has been described may disturb those who organise catering in medical (and other) institutions, and is highly relevant to debates concerning the generally poor status of hospital meals and the periodic outbursts of food-poisoning among patients. (Cited in Black *et al.*, 1984, p. 245)

Item F

Industrial–Academic Collaboration: The Interaction of Cultural Identities

This project funded by the ESRC (Economic and Social Research Council) aims to provide a detailed analysis of the process of research collaboration between academics and industrialists in the area of computer applications for manufacturing engineering. Employing an ethnographic case-study approach, it focuses in detail on a small number of projects organized around different collaboration models. It is intended that this approach will both give some insight into the cultural factors affecting collaboration and, in the process, contribute to the theoretical understanding of the constitution and interaction of cultural identities.

(*Source*: Research Initiative, Department of Sociology, University of Surrey, Project Director Geoff Cooper)

Exercise 3.13

Read Item F, and in small groups:

1. Discuss why the work appears to provide an example of here-and-now analysis.
2. Use recent journals/textbooks to identify *at least one* more example of research that adopts a here-and-now approach. Write down the full reference details and make brief notes on:

   (a) the research aim;
   (b) the research methodology adopted;
   (c) the key research findings;
   (d) criticisms levelled at the research (if any).

Here-and-now analysis – an evaluation

Exercise 3.14

Refer to the work outlined above and any other relevant research, and identify two strengths and two limitations of here-and-now analysis. Record them in a two-column summary chart.

Summary of the evolutionary view versus here-and-now analysis

Exercise 3.15

The following passage summarizes the evolutionary versus here-and-now debate. Complete the summary by selecting words from the list provided to fill in the gaps.

Researchers adopting an _____ view believe that the best way to understand social phenomena is to study them over time. Hence much attention is devoted to _____ analysis, tracing the evolution (that is, adaptation over time) of _____ . It is felt that this not only enables us to develop an insight into why society is as it is today, but also to make _____ about the future. More radical perhaps is the suggestion that studying the past and the present allows us to _____ the future. The evolutionary view is evident in the work of _____ (development of capitalism), _____ (development of the family) and Weber (the link between the rise of capitalism and Calvinism).

Here-and-now analysis is favoured by those who believe that social phenomena are the product of the _____ between individuals at a specific point in time. Research should aim to explore the _____ assigned in social _____ as it is this that structures social experience. There is little point in looking to the past because meaning systems are not fixed but _____ . Studying such meaning systems and _____ and the way they affect behaviour can have important practical applications. The work of _____ (on self), Goffman (on asylums) and Garfinkel (on social rules) are examples of here-and-now analysis.

Missing words

- interactions • Mead • fluid • evolutionary • predictions
- influence • Marx • historical • Engels • social phenomena
- Weber • meanings • contexts • personal constructs

POSITIVISM VERSUS ANTIPOSITIVISM

This debate concerns whether sociologists should adopt the research methods used in the natural sciences and aspire for sociology to be seen as scientific (see Chapter 10). Positivists argue that it would be valuable for sociology to associate itself with science. Anti-positivists disagree, seeing science and sociology as distinct disciplines with different subject matter and thus incompatible. They strongly reject the idea that scientific methods can and should be applied in sociological research.

ⒾⒶ

Link Exercise 3.1

Read the sections in Chapter 10 on positivism and antipositivism and draw up a list of the basic assumptions that underlie these approaches. It may be helpful to record your ideas in a chart copied from the one here.

Positivism versus antipositivism: summary of the key ideas

Positivism		Antipositivism	
Main writers	*Key ideas*	*Main writers*	*Key ideas*

Evaluation

Compare your work with that of at least one other sociology student. Did you arrive at the same understanding of the two positions in the debate?

The most famous example of an attempt to apply scientific methodology in sociology is undoubtedly Durkheim's (1897/1951) exploration of suicide. Durkheim was motivated by a desire to establish the credibility of sociology as an academic discipline. As Moore (1988, p. 21) notes:

> If he could prove that one of the most individual of human acts that any human being could perform – that is killing him/herself, could only explained through social factors, then surely any action could be examined in such a way.

Durkheim structured his research with reference to the hypothetico-deductive method, a framework commonly applied by scientists when studying the natural world. This involves researchers following a series of systematic steps, leading from their original ideas, through hypothesis formulation, to gathering and analysing data, to a decision about whether their hypotheses can be refuted or supported. Durkheim was probably attracted to the approach because of its logical and objective nature, both of which are valuable assets when dealing with a potentially emotive subject.

Exercise 3.16

1. Undertake some background reading on Durkheim's study of suicide. You will find it documented in most major introductory textbooks. Note down the definitions of the four types of suicide he identified, using a copy of the summary.

Summary of Durkheim's analysis of suicide

Type of suicide	Anomic	Altruistic	Fatalistic	E . . . . . .
Defining characteristics	Firm and deeply rooted commitment to a belief/cause leads to calculated death			Lack of social integration/ alienation from wider society
Applied example	Death of long-term partner. Unemployment with loss of status/ self-esteem		Asian girls living in West but under traditional constraints	

2. Now classify the suicide cases summarized below into Durkheim's categories. What reason would he give for the cause of death in each case?

Case 1: Death of Depressive Doctor

A middle-aged GP killed himself in the grounds of a mental hospital after being convicted for the manslaughter of his daughter. Prior to the crime the doctor had allegedly heard voices telling him to kill his daughter. Psychiatric reports note that the doctor had a history of depressive illness and alcohol and substance dependency.

Case 2: SOS from Suicide Centre

Staff at a young offenders centre in the Midlands have requested the help of the Samaritans to halt the rising tide of suicides in the last two years. A growing number of young offenders are taking their lives. The staff suspect that lack of access to a telephone may have affected the inmates' ability to talk through their problems.

Case 3: Overweight, Overwrought and 'On the Edge'

A young mum took her life, leaving a 16-month-old baby upon whom she doted. Neighbours commented that she had suffered from agoraphobia and lived with a much older man whom they described as 'unemployable'. She had recently appeared at the local shops with a black eye and scratches down her face. The shop assistant commented that she had really 'let herself go' in recent months and looked tearful and at 'her wits' end'.

Case 4: Caring Family United in Death

The bodies of an elderly married couple were found at a local beauty spot in a fume-filled car. The police were not looking for anyone else in connection with the tragedy. The couple had spent many years looking after their severely disabled child, who had died after an epileptic fit three weeks earlier.

Case 5: Miners' Misery Doubles Suicide Rate

A vicar has expressed his concern about the abnormally high suicide rate in his new parish. He reports that since moving to the North-Eastern mining town he has conducted more funerals for suicide victims than in the previous 25 years of his ministry in London and elsewhere in Britain. The majority were former miners, desperate to escape the despair that had blighted their lives since the mines were replaced by high-technology industry, rendering their skills useless.

For many years Durkheim's (1970) research was held up as an example of good methodological practice and good sociology. However, as Moore (1988, p. 24) notes, a number of criticisms were voiced in the 1960s as the anti-positivist movement gained momentum:

- His concept of social integration was too vague; he simply relied on intuitive ideas of what integration was.
- His variables of religion and the family were not as clear-cut as he suggested. How could these be 'isolated' as distinct influences on behaviour?
- The official statistics upon which he based his research left something to be desired. For example, in Catholic countries, where suicide is regarded as a sin, family doctors are reluctant to classify deaths as suicide.

Anti-positivists, for example Douglas (1967) and Atkinson (1971), condemn Durkheim's choice of research methodology as wholly inappropriate. They argue that in treating the suicide rate as a social fact he overlooks the subjective dimension of the way statistics are collected. Suicides are classified as such only if the coroner or the coroner's court chooses to do so. Thus some deaths may not be recorded as suicide for reasons such as those identified in the quote above. Conversely some non-accidental deaths may be regarded as suicide because the circumstances surrounding the death are ambiguous or misleading.

Thus anti-positivists advocate that if sociologists are to explore what Durkheim himself describes as 'the most individual of human acts', the emphasis of analysis should be upon the way deaths are classified rather than the number of deaths recorded. In addition, they would favour in-depth studies into the circumstances surrounding the death. This would provide valuable insight into the possible factors that cause individuals to take their own lives. However, it would not be possible to generalize from this analysis because each death is unique to the individual concerned. Whether anti-positivists would construe mass suicide in these terms is questionable.

Durkheim's research has provided a useful example of how the scientific method might feasibly be applied in sociology. But in highlighting the criticisms of his research, it is possible to see some of the limitations of the positivist argument, which raises questions about its suitability as a research method for sociologists. Critics of the positivist method would also argue against its use by drawing attention to the inability of science to provide precise explanations of social phenomena. Anti-positivists would see the shortfalls of science as another good reason to keep sociology free from positivist methodology. The following exercise will enable you to explore this line of argument in greater detail.

Item G

SCIENTISTS MAKE CHOCOLATE CHOCOLATIER

By Our Science Correspondent

Scientists working for a major confectioner have devised an ingenious solution to that age-old problem 'how chocolate-y should chocolate be?' By employing genetic splicing techniques, the scientists have altered the make-up of the bean that is used in the production of chocolate. This 'super bean' yields a more intense chocolate flavour that can be added to the confectioner's products. There is a problem with the process, however, in that the addition of the gene also reduces the nutritional value of the resulting bean. So, while the experience of eating chocolate will be even more pleasurable than it is at the moment, the known benefits of chocolate eating will be reduced.

Exercise 3.17

Consider the following fictional scenario:

You are an eminent anti-positivist employed by an anti-science pressure group. The government is due to pass a law banning all subjects except science in school. You have one final chance to persuade them not to adopt it. You have prepared an excellent speech detailing the evils of science and passionately extolling the virtues of all the non-scientific 'ologies'. You have been allocated a slot to address the cabinet at the party conference before the decision is made. As you jump out of the taxi and rush into the conference centre, you realize you have left your briefcase on the train. You only have five minutes before the conference starts and in this time you must prepare a speech on the shortfalls of science to demonstrate why society needs alternative subjects and alternative research methodologies.

With time running out, you realize you are still clutching a copy of an old newspaper you were reading on the train. Scanning it frantically for inspiration, you spot a small item by a science correspondent and realize it may be just the thing to draw attention to the frivolous nature of contemporary science and the difficulties of translating scientific discoveries into viable market products. Suddenly the ideas flow and a new speech starts to take shape.

1. Now read Item G and make brief notes on the following.

   (a) The main research findings expressed.
   (b) How these could be used as evidence to demonstrate the value of scientific research.
   (c) Refuting arguments – how the contents of the article could be ridiculed/used to provide evidence of 'science gone mad' – that is, losing direction, becoming obsessed with trivia at the expense of 'serious' issues.

   Try to use this as a basis for arguing that science alone cannot fully explain contemporary social life and that there is a need for non-scientific thinking and research. (Hint: You may strengthen your argument by citing a couple of examples of recent anti-positivist research with tangible and well-publicized practical applications. The internet would be a good place to start looking.

2. Use your notes to draft a speech outlining the limitations of science and the value of keeping anti-positivist subjects in the school curriculum.

Realism and suicide: people under trains

The work of Steve Taylor (1982, 1989, 1990) has gone some way to 'outdate' the positivism-versus-phenomenology disagreement. Taylor argues for using both the official figures on suicide (but with the precautionary view that they are unreliable) and a case-study approach to better understand suicide sociologically. In his research into deaths on the London underground over the period of a year he found that, although 32 people had died under trains, the causes of their deaths was by no means clear. However, 17 were classified as suicide, 5 as accidental and 10 had open verdicts recorded. Taylor found that deaths were more likely to be recorded as suicide if the person had a history of mental heath problems and/or had suffered some social failure. Crucially, witness testimony from families and friends played a part in the verdict. Taylor's research points to support for the view that suicides cannot be taken at face value, but he also attempts to find out about the underlying, unobservable structures that lead to an explanation of the verdict – this is based upon a realist approach which takes the view that the underlying causes of social phenomena cannot always be observed (see above).

Positivism versus antipositivism – an evaluation

Positivism advocates the use of scientific methodology to study the social world. It is assumed that such methodology offers a logical systematic and objective (that is, value-free) approach to conducting research. It is assumed that by rigorous hypothesis-testing through prescribed means sociologists can uncover laws governing the social world that are akin those discovered by scientists for the natural world.

Anti-positivists were adamant that the scientific approach cannot be applied to the study of the social world. The natural world and the social world are perceived as too different to warrant study by similar means. Also, it is recognized that any research is inevitably subjective because researchers cannot separate themselves from the values they hold. Anti-positivists advocate research through small-scale studies of individual cases. For them, this is the only way in which meaningful data can be collected.

The realist approach to scientific study takes a more pragmatic stance by arguing that in sociology the application of the scientific method can be useful up to a point and should not be dismissed out-of-hand, but must also be combined with the use of qualitative methods to uncover underlying causes for behaviour. (See Chapter 4 for more details.)

Exam focus: writing an essay

This section is designed to help you apply the knowledge you have acquired from this chapter and hone your essay-writing technique.

For the exam, a teacher set one exam question on sociological theory for her students. She wasn't that confident they would be able to answer it because she had spent a year and a half teaching them family and education, and only fitted in theory and methods the week before half-term.

Look at the question she set and read the answer of one of her students.

Questions

Describe and evaluate *one* of the following theoretical debates:

1. Structuralism versus social action.
2. Positivism versus antipositivism.
3. Evolutionary view versus here-and-now analysis.

(20 marks)

Student's answer

Positivists are positive that sociology should be a helpful and happy subject. The opposite of positivists must be negativists, who think sociology should be unhelpful and miserable probably. Now the theoretical debates are important and I intend to describe and evaluate positivism and antipositivism, structuralism versus social action and the evolutionary view versus here-and-now analysis. Oh, I've just noticed the opposite of positivism is antipositivism but they probably think the same as negativists but are just called something different. I remember doing this in class. It was a really good lesson because we had a student teacher and the fire alarm went off so we bunked off. Quite fancy being a teacher myself but I'm allergic to chalk, now where was I?, not that they use it mind, its all pens and OHPs that are a nightmare to copy down. Oops, I've only got five minutes left... better get on.

Now the theoretical debates are important and I intend to describe and evaluate positivism and antipositivism, structuralism versus social action and the evolutionary view versus here-and-now analysis. Structuralists think we should wear tight fitting clothes to halt the nation's decline. They're a branch of New Right with their main writer as Marshland. The opposite view is rupturalists, who think society might as well chill out and wear poncho capes because it's all falling apart anyway. That's to do with Guiness, a famous sociologist who came from California, I think, or went there for a while or something.

Here-and-now analysis is like that programme by Sue Lawley where that blonde woman called Alice rings people up and talks to them about saving money by wearing leather-look rubber hotpants. The evolutionary view must be the opposite, where you don't get on television and you sit at home hoping an understanding of society will evolve. Revolutionaries are the third view, which wasn't mentioned in the question but they are opposite somehow because they think differently.

So having looked at all sides of the debate, I think a mixture of all views is the best.

Out of time – sorry!

1. Try to identify ten classic exam gaffes that the student has made.

2. Learning from these mistakes, answer the question yourself. Remember, you are required to focus on *one,* not all, of the theoretical debates. Before making a start, it may be helpful to refer back to the advice given at the end of Chapter 2 on writing an essay. If you are intending to attempt debate (b) it would also be helpful to read the relevant material in Chapter 10 (see positivism versus antipositivism).

Important concepts

modernism • postmodernism • structuralism • epistemology • social action • *Verstehen* • here-and-now analysis • positivism • antipositivism

Critical thinking

- How far would you consider the four theoretical debates mutually exclusive?
- Think of ways in which elements of these different theoretical traditions could be combined to create another approach to the study of society. Are some parts of a sociological analysis of society more important than others – that is, is structure more important than action?
- In some ways postmodernism has been seen to supersede the more traditional theoretical sociological perspectives. How far do you agree?

Chapter 4

Contemporary Theory

By the end of this chapter you should be able to:

- identify seven interpretations of society advocated by contemporary theorists:

  1. Contemporary Left
  2. Realism
  3. New Right
  4. postmodernism
  5. postfeminism and critical race theory
  6. theories of sexuality and queer theory
  7. disability theory

- recognize the basic assumptions behind each approach
- provide examples of sociological research to demonstrate the applications of each approach
- identify the strengths and limitations of each approach and evaluate the contribution that each has made to sociological thinking and research
- understand the eclecticism underpinning contemporary social theory

INTRODUCTION

Sociology is evolving rapidly. While the theoretical assumptions considered in Chapter 2 on traditional theory still provide the foundations of the subject, in recent years sociologists have sought to develop new ways of analysing the world. Most have drawn their inspiration from the four main theoretical perspectives, although others have sought to develop ideas previously overlooked by sociologists.

This chapter will consider contemporary theoretical approaches. This does not mean that these are the only new theories that have been developed, but the selection here will provide a flavour of the new directions sociology is taking and the implications these have for the types of research now being conducted.

THE CONTEMPORARY LEFT

As Moore (1988) notes, the Contemporary Left approach arose from dissatisfaction with the existing sociological explanations of the reasons for crime and deviance in society:

> The Contemporary Left in Britain developed from the work of Taylor, Walton and Young in The New Criminology and also from the Centre for Contemporary Cultural Studies at Birmingham University... It combines the structural perspective of traditional Marxism with many of the insights of labelling theory – in particular, the belief that any understanding of society must include an awareness of the perceptions of individuals and the importance of societal reactions to perceived deviants. (Moore, 1988, p. 77)

Although the 'new criminology' approach was developed to aid our understanding of crime, it is possible to apply some of the basic ideas to other areas of social life.

Contemporary Left analysis attempts to investigate a number of issues simultaneously, as it is felt that to develop a full understanding it is necessary to broaden the focus of inquiry to incorporate both macro and micro features and the interplay between the two. Contemporary Left analysis seeks to understand the phenomenon itself – that is, the topic or issue under study, its defining characteristics and features, and so on. However, the phenomenon is not studied in isolation and attention is paid to the structural context in which the object or topic of study is located. Contemporary Left theorists attempt to explore the ways in which aspects of the social structure, most notably the economy, affect the issue under study. So, if they are conducting an analysis of crime, or education, or the family, they will inevitably explore the impact of the economic structure on their chosen topic.

Contemporary Left analysis also pays attention to interpersonal factors that might influence on the topic under study. Consideration is given both to individual factors – that is, the impact of individual motivation, choice and so on – and to societal factors – that is, society's response to particular phenomena, how societal responses vary in their effects, and the reasons why they do so.

Consideration is also given to historical, political and cultural factors that may have an underlying structural impact on the issue being studied. Such factors are perceived to be inherent in the structure of society and are influential not necessarily because they have a direct impact on the topic under study but because they shape the historical, political and cultural context in which the phenomenon exists.

Contemporary Left theorists imply that if we are to arrive at a complete understanding of an aspect of social life it is important to explore the interplay between all of the above issues. Only then is it possible to appreciate how all factors combine to provide a coherent explanation of the phenomenon under study.

Contemporary Left analysis is represented in diagrammatic form in Figure 4.1, which clearly illustrates the issues of interest to theorists and the interplay between them. The diagram provides a useful starting point for applying the Contemporary Left approach to aspects of social life.

To explore the approach a little further, we will look briefly at how the model can help us to understand the changing structure of the family in recent times. Many sociologists (for example, Goode, 1963; Anderson, 1971; Young

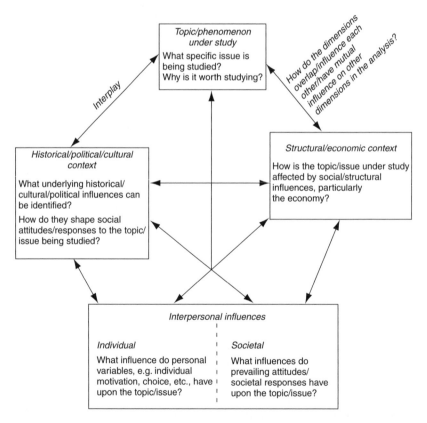

Figure 4.1 Components of Contemporary Left analysis

and Willmott, 1975) have tried to explore family change over time, but most analyses have tended to focus on unitary explanations rather than multifaceted ones. As a consequence our knowledge and understanding of how the family structure has changed is somewhat fragmented. What has been lacking is an overarching explanation of changing family structure that considers the influence of structural, societal, interpersonal, historical, political and cultural factors and the interplay between them. Figure 4.2 allows us to make sense of the various influences that contribute to change, and recognize the overlap between and mutual influence among the various factors.

The example shows how the ideas of Contemporary Left analysis can help us to develop an understanding of the changing family structure. As noted earlier, the approach was developed originally to further the understanding of crime, so in principle at least it should be even easier to apply the ideas to crime.

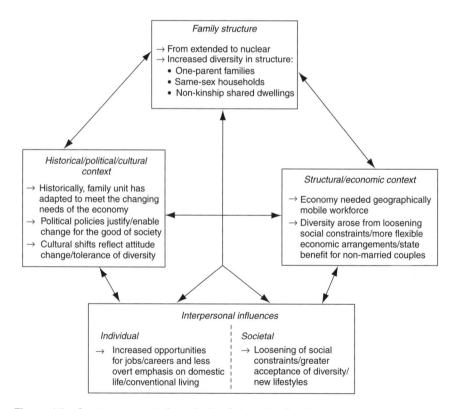

Figure 4.2 Contemporary Left analysis of changing family structure

Exercise 4.1

This exercise will help you to consider how Contemporary Left theorists might approach the analysis of crime.

1. Copy the diagram here and complete it by answering the questions posed in each box.

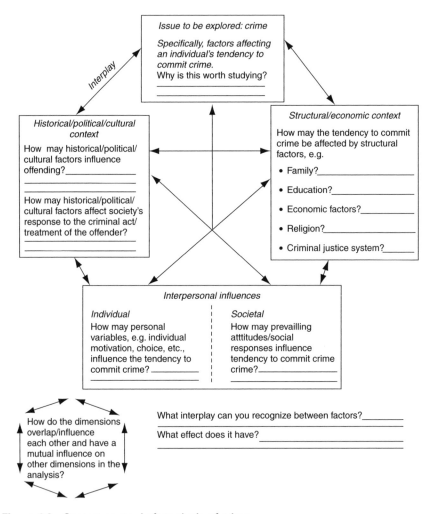

Figure 4.3 Contemporary Left analysis of crime

2. Now you have completed the diagram you should have some insight into the Contemporary Left analysis of crime. Check out the extent of your understanding by reading about the Contemporary Left approach to crime in a relevant sociology textbook, for example T. Lawson and T. Heaton, *Crime and Deviance (Skills-Based Sociology)* (2010).

Contemporary Left – an evaluation

Strengths

1. The Contemporary Left approach is a coherent and pragmatic way of combining the structuralist and action approaches.
2. Ideas related to crime can be reduced to basic analytical steps and applied to other areas of social life.

Limitations

1. An assumption is made that behaviour is motivated and that an element of choice is involved. Structuralists would dismiss this, arguing that people are merely puppets of the social structure and have little influence over their own lives.
2. Critics dismiss the Contemporary Left's assertion that explanations may need to be exceedingly complex, as complex explanations are of little use to those seeking to use theoretical models to develop an understanding of social life.

REALISM

The general approach to sociology from the realists is to argue that structures and institutions in society have an existence beyond that of the individuals that create and produce them. Structures and institutions exist, but their presence is not necessarily concrete and/or visible; they can however be experienced.

More recently, realism has emerged as a theoretical response to the positivism versus antipositivism debate. Realists seek to reconcile the difference between the two positions by proposing a new approach to the analysis of society that incorporates elements of both. Realism developed from the work of Keat and Urry (1975), Pawson (1989) and Layder (1990; 1993), who endeavoured to synthesize the useful components of positivism and antipositivism in a coherent way. Clarke and Layder (1994, p. 7) offer the following insight:

> Like positivism, realism suggests that there are some lessons to be learned from the natural sciences and that therefore some of their methods and procedures can be used. In particular a concern with how social processes and events are caused is an important question for sociologists to answer... Similarly, a concern with the objective nature of some aspects of society is a key aspect of realism that draws it closer to the natural science model. On the other hand, realism acknowledges that human beings are not objects like those studied by physical scientists. People are not simply moulded by 'external' social factors: they are conscious intentional agents who both create and recreate the social world.

Realism has a number of distinct features, including the following:

- It concentrates on the nature of society as a whole rather than the smaller elements that make it up.
- Its analysis combines interaction and institutions (for example, the economy, the political system, religion).
- It is interested in aspects of society that might go unnoticed but have a significant influence on the interplay between the individual and society.

The aim of realist analysis is to explore the underlying causes of social phenomena. To help achieve this, realists have tried to develop models of causal processes at work beneath the surface of events. They recognize that their models should also be able to accommodate the causal factors such as ideology, culture and power relationships. Figure 4.4 demonstrates the way these ideas fit together. The general model that underpins realism derives from a philosophical (ontological) position regarding the fundamental nature of social phenomena. The position resonates with C. Wright Mills's notion of 'the sociological imagination' set forth in his book so titled (1959) and can be explained by use of an example.

Suppose you are at an airport awaiting a flight for your summer holiday. This is a fairly unremarkable experience and one that is familiar to millions of people. Glancing outside you are likely to see a number of large passenger jets lined up next to the terminal building. We have all seen planes and many of us have travelled on one – the planes are part of our everyday experiences and one that we are unlikely to give a second thought to. However, if we move beyond this everyday unremarkable experience and deploy what Mills calls the

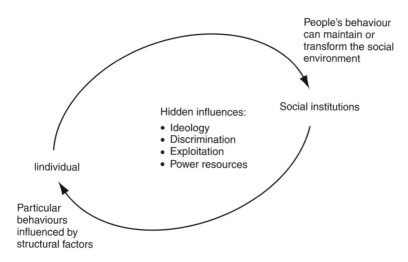

Figure 4.4 Realist approach to understanding social life

'sociological imagination' then we can begin to appreciate some of the wider sociological structures and processes that the plane represents. For example, the planes exist as part of a global system of production in which multinational businesses are privately owned and controlled, mostly by wealthy, white males. This raises issues of social class, ethnicity and gender within an overall capitalist system. The plane also represents globalization and development as forms of culture and leisure over time. However, unlike the plane or the airport, these are not open to observation and experience. Capitalism, globalization, class structures and so on exist, but because they are structural phenomena, because they refer to complex systems of social relations, we cannot know them through our everyday experiences. Moreover, what we do experience in our everyday lives is a consequence of these underlying structures and processes – planes and airports exist as a result of the capitalist system of production and consumption. This view of social phenomena, that they cause but cannot be known through direct observation and experience, is fundamental to realism.

But, if social phenomena cannot be directly experienced and understood, how can we describe and explain them – how can we have knowledge of things we cannot see? This is where social theory comes in. In order to 'know' underlying structures and processes we need to represent them in the form of theoretical models. There are many examples of this within sociology – alienation, anomie, collective conscience and so on cannot be observed in the way that trees, cars or planes can, but we can understand their nature in the context of their relevant theories. In summary, for realism, social life can be split into two realms – realm 1 refers to our everyday lives that we know and experience directly, while realm 2 refers to underlying structures and processes that are a backdrop to our realm-1 experiences but are beyond direct observation (see Exercise 4.2).

The realist approach has had an impact on the argument about whether it is possible for sociology to be a science, and most sociologists acknowledge that realists have made a useful contribution to the debate (see Chapter 10 for a review).

The influence of realism can also be seen in the study of crime and deviance, where a group of sociologists have sought to adapt the initial ideas and assumptions to provide a new approach to the study of criminality. The approach calls itself 'New Left realism', acknowledging its theoretical origins but demonstrating its radical departure from mainstream sociological thinking. New Left realism seeks to bridge the gap between Radical Left theories of crime, which focus on the economic structure, and New Right theories, which use the least powerful members of society (the 'undesirables') as scapegoats for the majority of criminal acts in society. New Left Realism has received critical acclaim from sociologists, criminologists and politicians, but has also been subject to fierce criticism.

(An)(E)
(A)

Exercise 4.2

Using the earlier example above of the airport and air travel, illustrate the meaning of Realism. Think of three more examples of realm-1 and realm-2 dimensions of our social lives.

Realism – an evaluation

(I)(A)

Exercise 4.3

Complete the following summary of Realism by selecting the missing words from those listed below:

Realism attempts to combine the most useful features of _____ and _____ . Realism concentrates on _____ as a whole rather than the smaller elements that make it up. Realism attempts to combine interest in _____ with the _____ elements of society, for example, the economy, politics, religion and so on _____ . Realism is interested in aspects of society that may not be obvious to the researcher but exert a significant influence. Realism has developed _____ to explain the _____ causes of social phenomena.

Realism has been adapted and applied to the study of _____ . The approach, known as _____ realism, attempts to explain crime in terms of three interrelated concepts: and _____ . Although welcomed by some criminologists and politicians, the approach has attracted fierce _____ . Although providing reasonable _____ explanations for crime, New Left realism has yet to give sufficient attention to the and _____ of the different adaptations to _____ and deprivation. Perhaps if it does, realism will bask in the reflected glory.

Missing words

- new left • marginalization • positivism • society • explanatory models • subcultures • injustice • meanings • relative deprivation • crime • underlying • institutional • human
- antipositivism • causes • criticism • structural • motives
- action • sophisticated

THE NEW RIGHT

The New Right is a socio-political approach which emerged as a radical perspective on welfare and social policy. The approach took its lead from the philosophies espoused by the Thatcher governments of the 1980s. Some theorists from that era, for example Marsland (1989), adopted the ideas of the New Right to explain poverty. The views of Marsland will be considered later. First, it will be helpful to explore the basic assumptions of New Right thinking.

The New Right approach is construed by its critics as anti-poor. This is because it appears to blame the disadvantaged for their disadvantaged position. Society is seen as partly responsible for social deprivation because mechanisms exist to maintain individuals in a state of dependence and vulnerability, rather than encouraging or forcing them to address their difficulties and improve their position.

A common argument levelled by New Right theorists is that welfare provision in Britain creates poverty, because people in disadvantaged positions come to rely on state handouts rather than taking responsibility for their economic position. The state creates and perpetuates what is termed 'a culture of dependency' – that is, the belief that reliance on state handouts is acceptable, even desirable. New Right theorists advocate a radical shake-up of the current welfare system to ensure that the government does not collude with the poor to keep them in poverty (see Exercise 4.4).

Item A

The New Right Approach to Social Policy

The central principle of the New Right is that people should be free from regulation by the state as much as is compatible with the maintenance of good order. Where the state attempts to run people's lives, social harm results. The reason is that, without competition and with an unfair advantage over private organizations, the state's activities always lead to inefficiency. This is as true in welfare policy as in any other sphere of activity. Rather than raise taxes to high levels to pay for a welfare state, taxpayers should be free to spend their money on the charities they wish to support. For example, they may wish to donate to the 'deserving poor', those who through no fault of their own are unable to work, but not to the 'undeserving poor', those who are not interested in finding work and contributing to society. The New Right argues that instead of using the state as a means of providing for the feckless, private provision of welfare and pension services is the most efficient way to organize the welfare industry.

Exercise 4.4

Read Item A and answer the following questions.

1. How is the argument in favour of private organization efficiency affected by the 'credit crunch' of 2008?
2. Identify one group of people who would fit the category of:
   (a) the deserving poor,
   (b) the undeserving poor.
3. To what extent do you agree that low taxes might affect the propensity to give to charity?
4. What difficulties would arise if charitable organizations depended solely on voluntary donations?
5. How might adopting New Right policies benefit the government?

Although New Right policies began to infiltrate and influence sociological thinking only in the late 1980s, examples of New Right research are not hard to find. The most famous of these is that by Marsland (1989), who applied New Right philosophy to the study of poverty. His argument closely follows the themes highlighted above by attacking 'universal welfare provision' that is, wide-ranging entitlement for all, delivered by the state and designed to address the basic needs of the entire population.

Marsland expands the argument to portray welfare provision as responsible for a multitude of social problems, including long-term unemployment, street crime, educational underachievement and the rise of one-parent families. The only salvation for this underclass is removal of the welfare state. Once liberated from 'erroneous ideas' and 'destructive policies' imposed on them by paternalists, socialists, and privileged members of the professional new class, such as social workers, the poor and disadvantaged should be well on the road to economic and social recovery. Thus for Marsland the answer to welfare reform is as follows: 'Instead of self-defeating socialist redistribution, the aim should be effective help for those in genuine need, and a return to self reliance as quickly as possible' (ibid., p. 55).

These controversial ideas have attracted criticism from those who are unprepared to allow the poor to be blamed for their poverty. For example, Jordan (1989) has directly challenged Marsland, arguing that if a culture of poverty exists, it is because the welfare system subjugates the poor to such an extent that they are marginalized from society and rendered incapable of making an economic contribution. Jordan's attack on Marsland provides an interesting insight into the limitations of New Right theory.

Despite criticism, New Right thinking has captured the imagination of those sociologists who are keen to apply a different perspective to ongoing concerns. The approach has become known as social authoritarianism, which attempts to exert a moral influence on society by advocating particular forms of behaviour or action that are seen as desirable for the common good. Social authoritarianism embraces convention and conformity and sees radicalism or originality as endangering the *status quo*. It seeks to reinforce common values by emphasizing shared responsibility, strict moral codes and sanctions to deter individuals from failing to comply.

Sociologists have used the approach to help develop their understanding of structural changes in society. Predictably, the perspective has been influential among those seeking to understand the family because its impact is easily detected. In the late 1980s and early 1990s conservative politicians declared that the rise of the one-parent family was in some way connected with the declining state of the nation's morality. The New Right approach highlighted the 'pathological' nature of the one-parent family and its relationship to state welfare. This was seen as a legitimate focus of concern owing to the growing number of such families, particularly those resulting from unmarried motherhood and divorce.

Much of the impetus behind the 'pathological' view of the one-parent family was provided by the leading right-wing politician Sir Keith Joseph, who argued that

> The balance of our population, our human stock is threatened... by inadequate parents, very frequently young unmarried women from social classes 4 and 5. Their children were problem children, future unmarried mothers, delinquents, denizens [inhabitants] of our borstals, subnormal educational establishments, prisons, hostels for drifters. (*Guardian*, 21 October 1974)

More recently, in the early years of the twenty-first century other groups have attracted attention in the form of media accounts, which have taken up the New Right's pathological view of certain groups. NEETs (young people Not in Education, Employment or Training) have been connected to crime, and Swale (2006) links their identification to the earlier writings of Charles Murray. NEETs have been described as a 'new tribe' (Winnett, 2005) or an underclass, demonized as workshy, benefit scroungers, singleparents with no qualifications. It is important to note the class prejudice which is inherent in much of New Right thinking – Chavs, NEETs, Hoodies all represent distinctly 'common-sense' views about the working class and the potential threat they pose to society.

The New Right approach dominated political thinking on the family in the early 1990s and beyond, with several New Right themes being taking up by the Labour government in the late 1990s and 2000s. Particularly prominent was the New Right concern about the effect that growth in the number of one-parent families would have on state welfare. This led to a range of (mostly unsubstantiated) articles in the media about young girls deliberately getting pregnant in order to obtain council housing or avoid custodial sentences. Although much New Right thinking on the family at the time was subject to heavy criticism (see Phoenix, 1988), even those who strongly opposed it recognized that it had some value. For example, McRobbie (1989), when commenting on the negative connotations of construing the one-parent family in pathological terms, conceded that 'it is unwise, however, in the desire to de-pathologise young motherhood, to end up suggesting it is unproblematic'.

More recently the New Right approach has been applied to the issue of children in the family. Wagg (1992) presents an analysis of childhood and politics in modern Britain that demonstrates how the construct of 'child' has been exploited for political ends. He makes the case that the New Right have portrayed children as 'vulnerable' in order to expose a whole host of groups to public scrutiny and accountability:

> [I]n the perception of many New Right activists, the family was menaced by an array of 'enemies within' – pornographers, drug pushers, left-wing teachers and doctors prescribing contraceptives for young girls – who directly subverted 'family life' and the traditional authority of parents over children. (Ibid., p. 12)

Teenage motherhood has not escaped the New Right approach. The increasing numbers of young women in the UK having children outside marriage has been viewed by the New Right as one of main indicators of the dependency culture and breakdown of family values. Politicians and New Right thinkers have sought to have welfare benefits and support withdrawn from such groups.

Critics of New Right thinking would argue that far from being an attempt to protect the moral fabric of society, the above are examples of the scapegoating of 'radical' groups who may pose a threat to the established social order. A similar trend is discernable in the New Right analysis of crime (see Van den Haag, 1975; Wilson, 1977; Friedman, 1980), which has been condemned for firmly locating the blame for criminality with vulnerable, disadvantaged or powerless groups in society or those who challenge the *status quo*.

The New Right – an evaluation

Strengths

1. There is little doubt that the approach pinpoints direct causes of social problems and offers solutions to them. In that sense it is very much a practical theory.
2. Adoption of the New Right approach to social problems would, theoretically at least, lead to a huge reduction in public spending. This would be popular with those responsible for managing welfare budgets and developing cost-effective solutions to social problems.

Limitations

1. The New Right approach stereotypes the poor and creates scapegoats for society's problems. It appears to blame the poor for their poverty, despite its claims to the contrary – that is, that universal welfare provision creates a dependent population.

2. Critics argue that far from being a pragmatic approach motivated by a desire for social reform, New Right philosophy is actually an ideological ploy to shift responsibility for poverty and other social problems from the government to the people.

POSTMODERNISM

The postmodernist influence has been felt in sociology since the mid 1980s. Much of the intellectual groundwork of postmodernism was laid by the debates arising from poststructuralism (see Chapter 5). Postmodernism represents a critical response to many of the basic assumptions upon which classical sociology is based. The ideas of postmodernism are really quite straightforward, but the language and discourse utilized by postmodernists have made it difficult for others to comprehend their ideas. Postmodernism does not provide a coherent theory of social life; rather it offers a series of interpretations of contemporary life in the latter part of the twentieth century and the twenty-first century. Central to the approach is the basic assumption that the world that exists now (the postmodern world) differs from that which preceded it (the modern world). The arguments surrounding this assumption will be considered in Chapter 5, but here we focus on the theoretical stance adopted by postmodernists.

Postmodernists take the ideas of the classical sociologists as their starting-point for the analysis of society. While postmodernists freely acknowledge that the classical sociological theories differ from each other (in fact this is an important feature of their analysis), they are seen as united by their acceptance of three basic assumptions. It is these assumptions that mark classical theories out as products of the modern age. For postmodernists the term 'modern' is very specific. It refers to the period stretching from the Enlightenment (an eighteenth-century movement) to the late twentieth century. 'Modern' is used in conjunction with 'modernism', which according to postmodernists refers to particular ways of thinking about the world that have their origin in the Enlightenment, in particular the belief in rational thought and the application of scientific knowledge to understand and explain the social world (Brown, 1996). Postmodernists believe that classical sociological theory is a product of the modern age and it is this which forms the basis of their critique of it.

As noted above, postmodernists see modern sociology as underpinned by three basic beliefs; these are: (1) that it is possible and desirable to generate objective (that is value-free/impartial) knowledge, the validity of which can be affirmed by empirical evidence; (2) that this knowledge, obtained through the systematic application of rigorous procedures, can be used to understand and alleviate social problems; and (3) that this knowledge can be generalized to provide an insight into entire societies and the structures and processes within those societies.

At first glance the postmodernist interpretation of modernism appears misleading. Consider the first point. Not all sociological theories see the production of objective, demonstrably valid knowledge as possible or desirable. Elements of Weberian sociology and interpretive sociology in its entirety reject the assertion that sociology should be about generating objective knowledge through empirical research. Second, not all sociologists advocate the use of systematic and rigorous procedures to gather data (see the discussion on antipositivism in Chapter 3). Nor do they accept that the primary aim of sociology should be to develop insights that can be used to tackle social problems and implement social change (see the section in Chapter 3 on here-and-now analysis). The third point is more a matter for debate. Not all sociologists advocate a structuralist interpretation of social life, but all appear to make the implicit assumption that their interpretation of social life is the most applicable and offers the greatest contribution to understanding the nature of the social world.

Setting aside the above objections to the postmodernist interpretation of classical sociology for a moment, it is interesting to explore how they provide a direct challenge to modern sociology. Brown (1996, p. 23) summarizes the Postmodern position into three polar opposites of the modernist assumptions:

1. Relativism: there is no such thing as valid (or invalid) knowledge.
2. Death of the subject: knowledge as control rather than liberation.
3. Grand theories are inadmissible.

This provides the framework for Postmodern social theory. To deal with the first point, postmodernists dismiss the attempts of classical sociologists to develop an objective body of knowledge that can be used to understand social life. Instead they argue that there is no objective reality behind social meaning – thus all knowledge is relative to context and constructs. All attempts by classical sociologists to gather empirical data to develop the knowledge base of the discipline are misguided and futile. They capture just one version of events, when the only 'reality' that exists consists of competing versions and the interpretation of events and social phenomena. Postmodernists are particularly critical of positivism, a modern approach that advocates the systematic study of the social world by scientific means. Their deconstruction (internal critique) of positivism is used to give credence to the claim that all knowledge is relative (see Brown, 1996, for a review).

Second, with regard to 'death of the subject', postmodernists point out that modernism gives great credence to the gathering of impartial knowledge and the application of this to alleviate social problems. In doing so, an assumption is made that the knowledge upon which they base their interventions is sound. However, given postmodernism's challenge to the absolute nature of knowledge, any social change advocated arises from one of the many, possibly infinite, interpretations of (or narratives about) the problem. Postmodernists use the concept 'death of the subject' to refer to the inability of specific specialists to arrive at a hard-and-fast understanding of social life and to locate social reform within an objective or real context.

Third, postmodernists argue that it is inappropriate for sociology to assume that knowledge can be extended to entire societies and the various structures and processes that make up those societies (ibid.). This argument logically follows their previous assertion that objective knowledge does not exist. If knowledge simply reflects any one of a number of possible narratives, it is obvious why generalizing and applying this knowledge on a wider scale is pointless. Hence postmodernists condemn grand theories as inadmissible. By this they mean that the overarching explanations that the classical sociologists claim to provide are not valid, basically because they are impossible. The expression 'demise of the metanarrative' is usually associated with this line of thinking. Here reference is made to the fall from grace of the large-scale, sweeping explanations (or social laws) advocated by modern sociologists. Postmodernists consider that such 'metanarratives' are redundant in the postmodern world because postmodern thinking has exposed their limitations. This issue will be explored further in Chapter 5.

From these criticisms of modernism it is possible to identify the defining characteristics of postmodernism. First, whereas classical sociologists seek to go beyond the relativity of social situations and establish some rational standpoint from which 'reality' can be described, postmodernists embrace diversity and fragmentation.

Their argument is that there is no 'objective reality' behind social meanings. Accounts and definition have no objective or external reference. They are elements in a free-floating system of images which are produced and reproduced through the media of mass communication. Through television advertising, soap operas and other forms of popular culture, these images actually come to define the 'reality' of the viewers. People live in an artificial world which is created and defined by the cultural processes of mass communications.

As shown above, postmodernists recognize that reality is now constructed largely by the media and popular culture. One interpretation of this is seen in the Postmodern analysis of popular culture, which emphasizes style and image over product function and utility. This point will be explored in Exercise 4.5.

Another principle identified as postmodernist is rejection of specific subject-orientated research and theorizing ('subject-centredness'). Instead, postmodernists advocate theoretical eclecticism, whereby ideas are borrowed from a range of theoretical perspectives to provide the basis for theoretical discourse and debate. The inspiration for this is rejection of the grand narrative. As Lyotard explains: 'Simplifying to the extreme, I define postmodern as incredulity to metanarratives...Let us wage war on totality...let us activate the differences' (Lyotard, 1984, pp. xxiv, 82). Consequently, postmodernism encompasses a range of different theoretical perspectives: 'Postmodern knowledge is not simply a tool of the authorities; it refines our sensitivity to differences and reinforces our ability to tolerate the incommensurable' (ibid., p. xxv).

Central to Postmodern theory is a desire to subvert or dismantle the boundaries between disciplines and subdisciplines and create a multidisciplinary, multidimensional perspective that synthesizes ideas from a range of fields and perspectives within a given discipline (Ritzer, 2008). Similarly, in the study of social life postmodernists advocate removal of the boundaries that segment society.

Postmodernists insist that sociology must move beyond the modern period into the Postmodern period. Both Lyotard (1984) and Baudrillard (1983) agree that in response to the demise of the metanarrative there is a need to develop 'small, localized narratives' – that is, low-level but detailed understandings of competing realities/social contexts. In developing such narratives, all social phenomena are seen as equally valid objects of study and none are beyond the realms of critical appraisal. This includes pre-existing intellectual theories, which are construed simply as texts, as the rhetorical constructions of theorists (Brown, 1990). This leaves postmodernists free to subvert the authority of theories and attack their privileged status. This has important implications: it 'leads to a view of science in general, and sociology in particular, as "a conversation of scholars/rhetors"' (Brown, 1990). In such a demystified conversation, theorists are free to borrow ideas from one another in an effort to create a new range of synthetic theories (Ritzer, 2008).

An important part of the study of social life is the study of the nature of sociological theory itself. Thus, postmodernists seek not simply to analyse society, but also systematically to study sociological theory itself. This explains their preoccupation with the limitations of the classical sociological theories as well as what Ritzer (1992) identifies as their interest in 'developing new concatenations (linkages) of Marxism, critical theory, feminism, postmodern social theory, and other currents of critical social theory to solve the theoretical and political problems confronting us today'.

The impact of postmodernism

Having outlined some of the basic ideas of postmodernism, it is now important to explore the impact that postmodernism has had on sociological theory and research.

The late 1980s and 1990s saw an explosion of attempts to apply Postmodern ideas to various aspects of social life. Most effort has been directed at developing an understanding of popular culture (see Strinati, 1992; Sugrue and Taylor, 1996), although there have also been notable attempts to apply Postmodern ideas in analyses of health (Senior, 1996), the workplace (Warde, 1989), relationships (Giddens, 1990), organizations (Clegg, 1992) and new technology (Tattersall, 1997). In addition, Brown (1996) notes the influence that postmodernism has had on the study of economics, business, education and the state.

Much of this research has sought not only to investigate the applicability of Postmodern assumptions but also to explore the Postmodern claim that a Postmodern society has emerged, distinct from the modern society that preceded it. Such attempts seek to combine analysis of modern and Postmodern features of the topic under study with interpretation of the usefulness of Postmodern concepts such as metanarratives, discourse, fragmentation and so on (see Senior, 1996). Postmodernists in turn are able to use sociological inquiry such as this to reflect upon the validity of their ideas/assertions.

Item B

Postmodernism and Popular Culture in a Postmodern Society

Strinati (1992) highlights five key postmodernist features that have implications for the impact of popular culture upon individuals and social life:

1. *The breakdown of the distinction between culture and society* – Popular culture has emerged as a significant player in Postmodern cultures, as it permeates our consciousness, influencing patterns of consumption. The images of popular culture interpenetrate the media and provide our dominant view of the society in which we live.

2. *An emphasis on style at the expense of content* – We have become obsessed with designer images, such that we buy products not for their utility or intrinsic worth, but because we respond to the label associated with them. The image is more important than the substance and we are prepared to pay high prices to sustain the image.

3. *The breakdown of the distinction between high culture (art) and popular culture* – This is most evident in the world of advertising, where products are marketed through a mixing of popular and high culture. The traditional distinctions between an elite 'high' culture and a mass 'popular' culture are dissolved.

4. *Confusion over time and space* – The development of extremely rapid communications and transport systems has served to shrink the world, in terms of both time and space. We can access information about real world events in faraway places much faster than in the past. We can travel to distant places relatively quickly, often into environments however that are remarkably similar to each other.

5. *The decline of the metanarrative* – We are no longer certain about any knowledge in the world, which presents itself as a place of unknown risks and opportunities, but which cannot be explained or understood in any meaningful sense. There is no 'truth' that art and culture can represent and thus culture cannot be 'representative' of some underlying verity. As a result, culture and art turn to borrowing ideas from different sources and present themselves, not as 'true' art but as 'collage'.

Exercise 4.5

This exercise will enable you to explore how Postmodern ideas can help us to develop an understanding of popular culture. Read Item B and conduct the following task.

The following phenomena are a familiar part of modern life. Consider the list carefully and try to identify which of the features of postmodernism outlined in Item B (numbers 1–5) they can best be identified with.

- The popularity of reality TV programmes such as *Big Brother, The X Factor* and *Britain's Got Talent* where members of the public become part of the 'performance'.
- Participation of celebrities in singing, dancing and 'living in the jungle' programmes where their performance is judged by the public.
- Global hotel chains that have a similar decoration and style wherever their hotels happen to be located.
- Use of classical music to publicize football tournaments like the World Cup.

- Pop programmes 'zapping' from topic to topic with fast-forward/rewind graphics evident on the TV screen.
- Oasis/Franz Ferdinand 'borrowing' ideas from the Beatles and other bands from the 1960s or the multilayered music genres used by rap and hiphop artists.
- High sales figures for 'designer' bottled waters, for example, Perrier, Evian.
- Live news reports from war zones, for example, Afghanistan, the Gulf, Kosovo, Iraq.
- The dominance of Cable News Network and Sky Television in the global media.

Postmodernism has affected not only sociological research; its impact can also be seen in sociological theory. It is now possible to identify examples of classical theories that have sought to respond to the challenges posed by postmodernists in order to provide a relevant and purposeful analysis of society in the late twentieth century. For example, Wood (1986) identifies the influence that Laclau and Mouffe (1985) have had in developing Postmodern Marxist theory. Wood (1986, p. 47) notes how this approach differs from what has gone before: '[T]his work, accepting the focus on linguistics, texts, and discourse in postmodernism, detaches ideology from its material base and ultimately dissolves the society altogether into ideology or 'discourse'.

Similarly Walby (1994) applies postmodernism to her analysis of gender. However while Walby recognizes the value of some Postmodern ideas in highlighting the inadequacies of overarching theories of patriarchy, racism and capitalism, she criticizes postmodernism as being of little use to those seeking to understand gender relations in the late twentieth century: '[T]he fragmentation has gone too far, resulting in a denial of significant structuring of power, and leading toward mere empiricism' (ibid., p. 225). The impact of postmodernism on feminist thinking will be given further consideration when we explore our next contemporary theory below.

Postmodernism – an evaluation

Strengths

1. Postmodernism is an original attempt to encompass a range of historical and cultural changes within a single theoretical framework.
2. It has been an influential force behind the analysis of diverse areas of social life.

3. It has forced a reappraisal of existing theories. Classical theorists have been inspired to revise some of their basic assumptions and respond reflexively to develop a more tenable (defensible) analysis of contemporary life.

Limitations

1. The ideas of postmodernism are essentially simple but the language and discourse of postmodernism are not easily understood. It is regarded by some as an abstract analysis that does little to aid understanding of the practical problems of everyday life.
2. By proclaiming the 'death of the subject' it devalues the contributions made by those who have addressed social problems. Giddens (cited in Tattersall, 1997) argues that rejection of the metanarrative is unhelpful, and suggests that postmodernists should acknowledge the limitations of the existing body of knowledge and seek to build upon it.
3. Critics argue that postmodernism is as 'subject-centred' as those it condemns. By making public their ideas, postmodernists must be assuming that these ideas can be used to further the understanding of life in the twentieth century and twenty-first centuries. This leaves them open to the same criticism they level at others. This contradiction in Postmodern theory is embarrassingly difficult to conceal.

In defence of modernism

Postmodernism seems to have reduced the accounts of sociologists to narratives or stories that are no more valid than stories told by any ordinary person. Postmodernists use the terms 'narratives' or 'stories' to emphasize their view that social reality is constructed through language rather than existing in some sort of objective form that can be discovered or described through social scientific methods. There are as many 'realities' as there are constructions of it – all are 'stories', none can be shown to be better than others – including those of sociologists! We have no reference outside of language that we can use to legitimate our sociological 'knowledge of society' or the accounts of our informants (social agents). The 'real' world we wish to capture in sociological theory is also the means by which we construct it! Similarly, epistemology is exposed as a self-justifying project that is based upon uncertain principles (see Chapter 3). Such views are, to say the least, not ideal for sociologists wishing to describe and explain the social world.

In defence of modernism and therefore of modern sociology we can argue that it is possible for postmodernism to deliver such a critique of sociology *only* by setting up two entirely false choices:

1. Either we can provide objectively verifiable knowledge of society (modernism) or we have to accept complete relativism (postmodernism).

    Social accounts are therefore either scientific (verifiable using epistemology) or entirely relative (no judgement can be made between them). However, we may wish to consider the following points:

    (a) Lack of **absolute** proof in the epistemological sense does not mean that producing evidence through sociological research is a worthless exercise. Some descriptions of the social world are more factually accurate than others. For example, a reference to World War Two has more credibility than one to the Anglo-Scottish War of 1998 precisely because there was no war between England and Scotland in that year. Similarly, the statement that educational performance is in part related to the socio-economic background of children, supported with appropriate statistical evidence, is rightly taken more seriously than an alternative statement that is simply made up. In other words we do not have to accept relativism even if we accept an absence of absolute certainty. There can be means by which we can make judgements about social phenomena which do bring us closer to causal explanations for what is happening. We **know** that aspects of our health, welfare and education for example are closely related to our socio-economic position in society.

    (b) In addition, postmodernism is itself 'epistemological' in that it claims truth for its own pronouncements which it denies for others. Postmodernism contradicts itself.

2. Either we accept the possibility of social progress resulting from human intervention based upon sociological knowledge or we must abandon any notion of social improvement.

    But, if we can argue that it is possible to judge between accounts based upon the production of evidence (as in (1) above), then this suggests a movement from less adequate to more adequate explanation, even if the concept of *absolute* proof is problematic (see Exercise 4.6). For this reason, the outcome of empirical research into the causes of delinquency, for example, is not equivalent to the opinion of anyone you might happen to meet on the street and can therefore be used as a basis for changes in social policy and the criminal justice system. Modern sociology, there-fore, allows us to engage with society in a positive and political manner, whereas the relativism of postmodernism seems to imply scepticism and political disengagement.

Exercise 4.6

Princess Diana died tragically in a car crash in Paris on 31 August 1997. Since that time there has been speculation about the cause of the accident. Some argue that her death was in fact murder. Some have pointed a finger at the British royal family itself as responsible, others have attacked the press and media for their obsessive coverage of all her movements. An 18-month-long judicial investigation ended in France in 1999, followed in Britain by a long police inquiry concluding in 2006 and long inquests concluding in 2008 which found no substance to the conspiracy claims. Princess Diana, the inquest jury found, was 'unlawfully killed by the grossly negligent driving of chauffeur Henri Paul and paparazzi photographers'. However, samples of blood tests and other medical evidence had gone missing and this has led to further speculation surrounding the events of 31 August 1997.

Use the internet to read some accounts of the investigations and inquests and attempt to answer the question below:

Is it possible to establish the truth about what happened in the death of Princess Diana? (Note: The question is not asking you to establish the truth – it is asking whether or not the truth could be established.)

POSTFEMINISM

Postfeminism refers to the state of feminism in the late 1990s and 2000s. Some of the issues and areas of concern today are different from those which dominated thinking in the 1960s and 1970s. Some argue that this marks a Postfeminist era, typified by 'the belief that earlier battles have been won: women have achieved economic, political and legal equality, therefore making feminist theory practically obsolete' (Clarke, 1996). However this optimistic view about the changes to women's position in society is not always borne out by the evidence in relation to work, equal pay, housework and childcare responsibilities, domestic violence and rape convictions.

The days when feminism was assumed to have a broad agenda, which tack-led many of these issues and others ranging from equal opportunities in the workplace to improved child care facilities and campaigns against pornogra-phy and sexual violence/harassment, do seem to have been assigned to the past with the rise of 'Girl Power' and other media inventions (ibid.). Nonetheless a range of feminisms still exist (see Chapter 2 for a review), united by the common aim of improving the disadvantaged position of women in society. Some conceptualize 'women' in unitary or homogeneous terms – that is, they share a common experience of exploitation, which serves to define their position in society. An important feature of feminist analysis is the concept of 'patriarchy', a term used to refer to the ideology of male domination that pervades all institutions and social life.

Feminism in more recent times has faced three main challenges that have served to fuel the debate about whether the approach is of relevance in the twenty-first century. The first is research evidence of a marked improvement in some aspects of the economic and social position of women (see Wilkinson, 1994; EOC, 2005; see below). The second is what Clarke (1996) terms the 'anti-feminist backlash' – that is, a politically motivated move to erode the status of feminism and reverse the advances made by women. The third stems from the rise of postmodernism, which has offered a critique of 'modern' sociological theories, feminism included. The significance of each of these challenges will be considered in turn.

Much of the impetus for the debate on women's improved position has stemmed from Wilkinson's (1994) research on what she calls 'genderquake', a social phenomenon that is reversing centuries of gender inequality. Wilkinson identifies a number of ways in which women are now surpassing men's achievements in the labour market. Media articles in the mid 1990s ceased to highlight the disadvantaged position of women and began to focus on the difficulties faced by men in an increasingly female-dominated labour market. Smith and Thomas (1996), citing British Household Panel Survey data, note that the shift towards female breadwinners is increasing year by year. In contrast, male unemployment has risen to record levels and men have been forced to reconsider their role in the labour market, leading research agencies, such as the Policy Studies Institute, to highlight the discrimination faced by men. The EOC (2005) also pointed to particular areas were women have been successful, the increasing number of women MPs – 19.7 per cent in 2005 compared with 4.3 per cent in 1975, 42 per cent of solicitors in 2005 compared with 7 per cent in 1975 and the fact that girls do better than boys in SATs (with exceptions), GCSEs and A levels and now constitute the majority of undergraduates in higher education. This progress is put down to the tackling of direct discrimination since the implementation of the Equal Pay and Sex Discrimination Acts of 1975.

Such research has been exploited by those involved in the anti-feminist backlash to argue that feminism is an outdated and outmoded social movement that is of little relevance in contemporary Britain. However sociologists would disagree. Much sociological evidence (see Pascall, 1995, for a review of this) suggests that women continue to experience disadvantage in the workplace in relation to pay, promotion and pensions, and that while improvements may have been made in certain areas, in others regression has taken place. Initiatives such as care in the community have left women with the double burden of paid employment and family responsibilities. In many cases this has caused women to retreat into the private sphere and made them dependent once more. This process has been influenced by inequality in the workplace:

> Women have been left to manage these contradictory trends: they organise their own childcare, and care for older relatives. This is at high cost in terms of continuity of employment and career in its traditional sense. Cultural expectations are one factor in making these obligations women's more than men's. But discrimination at work is another factor: in most households women are paid less than men, and in these circumstances economic logic will dictate whose 'career' will take priority. (Pascall, 1995, p. 6)

In relation to the types of work women do outside the home there are still marked gender boundaries, with women concentrated in the social and caring spheres. Even within education post-GCSE, girls and boys move into traditional subject and vocational areas. At work, women are more likely to be part-time – 78 per cent according to the EOC – which carries a career, earnings and pension penalty as well as less likelihood of training and staff development. Similarly, women's earnings in all occupational areas are less than men's (Economic and Social Research Council (ESRC), *Society Today*, 2005).

Increasingly, sociologists are recognizing that to lump all women together into a single category is no longer appropriate. Writers have begun to acknowledge that the differences between women, for example as a result of social class or ethnicity, may be far greater than the common experiences that stem from gender. Low pay, poverty, lower educational qualifications and low-status work are common for women from certain minority groups such as those of Pakistani and Bangladeshi heritage. The evidence and arguments are not new. As noted in Chapter 2 (pp. 77–8), black feminists have long objected to the idea that gender is the primary shaper of social experience and that women are a homogeneous group. Black feminists argue that black women's experiences of racism means that they have more in common with black men than with white women. In recent times it has become so significant that feminists have been forced to reappraise and adapt their theories to accommodate diversity of experience within overarching theories of gender inequality (see below).

To turn to the second challenge to feminism, the anti-feminist backlash, Wilkinson (1994) notes a growing reluctance, particularly among young women, to identify with the women's movement. This is somewhat surprising as public opinion polls show that the majority of women do not believe that attitudes towards women have changed for the better or that sexual discrimination has reduced. Clarke (1996, p. 23) cites a possible explanation for this:

> The growth in the 1980s of the New Right, with its emphasis on traditional family values and sex roles, can also be identified as part of the backlash against feminism and the transformations that are taking place in women's lives. John Major's 'Back to Basics' campaign idealized the nuclear family and attributed many social problems to the increase in the number of lone parent families, the majority of which are headed by women.

It appears that far from harnessing political power to liberate women, feminism has contributed to the subjugation of women by making them a scapegoat for society's problems. If this is the case, feminists would argue that it is now as important as ever to fight for women's rights and sexual liberation, and indeed it has added new vigour to specific campaigns on women's rights issues such as rape within marriage, unfair dismissal as a result of pregnancy, the sex trade and pornography and domestic murder. The success of such campaigns has been much publicized and enshrined in law through changes to the law on domestic murder, the criminalization of rape within marriage and amendments to employment legislation to safeguard the rights of pregnant women. It is still worth noting that high-profile industrial tribunal cases still involve cases where women have to fight for equal pay not just against their employers but also against their trade unions, often in the public sector.

This, alongside the huge impact that feminism has had in the 30 years since it began, appears to offer an embarrassing legacy to the antifeminist movement. As Clarke (1996, p. 23) highlights, feminists have not just engineered structural change; they have also engendered attitudinal change and it is this which is probably the most significant and resilient contribution of the movement:

> [A]n enormous achievement of feminism over the past 20 years has been the change it has brought about in female consciousness. The founding aims of the women's movement: reproductive choice, equal pay, access to childcare and freedom from sexual abuse are now supported by vast numbers of women who might not identify themselves as feminists.

Walby (1994) provides a useful insight into the third challenge – the impact of postmodernism on feminism. Walby looks at the key assumptions of postmodernism and identifies the way these ideas have been used to attack feminism. She takes her own definition of postmodernism as the starting-point for the discussion:

> I use the concept of 'postmodern' to refer to the changes which lead to fragmentation on a number of different levels, from substantive social reality to modes of social analysis. It is my claim that these have common features. I am not arguing that postmodernism simply follows on temporally from modernism. Rather it catches an analytic grouping of themes which are current in contemporary social science, the main aspect of which is fragmentation. (Walby, 1994, p. 226)

She goes on to argue that while some of the issues raised by postmodernists do provide feminists with food for thought, postmodernism has gone too far. Walby bases her debate upon three fundamental assertions of postmodernism: (1) that the concepts 'gender' and 'race' have no value and that capitalism is disorganized; (2) that theorizing based upon structuralist notions of 'patriarchy' and 'capitalism' are inadmissible; and (3) that there is no place for grand narratives in contemporary sociological thinking and social life.

Walby refutes the first point, conceding that while social relations in terms of gender, ethnicity and class have changed, postmodernists have gone too far in attempting to dismiss such concepts. Walby acknowledges that despite widespread recognition of the differences between ethnic groups and between women, they are united by their disadvantaged position relative to men. She also asserts that although capitalism in the twenty-first century has been re-defined, its influence is still marked: 'Gender and ethnicity, or more precisely, patriarchy and racism, remain potent social forces, and capitalism has not withered away despite its new form' (ibid., p. 226).

With regard to the second point, Walby states that Postmodern critics go too far in asserting the necessary impossibility and unproductive nature of investigating gender inequality. She argues that although it is reasonable to highlight that gender relations could potentially take an infinite number of forms, in reality there are some widely repeated features and considerable historical continuity:

> The signifiers of 'woman' and 'man' have sufficient historical and cross-cultural continuity, despite some variations, to warrant using such terms. It is a contingent question as to whether gender relations do have sufficient

continuity of patterning to make generalisations about a century or two and a continent or so. While the answer to this cannot be given at a theoretical level, I would argue that in practice such generalisation is possible. There are sufficient common features and sufficient routinized interconnections for it to make sense to talk of patriarchy. (Ibid., p. 229)

However, despite her interest in generalization, Walby makes it clear she does not advocate a return to the 'totalising framework of traditional Marxism, which attempted to tuck all other forms of social inequality under that of class' (ibid., p. 27). Instead she proposes analysis of the mutual determination (inter-relationship) among the three systems of race, class and gender.

Finally, Walby makes the case for theory beyond the realm of the small, localized narratives advocated by postmodernists. She argues that it is both possible and desirable to develop grand narratives about social life, and that these are important for the development of a truly global understanding of gender inequality. Drawing on the work of global systems theorists (see the section in Chapter 5 on globalization) and feminists working within this field (Mies, 1986; Mitter, 1986), Walby (1994, p. 227) makes the case for global as opposed to national or local analysis of gender relations:

I am arguing for an international perspective. Neither class, nor race, nor gender can be understood within one country alone. We live in a world system, which is limited only marginally by national sovereignties. However, this world system is not only one of capitalism (as Wallerstein would argue), but also of racism and patriarchy.

Where does this leave feminism? Feminist writers have sought to respond reflexively to the challenges they face. Researchers will continue to explore women's disadvantaged position in society and the fight for economic, political and legal reform will no doubt continue, albeit at the local rather than the national level. However, feminist theory will seek to transcend the local and national scene and undertake global analyses of gender inequality (Swasti Mittar, 1986). Some work will be inspired by Postmodern thinking, although this will not mean full acceptance of the assumptions of postmodernism.

It is likely that feminists will seek to reconcile the internal contradictions and limitations of the various theories they espouse and attempt to synthesize the most productive and relevant ideas (Abbott and Wallace, 1990). What is certain is that their fight to establish gender equality in sociology, as a basis for equality in social life, will continue:

What is necessary is a total rethinking of sociological knowledge and the ways in which that knowledge is produced. This is because it is not accidental or the result of an oversight that women have been ignored, marginalized, or distorted in sociology, but the outcome of the theoretical underpinning of the discipline. Malestream sociology failed to confront the view that women are naturally determined and women's role the outcome of biological imperatives. Consequently, the concepts developed to carry out sociological research, and the issues seen as there to be researched, ignored women. To produce adequate sociological knowledge it is necessary to reformulate these concepts and questions so that women become central to the concerns of the discipline. (Ibid.)

Dorothy Smith (1990) uses the concept of 'relations of ruling' to reconceptualize the notion that all social relations can be said to be gender-saturated. Drawing on a Marxist discourse, Smith argues that, from dominant regulatory institutions such as the government, business and the law to our everyday practices and processes in family life, education and work, women's oppression is underpinned and women's subordination maintained. Smith employs the notion of the public and private spheres of social life to show how 'relations of ruling' are often hidden but nonetheless powerful mechanisms and means of oppression. The 'textual' dimensions of the everyday world (claiming state benefits, filling in tax forms, taking exams) she sees as subordinating people to the power of the ruling class or state in an administrative forum which maintains both gender and class inequalities. Smith also drew upon phenomenology to argue that the standpoint of women (and ethnic minorities, gays and other groups) is not just a matter of definition by dominant discourses, but also includes subjective, non-rational understandings of women. Women and men 'do' gender in their everyday lives by drawing upon individual and collective assumptions about what it is to be a man or a woman (Smith, 2005).

A final postscript to the lack of interest and commitment to feminism by the younger generation is the role the media played and plays in our perceptions of what feminism is. In the 1970s and 1980s the radical feminists were misrepresented as 'bra-burning' man-haters, and in the 1990s the view of the unfeminine feminist, denying aspects of what being a woman might mean to many women, such as wearing make-up or remaining childfree, was prevalent. Towards the end of the 1990s and into the twenty-first century the idea that women could compete on men's terms and win became part of media hype. The notion of the working mother as an equal partner with the working man was prevalent and maternity rights and benefits continued to improve throughout the 1990s and 2000s. More women in parliament, in the professions, the phenomenon of successful women in the media and in entertainment – such as female pop bands like the The Spice Girls and the phenomenon of ladettes, all became seen with help from the media as women having finally taken their place alongside men in society. However on closer inspection the role models were in fact pretty traditional and did nothing to illuminate the lack of equality for women in many areas of social life. The sexualized imagery presented of many of the younger female entertainers suggested their 'managers' also held the traditional perspective on the nature of women's role in society. The cult of celebrity and increased use of cosmetic surgery further reinforced stereotypical images of women's role and what women's bodies should be like.

Furthermore the sexual exploitation and abuse of women has also been highlighted – the low conviction rate for rape has been a cause for concern over many years and despite changes to police management of cases and the ways the courts handle cases there has been little improvement. There was a doubling of the number of lap dancing clubs in the UK to 300 between 2004 and 2008. According to Andy Bloxham writing in the *Daily Telegraph* in June 2008 there are moves afoot to re-classify such clubs as 'sex encounter' venues which have come into existence because of uncertainties in the licensing laws and which are to some degree venues similar to legalized brothels or 'glorified strip clubs'.

Men's studies and masculinity

Part of the 'postfeminist' era has seen an increasing interest in and analysis of masculinity on the part of sociologists which led to the development of men's studies. As Parker and Lyle (2005) point out, the emergence of men as consumers of fashion, style and cosmetics in the 1970s brought about a wider academic and popular debate about the nature of masculinity. The 1980s in particular saw the emergence of the 'yuppie' (young upwardly mobile professional) and the 'new man' – the more family-centred, emotional, caring type who looked after his children and shared the housework. Both of these male identities were staunchly heterosexual but fairly short-lived in terms of making any lasting changes to our conceptions of masculinity, if they ever did indeed exist in any meaningful form. The seeming 'disappearance' of these examples of new masculinities gave rise to two other masculine 'types' –'lads' and 'metrosexuals'. 'Lads' culture was characterized by some excessively stereotypical masculine, often working-class traits – heavy drinking, hedonism, misogyny, anti-feminism – whereas 'metrosexuals' were concerned with appearance, fashion, lifestyle choices and a more feminized persona, in short the opposite of 'laddism'. These developments led to a new approach to studying masculinity which was rooted in sociology and used feminist-based theory to look at gender as a part of the structure of social relations in society.

Hence, some of the concerns established by traditional feminists about gender and issues such as socialization, stereotypes, power relations, role expectations and so on have been considered sociologically from a male perspective. Questions such as how boys are brought up and socialized into masculine roles, what are the male stereotypes that boys and men are labelled by, and what is the role of the male in the family, education and work in the changing twenty-first century have been addressed by sociologists such as Francis (2000), Mac an Ghaill (1992) and Connolly (2006). Increasingly research challenges the accepted male role models and attempts to understand the underpinnings of what it is to be male and exhibit masculine behaviour in modern society.

Anthropological and ethnographic research has shown that cultural norms play a significant role in defining what ways are approved of in any given society of 'being an adult male' (Gilmore, 1990). Although Gilmore argues that many societies define masculinity in similar ways, there are also considerable societal differences. For example displays of male-to-male affection are taboo in the UK (except in certain circumstances such as when a goal in scored on a football pitch) but common in other European countries like Turkey and Greece. Also there are societies where masculine and feminine behaviour are not very clearly demarcated.

Connell (2000) has challenged the use of both biological and cultural explanations of masculinity. He argues that biological and cultural factors should be used jointly to understand the nature of the body within its social context. The role of men in some sports is an example of how bodily activity symbolizes masculinity and gives meaning to what is to be male. Also men can change their masculine status depending on the context they are in, at home, at work, with friends and so on.

Messerschmidt (1995) has argued that there can be two variations in masculine types and traits. The first is *hegemonic masculinity*, based on dominance over women and achievement of high status through work, sport or power. This is a highly sought-after type of masculinity compared with the second type – *subordinate masculinity* associated with males from minority ethnic groups or homosexuals.

Sociologists have also discussed 'accomplishing' masculinity – how men become masculine and define themselves in society. In his research on masculinity in primary schools Connolly (2006) has shown that boys enter school already with ways of thinking about masculinity, femininity and ethnicity. These can be brought from home, neighbourhood, prior role models or even from media influence and common computer games. These ways of thinking have important consequences for developing relationships in school. Connolly observed how notions of 'hypermasculinity' were displayed even at quite a young age to achieve high status. Displaying toughness, being non-academic, being good at football seemed to earn respect from peers as well being attractive to girls. However, he also cautions against treating males as a homogenous group, as his research shows that there are significant differences in conceptions of jobs between middle-class and working-class boys.

Studies into male criminality have also analysed the role of masculinity in determining who gets involved in crime and deviance as well as the differences in meanings applied to criminal behaviour of different male groups. Some predominantly male examples of criminality such as the 'rogue trader' in the financial markets would not necessarily even be considered as dishonest or criminal, since the background he is likely to come from affords some protection from the traditional male criminal stereotype.

What counts as masculine can be fluid and changing, depending on age, status, ethnicity, sexuality and social class. Furthermore, over time patterns of social relations change with the necessity to change perspective on what it is to be male and female and what counts as masculine and feminine behaviour. The world of work is an example of these changes with women now constituting half of the workforce, albeit in predominantly part-time work, men no longer have as secure a foothold in as many occupational areas as their fathers did. Men are no longer the sole or main breadwinner in the family in many circumstances. The industrial labour market has changed beyond recognition since the end of the Second World War and so have the certainties that gave rise to gender divisions in society.

Part of the Postfeminist and postmodernist perspective that relates to gender is the notion of the personal construction of femininity and masculinity – men and women have a range of choices about the ways they construct their gender identity. Butler (1990) for example argued that gender is performance – behaviour exhibited depending upon where we are, what we are doing and who we are with. She argues that men and women should no longer be seen as separate or distinctive sexes but we should see gender as a range of social processes whereby men can adopt characteristics previously associated with women such as looking after their appearance and women can adopt traits associated with men such as aggression and pursuit of a career. Popular culture and the media personalities associated with it such as Gok Wan further underpin these changes. The term 'transgression' has been used to describe this crossing of the gender identity boundaries (Livesey and Lawson 2005).

Leach (1994) has criticized analyses of masculinity that rely upon sociobiological or cultural explanations as being able to provide only a partial understanding of the role of gender identity in society. Leach argues that masculinity as gender identity can be understood only as an economic, social, political and ideological construction. The 'breadwinner' dimension of masculinity is part of industrial capitalism's need to create a compliant work-force with responsibilities for providing for the family. The breadwinner role also legitimizes the sexual division of labour, which sustains the economic sub-ordination of women. Ideologically, traditional masculinity also maintains the sexual oppression of women since it is defined by sexism, misogyny, aggression, homophobia and the behaviour which supports the ideology such as domestic and sexual violence against women. Leach is arguing that masculinity and fem-ininity are part of wider structures of power and social processes that maintain male dominance and can be understood only in these terms.

Exercise 4.7

Using the knowledge you have gained of feminist perspectives in Chapter 2, write a short paragraph to explain how each feminist perspective would view the social construction of masculinity. Marxist feminists, for example, would argue that capitalism had created a particular form of masculinity that is linked to the maintenance of the industrial economy and that also leads to the oppres-sion of women. Hence the dominance of men is linked to the structure and organization of society that creates a vested interest for men in the continuance of an unequal discriminatory system.

Drawing on the information presented in this section, write down at least two strengths and two limitations of Postfeminist theory.

CRITICAL RACE THEORY

Paralleling the emergence of postfeminism, there have been similar develop-ments in theories of race and racism. Drawing on sociological theories such as Post-Marxism and poststructuralism, as well as influences from beyond soci-ology, critical race theory developed a social constructionist approach to race and racism. The emphasis in American sociology was on the way that legal and social arrangements were not neutral in terms of race, but were manipulated by social and economic elites to serve their interests (see Matsuda *et al.*, 2003). In particular, the American courts were not colour-blind, as was often claimed, but interpreted the law to suit the needs of a particular time, for example in redefining social groups as minorities as the economy needed. Indeed the whole notion that the United States has become 'colour-blind', as evidenced by the election of Barak Obama has come under attack from critical race theorists as a smokescreen that perpetuates racism in new forms (see Bonilla-Silva, 2003).

A key insight of critical race theory was that race could not be considered separately from other identities. Instead, ethnicity operates at the intersection of other identities that creates the potential for conflictful feelings in individuals as loyalties overlap or come into tension. Identities that are at this intersection are class, sexuality, religion and gender among others. It was therefore important for sociologists to allow the voices of ethnic minorities (and majorities) to be heard, so that the experiences of oppressing and being oppressed can be expressed (see Delgado and Stefancic, 2001). However, other critical race theorists argue that it is not enough to give voice to oppressed minorities, as a micro approach such as this can lead to the conclusion that racial discrimination is in terminal decline. Brown *et al.* (2003) suggest that structural inequalities are not just historical but continue and are perpetuated in American society, and it is in the areas of housing, education, and the economy that racism needs to be exposed and remedied.

Another emphasis of critical race theory is global in its scope. Theorists have shifted focus from the national position of ethnic groups, such as Afro-Americans in the United States, to examine race and racism across the world and through history. The processes of imperialism, decolonization and neo-colonialism are central to understanding the development of ethnonationalism, as exhibited in places as diverse as Kosovo, Rwanda and Sri Lanka (see, for example, Darder and Torres, 2004).

THEORIES OF SEXUALITY AND QUEER THEORY

Sociologists have long recognized that societies have powerful patterns, rules and regulations governing sexual behaviour. Laws, religions and family systems all seek to control sexual activity and behaviour. Foucault's *History of Sexuality* (1979) was an influential starting-point in sociology for ways of thinking about sexual behaviour. Through the structure of language we come to have particular ways in which we perceive sex which then become organized as part of the power relations in society, such as those based on gender. Foucault argues that during the nineteenth century sexual talk took place in negative ways and sexualities became reorganized to take account of new categories (linked to psychiatry) and organized into new patterns of power relations. (An important concept in Foucault's work is 'discourse' – discourses are bodies of ideas and language often mediated through institutions which indicate what the dominant thinking is at that particular time. We might think of medical discourses, criminological discourses, scientific discourses as well as sexual discourses and so on.)

Discussions concerning the nature of sexuality have been aligned with the work of feminists and the feminist tradition since its early days but have not been without controversy and debate. Radical feminists see sexuality as one of the main ways in which men control and regulate women's lives. Men from this perspective use sex in a variety of forms as mechanisms by which all women can be subordinated to men. It is men who rape, abuse and harass women, men own the sex industry in the form of pornography and the sex trade, as well as buy and use pornography, and pay sex workers. It is men who are sex offenders and sex killers. Central to this thinking is how women's lives are surrounded and for some engulfed by sexual violence. There is a massive range of sexual experiences which are part of every woman's life – pornographic images in magazines in newsagents, posters hung in work places, stalking, obscene phone calls, sexual harassment at work, being told to be careful if outdoors after dark, date-rape and coercive sex. Radical feminists have campaigned against these forms of oppression since the 1970s and there have been changes for example to the law on sexual harassment and the setting up of rape crisis centres and specialist units within the police to secure higher conviction rates for rape.

Not all feminists however agree with these arguments and view the emphasis on sexual violence and pornography as deflecting too much attention away from the real everyday issues such as women's position in the labour market. Others argue that the focus on male dominance in pornography has treated women as passive victims and therefore failed to acknowledge that women's sexuality may be more diverse and open to eroticism (see Exercise 4.8).

(E)

Exercise 4.8

Evaluate the idea that sexuality is largely defined by men. Think about the everyday images that appear in the media that many people tend to take for granted, which portray a particular view and attitude about the nature of women's role in society. Tabloid newspapers, magazines and men's magazines like GQ for example regularly contain pictures of semi-naked women. Pop music videos often have young female singers dressed in sexually provocative clothing, dancing in an overtly sexualized manner. Are there equivalents for men?

Heterosexuality and homosexuality

Heterosexuality has been seen as the norm in society, with the nature of the roles women and men play in heterosexual relationships as driven largely by 'nature' – men as dominant, aggressive and active; women as subordinate, passive and secondary. Mainstream sociology has also had its origins in this notion, especially in traditional family research for example. Rubin (1989) discusses 'hierarchies of sex', with heterosexual, monogamous, stable relationships based on reproduction, at the top. The sexual discourse here is fairly clear and although devised in the 1980s it is interesting to revisit.

Throughout the most part of the twentieth century homosexual behaviour was punishable by law in most European countries and the USA. Influenced by research in the nineteenth century which classified homosexuality as pathological and only to be understood in medical terms which would seek a 'cure' or treatment for the disease, for the most part homosexuals were hidden 'outsiders', abused, discriminated against, treated as different and condemned by society. However as more and more evidence pointed to the prevalence of homosexuality (*Kinsey Reports*, 1948, 1953; Humphreys 1975; Plummer 1981) campaigns began which tried to challenge the dominant discourse, seek changes to discriminatory laws and practice as well as establishing 'gay rights'. A gay movement in the 1970s began the process of changing perceptions and prejudice against the homosexual community which resulted in equal rights in law and eventually the establishment of 'gay marriage' in civil law in the UK.

Within the social sciences, with the increasing acceptance in society of homosexuality, there has been the associated growth in the study of gay and lesbian sexuality. Plummer was one of the early researchers into the field with his ground-breaking *Sexual Stigma* (1975) and *The Making of the Modern Homosexual* (1981). More recently he has produced life histories and accounts of the experiences of gay people in 'coming out' (Plummer, 1992, 1995), In the 1980s this focus has become known more generally known as 'queer theory' but was perhaps more firmly established in the work of Sedgewick (1990). Despite the more general acceptance of homosexuality in society, queer theory argues that much of sociological theory and practice is biased towards heterosexuality and against homosexuality, and that common sociological topics and areas such as family, education and stratification are still geared towards traditional sexuality. The notion of the ways in which we conceptualize gender has been a key interest in queer theory. How do we understand the nature of transgender and transsexualism? Could it be that the male and female genders are at two ends of a continuum with a range and variety of other sexualities in between? Is it possible that people can change and redefine their sexual identities? Is it possible that we have multiple sexualities at the same time? These are some of the important questions which queer theory has given rise to and which are now becoming part of mainstream sociology. The development of a queer ethnography is also taking place which began with the work of Plummer (1995) and is continuing in the work of others (see Lambevski,

1999). Many queer theorists resist the restriction that the label implies and broaden the theory to transcend any sexual identities. Piontek (2006) for example argued that queer theory was not concerned with homosexuality *per se* but was a critical stance towards any orthodoxy, which allowed practitioners to question taken-for-granted attitudes and behaviours within society.

Stein and Plummer (1994) defined the characteristics of queer theory as involving the use of sexual power in many areas of social life (even those not usually seen as involving sexuality) to separate out a normative heterosexuality from a deviant homosexuality. This policing of the boundaries of what is acceptable can occur even at music events (Morris, 2003) and commonly in popular culture (Sullivan, 2003). In addition, queer theory rejects the idea that homosexuality is a state of being, but it is rather a process of doing, so that the boundaries between gay and straight are permeable rather than rigid and the politics of carnival are embraced in preference to traditional political action for equality. In these ways, queer theory differs from Gay and Lesbian studies, which accept the binary definition of straight and gay. In contrast, queer theory seeks to explore how both sexualities are continuously constructed and policed (Giffney, 2004).

Like the backlash to feminism there has been considerable resistance to and criticism of queer theory. Traditionalists argue that gender is still the foundation of identity and society and the moral order. A return to traditional sexual values has been a recurrent theme in the US and UK with the support of Christian and Islamic religions which disapprove of sex before or outside marriage, sex instruction in schools and homosexuality.

Queer theory – an evaluation

Strengths

1. It provides a new dimension to sociology which makes the subject more inclusive and considers the lives of people who have been previously marginalized in society and sociology.
2. It has opened up the possibility of incorporating the study and understanding of the gay community into existing areas of sociology such as culture and identity, the family, marriage and households, the sociology of work and so on.
3. It has an ever-widening focus, with new areas of interest appearing all the time – see the periodical *Sexualities* for examples.

Limitations

■ The possibility of achievement of mainstream status as an area of study may be limited because of the narrow focus on homosexuality/ heterosexuality.

■ There are limitations in the scope of the area which may do little to prevent the continued persecution and abuse of sexual minorities.

■ The links between campaigners in the gay national and international movements and queer theory may attract criticism of its academic credentials.

DISABILITY THEORY

The popular encyclopedia website, *Wikipedia*, offers a 'common-sense' definition of disability as 'a lack of ability relative to a personal or group standard or norm' (www.wikipedia.org/wiki/Disability), illustrating how everyday notions of the concept are limited and do not necessarily accurately encompass the full meaning of disability, and has negative connotations in the phrase 'lack of ability'.

The International Classification of Functioning, Disability and Health (ICF) produced by the World Health Organization lists nine domains of functioning which can be affected by disability – these are learning and applying knowledge, general tasks and skills, communication, mobility, self-care, domestic life, personal relationships and community life. The view of disablement as negative is underpinned by such definitions and classifications. It also overlooks the views, opinions and voices of the disabled. The late Swedish prime minister Olof Palme summed up the general approach to disability in many societies as subconsciously thinking of the disabled and non-disabled as two separate species, whereas disabled people should be thought of as a 'different' life-stage which can be accommodated through strategic thinking and actions. Visual impairment in Sweden is thought of as a minor convenience which has largely been overcome through the provision of touch sensitive equipment and facilities. There has also been the development of the sociology of disablement which has come from those who themselves are disabled and have had experience of the barriers, discrimination and inequality in society faced by disabled people.

Previous models or perspectives on disability have been largely rejected by disability theory such as the tragedy/charity model that depicted disabled people as victims of cruel circumstances and deserving of pity. Also rejected is the medical model that presented the view that disability is caused by trauma, disease or health conditions and is therefore a problem of the person. The disabled person, according to this view, needs medical intervention and care by professionals to 'manage' their life. Ultimately the focus of 'treatment' is to 'normalize' the life of the patient so that they are almost cured or the disability is overcome and they can take part in society. Both of these perspectives on disability use derogatory terminology about those with an impairment and treat those with disabilities as outsiders. Hence, these perspectives are rejected by sociologists.

The social model sees 'disability' as a socially constructed problem (Shakespeare, 2006). The view of disablement being a quality or attribute of the individual is largely rejected and replaced by the notion that it is created by the social environment and cultural representations. Social action which leads to the full inclusion of those with disabilities in society is the political dimension of this model. Hence, there is a human rights issue related to our treatment of and behaviour towards the disabled. Tom Shakespeare leads a project which gives information to prospective parents on antenatal screening for conditions such as Down's syndrome and spina bifida so that they can make informed decisions based on a variety of sources including information from disabled people themselves.

Disability theory works with the social model of disability and has its roots in campaigns against discrimination which have been organized by the disabled themselves. Part of disability theory is to challenge the ideology and practice of 'able-bodied society' in a number of ways. Rethinking of building design and construction is one area of focus, and now through pressure from disabled groups planning applications must provide for access to those who use wheelchairs and have appropriate facilities for those with other impairments such as limited vision and hearing, such as hearing loops in cinemas. Access to the countryside has also improved with the provision of wheelchair-friendly routes and gates to public footpaths. Another area is to challenge use of 'ableist' language, imagery, attitudes and stereotypes – to use non-discriminatory terminology such as 'wheelchair user' rather than 'wheelchair-bound' for example. Also challenged is the unconscious use of derogatory words such as 'handicapped', 'backward', 'crippled' that denote stereotypical views.

Disability charities also come in for criticism in that they have either non-disabled fundraisers, managers and executives which do not represent the group the charity has been set up for and/or for perpetuating the negative/tragedy/pity culture which is inherent in society. Some have had titles which were overtly discriminatory: for example the charity representing those with cerebral palsy SCOPE was until 1994 called The Spastics Society. Education has been another area that arguably draws on the medical model of disability when children are 'diagnosed' as having learning difficulties such as autism, dyslexia, ADHD and other disabilities which may impair their learning development. The implication again here is that intervention by quasi-medical practitioners such as educational psychologists will help teachers to 'manage' these conditions in the classroom.

Disability theory is bound closely to political campaigning around issues related to equal rights in employment, housing and education as well as equal access to the environment, leisure facilities, transport, buildings and representation (see Exercise 4.9).

Exercise 4.9

Look at some disability charity websites, publicity material, means used to raise money, images of the disabled and TV campaigns like Children in Need. Provide a critical assessment of their approach. Which model of disability are there more examples of in the material you have accessed? (Children in Need is a national British charity which raises money in a once-a-year TV programme involving many national celebrities headed by Terry Wogan for a range of children's causes. People are encouraged to pledge money during the evenings viewing of celebrities singing, dancing and doing silly sketches. It usually raises many millions of pounds which are distributed to children's charities around the UK.)

Exercise 4.10

Drawing on the knowledge you have acquired when reading this chapter, complete a copy of the following table by summarizing the contribution made by contemporary theories to the understanding of social life.

Summary of contemporary theories

	Contemporary Left	New Realism Right	Postmodernism	Postfeminism	Queer theory	Disability theory
Basic idea						
Key writers						
Key studies/ applied examples						
Strengths						
Limitations						

<hr>

Exam focus: writing an essay

Working in pairs, *plan* answers to the following questions. Use these to select and *answer* one question each in full. Answer a different question from that chosen by your partner, as once they are marked you can swap answers and learn from each other's work.

1. 'I define "postmodernism" as incredulity towards meta-narratives' (Lyotard, 1984).

   (a) Describe the basic assumptions of postmodernism and the foundations upon which they are based.
   (b) With reference to alternative contemporary perspectives, critically evaluate the contribution made by postmodernism to the understanding of social life in the late twentieth century.

2. Compare and contrast Contemporary Left and New Right sociological perspectives.

3. Evaluate the view that the rise of contemporary sociological perspectives signals the decline of the grand theory in sociology.

4. It is no longer appropriate to speak of sociology, only sociologies. Evaluate the claim that contemporary diversity has led to the destruction of traditional sociology.

<hr>

Important concepts

realism • Contemporary Left • New Right • postmodernism •
queer theory • disability theory • postfeminism

<hr>

Critical thinking

- Do you agree that 'new voices' in sociology such as queer theory and disability theory are rendering traditional approaches redundant?
- Has the 'Postfeminist' phase adequately addressed issues of concern to women in the twenty-first century?
- How far have recent world events such as the war in Iraq and the 2008 global economic recession rendered postmodernism bankrupt?

Chapter 5

Contemporary Debates

By the end of this chapter you should be able to:

- Recognize the main philosophical debates of significance in contemporary sociology:

    1. poststructuralism versus anti-structuralism
    2. structuration or action versus structure
    3. modernity versus postmodernity
    4. classical and contemporary theories of globalization
    5. sociology of society versus sociology of self
    6. the risk society

- Identify the contribution made by key writers in each debate
- Outline the basic assumptions underlying each debate
- Evaluate the validity of each debate in the light of criticism levelled at it
- Speculate about the implications current debates may have for the future of sociology

INTRODUCTION

As sociological theory has developed, so too has sociological debate. Although the debates outlined in Chapter 3 are still of central importance to the subject, new debates have arisen. Many have taken traditional ideas as their starting-point; for example, poststructuralism has it roots in structuralism, structuration stems from the action-versus-structure debate and so on. Others have been inspired by new developments in sociological theory, such as the modernity/postmodernity debate and issues to do with globalization. This chapter aims to explore contemporary debates in a clear and concise way to enable you to develop a sound understanding of current controversies and consider their implications for the future of sociology.

POSTSTRUCTURALISM

Poststructuralism stems from the work conducted by structuralists on the nature of language (see Chapter 3) and seeks to respond to the postmodernist critique of absolute knowledge. As discussed in Chapter 3, structuralism presents an analysis of social life that is based largely upon the nature of language. The most famous proponent of structuralism, Levi-Strauss (1967), argued that language derives from society and is a constraining influence rather than a liberating one. Strauss rejected the claims of action theorists who argued that what marks out human beings as different from animals is their ability to use language. Instead Strauss argued that humans do not control language, it controls them. Poststructuralists sought to build upon this argument, particularly Foucault (1965).

The second influence on the development of poststructuralism has been postmodernism. An issue of particular relevance is postmodernism's rejection of the modernist claim that objective knowledge exists and can be uncovered through systematic and rigorous study. Instead, postmodernists argue that knowledge is merely a matter of interpretation – that is, it is a collection of narratives or versions of social reality. Knowledge is not social fact but social 'fiction'. Poststructuralists have seized upon this idea and analysed society in terms of how competing narratives serve to define the social world and individuals' 'experience' of knowledge.

The poststructuralist debate therefore involves two main arguments: (1) language shapes thought and structures life experiences, and (2) knowledge is nothing more than a myriad of competing versions of reality. The potential of language and the relative nature of knowledge form the starting point of Foucault's analysis of society.

As Jones (1993) notes, Foucault's work constitutes a direct response to Levi-Strauss's claims about the nature of language. However, Foucault seeks to develop Levi-Strauss's ideas in a significant direction:

Though agreeing about linguistic authorship of human life-stories, Foucault goes beyond the kinds of ideas produced by Levi-Strauss in two ways. First, he rejects the idea that there are universal features underpinning all languages. Second, he is principally interested in the exercise of power involved in the establishment and use of language. (Jones, 1993)

Foucault's rejection of Levi-Strauss's view that language is universal reflects the Postmodern influence in his work. Foucault adopts a broad view of language, using the term to refer not to the speaking of a dialect or mother tongue (English, French, German, Japanese and so on) but to specific ways of thinking and talking about the world (ibid.). It would be impossible for such a phenomenon to be underpinned by rules because there are a multitude of ways of thinking and talking about the world. Foucault adopts the term 'discourse' to refer to this phenomenon. He sees discourse as significant because it embodies a form of knowledge. Each discourse represents a version of reality and provides us with a way of knowing about reality.

In essence, Foucault makes the following points: (1) we can only speak in words that exist, (2) we can only think in terms of ideas that exist and (3) we can only communicate with others through the common concepts and shared meanings that exist. So our reality is constructed by mechanisms that pre-exist to help us connect with it. In connecting with our world through discourse, we are acquiring and applying knowledge. Because there are a multitude of ways of thinking and talking about aspects of the world, and these discourses provide us with knowledge, there can be no absolute knowledge because knowledge is dependent upon discourse.

Foucault uses his concept of discourse to analyse society. From the above, it would seem that the world of discourse is liberating: there are an infinite number of discourses and thus individuals are free to develop their knowledge as they will; and all knowledge is equally valid because there is no absolute truth. However, far from this being a source of liberation, Foucault argues that discourse can be coercive, and from this he develops his analysis of the exercise of power in society.

Foucault argues that power stems from the ways in which language is established and used. Once established, language is all-powerful and renders the user powerless as he or she is dependent on it to communicate or connect with reality. Creativity, imagination and the manner of human thought are all constrained by discourse:

Since we are compelled to know by means of discourses, they exercise power over us. Who we are – what we think, what we know, and what we talk about – is produced by the various discourses we encounter and use. Thus, the 'subject' – the creative, freely choosing and interpreting agent at the centre of action theory (and at the heart of philosophies like Existentialism) doesn't exist. People's subjectivity and identity – what they think, know and talk about – is created by the discourses in which they are implicated. (Jones, 1993)

When developing his analysis of power in society, Foucault saw the study of history as important. Through historical analysis, he felt it was possible to work out how and why different discourses came to be established when they did (ibid.). He considered it important to explore the impact of various discourses upon knowledge and thought.

Although Foucault's work is varied, the central theme that unites most of his analyses relates to his desire to document how discourse has emerged alongside the development of social organization and structures. Discourse has pervaded the social structure and served to define the knowledge base of society at given times. For example, in his historical analysis of the development of psychiatry, *Madness and Civilisation* (1965), Foucault traces the development of mental health discourse. He highlights how changes in thinking on the nature of the mental condition have had implications for the way the mentally ill are perceived in society and the nature of the treatment they receive. Foucault notes that during the Renaissance the 'mad' were afforded the same rights as the sane. After that, however, during the seventeenth and eighteenth centuries reason (rationality) came to subjugate madness (irrationality) and it became the responsibility of the sane to 'help' the insane. Foucault sees psychology as a moral weapon aimed at oppressing the vulnerable and mentally infirm.

Similar ideas are evident in Foucault's other works, which focus on the ways that discourse provides knowledge that can be used to exercise power over individuals and social groups. His later work moved away from structuralism and discourse to concentrate on the link between power and knowledge. His analysis rests on the assertion that power and knowledge imply one another. *Discipline and Punish* (1979), his analysis of prison life, provides an example of this approach. Here he provides a complex analysis of what he terms the 'technology of disciplinary power', whereby a system of micro powers is perceived to be infiltrating social life and contributing to the growth of a disciplinary society: 'Eventually most major institutions are affected.' Foucault asks rhetorically, "Is it surprising that prisons resemble factories, schools, barracks, hospitals, which all resemble prisons?" (1979, p. 226). In the end, Foucault sees the development of a carceral system in which discipline migrates from the penal/justice system to the entire social body (1979, p. 298).

So the picture Foucault paints is a bleak one. Like structuralists he argues that language, far from being a source of creative expression, is a form of oppression. The ways of thinking and talking about aspects of the world (discourses) are produced by the world, and since we can think or talk only in such ways we are prisoners of discourse (try Exercise 5.1 for an application of this concept). Knowledge is shaped by discourse and this has significant implications for the way control can be exercised in society. Perhaps the bleakest picture of all is provided in his later work, where he appears to reject discourse in favour of the knowledge/power issue. Here he traces the rationalization of power through bureaucratic means to create a more efficient, sober and disciplined society.

Item A

Privatization of Education

The Labour government of the late 1990s took grant-maintained schools back into local authority control. However, different forms of what Ball (2000) called privatization of education emerged. In the early years of the twenty-first century schools could bid to have 'specialist status' in subject areas such as business, ICT, performing arts, visual arts, science and so on. Once established these schools attracted additional funding from government. Also there has been the growth of academies in several cities which are sponsored by private businesses such as Reg Vardy, the Samworth Brothers and religious organizations, the voluntary sector and individual philanthropists. Although the government argues that academies are state-funded, being backed by local authorities with sponsors having the role of establishing and managing the schools, these developments have been seen as a further diversification of the education system and are not without their critics. This proliferation in types of schools has been justified by the government on the grounds of diversity of provision and meeting the demands of parental choice of school. These new arrangements stand in stark contrast to the situation where most schools were comprehensive in their intake and provision.

Exercise 5.1

This exercise will enable you to apply some of the ideas expressed in the structuralism/poststructuralism debate. Read Item A and in small groups discuss the following questions.

(A) 1. What evidence is there contained in Item A to support the notion that a new
(A) discourse is emerging in education in the twenty-first century?
(E) 2. What is the nature of this discourse?
(An) 3. What are its implications?
(E)
(An) 4. Other changes in education in the twenty-first century include the intro-
(E) duction of Applied A levels, vocational GCSEs, specialized diplomas and
the 14–19 curriculum. How would these policies relate to the structuralism/
poststructuralism debate?

While poststructuralism has made its mark on sociology, it has not been allowed to go unchallenged. Anti-structuralists have refuted the claim that human beings are constrained by discourse and knowledge. For example, Douglas and Johnson (1977) highlight the objections of the existentialists. Douglas and Johnson define existential sociology as the study of human experience in the world in all its forms. The basis for the existential critique of Poststructuralists is their assertion that although humanity is constrained in some respects, constraint coexists with freedom: 'Man is varied, changeable, uncertain, conflictual, and partially free to choose what he will do and what he will become, because he must be so to exist in a world that is varied, changeable, uncertain and conflictual' (Douglas and Johnson, 1977, p. 14). By accepting such a view, existential sociology rejects any monocausal (that is, structural) view of human life.

Post-structuralism – an evaluation

Link Exercise 5.1

(E) Identify two strengths and two limitations of poststructuralism. Use the evaluations of structuralism (Chapter 3) and postmodernism (Chapter 4) to help you. Note down your ideas in a two-column table.

STRUCTURATION

The structuration concept arose from the traditional structure-versus-action debate in sociology (see the section in Chapter 3 on structuralism versus social action). Sociologists have become increasingly interested in developing ways to accommodate this apparent contradiction in a coherent analysis of social structure. Structuration is both a debate and a theory. It is an argument that centres on whether we can consider society in terms of the relationship between action and social structure, and it presents a model for analysing society in terms of this relationship. Structuration is only one of a series of attempts to reconcile the structure versus action debate, as we shall see below. However, it is probably the most influential and was developed by British sociologist Anthony Giddens.

Giddens's (1984) structuration signals a rejection of the arguments of structuralism and poststructuralism. As New (1994, p. 4) notes:

> Giddens has steadfastly insisted, against both structuralism and Post-structuralism, that societies are made up of knowledgeable agents, whose observance of social rules is action not reaction (1984, p. 21). His 'structuration theory' (1984, p. 170) stresses that while society is external to individuals, who are formed by it, it is also their creation which through their actions they reproduce and transform.

So structuration acknowledges the interaction between individuals and structures in shaping the social world. Giddens not only dismisses theories of social structure as unitary explanations of society; he also dismisses sole dependence on action theories. This is largely because, for Giddens, our actions are influenced by the structural characteristics of societies, but at the same time we recreate and sometimes alter ('transform') structural characteristics by our actions.

If this seems a little abstract, Haralambos and Holborn (2004) provide an applied example to clarify the matter, drawn from Giddens's own work:

> The English language is to Giddens a structure; it is a set of rules about how to communicate, which seems independent of any individual. The grammar and vocabulary of English cannot simply be changed at will by members of society. Yet if that language is to be reproduced, if it is to survive, it must be spoken or written about by individuals in ways which follow its existing rules. Thus, Giddens says, 'when I utter a grammatical English sentence, I contribute to the reproduction of the English language as a whole'. The structure of the language ultimately depends

upon the rules of the people who use it. For the most part, competent English speakers will follow the rules of English and reproduction will take place. However, this is not inevitable. Languages change, new words are invented and accepted by being used, some old words are forgotten and fall into disuse. Human agents, by their actions, can therefore transform as well as produce human structures. (Haralambos and Holborn, 2004, p. 969)

Link Exercise 5.2

Compare Giddens's ideas on language with those of:

1. Levi-Strauss (see the discussion on structuralism in Chapter 3, pp. **90–5**).
2. Foucault (see the previous section on poststructuralism).
   In each case identify:

   (a) Their similarities.
   (b) Their differences.

Exercise 5.2

This exercise will enable you to explore the validity of Giddens's ideas on the structure of language in the light of contemporary scientific thought. Read Item B and answer the following questions.

1. Consider how Giddens might interpret the contents of the article, using the following questions to help you structure your thoughts:

   (a) What evidence does the extract contain to support Giddens's view that language is a set of rules independent of the individual?
   (b) How does the article demonstrate Giddens's view that the English language is reproduced by those who speak it?
   (c) How does the article provide support for Giddens's view that the reproduction of language is not inevitable?

2. What do you understand by Aitchison's assertion (Item B) that 'today's swearwords are undergoing a bleaching process'?
3. To what extent do you agree with Aitchison's view?

Item B

How children instinctively know the laws of language

REITH LECTURE

In her third Reith lecture, the technical tone of which was more pronounced that the first two, Jean Aitchison talked last night about the way in which human young acquire their language.

Professor Aitchison, the first holder of the Rupert Murdoch chair of language and communication at Oxford University, spun her lLanguage Web lseries in a new and provocative direction.

Citing the linguist Eríc Lenneberg, whose *Biological Foundations of Language*, published in 1967, she described as a "major landmark", she emphasised that language was effectively pre-ordained in children.

"Children talk so readily because they instinctively know in advance what languages are like. As in a spider's web, the outline is pre-programmed..."

Children, she argued, do not always get language right the first time. "The doll shuts she's eyes" and "My teacher holded the baby rabbbits" are examples of effective biologically programmed speech, which children will later reform after learning the rules from the speech around them.

Professor Aitchison also referred to the American linguist Noam Chomsky, on whose work she has nourished herself and whose ideas she has done her best to simplify. Chomsky, she said, believed not only that children were biologically endowed with language, but also that they possessed the means of distinguishing between one language type and another.

A child, she said, was able to discover whether "it is dealing with an English-type language, which puts verbs in front of its objects, or a Turkish-type one which does the reverse".

Inevitably, language becomes a tool with which differences in generation are expressed. Professor Aitchison here referred back to the theme of her first lecture – trivial worries about language – and pointed out that parents often wanted their off-spring to use "so-called standard English Language suddenly becomes a mud-slinging match between generations, at least in England".

Teenagers often want to talk as their peers do, "with predictable kicks at convention". Mateyness and casualness, Professor Aitchison said, were sometimes emphasised by swearing. This was not a solely adolescent phenomenon.

Referring, no doubt to works such as James Kelman's Booker Prize winner *How Late It Was, How Late*, she said: "F-words swarm like bees in some recent literature." Yet she added; "Today's swearwords are undergoing a bleaching process, a fading of meaning that happens in all semantic change."

Just as oaths using the name of God were widely disapproved of in the last century, but have now lost their power to shock, "these days F-words and S-words no longer horrify so many people". Their meaning has weakened clearly, as their original connection with sex and excrement fades.

Tanku Varadarajan

(*Source*: Tunku Varadarajan, *The Times*, 21 February 1996)

Giddens's (1984) analysis of the social system explores both structure and 'agency' (that is, action) and details how the relationship between them shapes the social system. When considering structure and agency Giddens explores two important themes: (1) how each can contribute to the maintenance of the social system and (2) how each can contribute to change or 'transformation'. He also considers the implications his analysis has for the free will/determinism debate.

Giddens first conceptualizes the social structure and outlines the way in which it maintains and transforms the social system. When analysing the social structure Giddens identifies two key features: 'rules' and 'resources'. He uses the term 'rules' to refer to the procedures or routines that underlie everyday interaction. However, for Giddens such rules are not static but dynamic – that is, open to revision through new patterns of interaction. Rules can either be reproduced (maintained) or altered (transformed), depending on whether the patterns of interaction remain the same or change.

To give an example of this, in the 1950s and 1960s people travelling in cars didn't necessarily put on a seatbelt, thus the 'rules' involved in car travel were reproduced from one decade to the next. However in the 1960s, owing to increased public awareness of the danger of road accidents, wearing a seatbelt became law. Hence the rules for travelling in a car were transformed because 'belting' became a feature of the process.

Rules do not necessarily have to be represented in law. It was once usual for young people to give up their seats on buses to older people. However, in recent years, changing attitudes have eroded this practice and such behaviour is probably now the exception rather than the rule. A 'transformation' has taken place. This right to a seat on public transport is no longer defined by age or respect for authority. Instead the rule is that occupation is possession – at least for the duration of the bus journey!

Giddens's second key feature – resources – can also be reproduced or transformed by human action. Resources are the means by which the material and social structures of society are defined. The material aspects of society are converted by human action into resources – for example, land becomes a resource through farming. Similarly, social relations become resources when individuals use them to attain dominance over others – for example, authority becomes a resource only when one person exerts influence over another.

When analysing social action or 'agency', Giddens uses the concept 'duality of structure' to reflect the way individuals both affect and are affected by structures. He argues that individuals can help to both reproduce and transform structures through their actions. They reproduce society when they routinely behave in ways that are prescribed by society – that is, by enacting structural rules. They also reproduce society when they utilize the resources of society in ways that are expected.

However, they also have the power to intervene in society by developing new patterns of interaction and transforming the rules and resources of society. Much of the time this is unlikely, because according to Giddens human beings crave predictability and routine. Giddens saw this desire for 'ontological security' as a basic human need. However, individuals are never fully constrained because change is always an option. Social structures may determine the options open to individuals throughout their lives, but it is their values, beliefs, abilities and experiences that shape the choice they make.

In his analysis of agency, Giddens not only draws attention to the intentional consequences of action that arise from choice; he also recognizes structural components beyond the individual's control that can lead to unintentional consequences.

Giddens (1984) acknowledges that individuals have the unique ability to reflect upon their action and change subsequent behaviour ('intervention') in the light of this feedback. He calls this 'reflexivity'. This is not limited just to individuals – social groups also have the capacity to reflect upon structural issues and intervene in the light of this. Thus, Giddens makes a distinction between personal reflection and the decision-making that is typical of our everyday lives (as in deciding whether or not to get married) and social reflexivity, where people in wider political or social groups make decisions based on discussions, for example what to do about global warming (Chignell and Abbott, 1995).

We turn now to Giddens's view of the social system, central to which is his concept of structuration. Giddens (1984) defines social systems as reproduced social practices, or 'reproduced relations between actors or collectivities organised as regular social practices' (Giddens, 1984). Social systems do not have structures but they exhibit structural properties. They do not exist in time or space but are dynamically created through reproduced practices (that is, rules/resources). While some systems may be the product of intentional action, Giddens strongly emphasizes the fact that such systems are often the unanticipated consequences of human action. These unanticipated consequences may become unrecognized conditions of action and feed back into it. These conditions may resist attempts to bring them under control, but actors nevertheless continue their efforts to exert such control.

'Structuration' provides Giddens with a means of integrating action and structure. What follows is a vision of the social system, characterized by the mutual interdependence of agency and structure (that is, duality) rather than power of one over the other (dualism). It is not surprising that Giddens's response to the free-will-versus-determinism debate is to argue that human behaviour is neither entirely determined by outside forces (determinism) nor entirely voluntary (free will). Instead he proposes that absolute external constraint is rare and that the constraints that exist in society can be mediated by individual choice. It is nearly always possible to 'do otherwise', to do something different. Therefore constraints, according to Giddens, do not determine actions, but operate 'by placing limits upon the range of options open to an actor' (Haralambos and Holborn, 2004, p. 971).

Exercise 5.3

Before moving on to consider the impact of Giddens's work on structuration it would be useful to recap on the main ideas. You can do this by answering the following questions:

Ⓤ 1. To what does the term 'structuration' refer?
Ⓐ 2. How does Giddens use language as an example to demonstrate his argument about the mutual interdependence of agency and structure?
Ⓐ 3. How does Giddens conceptualize the social system?
Ⓤ 4. What two aspects of structure does Giddens identify and what key functions do they perform?
Ⓤ 5. What is 'agency'?
Ⓐ 6. How do agency and structure relate to each other?
Ⓤ 7. What is 'reflexivity'?
Ⓔ 8. Why is reflexivity so central to Giddens's analysis?
Ⓐⓝ 9. How do 'dualism' and 'duality' differ? Which position does Giddens
Ⓔ adopt?
Ⓔ 10. What implications does Giddens's theorizing have for the free-will-versus-determinism debate?

It is difficult to quantify the impact of Giddens's work because his structuration theory is largely abstract. Although it is presented as a potential mode of analysis, he has not sought to apply his ideas to empirical research. However he draws attention to works that provide examples of the agency/structure duality. One such is Willis's *Learning to Labour* (1977), which, according to Giddens, demonstrates how structures are actively reproduced by the actions of agents as an unintended consequence of their actions. By turning their back on education, lads self-select themselves for poorly paid, dead-end jobs that render them powerless to change their lives.

Exercise 5.4

(A)(E) Giddens claims that if sociology is to progress beyond the division between action and structure, it requires more studies like that by Willis to show how structures are reproduced by purposeful human agents. Another example is the work of Eileen Barker on religion, specifically *The Making of a Moonie* (1984).

Given that Giddens began to theorize about structuration in the mid 1980s, it is possible that further studies now exist. Look through textbooks and journals such as *Sociology Review* and try to identify contemporary research examples that fit Giddens's ideal-type. Make brief notes on:

1. The background or context of the study.
2. The key methodology(ies).
3. The key findings. And crucially,
4. Why it provides an example of structuration analysis in action.

Structuration – an evaluation

Inevitably, Giddens's work on structuration has attracted criticism, but as Chignell and Abbott (1995, p. 14) remark, 'Giddens himself would be dismayed if there was any uncritical reading of his remarks'. The bulk of the criticism of structuration appears to have come from Archer (1988), although others (for example Abbott, 1994; Craib, 1994; New, 1994;) have followed her lead. First, criticism has been levelled at Giddens for overemphasizing the mutual interdependence of structure and action (that is, duality). Archer argues that to reject dualism is to lose sight of important differences between agency and structure and to limit the potential for the relationship between them to be analysed: '[T]oo many have concluded too quickly that the task is how to look at both faces of the same medallion at once...This forgoes the possibility of examining the interplay between them over time' (Archer, 1988, p. xii).

Second, the notion that constraints can be enabling (because individuals can choose a course of action) has not been well received. New (1994, pp. 4–5) logically points out that not all individuals are as free to choose as others, thus some are more constrained whereas others are more enabled:

> Giddens's stress on the width of the category of action, on the duality of constraint/enablement, moves the emphasis away from the ways in which our options are determined by our place in the structure, and from the way in which our place in the structure determines our power to change it.

A third but related criticism is that Giddens has overemphasized the ability of agents to transform structures simply by changing their behaviour. Archer cites several cases where changes in behaviour have not brought about changes in society owing to inadequacies within the infrastructure of society. For example, to take the case of the Gulf War in 1991, although Saddam Hussein wanted to retain control of Kuwait, and thus change power relations in the Middle East, his army was inadequate and he was thus forced to relinquish control. Ironically, in 1998 another example of the inability to transform structures was provided by the United Nations's failure to get Iraq to comply with international disarmament agreements and stabilize military power. The war that followed in 2003 was the military response from the USA, the UK and other European countries to force Iraq to comply with Western instructions despite there being no evidence that weapons of mass destruction were being built in Iraq. Nevertheless the regime was destroyed, Saddam Hussein eventually executed and Western-style 'democracy' imposed. This last example might provide evidence of the ability to change structure by force.

Archer also takes issue with Giddens's claim that material resources come into being only when humans choose to make use of them (Haralambos and Holborn, 2004). This appears nonsensical because natural resources existed before humankind and will continue to exist even if the latter become extinct, provided they are not overexploited in the meantime. Human control of the physical environment is limited.

On a practical note, Giddens has been criticized for excessive use of complex language to express his ideas on structuration. Cynics might argue that his ideas are essentially quite straightforward and his use of pretentious jargon serves to make simple ideas inaccessible (see Exercise 5.5).

Exercise 5.5

Identify at least two strengths and two limitations of Giddens's structuration concept. Record your ideas in a two-column chart.

Think of some applications of structuration to your everyday life. Giddens gave the example of drinking a cup of coffee – a seemingly trivial, common and easily understood activity, until you begin to think more theoretically about it and realize the global implications. Take the following points for consideration:

- Coffee is grown only in particular parts of the world with suitable climates – it must be transported from many other places, such as Colombia, Brazil, Kenya. Hence the developed world has a relationship with poorer, often exploited adults and children who farm and harvest the coffee beans. People in the developed world have little other contact with these countries besides our desire to buy and drink the coffee they grow.
- Coffee in the West has a cultural significance: we meet friends to drink coffee, we go to cafés to drink coffee, we have coffee-breaks from work. Sometimes the cultural significance is more to do with the rules of social behaviour than it is to the act of drinking coffee.
- Caffeine contained in coffee is a mildly addictive drug that, if taken in frequent and large doses, can affect our health. Why do we not consider the action of taking caffeine alongside other drugs like tobacco, cannabis, ecstasy as dangerous?

Can you now think of other examples which you can apply structuration theory to?

ACTOR–NETWORK THEORY (ANT)

An alternative to structuration theory has been developed by theorists who are critical of Giddens's approach and who have adopted insights from semiology and from other academic disciplines such as natural science and geography. This theory starts from the premise that individuals exist only in relationships (hence 'actor–network'), but differs from other theories in that it includes material objects and not just other individuals in these networks. Human beings have no essential qualities or attributes and there are no such things as structures. Rather, 'actors' exist only in networks and the individuals and material objects that they contain. By rejecting all 'dualisms', actor–network theorists dismiss the structure–agency binary to focus on the nature of networks that individuals and objects enter on a temporary or more long-lasting basis. Networks are seen as processes; activities built out of the relationships of the 'actants' (both human and material) that operate only on a local (not societal) and a practical (not theoretical) basis (Crawford, 2005).

Networks are therefore constantly faced with the prospect of dissolution, as they exist only on the relationships between individuals and objects included within the network. Durability is achieved as networks hold their shape as they move through time and space, but they are also susceptible to falling apart at any time (see Law and Hetherington, 2002). In including material objects with networks, ANT theorists argue that material objects also 'act' within networks, such that even objects such as carpets carry messages about power relations within a network. The explosion of new technological objects such as the internet is argued to have changed the processes of networks in a 'postsocial' direction. Knorr-Cetina (2007) suggested that traditional sociality is being 'emptied out' as fewer face-to-face interactions are required by networks in which email, keyboards and websites are key 'actants'. The challenge for sociologists is to analyse these networks to explore the new forms of sociality that are likely to emerge from postsocial networks. By producing complex accounts of networks, ANT theorists argued that they are being true to the complexity of social life and releasing sociology from the structure–action bind.

MODERNITY VERSUS POSTMODERNITY

This debate relates to the development of postmodernism (see Chapter 4) and whether there has been a change from one type of society to another – that is, from 'modern' to 'postmodern'. The terms used to encompass the features of the two types of society are 'modernity' and 'postmodernity'. Modernity refers to the nature of social relations and social conditions from around the period of the Enlightenment until far into the twentieth century. Postmodernity refers to the nature of social conditions in the late twentieth and early twenty-first centuries.

The modernity-versus-postmodernity debate concerns not just whether changes have occurred, but whether these changes can be seen as heralding a new era, distinct from the old, or whether they are simply evidence of the evolution of society. Thus, there are several responses to the claim that postmodernity is upon us. First, there are those who do not believe that the changes identified by the postmodernists are as significant or as widespread as we are led to think. Thus, it is assumed that society has retained many of the features of modernity. Second, there are those who recognize that important changes have occurred but these have simply evolved from existing (or 'modern') society rather than developed in response to a critique of it. Thus, late twentieth- and early twenty-first-century society is simply a more sophisticated and complex version of what has gone before. Third, there are those who believe that the late twentieth- and early twenty-first centuries are characterized by rejection of the assumptions upon which modern society was based, signalling the emergence of a new social order – postmodernity. Before exploring the validity of these viewpoints it is important to identify the changes that have taken place.

The main features of modern society are associated with three areas of social life: the economy; politics; and culture.

- The modern *economy* was characterized by the growth of capitalist practices, for example, production for profit, reliance upon technological innovation and an increasingly divided, waged labour force.
- Modern *politics* involved the spread of centralized bureaucratic and government practices, the strengthening of the nation-state and the rise of democratic party politics.
- Modern *culture* embraced technical and scientific knowledge at the expense of tradition. Religion was usurped by reason.
- Modernity is associated with the dominance of rational scientific thought and knowledge.

Link Exercise 5.3

Looking at the features of modern society, it is not surprising that the classical sociologists developed the interests they did. Refer back to Chapter 3 and identify three sociologists whose work appears to have been motivated by a need to describe and explain the themes described above. Make a note of their names and why their work demonstrates an interest in one or more aspects of modernity. The accompanying table should help you to get started and structure your ideas clearly.

Traditional sociologists' interest in modernity – a summary

Sociologist	Feature of modernity	Contribution
Weber	Politics	Interested in the development of capitalism and the impact it had on the production process and labour relations (Hint: Look at work on bureaucracy.) (Hint: Look at work on religion.)

Modernity affected all areas of social life. In economic terms, for example, modern society became a society of mass production and consumption, of corporate capital and organized labour. The postwar period in Europe and the

United States (1945 to around 1973) typified such practices. Henry Ford's contribution to this via mass production of the motor car typified economic relations to such an extent that the term 'Fordist' came into being to embody these modern economic production and consumption practices.

In political terms, society was characterized by an interventionist state, full employment, demand management and public investment in health and education. The 1940s was a particularly significant period for modernist ideals, for it was then that the British government assumed responsibility for the education and welfare of the nation by establishing a system of compulsory education for all, the National Health Service and the Welfare State.

Culturally, art and architecture became increasing influenced by rationality and science. Attention turned from aesthetic flamboyance to mechanistic pragmatism. Rather than emphasizing style and visual or physical appeal, art and architecture stressed functional utility. The high-rise blocks of flats that dominate Britain's cities are a legacy of modernity, as are multistorey car parks and the 'modern art' canvasses gathering dust in contemporary art galleries. Scientific thought dominated our ideas and beliefs about the nature of the physical world, medicine, technology and progress.

Postmodernity can be explored with reference to the above features of modernity. Postmodernists argue that most if not all of the key aspects of modernity have disappeared. Economic processes have altered dramatically in the light of developments in technology and employment relations. Political ideologies such as nationalism and state responsibility have given way to privatization and personal responsibility. The cultural realm has seen an explosion of 'anti-modernist' ideas from the late 1960s onwards with the arrival of new forms of art and architecture, which have allegedly been developed to counter the dehumanizing effects of modern society. Similarly, the anti-positivist movement has advocated the rejection of traditional scientific and rational knowledge in favour of humane modes of inquiry.

Item C

Defining Postmodernity?

There is a distinction to be made between postmodernism (the theory that advocates that we now live in a postmodern society) and postmodernity (the actual lived conditions of a postmodern state).

In other words, postmodernity is concerned with what a postmodern society actually looks like. Postmodern societies are different culturally from modern societies in that the focus in postmodernity is not on the unchanging and abiding truths, but on the short-lived and surface image of things. What matters culturally is not the expression of some underlying reality, but the throwaway, the new and the mass. Boundaries between areas of social life, such as that between art and advertising, have broken down.

In economics, a postmodern society differs markedly from a modernist one. Postfordist working patterns emerge that reject the modernist production line in favour of flexible working, reducing the role and importance of trade unions and involving a shift away from manufacturing and towards the service industries. This development has been described as disorganized capitalism, as large corporations franchise out routine activities to smaller firms, who pay much lower wages to their workforce and employ many more part-time and peripheral workers.

The political expression of these developments is neo-conservatism, the deregulation of financial markets and the introduction of private provision into areas previously delivered by the state, such as welfare services. This is done in order to reduce taxation and allow taxpayers the freedom to spend their cash as they like (choice). Financial discipline is maintained through control of the money supply, but any further regulation of the wealth-creators is viewed as a bad thing.

Exercise 5.6

This exercise will enable you to explore these ideas in more detail. Read Item C and answer the following questions.

(K)(U)
(E)
1. What does the term post-Fordism mean and what is its significance to the modernity/postmodernity debate?

(A)(An)
(E)
2. How might feminists (see Chapters 2 and 4) construe the impact of modernity? Would they view postmodernity as better?

(K)(U)
3. To what does the term 'disorganized capitalism' refer?

(K)(U)
4. What thinking underlies neo-conservativism?

(A)(An)
(E)
5. How might Giddens (see p. 166) use structuration theory to interpret neo-conservatism's philosophy of tax cuts leading to choice (see previous section)?

(E)
6. What alternative interpretation of tax cuts could be offered?

(A)(U)
7. Which contemporary perspective aligns itself with notions of personal responsibility for welfare and the dismantling of public services (see Chapter 4)?

(An)(E)
8. Why are fashion and image, consumerism and mass consumption seen as inextricably linked in postmodernity?

Ⓐ 9. Which sociologist undertook an analysis of mass culture, taking the main assumptions of postmodernism as a starting-point? (See Chapter 4.)

Ⓔ 10. Give one example of the way the boundary between advertising and art has broken down.

Ⓐⁿ
Ⓔ

Exercise 5.7

Using the knowledge you have acquired by answering the questions above and reading this section, copy and complete the accompanying summary chart, highlighting the key differences between modernity and postmodernity.

Modernity and postmodernity – summary of key features

	Modernity	Postmodernity
Time period		Late 1970s
Economy	'Fordist' Mass production Wage labour Industrial technology Division of labour	
Politics		Neo-conservatism/ Ergonomics Privatization Decentralization of responsibility Monetarism Fiscal conservatism
Culture	Celebration of science/reason Emphasis on functional utility/mechanism/rationalization, e.g. high-rise architecture, modern art	

Postmodernism and the modernity-versus-postmodernity debate have had a considerable impact on contemporary sociology. For example, in the previous section we saw how Giddens (1984) has sought to respond to these arguments. Feminists have also reflected on the implication of postmodernism in their work (see Walby, 1994) and recently there have been a number of attempts to explore the modernity-versus-postmodernity debate in studies of aspects of social life (see Strinati, 1992; Sugrue and Taylor, 1996; Tattersall, 1997). Much of this work has focused on culture, which is not surprising given that cultural postmodernity has become the basis of a whole social theory. Contemporary analyses of culture contribute to the modernity-versus-postmodernity debate because most writers explore whether culture exhibits features of postmodernism.

An important contribution to the understanding of postmodernism and popular culture is provided by Strinati (1992), who explores the nature of late twentieth-century popular culture within a postmodern framework. He takes the distinguishing features of postmodernism as a starting-point for his analysis and uses them to identify postmodern trends in popular culture. He speculates that the emergence of such trends might indicate the development of a postmodern society.

Strinati identifies a number of emergent trends in popular culture that would appear to reflect postmodern influences. He notes postmodern trends in art and architecture, and provides examples of buildings that appear to represent a rejection of the metanarrative of the rational, scientific and technical construction of built space. He highlights the shift in film making towards films that emphasize style and visual appearance at the expense of content, character, narrative and comment. In television, Strinati notes a trend towards the production of regular daily and nighttime flows of images and information that splice together bits and pieces from elsewhere, where programmes are constructed on the basic of collage techniques and surface simulations (ibid., p. 5). In advertising, he recognizes a shift towards marketing style at the expense of substance and content and the meshing of high and popular culture to publicize goods. In music there are similar trends – towards manufactured pop and away from new and distinct sounds. Turkle (1996) has argued that the media represent a simulated world; we identify more readily with the images and signs displayed in the media than we do with the actual world we live in. The postmodern world involves a 'culture of simulation'.

According to Strinati, cultural trends do not occur in isolation but reflect wider changes in society. He identifies three structural trends as significant. First, the rise of the media-saturated society, which has greatly increased the mass status of popular culture:

> The world has come to consist of media screens and cultural surfaces – TVs, VDUs, videos, computers, computer games, personal stereos, ads, theme

parks, shopping malls, 'fictitious capital or credit', money as a set of figures on a luminous display screen -and these have become part and parcel of the trend towards postmodern popular culture. (Ibid., p. 6)

Second, Strinati notes that new occupations and consumer markets have arisen as a consequence of the increasing importance of both consumption and the media in modern societies. Basically, the media have created consumption needs that can be met only by the expansion of certain professions, for example, journalism and advertising, which are influential in the development of popular styles, values and ideologies. A simple example of this is the 'What's Hot And What's Not' columns that appear in popular magazines, which not only report but also affirm fashion trends.

Third, Strinati argues that significant changes in society have led to the erosion of traditional sources of collective and personal identity, for example, class, family, religion, trade unions and so on. This is largely attributed to a process known as 'economic globalization' – that is, the tendency for the production, financing and selling of goods and services to take place without regard to, and going above and beyond, the realities of the nation-state and local communities. Thus individuals are left with a void to fill, with no meaningful source of identity. This leaves them vulnerable to the superficial trivia of the mass media and ephemeral trends of popular culture, which further threaten their sense of stability and in turn the stability of society:

[T]hese new trends are part of the problem, rather than the solution. They encourage superficiality rather than substance, cynicism rather than belief, the thirst for constant change rather than security of stable traditions, the desires of the moment rather than the truths of history. (Ibid., p. 7)

Strinati infers that popular culture has become postmodern in order to reflect the trend towards postmodernism in society. However, the question of whether these features of postmodernism are enough to indicate the onset of post-modernity is left unanswered by Strinati. With this in mind, let us consider the various positions in the debate:

1. A postmodern era is upon us.
2. The changes identified by postmodernists are neither as significant nor as wide-ranging as they would have us believe.

3. Significant social change has occurred but in an evolutionary rather than a revolutionary way.

Each of these will be discussed in turn.

Is a postmodern era upon us?

Lyotard (1984), Jameson (1984) and Baudrillard (1983) consider that recent developments in society are significant enough to signal the dawn of a new, postmodern era. Postmodern society is seen as qualitatively different in nature from modern society, signifying a break from the past and a transition to a new, diverse and fragmented future. Objective social reality is rejected in favour of a view of the social world as a dynamic, reflexive system of images and ideas produced and reproduced by individuals interacting with and experiencing the social world.

An illustration of the notion of postmodern imagery, reflexivity and diversity is often given by reference to the increasing media-saturation of society. The introduction of satellite broadcasting and digital technology has brought a global perspective to our use of the mass media. The division between the real world and the media is becoming increasing blurred according to commentators such as Baudrillard (1988). We view reality through the media whether in terms of news coverage, sporting events, reality TV or lifestyle choices. The war in Iraq was played out to us on our TV screens 'as it happened', apparently. We are led to believe that what we are witnessing are events as they are happening across time zones and in other parts of the world – we have a sense of hyperreality; our knowledge of the world is drawn from media images rather than direct experience. However, critics would argue that the media are a construction by journalists, editors and owners of media companies such as Rupert Murdoch.

Change is not as significant as postmodernists believe

Those who object to the notion of radical social change cite historical examples of similar phenomena, which at the time were perceived to be of great social significance but were later dismissed as fads or phases. This point is developed by Tattersall (1997, p. 23):

> Lyotard is amongst those who are convinced that recent developments signify the arrival of a postmodern age. However, it is possible to view the

changes examined as matters of style or degree rather than of kind; young people have never shown much interest in the past, culture has been commoditized and sold since the invention of the printing press, the telegraph was as big a breakthrough in information technology as the computer and the art movement Dada posed a more fundamental challenge in cultural terms than anything that has happened since.

There is no new thing under the sun, and it's possible that post-modernity is a *chimera* – no more than a complex myth – created, perhaps by an over-zealous playing of obscure language games. If it lacks any concrete reality, well, what else would you expect from a concept devised by philosophers such as Lyotard, who deny that a sense of the real can ever be arrived at through rational processes.

If the basic ideas of postmodernity are revisited, it is possible to shed further doubt on claims that a new era has dawned. Although many of the features identified appear to typify the late twentieth and early twenty-first centuries, others are a matter for debate. For example, postmodernists argue that the economy has rejected Fordist mass production in favour of flexible working patterns and a flexible labour force. However there are many examples of Fordist practices still in operation.

In politics, the trends identified by postmodernists show signs of reversal. For example, Britain's New Labour appears to be favouring increased state intervention in the management of private assets. An example of this is government intervention in the rail franchise for the high-speed Eurolink service and the 'nationalization' of the Northern Rock and the Bradford and Bingley banks after their near collapses in 2007 and 2008. Also, the increasing politicization and central government control of the curriculum and education as well as welfare policies could be construed as a return to the interventionist state of the 1940s.

Finally, as demonstrated by Tattersall above, fashion and fads have always been a feature of culture, and probably always will. The current tendency to seek out and revamp earlier styles of music and lyrics could indicate a desire to make the past appealing and accessible to contemporary generations, rather than a conscious juxtaposition of styles in a postmodern genre.

Evolutionary change has occurred

The third view is that change has occurred but this does not indicate the dawn of a new era, merely a more advanced form of the existing one.

Several theorists have rejected the thesis that we are entering a postmodern epoch. As Thompson (1992) notes, probably the most vehement critics of the thesis are orthodox Marxists (see Callinicos, 1989), who seek to reaffirm the revolutionary socialist tradition of the primacy of class-based politics against those they regard as 'revisionists' or proponents of the more pluralistic 'New Times':

> Callinicos' criticisms of the thesis of New Times and the era of post-modernity include detailed arguments about the extent to which Fordist mass production has declined, and whether postmodernity cultural trends are any different from modernism. He makes a strong case against the thesis that there has been a decisive shift from a modern to a postmodern era, although the case against the more moderate thesis of gradual change is less conclusive. (Thompson, 1992, p. 239)

Adopting a less radical position, neo-Marxists have acknowledged that in the early years of the twenty-first century we have witnessed significant developments across the whole range of human experience (Tattersall, 1997). They do not see this as signalling the onset of a new era, but rather the development of a more complex form of modernity. Several writers have adopted this view, using a range of terms to describe it:

> Some theorists, especially neo-Marxists, prefer such terms as 'late capitalism' and 'third phase capitalism' to postmodernity. Giddens's formulation is 'radical modernity', although he does say we have moved 'into a new and disturbing universe of experience'. Jameson accepts there is a distinct postmodern culture but maintains it is only the 'logic of late capitalism'. (Ibid., p. 23)

When rejecting postmodernity, critics don't necessarily dismiss all the concepts associated with the thesis. For example, the impact of globalization has become a central topic of debate among many contemporary sociologists, including Giddens. However unlike the post-modernists, who regard globalization as both cause and consequence of postmodernity, Giddens regards it as a feature of modernity. We have entered the stage of high or late modernity, signalling a radical end to tradition on a global scale. Modernity has become global in its impact, with all parts of the world forming elements of a globalized system of modernity (Scott, 1992).

The accompanying table summarizes the key viewpoints in the modernity-versus-postmodernity debate. It contains a number of deliberate mistakes. Use the knowledge you have acquired to identify and correct the errors. Copy out the table and write the correct information in the boxes. This will be a useful revision aid later in your course.

The modernity/postmodernity debate – summary of the key viewpoints

Viewpoint	Key writers	Key arguments
Modernity	Lyotard Baudrillard	Society has undergone change in three spheres of social life: 1. Economy – post-Fordist. 2. Politics – decentralization/privatization. 3. Culture – ephemeral: fashion/image. The trends in each sphere reflect broader trends in wider society. We have moved into an era with distinct features. The most influential area of life is culture. Mass communication and popular culture underlie economic and political trends and define social reality.
Postmodernity	Tattersall Walby Callinicos	We have entered a historical phase within a broader epoch rather than a new era. There have been significant developments in many social spheres, although this signifies a more complex form of modernity rather than its disappearance and the succession of postmodernity. Several names have been given to this, e.g. high modernity, 'late capitalism', 'third-phase capitalism'. Jameson accepts there is a distinct postmodern culture ('the cultural logic of late capitalism') but asserts that this does not generalize to a postmodern society, i.e. give rise to postmodernity.
High modernity/ alternatives	Giddens Jameson	The 'changes' identified by postmodernists are not as widespread or significant as they would have us believe: 1. Economically – mass production still prevails and capitalism is not 'disorganized'.

2. Politically – the recent change of government in the US has led to a resurgence of nationalization and centralized state intervention.
3. Culturally – fashion and fad are nothing new and do appear to go in historical cycles.

If there are changes they are likely to be of 'style or degree rather than kind'. 'There is nothing new under the sun.' Postmodernity is a 'complex myth'.

A common theme in postmodern writing is that tradition has no place in contemporary life and that people are now more interested in short-lived fads and fashions than established features of society. Presumably, if a postmodern society has emerged there should be evidence of rejection of tradition in favour of trivia. This would pose a threat to traditional institutions unless they chose to present a more contemporary image.

This theme is a familiar one, and recently much attention has focused on the British royal family because public opinion, as reported by the mass media, appears to be calling for the monarchy to modernize and bring itself more in line with the people. This raises important questions about what the monarchy is trying to represent, whether it is still relevant and whether it would betray its historical roots if it 'modernized' itself (see Exercise 5.9).

Item D

The royal family and postmodernity

As the living embodiment of tradition, the monarch and the royal family generally find themselves in something of a quandary. While locating themselves as the lynchpin of society worked when modernist notions of order, stability and continuity were dominant, in the fast-moving world of postmodernity, where image and surface appearance count more than solidity, the monarchy could be in danger of being seen as an anachronism (that is, out of its time). This was highlighted by the public response to the royal family's reaction to the death of Princess Diana. Some members of the public expressed the view that the royal family had shown how remote and out-of-touch with popular sentiment they were. One potential solution is that the royal family needs to employ better public relations strategies in its presentation of its image to the world at large.

Exercise 5.9

This exercise will enable you to consider some of the issues raised above. Read Item D and discuss the following in small groups.

Ⓔ 1. To what extent does the Diana phenomenon reflect comments about post-modern culture?
(Hint: Use the following questions to help you structure your discussion:

- Was Diana popular because she embodied trivia?
- Did her popularity stem from her 'playful' rejection of previously accepted rules and conventions?
- If there had been no Diana, would the monarchy have been allowed to continue with tradition unchallenged?
- Was she a postmodern princess?)

Ⓔ 2. Should the Royal Family 'modernize' itself in response to public opinion?
(Hint: Think about the following issues:

- What are the dangers of this? Think of the ephemeral nature of postmodern culture.
- What implications might this have for British sovereignty and Britain as a nation-state?)

Modernity/postmodernity – an evaluation

Ⓐ

Exercise 5.10

The following passage explores the contribution this debate has made to contemporary sociology. Find the missing words in the list below.

Reconstructions in Postmodernity, or New Times

Most of the theorists who have written about _____ have viewed it as some kind of _____ period in which older _____ are giving way to newer ones, as in the change from _____ to _____ production; services are overtaking _____ ; suprana-tional _____ are proliferating; 'civil society' is expanding and becoming more _____ , not only in terms of different _____ groups and _____ , but also with respect to the _____ of social life, in which ordinary people in industrialized societies have a greater range of positions and _____ available in their everyday and _____ lives. There are different opinions about the extent of these changes (particularly about whether they only apply to industrialized countries and the _____ two-thirds of the people in those countries) and also about whether they are capable of being subsumed under the logic of a new stage of _____ . However, leaving aside the question of whether it is possible to predict a future stage of in the way that the project envisaged, there is no doubt that analyses of postmodernity or _____ are attempting to develop new _____ and categories that are adequate to the rich kaleidoscope of social life and that they have succeeded in opening up fresh and stimulating debates. (Adapted from Thompson, 1992)

Missing words

- consumer • social • concepts • better off • Fordist • diversified
- working • global capitalism • identities • production systems
- lifestyles • post-Fordist • pluralization • social development
- manufacturing • family • Enlightenment • contemporary
- organizations • transition • postmodernity • new times

GLOBALIZATION: ONE WORLD OR A SOCIETY OF STATES?

'From now on, nothing that happens on our planet is only a limited local event' (Ulrick Beck, quoted in Macionis and Plummer, 2005).

Globalization has become an increasingly important area of interest to sociologists. Not only can it be explored as a topic in its own right, but the impact of globalization has also featured in many of the debates covered above. This section will discuss the definition of globalization, some of its basic features and theories about the causes of globalization and its implications. This should enable us to establish whether it is now more appropriate to construe society in world terms, rather than as constrained by structural or geographical boundaries. Also, we will look at the question of whether the territorial state has ceased to be a central unit in world affairs or whether it still has a place in modern politics.

Many definitions of globalization are offered (see for example, Wallerstein, 1991; McGrew, 1992; Sklair, 1993; Robins, 1997), but in essence they all appear to be similar. Globalization is identified as a process whereby national and international boundaries are broken down by economic, political and cultural activity on a world-wide scale. This has been attributed to the rise of transnational corporations, the new international division of labour and the development of global communication networks (Sklair, 2003).

Globalization is a relative process – that is, its impact is not universal and in different areas people will experience globalization differently. Globalization does not emerge logically or coherently within a fixed time scale, because its development is related to prevailing social conditions. Because the impact of globalization appears to have been more visible in the Western world, some writers have argued that globalization is a Western experience rather than a truly global one. However, critics have argued that what makes globalization a truly global experience is the effects that developments in one area of the world have upon another. Although regions may not appear to have been directly affected by globalization, they are affected through their relations with other countries of the world.

Although there is considerable disagreement about the causes and implications of globalization, sociologists do recognize a number of features that appear to reflect globalization.

- Growing mobility across frontiers (that is, of goods, commodities, information, communication, products, services and people).
- Changes in social and cultural life, the synchronization of national economies through 'real time' (that is, international business is being conducted in common time zones).
- The growing significance of knowledge and information in the changing world economy.

Macionis and Plummer (2005) pointed to six key features of globalization (see also Exercise 5.11).

1. The shifting of borders of economic transactions.
2. Expanded communication in a global network.
3. The creation of a global culture.
4. New forms of international governance.
5. An awareness of shared world problems.
6. The creation of a risk society.

Exercise 5.11

Give an example for each of Macionis and Plummer's six points.

Global and local features

Much attention has been directed at the relationship between emerging global features and existing local features. 'Local' is also a relative concept in writings on globalization. It does not refer literally to the local community, but to the polar opposite of global. Thus local could feasibly refer to locality, region, nation or even a multinational sphere of activity (Sklair, 1993). Writers have sought to explore how the 'local' has responded to the 'global' to ensure that it is not cast aside in the globalization process. For example, cities have tried to market themselves as preferential locations, exploiting local assets and resources to attract not only industrial and business investment, but also more mobile ventures such as conferences and conventions, sporting events, science parks, theme parks, expositions and so on (Robins, 1997).

Simultaneously, local resistance to globalization has been noted. For example, some groups have sought to preserve their unique cultural identity in the face of increasing pressure to adopt a global identity. Globalization has given rise to active cultural campaigning to defend local and particularistic identities (Robins, 1997). Also, local campaigns to protect territory and culture have been a feature of resistance to global demand for wood and food, especially in the Amazon rainforest. An example would be the indigenous Kayapo people who live traditionally in the Brazilian rainforest. They are expert at making use of the international media and celebrities such as Sting to make their case against the loggers and cattle-farmers in Amazonia. They have managed to protect their tribal land through the creation of a reserve and successfully lobbied the government to support their case. It is accepted that the Kayapo own their land and can prevent other groups from using it.

Theories of globalization

McGrew (1992) makes a useful distinction between single and multi-causal explanations of globalization. Single explanations (see Wallerstein, 1984; Gilpin, 1987; Rosenau, 1990) identify one main factor as responsible for the development of globalization. Multi-causal explanations tend to focus on the influence of various overlapping factors (see Robertson, 1991; Sklair, 1991; Giddens, 1992). Some attention is paid to the interrelationship between the factors, but more is paid to the impact of globalization.

Wallerstein (1991), a proponent of world-systems theory (the interconnectedness of national systems of government, economy, media and so on), argues that globalization is linked with the dynamics of historical capitalism. For Wallerstein, the logic of historical capitalism is necessarily global in reach (McGrew, 1992). Wallerstein perceives globalization as largely an economic process. Whereas capitalism has gradually created a global economic order, the political structure remains at the level of the nation-state and rule remains with the sovereign state. The world economy retains the unequal structure so characteristic of capitalism through the years.

However, this structure is not thought of as hierarchical. Instead, Wallerstein presents a geographical analysis of power distribution, locating primary economic power within the core and progressively less power within semi-peripheral and peripheral areas. Each has a role to play in sustaining the overall integrity of the system. However, this is not met with universal acceptance by all sections of the world; rather, global economic relations are met with resistance on a global scale in the form of anti-systemic movements – for example, environmental, socialist and national movements (McGrew, 1992). For Wallerstein, it is this resistance and conflict of interests that will lead to the eventual collapse of the world capitalist economy.

Friedman (2000) suggests that Western societies have brought about not just globalization but an American version of it. From the global 'brands' like Coca-Cola and McDonalds to computer systems and Mickey Mouse, the United States has come to be a dominant international economic, military, cultural and social force.

Rosenau (1990) presents a different view of the cause of globalization, locating it within the technological realm. The key concept for him is global interdependence, which has arisen as a result of technological breakthroughs. He presents a vision of the world where boundaries are being transcended by advanced transportation and information networks. The relocation of businesses such as Dyson vacuum cleaners, Rover cars, and banking and insurance call centres from Western industrial societies to the Far East and the Indian subcontinent could be examples but could equally be explained in terms of exploitation of cheaper labour in those countries This has led to a transformation of the human condition on two fronts – the industrial and the political. Rosenau proposes that a post-industrial society exists and that international politics has been superseded by post-international politics – an era in which nation-states have to share the global stage with international organizations, transnational corporations and transnational movements. The state is no longer the primary unit of global affairs (McGrew, 1992, p. 71).

Unlike the above writers, Giddens (2003), suggests that more than one factor causes globalization. He sees globalization as having four dimensions: the nation-state system, the world military order, the international division of labour and the world capitalist economy. For Giddens, globalization is a product of modernity itself and is linked to the notion that we all now live in one world. Each factor has a distinct influence on globalization and its influence depends on institutional forces and contingencies. McGrew (1992, p. 72) notes:

> Thus, the logic and contradictions of the capitalist world economy influence the pace and pattern of economic globalisation, whilst, within the inter-state system, it is the 'universalism of the nation state' form which is responsible for the creation of a single world (Giddens, 1987, p. 283). Similarly, the 'globalising of military power' (Giddens, 1990, p. 75) is tied to the logic of militarism, whilst the changing global division of labour is conditioned by the logic of industrialism.

Giddens's interest lies in exploring the interconnections between these factors as well as their consequences for globalization as a process. The invasion of Iraq in 2003 by American, British, Australian, Polish and Danish forces has been seen by observers such as Harvey (2005) as an example of the interconnection between the need to secure increasingly scarce industrial resources such as oil, military power and the imposition of particular forms of government such as 'democracy over dictatorship'. This 'new imperialism' could be seen as a more sophisticated version of the old colonialism of the eighteenth and nineteenth centuries, where ideological control is used alongside economic, military, industrial and political power. Hence the war in Iraq has been justified by linking all Muslims to the attack on the World Trade Centre in New York in 2001.

Robertson's (1991) multidimensional analysis incorporates the economic, political and cultural aspects of globalization. He advocates the exploration of each as a separate influence, as each has a distinct logic. He usefully used the term 'glocalization' to describe the process by which local communities respond distinctively to global changes. Macionis and Plummer (2005) point out the example that Thai cuisine has become globalized but is modified and distinctive depending where it is being eaten; Thai cuisine is different in London, New York, Bangkok and Dubai. Of particular interest to Robertson is the way that globalization universalizes some aspects of modern life (the nation-state, assembly line production, consumer fashions and so on) while at the same time fostering uniqueness (for example, the resurgence of nationalism and ethnic identities).

Another multi-causal explanation for globalization is provided by Sklair (1993), who focuses on transnational practices. Sklair argues that global means more than simply 'relations between states' (ibid., p. 9) and defines transnational practices as:

practices that originate with non-state actors and cross state borders. They are analytically distinguished in three spheres: economic, political and cultural–ideological. Each of these practices is...characterised by a major institution. The transnational corporation (TNC) is the most important institution for economic transnational practices; the transnational capitalist class (TCC) for political transnational practices and the culture-ideology of consumerism for transnational cultural-ideological practices. (Ibid., p. 9)

This model moves beyond the focus on the state as central, as according to Giddens globalization can be understood only in terms of the economic power of the transnational corporation, the political organization of the transnational class and control over global media to 'propagate the culture-ideology of consumerism all over the world' (Sklair, 1993, p. 9). Furthermore, the location and influence of companies and business from 'third-world' locations to industrial settings and vice versa is an increasing common phenomenon of the twenty-first century.

Globalization and sport

Sport is an area which illustrates well the impact of globalization. Whereas in the past sport might have been seen as part of the fabric of a local community – a local football team, say – it has now become part of the globalization process. Top sportspeople become international, hugely rich superstars travelling the world followed by their supporters. The mass media coverage of international events such as the World Cup, Wimbledon, Formula One, the Olympics, along with advertising, sponsorship and sale of commercial products, has brought the sporting arena into everyone's living room. Companies which have a major impact upon the global nature of sport are Sky, Disney, Coca-Cola and Nike to name but a few and the powerful merchandizing of sporting commodities is part of the globalization of sport and sporting events. The staging of the 2008 Olympics in Beijing and the topping of the medals table by China announced to the world the place of developing and communist states as major players in the international sporting arena. (See Macionis and Plummer, 2005, and Exercise 5.12 for an extension activity.)

Exercise 5.12

Go to the 2012 London Olympics website and find out who is sponsoring the games. What have these companies got in common and what motivates them to provide the support for the games? Provide a critical assessment of the acceptance of Coca-Cola, McDonald's and Cadbury as sponsors.

Globalization and religion

The increased access to and use of computer and information technology has led to the globalization of religion according to some sociologists. The internet is a source of information about religious belief and values and is used by some as an alternative to locally based expression of religiosity such as attending church (Lyon, 2000). The use of websites to recruit and inform followers by a variety of religious groups has also grown. Furthermore, the increase in consumerism can also be applied to religious expression. People may adopt a 'pick-'n'-mix' approach to which aspects of religion they choose to follow or believe in. For Lyon (2000) this indicates that religion is changing and differentiating in the postmodern world rather than declining. He gives the example of how religion is adapting to postmodern society in his description of the Harvest Day Crusade at Disneyland in California, whereby a variety of evangelists performed – preaching and singing – the Christian gospel in this well-known fantasy kingdom. Hence religion is no longer confined to traditional settings, institutions or boundaries.

Reverse colonialism

'Reverse colonialism' is the term used by Giddens (2003) to describe the ways in which non-Western, previously third-world economies are having an impact upon previously globalizing countries in the West. In particular the twenty-first century according to Baracco (2006) has a distinctly cosmopolitan atmosphere, with Asia and China being the new economies to stamp their footprint in the global market place. A glance at the labels in the clothes you are wearing will provide evidence of the manufacturing prowess of India and China. The relocation of successful European companies to third-world sites and the increasing influence of Indian companies and Chinese manufacturing in Europe are examples of reverse globalization. These developments may lead to less Americanization rather than more in the global village. Baracco also points to the emergence of a 'global cosmopolitan culture' that has its origins in global systems rather than individual nations or communities. Such developments are likely to be 'anarchic, haphazard' and largely independent of the will of any one nation or collective enterprise.

Exercise 5.13

Draw up a larger version of the table here and summarize the key ideas on the causes of globalization. It may be helpful to reread each theory and make brief notes before finalizing your table. Once completed, it should provide a quick reference tool when you come to revise.

Causes of globalization – a summary of key ideas

	Monocausal theories	
Wallerstein (1983)	Rosenau (1990)	Gilpin (1987)
	Multicausal theories	
Giddens (1990)	Robertson (1991)	Sklair (1993)

The implications of globalization for society

Regardless of the cause(s) of globalization, it is commonly acknowledged that globalization is characterized by considerable complexity. This relates to the point made earlier about the relative nature of globalization. Causal factors do not result in a universal globalization process whereby everybody in the world shares a common experience of globalization and/or globalization has certain fixed characteristics. Globalization is more complex than that and its effects are perceived to be 'dynamic' – that is, relative to space and time. Globalization is a dialectical process because it does not bring a generalized set of changes acting in a uniform direction but consists of mutually opposed tendencies (Giddens, 1990, p. 164).

Thus, it is logical that various interpretations exist of the implications of globalization, some of which suggest that we are moving closer to a global society (Perlmutter, 1991; Modelski, 1972) whereas others argue that globalization has led to a fracturing of the world into a society of states. McGrew (1992) identifies four conceptualizations of globalization, two of which offer support for a global society and two of which suggest that globalization is not all pervasive and that the nation-state and the inter-state system prevail.

Five views of globalization

1. *World society* – Perlmutter (1991) presents the view that globalization is leading to a world society. This involves rejection of the idea that the world is organized into discrete nation-states and argues that instead a universal 'community of fate' prevails. Several writers elaborate upon this

'global civilization'. For example, 'today's extensive patterns of global interaction and global awareness, combined with the deepening of universal values (i.e. environmentalism, human rights, survival) point to the reality of world society' (Modelski, 1972, p. 227).

2. *Capitalist world economy* – A different interpretation of the global nature of society is provided by Wallerstein (1984). He proposes that a single capitalist world economy exists and that this economic structure affects the constituent parts of that economy (states, people, communities and households) (McGrew, 1992, p. 79). New technology has extended the reach of capitalism and few can opt out of the global economic structure. Those who do, risk being marginalized. So, global capitalism is a contradictory process, including some and excluding others. Central to the single capitalist world economy is the existence of transnational corporations (Sklair, 1993), which increasingly exploit transnational relations and industrial opportunities to maximize profit and economic power. The national territorial boundaries that limited trade and production in the past have given way to transnational practices in the global capitalist economy.

3. *Fragmentation* – Rosenau (1990) argues that far from there being a global system based on transnational or humanitarian cohesion, the world has become fragmented by globalization. Two societies now exist: a society of states, displaying the traditional relationships and interests that have typified international relations over a number of years (state-centric); and a multicentric world of transnational groups with diverse and sometimes conflicting interests, outside the control of any nation-state. Global society involves the interaction of these two groups, but relations are turbulent rather than stable and as a result the global order appears to be breaking down.

4. *Realism* – The fourth view is provided by Gilpin (1987), who rejects the idea that interconnectedness necessarily means that a world society has arrived. For Gilpin, if the nation-state is bypassed, the potential for conflict and instability is great. Global society, far from being liberating, is volatile and ridden with confrontation. Thus Gilpin proposes a 'realist' view of globalization, viewing the global states system as a system of power politics in which conflict and insecurity are the norm (McGrew, 1992, p. 84). Gilpin rejects the view that a global civilization is emerging and that global economic development is creating a truly global infrastructure. He also rejects the two-state system, arguing in favour of the continuation of the nation-state. He draws attention to the ephemeral (short-lived) nature of globalization throughout history and highlights that

its survival is dependent upon certain conducive conditions, and given the transient nature of power relations its future is less certain than that of the nation-state.

5. *New global culture* – Baracco (2006) argues that globalization has reached a distinctive stage in world history characterized by interrelated economic/ financial, political and cultural networks. These interconnections can be seen in the 'knock-on' effects of the events in one country/continent on the rest of the world. Also the connections between members of the international banking sector became evident in the economic crisis of 2008.

These networks have been facilitated through developments in electronic communication technologies. The world has a more cosmopolitan feel to it with the rise of economies of Asia in the twenty-first century. Baracco believes that American dominance is declining and will be the subject of challenges in the future. He argues that we will have an increasing sense of 'the runaway world' rather than the Americanized one in the global system. The economic recession which began with the sub-prime property markets in the USA certainly had enormous repercussions in the financial markets across the globe and led to the bankruptcy of several banks and a global recession in 2008. Certainly the reliance on American systems of power, finance and government came under increasing pressure, and as Baracco said presented a 'serious challenge' to the dominance of the USA.

Exercise 5.14

Draw a larger version of the accompanying chart and summarize the five viewpoints that have been offered on globalization.

The implications of globalization – a summary of key ideas

One world		
Global civilization Perlmutter:		Capitalist world society Wallerstein:
	5 views on globalization	
Rosenau: Bifurcated world	Baracco New global culture A society of states	Gilpin: Global states

Globalization – an evaluation

The debates on globalization have important implications for the way we view society. Until the present day, attempts to understand society have been based on the premise that society is a cohesive, bound totality, an integrated social system. In effect, therefore society is indistinguishable from the nation-state (McGrew, 1992, p. 63). However, because of the emergence of transnational forces, global relations and worldwide technology, it is now increasingly difficult to study the nation-state without taking consideration of the global scene. As a consequence some writers (for example, McGrew, 1992; Sklair, 1993; Robins, 1997) have questioned whether there is a need to reappraise our conception of society (and by association the nation-state):

> If, as many would argue, globalization is reconstituting the world as 'one place', then a refocusing of the sociological project – away from 'society' and the 'nation state' towards the emerging 'world society' – would seem a logical prerequisite for making sense of the contemporary human condition. (McGrew, 1992, p. 64)

Much of the discussion on refocusing has concentrated on the nature of the nation-state. Some have argued that the nation-state has been stripped of its functions and no longer plays a central role in international relations (Jameson, 1991), whereas others have cited the transformation of the agenda of the nation-state to focus on international problems (Bell, 1987), for example, the environment, potential threats to world cohesion and stability, the activities of transnational corporations and so on. Leading states have formed cohesive forums for debate. For example, the G8 summit gives the most wealthy and powerful states in the world the opportunity to discuss world issues.

It is unclear whether this provides evidence of global politics or whether it reflects the 'internationalization' of the state, whereby national concerns give way to international issues and national concerns are addressed with regard to international goals (Kaiser, 1972). It is also difficult to establish whether this is a stage in the transition from national to world politics, or a new set of relationships that reflect the need to address 'local' (national) and 'global' (international) issues simultaneously. Writers will no doubt continue to debate the effects that globalization may have upon the role and functions of the nation-state.

Globalization has pervasive effects but understanding its impact is difficult. The causes of globalization appear to be varied and its impact depends on prevailing 'local' conditions. The effects of globalization are ambiguous, and various interpretations have been offered. Regardless of which is accepted, sociologists will no doubt continue to explore the economic, political and cultural aspects of globalization to confirm whether it is necessary to 'refocus the sociological project' in favour of one world sociology. The emergence of a global, cosmopolitan culture rather than single nation-states seems to characterize the twenty-first century, according to Baracco (2006). This development will necessarily be 'anarchic' and unpredictable but will gather momentum with the entry of China, Asia and other continents in the global system. It may become out of control as Giddens predicted and head in many different directions, but as the global credit crisis in 2008 showed what happens in one part of the world has repercussions almost everywhere else.

SOCIOLOGY OF SOCIETY OR SOCIOLOGY OF SELF?

Throughout this chapter we have seen how contemporary life poses new challenges for those who try to study it. One theme that emerged in the previous section was whether it is appropriate for sociology to continue to study society, or whether a reconceptualization is needed to accommodate the global changes that have emerged. In previous chapters we focused on whether it is appropriate to study the structures of society or the actions and interactions of the individuals who make up that society. Recently there have been attempts to reconcile the debate by advocating analysis of the dynamic relationship between agency (that is, action) and structure (see Bourdieu, 1984; Giddens, 1984; Habermas, 1987; Archer, 1988). Such attempts have focused on the importance of agency in developing an understanding of structure – so much so that some of the ideas arising from this research are starting to change the direction of sociological theorizing and research. Instead of focusing on the sociology of society, there is a growing interest in the sociology of self. This will form the basis of the discussion in the final section of this chapter. Craib (1994, p. 12) identifies interest in 'self' as associated with the work of Giddens:

> While Anthony Giddens was developing his structuration theory, sociology journals seemed full of papers discussing what he was doing; then in 1991 he published the first of two books *Modernity and Self Identity* to be followed a year later by *The Transformation of Intimacy*, which...moved on to consider the nature of the self, emotions, intimacy and identity in late modernity.

Giddens's (1991) analysis of self builds upon – but differs from – earlier work by symbolic interactionists such as Mead (see Chapter 2 for a review). Whereas

Mead identified two processes within the self, the 'I' and the 'Me', and paid little attention to the nature of the self independently of these, Giddens focuses solely on self. When doing so he applies a number of concepts from his earlier work on modernity, the most important being reflexivity. Giddens construes the self as reflexive, resulting from the process of thinking about what we are doing, making decisions and choices (Craib, 1994). Thus, the self is dynamic rather than fixed and relative rather than absolute.

As the self results from reflexivity, so does society. Giddens draws upon symbolic interactionism to present society as largely the manifestation of action and interaction. For Giddens, late modern society is also reflexive. Nothing can be rooted in the past; it must be continually invented and reinvented in the present. Crucial to this are the processes of reproduction and transformation, arising from agency and structural influences (see the section on structuration earlier in this chapter). Thus for institutions, relations and social practices to be maintained they must be justified, having been examined in the light of new circumstances and information. Nothing can be taken for granted. Late modernity is ephemeral in nature and as a consequence individuals are permanently engaged in appraising and reappraising action in the light of feedback. As Craib (ibid., p. 14) notes, this has consequences for the self: 'We are constantly involved in constituting and reconstituting ourselves; we can never take anything for granted, we have to justify to ourselves and to others what we are and what we are doing.'

Item E

Anorexia: The Late Modern Disease

Giddens extends his analysis of self to include the act of taking control over one's own body. He regards anorexia as possibly a typical illness of late modernity and presumably sees anorexia as a way in which individuals can constitute and reconstitute themselves to alter the image they present to others. The onset of anorexia can be a slow buildup from the counting of calories and the avoidance of certain types of food to actual starvation, as the victim attempts to craft their body into an 'ideal' shape. Anorexia is most commonly associated with women, but men can also be victims, responding to the stresses of late modernity by restricting the intake of food. Food is therefore one way in which an individual can seek to control their lives, which they often feel is out of their control.

Exercise 5.15

This exercise enables you to explore the phenomenon of anorexia and to consider the validity of Giddens's ideas. Read Item E and answer the following questions.

1. What evidence is there in Item E to support Giddens's view that anorexia is a form of image control?
2. What other explanation(s) could be offered for the onset of anorexia? (Hint: You could do some research in the library, or perhaps on the internet, to identify other factors associated with the onset of anorexia.)
3. Which argument do you think most convincingly explains anorexia? Why?
4. Why might some argue that Giddens's analysis of anorexia is more applicable to female than to male anorexics? Give reasons to justify your answer. (Hint: Who is under more social pressure to maintain a particular body image?)

Through his analysis of self, Giddens (1992) explores the nature of intimacy. He recognizes that relationships in late modern society have undergone a transformation as some of the factors that made them inequitable in the past have been stripped away. For example, contraception now means that sexual relations do not necessarily lead to reproduction, hence they have been redefined as a mechanism for intimacy. Giddens's interpretation of intimacy is interesting. He sees it as involving a balance of autonomy, sharing and trust. Late modern relationships are characterized by 'effort bargaining', whereby partners negotiate to reconcile differences and overcome difficulties. Thus, like the self, relationships involve perpetual assessment and reassessment of possible outcomes. This is different from relationships in the past when they remained structurally sound in the face of difficulties – difficulties were endured rather than addressed dynamically through negotiation and reappraisal.

For Giddens (1992) the commitment embodied in the relationships of today is different from that of the past. Commitment today now means recognizing the uncertainties and difficulties of a relationship but nonetheless being willing to take the risk because of the satisfaction it offers, at least in the medium term (Craib, 1994, p. 14). To use a betting analogy, it seems to follow that the most successful relationships are those where the 'odds' have been considered and a safe bet placed. Unsuccessful relationships are those where the odds are not considered fully, or a bad bet is placed, despite them.

Giddens's (1992) analysis of relationships places heavy emphasis on autonomy and self-realization. Relationships are managed to benefit partners in the way that best suits them. This idea is not new. Social psychologists were identifying the importance of processes such as balance and perceived equity in relationships as early as the 1950s. For example, Thibaut and Kelley (1959), following the social exchange model, proposed a four-stage model of relationships based on economic principles – that is, the potential costs and benefits. This was later extended in equity theory (Walster *et al.*, 1978) to emphasize a long-term balance in the distribution of rewards and incentives, rather than a short-term, immediately 'fair' exchange (Banyard and Hayes, 1994). Applying this approach to relationships, Walster *et al.* identify four basic principles of equitable relationships: (1) people try to maximize reward and minimize unpleasant experiences; (2) rewards may be shared out in different ways – a group or couple may develop their own 'fair' system; (3) inequitable (unfair) relationships produce personal distress; and (4) someone in an inequitable relationship will try to restore equity to the relationship – the greater the inequity, the more effort they will make to do so.

However, Giddens's (1992) analysis differs from that of social psychologists by focusing not just on inequity of reward but also on inequity of power in relationships. He also tries to understand relationships not just in the here and now, but also their potential for the future. He foresees an ideal relationship where democracy prevails and where the structural inequalities that contribute to inequity are eliminated. The role of self is important in this process. For relationships to become 'pure', all economic and psychological differences between the sexes will have to be eroded. Reflexivity can contribute to this process, as the self increasingly creates and recreates harmonious relationships where abuse and exploitation have no place.

Giddens's (1992) writing on intimacy has attracted critical commentary and his portrayal of the self has been debated. Giddens implies that ideal relationships are those where democracy prevails, where 'effort bargaining' has been successful. However, this presents problems if it is taken as the basis for understanding relationships in wider society. For example, Giddens presents society as constituted (defined/developed) through human reflexivity and social institutions as a human product. Emphasis is on the role of the individual in constituting and reconstituting society. Critics argue that this denies the role of collaborative action in shaping society. It presents the image of an egotistic self that is only interested in what it can get out of relationships, with little concern for others' needs and interests. This contradicts the view of other sociologists (Weber, Marx, Durkheim), who regard human self-realization (that is, maximization of human potential) as stemming from collective consciousness and mutual responsibility. Like Giddens, they recognize the role the individual has to play, but their interpretation is somewhat different. In their view, the individual is not driven by a desire to exploit relationships for personal gain. Instead people regulate their behaviour through their own morality, and decisions and actions are based on collaboration or bargaining for mutual gain.

Giddens's (1992) views on intimacy have generated discussion about the nature of the self and human action. Arising from his writing on structuration, these views provide interesting new insights into an aspect of social life that until now has been largely unstudied. Although interpretive sociology has considered the role that individuals play in shaping society, it has yet to explore in depth the motives behind human action. Giddens has started to address this in his work. Although criticized, there is little doubt that some of the features he identifies in modern relationships are valid. Popular magazines often contain advice on 'how to get the most out of relationships'. It is difficult to know whether this sets the tone for 'effort bargaining' in relationships or merely follows on from it. What is clear is that despite the criticism that Giddens's view of the individual is egotistical or self-centred, it is recognized in popular culture. Given the power of mass communication in the late twentieth century, if an egocentric route to human fulfilment is espoused it is likely to become a reality, regardless of claims that it marginalizes the role of mutual reliance and civic responsibility.

Exercise 5.16

Using the information presented in the passage above, write a paragraph summarizing the contribution Giddens has made to our understanding of self. Identify at least one strength and one limitation of his work. Try to arrive at a judgement about the implications of his work for the future of sociological theory.

Sociology of society or sociology of self – an evaluation

Giddens's writing on the sociology of self is interesting but it does not herald the demise of the sociology of society. In his work on intimacy in late modernity, he takes the individual as the starting-point for understanding how society is constituted. However, in the broader context of structuration, developing an understanding of society is still as important. Sociologists such as Giddens are recognizing that rather than becoming embroiled in traditional debates about approaches and philosophies, these should be used as a springboard to further theorizing and research. Sociological analysis in the late twentieth century appears to be devoted to new lines of inquiry aimed at a better understanding of society. Even if the sociological project is reconstituted and 'society' is reconceptualized to reflect contemporary trends, society will always be at the centre of sociology and attention will continue to focus on how self, agency and structure interrelate to constitute that society.

THE RISK SOCIETY

Sociology has been influenced since the 1990s by the notion of 'risk' in society. Indeed the early years of the twenty-first century could be said to be 'risk-obsessed'. From both an individual and society perspective we could argue that 'risks' are part of life. We might take risks with our health by smoking or we may be at risk from the environment we live in through pollution, pesticides in food or traffic accidents. These examples are aspects of our everyday lives which most of us can recognize as familiar. Giddens (1999) distinguishes two types of risk: first, external risk which comes from 'outside' us – that is from nature; and second, manufactured risk which human beings themselves have created.

Ulrich Beck (1992) describes these risks as characteristic of a 'new modernity' in society rather than postmodernity – a conceptualization of society that he rejects. Beck argues that while we once put our trust in science and scientists to improve our lives we no longer have such a positive relationship or belief. The notion that science will lead to a golden future where all ills will be overcome has broken down. The twenty-first century is characterized by more and more uncertainty in terms of what we can assume about the future. Rapid and constant change at global and institutional levels impacts upon the ways we establish and sustain our individual identities. Hence there is a complex interplay between change at the whole society level and our individual social worlds – some aspects of our lives may be immediately controllable, for example whether we engage in risk-taking behaviour such as smoking, while other aspects are somewhat out of our control, such as global warming or pollution. Even with these examples we can see how our individual actions may make a difference at the whole societal or even global level. The difference between the past and present according to Beck (1992) is that modern hazards and dangers are more abstract in nature than they were in the past and therefore less easy to resolve. Individuals have become more pessimistic about the future and seek to prevent danger and risk rather than achieve 'the good'. We have moved from a society based on class to one where everyone faces risk and the driving force of contemporary society is safety.

Risk management involves 'reflexivity' at both the individual and institutional level. This means that we are constantly establishing, re-establishing, renewing and maintaining our social networks. In the past there were what Giddens has called 'ontological certainties' – community, family life, marriage, work; areas which we were defined by – but these no longer exist in any stable or permanent sense (see Exercise 5.15). We no longer have clear knowledge or understanding of the meanings of these aspects of our lives, so we make and remake ourselves in order to cope with constant change. 'R'eflexivity is the name Giddens has given to the search for ontological security because of the absence of traditional signposts which helped us define ourselves and who we were within a cultural context.

Risk theory is essentially an attempt to understand social change in the contemporary world. The use of advanced technology which challenges the traditional categories of time and space to transform human communication is an example to consider. A relatively short time ago mobile phones, computers and digital technology were unheard of; certainly people in their 60s and 70s would not have known them in most of their adult lives. The younger generation have not known life without such technology; indeed they define themselves by ownership of iPods, iPhones, MP3s and so on. Hence the impact of change upon our identity is profound. As individuals make their 'lifestyle' choices from the vast array that is available they are therefore making risk calculations, or, as Giddens has put it, entering into a 'positive engagement with risk'. Importantly, this also illustrates Giddens's point about the duality of structure – structure brings about action and action reinforces or reproduces the structure within which the action takes place.

Furlong and Cartmel (1997) have argued that young people are in the forefront of the risk society. They are experiencing the most diverse, challenging and changing society with opportunities and threats strewn across their path to adulthood. Youth lifestyles reflect the prolonged transition into adulthood and the associated risky behaviour such as drug-taking, binge drinking and unprotected sex – described by Kelly (1999) as 'wild zones'.

Ⓐ
Ⓔ

Exercise 5.17

Try to operationalize Giddens's concept of ontological certainty. Make a list of the key aspects of your own identity. When you think of yourself, what are your defining characteristics – your sex, gender, ethnicity, age, social class? Is your geographical location important to you? Is your educational setting a defining aspect or your identity – are you an adult or child? Once you have done this put the characteristics in order of importance. Finally, compare your list with that of an older or younger member of your family. Is there a change in importance of the characteristics noted down by different people at different times in their lives?

The risk society – an evaluation

Although there are elements of truism in the notion of the risk society that we can all identify with and understand at the individual and societal level, we must question whether this is a new phenomenon. Past societies could easily be described as more risky – certainly in relation to health, as any visit to life expectancy statistics will tell us. Is risk as great as some of the commentators would have us believe? Were children at any more risk in the past when playing out in the street or park than they are today, or is this heightened risk a perception brought about by the media? Social theory can be used as a tool in this context to provide a critical approach to understand these aspects of our daily lives.

Exam focus: writing an essay

Drawing upon the techniques and skills you have developed in previous chapters, select *one* of the six contemporary debates featured above and:

1. Describe the main issues raised in the debate.
2. Evaluate the contribution made by the debate to our understanding of society.

(Hints: Either pick a debate you feel comfortable with – that is, where you are confident you can identify the main arguments put forward *and* understand their implications/impact – or, alternatively, choose a debate which you want to improve your understanding of.)

Description

1. Clearly state the debate you have chosen and identify the distinct viewpoints expressed within the debate.
2. Detail each viewpoint with reference to key writers and supportive research/applied analysis (if appropriate).
3. Provide a brief (two to three sentences) summary of the salient themes that emerge from your description. This will help you to focus more clearly when considering the implication/impact of the debate.

Evaluation

1. Why did the debate develop? What did it hope to achieve (for example, to clarify current ideas about society, to offer a new insight and so on)?
2. Consider the impact of each viewpoint in turn. Avoid going over ground covered in your description of the viewpoints. Focus instead on what they have contributed. Have they offered valuable insights? How? Why?
3. Bring the ideas together. Do the ideas raised in the debate help us better to understand society? How? Why?

Aim to write roughly four pages in total. Divide your time appropriately between the two parts of the question to reflect the difference between the marks allotted. If you need additional help, look at the hints on writing an essay at the end of Chapter 2.

Important concepts

poststructuralism • structuration • modernity • postmodernity • globalization • glocalization • risk

Critical thinking

- Apply the theories of globalization to the international economic crisis of 2008 which began with the bankruptcy of several banks and the collapse of the sub-prime market in the USA.
- How far do you agree that we live in a 'risk' society? Have there always been risks in society?
- Does the concept of structuration go some way to solving the traditional dichotomy between structure and action in sociology?

Chapter 6

Research Concepts

> By the end of this chapter, you should be able to:
>
> - identify and understand the importance of the key concepts that sociologists use in their work
> - highlight examples of research where research decisions have been affected by consideration of particular concepts
> - recognize the types of data sociologists might collect and the reasons for their choice
> - recognize concepts that relate to sampling and identify and evaluate various techniques for selecting research participants
> - understand the issues surrounding the debate on the nature of social facts

INTRODUCTION

By now you should have gained an understanding of the traditional and contemporary theoretical perspectives and key debates. The following chapters are designed to build upon this. By reading them and completing the exercises you will become familiar with traditional research concepts and methodologies, and develop an understanding of the impact that contemporary sociological thinking has had upon sociological research.

In order to conduct sociological research it is important to be aware of and understand some important concepts that influence sociological research. Like any subject, sociology involves learning a new language. The important thing about the language of sociological research is that each piece of jargon refers to something quite specific. Anyone trying to get to grips with research in sociology needs to be confident they understand the precise meaning of each concept.

This chapter outlines some of the most commonly used research concepts. Definitions and examples of each are given and exercises are included to enable you to test your understanding of the concepts. Each concept is evaluated in terms of its importance in sociological research. Consideration is given to the types of data sociologists may utilize in their research. Attention is also paid to the concepts and techniques that help sociologists to select people to be involved in the research. The chapter concludes with a review of a very important debate in sociology, that on the nature of social facts. This issue links with ideas presented in earlier chapters about the way different sociologists conceptualize and interpret the information they collect (see the discussion on Durkheim in Chapter 2 and of positivism in Chapter 3).

KEY RESEARCH CONCERNS

Reliability

Reliability refers to the capacity of the results of research to stand up to re-testing. If research is said to be reliable, this means that if it is replicated (repeated under identical research conditions), identical results will be achieved. Coolican (1994) succinctly states that reliability 'refers to a measure's consistency in producing similar results on different but comparable occasions'.

Reliability is important if generalizations are to be made. If researchers can establish that their research is reliable there is less risk of their taking a chance pattern or trend exhibited by their sample (the group being studied) and using it to make inferences or assumptions about the population as a whole.

If research has been completed twice under the same research conditions and the results are not similar it is dangerous to generalize. If research has only been completed once and there is no verification (double check) of the findings, it is unwise to use the results to make inferences or assumptions. However, given the pressure on sociologists to complete their research quickly and economically (see Chapter 9), many do in fact do this.

Item A

Researching Race

A sociology student decides to research ethnicity for his dissertation as she knows about the topic of 'culture and identity'. She wants to do something a bit different from the standard projects and chooses the area of environmental sociology. She decides to do a small survey on ethnicity and recycling in order to find out whether there are cultural differences in recycling habits.

She thinks about sending out questionnaires as a means to gather material which is relatively cheap. She considers interviews, but really hasn't got the time to organize them as she knows they take ages to do. Suddenly an idea strikes her: she can go to the new out-of-town superstore and simply count the people who deposit their bottles in the bottle bank in the car park. By devising simple categories for different ethnic groups (black, white and other), she can obtain quick and easy data that won't take long to analyse. Her teacher describes this method as structured non-participant observation, though she doesn't understand why as she will be joining in by standing in the car park. Never mind – he'll be pleased she has remembered something he has taught her anyway.

Next day, dressed in a balaclava knitted by her mum to keep out the winter chill, she positions herself in the car park with a clipboard. An hour goes by and she counts 20 people: 15 black, 3 white and 2 other – she has to class the latter as 'other' as they are so wrapped up in scarves, woolly hats and gloves that she can't really tell their ethnic origin and she needs some people in the 'other' category to make the data more interesting to analyse.

Getting chilly, she decides to nip into the shop for a coffee and 'invents' a few people to make up for those who use the bottle bank while she is gone. After another half an hour she decides to call it a day. As she crosses the road to the bus stop she notices another set of recycling bins that she didn't know existed. She doesn't think this is important – after all, the same proportion of people will use these bins as the ones in the car park. She hops on the bus, safe in the knowledge that she has collected reliable data.

A week later, she writes up her research. She copies out an article in *Sociology Review* for her 'Context' section. She then writes up her results. She draws a pie chart to represent her data: 26 'black', 24 'white' and 14 'other' – a total sample of 54. She writes: 'From the data, Asians appear to be particularly environmentally aware, whereas West Indians and Chinese people don't recycle because they don't drink enough wine. White women are better at recycling than white men but not as good as West Indians.' Pleased with her work, she concludes boldly that her research has found 'clear and significant differences between the recycling habits of different racial groups, with Asians being the most environmentally friendly ethnic group'. Putting down her pen, she can't help grinning – after all her teacher had said that sociological research is really difficult!

Exercise 6.1

This exercise is designed to get you to think about the importance of 'reliability' in sociological research. The scenario is deliberately exaggerated to demonstrate some of the problems that arise from making generalizations from unreliable data. Read Item A and answer the following questions.

1. Given what you know about reliability, how reliable was the research?
2. What aspects of her data collection leave a question mark over the reliability of the data?
3. To what extent should she have generalized from the data she collected?
4. What conclusions would you have drawn?
5. If you were to redesign this research to increase its reliability, what changes would you make? Why?

Validity

Validity refers to the extent to which the results of research provide a true picture of what is being studied. If research is said to be valid, this means that it is really measuring what it is intended to measure and gives an accurate insight into the research area – that is, it 'mirrors' reality.

Validity is important if researchers are seeking to obtain an in-depth insight into individuals, small groups or situations. If researchers can establish that their research is valid, they can be confident that their findings really do portray the uniqueness of the issue being studied. If the research lacks validity, this means that the researchers cannot guarantee that their findings reflect the truth.

It is very difficult to establish absolute (total) validity in sociological research because inevitably all topics are studied from the perspective/viewpoint of the investigating sociologists and no matter how much they try to empathize (achieve mutual understanding) with those interviewed about the issue or topic in question, they can never enter another's personality or experience another's feelings. For example, you may gather considerable information on bereavement and talk to bereaved people and bereavement counsellors, but unless you have experienced bereavement you can never fully understand how it feels.

Establishing validity is further complicated by the fact that even when two people share a similar experience, they do not necessarily understand or react to it in a similar way. Individual differences such as genetic factors, heredity, culture, predisposition/susceptibility to environmental factors and so on all operate to make people's interpretation of and response to situations unique.

Sociologists who care about the validity of their research must be sensitive to the fact that they will probably never gain a full picture of the truth; at best they can simply come close by ensuring that their reporting of events draws heavily upon the perceptions and interpretations of the group under study.

Item B

Handling Grief

No one can prepare you for the death of a loved one, no matter how much you read and talk about it. Even when you know it is going to happen, because of a long illness or the sheer deterioration in their condition, it still takes you by surprise. The emotions that a death stirs up are surprisingly mixed and guilt-inducing. One part of you is screaming inside about **your** loss (how selfish is that?) and another part might be relieved because of the pain your loved one was enduring. It is not only the immediate emotions that are paramount here. The inner turmoil is often hidden behind a public face of mourning, in which you think you know how you should act and feel in the public arena, but these might not match the internal thoughts and actions in the privacy of your own company. You catch yourself looking around and seeing how others are coping with the loss. The trick is not to be judgmental about those whose way of handling grief differs from yours. 'Whatever gets you through' must be the watchword.

Exercise 6.2

This exercise is designed to get you to think about the importance of 'validity' in sociological research. Item B is a fictitious account of an individual's reaction to the loss of a loved one. Information such as that contained in the item could well be used by a sociologist who is studying the experience of grief but is unable or chooses not to collect original (primary) data. Data that have been collated by one individual or agency and then studied by others are termed 'secondary' data. Read the item and answer the following questions.

1. What aspects of this account make it valid – that is, a picture of truth?
2. What are the strengths and limitations of this extract in terms of its usefulness to a sociologist? A table like the one below will help you to structure your thinking. Entries are included to get you started.

Valid data – an evaluation

Strengths	Limitations
1. Gives a true picture of one person's experience.	1. Cannot be generalized.
2.	2.
3.	3.

Ⓔ 3. To what extent can an account such as the one in Item B be seen as reliable?

Ⓐ 4. What other sources could provide the sociologist with data about the experience of illness? Which of these could be considered valid?

Representativeness

Representativeness refers to the extent to which data collected from a research sample (the group of people selected for study) 'mirrors' society at large. Data are said to be representative if the findings obtained from the research sample are a fair reflection of all the possibilities that might occur in the research population as a whole.

Representativeness is important if generalizations are to be made. If researchers are confident that their research is representative, they can be more confident about extending inferences or assumptions from the research sample to the research population.

Normally, if sociologists intend their research to be representative they use certain sampling techniques. Such techniques involve selecting a sample group where all possibilities are covered and the sample reflects in proportional terms all those existing in the wider population. Without this, any generalizations made would need to be interpreted with caution, as the data could be unrepresentative and may lead to inaccurate assumptions/inferences. While not all sampling techniques are representative, they are still of use to sociologists for specific purposes.

Item C

'Media for Middle-Class Men?'

Background to the research
Having studied bias in the mass media, and having a personal interest in pursuing a career in the media, I decided I wanted to investigate the ideas of the hegemonic model – that is that bias in the media stems from journalists who, due to their privileged background, present only one view of the world. Because the mass media are such a big area and it would be difficult to test the ideas of the hegemonic model in general terms, I decided to focus upon the claim that 'media professionals are generally middle-class, affluent men'. If I could find support for this hypothesis (statement to be tested), then it would validate (confirm) the ideas of the hegemonic model.

Selecting the sample
I decided to collect data from two groups: (1) those currently working in the media and (2) those applying for university courses in media studies, communications, journalism and so on. This would give me a representative view of the background of media personnel. I devised two questionnaires – one for each group – on their reasons for wanting to enter the media, gender, qualifications, social class background, career ambitions and so on.

My uncle, who works for the *Bournemouth Echo,* gave out 15 copies of the first questionnaire to people he knows in the finance and sport sections of the paper. He left a few questionnaires in the staff restroom for journalists from other sections to complete during their tea break. I was attending university interviews to get onto a media course at the time, so I took copies of the second questionnaire with me. At 4 interviews (Kent, Bristol, Exeter and Brighton), I managed to get 20 questionnaires completed. The Kent candidates were particularly helpful, delaying the group discussion part of the interview so that they could fill in their questionnaires together.

Exercise 6.3

Item C is a fictitious extract from a sociology student's research project. Using your knowledge and understanding of the concept 'representativeness', interpret the information and evaluate the extent to which her research is representative. Use the following questions to guide you.

1. To what extent did the student attempt to make her study representative?
2. Which design flaws weakened the representativeness of the study?
3. Why would it be very difficult to obtain representative data to test the hypothesis that 'media professionals are generally middle-class, affluent men'?

Standardization

The term 'standardization' refers to the systematic nature of research. When research is described as 'standardized', this normally implies that it follows a logical procedure and that controls exist to ensure that anyone attempting to replicate (repeat) the research will follow a similar pattern.

The purest example of standardization is experimental research conducted under laboratory conditions (see the section in Chapter 7 on scientific method), where all procedures are strictly controlled and systematically followed so that the experimental hypothesis (statement/predictions) can be tested precisely.

Once the predictions have been tested and conclusions drawn, the research must be replicated to establish the reliability of the data (see the previous section on reliability). If standardized procedures are followed the research is relatively easy to replicate (repeat under the same or similar conditions). If the procedures are not standardized the researchers can never be sure whether data collected in different circumstances or by different members of the research team are directly comparable.

Exercise 6.4

This exercise requires you to evaluate the importance of standardization in sociological research. Read the following paragraph and answer the questions below. Compare your ideas with those of other sociology students and assess the extent to which you agree.

You read somewhere that the proportion of children in the total UK population has declined, that fertility rates have fallen across Europe and that more and more women are choosing not to have children. This seems like an interesting area of research to increase your understanding of changing patterns and trends in family life.

You decide to do a quick survey of women's attitudes towards having children. Time is limited, so you enlist the help of four friends, all of whom are students but only two of whom are doing sociology. You decide to conduct short, semi-structured interviews. Each of you will conduct two 15-minute interviews on a mixture of volunteers and female friends. This will give you plenty of data to analyse and generalize from.

1. Why would you need to standardize the data collection in this case?
2. What steps would you take to standardize the data collection procedure?
3. What problems would occur if these steps were not taken?
4. If you suspect that the data collection has not followed the standard procedure, what precautions should you take when analysing the data and presenting the results?

Link Exercise 6.1

Bearing in mind the above considerations, devise a standardized interview schedule (a logical list or series of appropriate questions) for a structured interview that could be used to gather the type of data in which you are interested. To do this, you will need to look at the information on devising and conducting interviews in Chapter 7.

Generalization

If the size and composition of a sample is representative of all those people you are interested in, the results of researching the sample can be said to apply to that larger population – that is, the results can be generalized. 'Propositions derived from studying a sample of people with specific characteristics which can be applied to all people who have those characteristics' (Lawson and Garrod, 2009). Sociologists would not have sufficient time or resources to study all the people in a population so they use smaller representative samples of people which reflect the whole population under study as a cost-effective way to study society as a whole.

Objectivity

Objectivity refers to the extent to which research is free from personal bias or opinion. Positivists (see Chapters 3 and 10) argue that research should strive to be objective and value-free (see below). If it fails to achieve this aim it is of limited use to researchers. Positivists also argue that for a judgement to be objective it must be based on fact, not opinion.

Realists (see Chapter 10) argue that while it is desirable for researchers to try to be objective, in reality it is almost impossible to keep opinions out of research. This is because sociologists are human beings, and their own personal views, attitudes, outlooks and so on form an integral part of their 'self' and cannot be ignored (see Chapter 9). To overcome this problem, realists argue, sociologists should adopt a systematic, logical approach to research that maximizes objectivity and minimizes the subjective nature of research.

Exercise 6.5

Interpret the following statements using your knowledge of the concept of objectivity. Which statements can be termed 'objective'? Which ones are not? Are there any that are difficult to categorize? Why? Insert each sentence in a three-column table under one of the following headings: 'Objective', 'Not objective', 'Difficult to categorize'.

1. Looking at the weather forecast, it will probably rain today.
2. I've seen clouds like that before. I think there'll be a storm tonight.
3. *Social Trends* data indicate that 75 per cent of unskilled manual adults but only 32 per cent of professional adults over the age of 75 have no natural teeth.
4. Obviously, unskilled manual workers' teeth drop out because they don't clean them.

5. Unskilled manual workers are more likely to lose their teeth than professional people.
6. Women eat more chocolate than men.
7. Eight out of ten cat owners who expressed a preference said that their cats preferred Whiskas.
8. Little boys are more likely to be aggressive than little girls.

Subjectivity

Subjectivity refers to the extent to which research reflects the personal views and opinions of the sociologist. While positivists (see above) regard subjectivity as unscientific and thus undesirable, anti-positivists (see Chapter 3), like realists, accept that research is inevitably a subjective process. However, unlike realists, anti-positivists do not believe that research should strive to be as objective as possible.

Anti-positivists do not agree that objectivity is desirable in research, arguing that it is only by becoming involved with the individual, group or situation being studied that the researcher can ever hope to understand fully what is going on. Anti-positivists accept that research is a subjective process. Subjectivity follows from anti-positivist research because empathy (mutual understanding) is central to valid (true) data.

Item D

In-Depth Informal Interviews

One strategy adopted by qualitative researchers intent on delving deeply into individual's meanings, intentions and understandings of the social world is to adopt an intensive round of informal interviews. Unlike more formal interviews, the questions used are open-ended and allow the respondents time and space to develop their answers fully in a conversational exchange. By returning to interviewees again and again, the researcher is able to follow up interesting lines of enquiry and ensure that they have fully understood what the interviewee is saying. Such is the intensity of the relationship that can develop in such types of interview that the researcher can be in danger of becoming over-friendly with the interviewees. This danger means that the researcher must always be open about the purpose of the interviews and remind her or himself constantly of the sociological nature of the exchanges.

This exercise will enable you to explore the concept of subjectivity in more detail. Read Item D and answer the following questions.

ⓘⒶ 1. Why are interviews that use open-ended questions and are more conversational prone to subjectivity?

Ⓔ 2. To what extent can unstructured interviews that are 'over-friendly' produce worthwhile research data?

Ⓔ 3. Why might having 'empathy' with respondents compromise the validity of the research?

TYPES OF DATA

Primary data

Data are referred to as 'primary' if they have been collected by a sociologist herself or himself for a specific research purpose. The data are collected in a format decided in advance by the sociologist and analysed in accordance with the research purpose. Examples of primary data include statistics, survey responses, interview transcripts, questionnaire responses, observation records, oral history, tapes and so on.

Data collection can be a time-consuming and expensive process and it is not always possible to gain access to the information needed, but once obtained, primary data can be quite versatile. For example, the 'raw' (untreated) information can be sorted, classified, reclassified and presented as descriptive statistics – mean, median, mode, percentages and so on. The data can also be presented in graphical form (pie charts, bar charts, histograms, frequency polygons (line charts) and so on), interpreted through content analysis and categorized or summarized. Such processing enables sociologists to interpret the data and investigate patterns and trends or emergent themes.

Inferential statistics (for example, statistical tests) can also be used to test assumptions about data. Such tests can investigate differences, correlations and associations in data and the results can be compared against critical value tables to establish the significance (in statistical terms) of the findings. These tests are likely to be used by psychologists and sociologists interested in investigating specific cause-and-effect relationships as opposed to general social trends.

Primary data can take a variety of forms, depending on the research technique adopted when collecting it (see Chapters 7 and 8 for an overview of research techniques) and the type of information (see below) the sociologist needs for the issue being studied. Sociologists must be sensitive when working with primary data to respect the privacy of those comprising the research sample. Strict guidelines exist to shape this aspect of sociological research (see Chapter 9). Considering the rights of respondents is becoming increasingly important with the increased use of information technology to analyse data for research purposes. Sociologists are able to analyse data with the aid of sophisticated computers with advanced statistics and graphics packages, presuming they have the funding to support this.

Exercise 6.7

This exercise will give you practice at evaluating the usefulness of primary data. Copy and complete the accompanying table and answer the questions that follow. Examples are included to help you get started.

Primary data – an evaluation

Advantages	Disadvantages
1. The data will be in the format the sociologist wants.	1. It is time-consuming to collect your own data.
2.	2.
3.	3.

1. List as many research areas as you can think of where you would *not* be able to collect primary data. Justify your answer.
2. Select one item from your list and discuss what other options would be available to you for data collection.
3. Evaluate the relative merits of these options – overall, which would be the most appropriate/useful?
4. Evaluate the relative merits of the above technique against the use of primary data if they were obtainable.

Secondary data

Data are referred to as 'secondary' if they have been collected by someone other than the sociologist and not specifically for her or his own research purposes – that is, the sociologist uses existing data rather than collecting 'raw' information. If sociologist A uses the results of sociologist B then he or she is using secondary data. Examples of secondary data include Office of Population Census and Surveys data, *Social Trends* figures, Crime Victim Survey data, personal documents and diaries, photographs, media material and so on.

Secondary data can be very useful if researchers cannot gain access to the necessary sources to collect their own data. If large amounts of data are needed from large samples, or data are to be collected on sensitive topics, it is sometimes impossible for sociologists to rely on anything other than secondary data from sources such as those listed above. It can be relatively quick and cheap to use previously collected data, and it can be convenient if the original data have been presented and/or analysed in the format required, but this is not always the case.

Sometimes vital information is not included, or the way the data are categorized or presented is unhelpful. It is difficult to rework previously collected data, especially as it is very unlikely that the sociologist will know how the original data were collected. Also, owing to the passage of time, the data may no longer be relevant or recent enough to be useful.

Exercise 6.8

Using the knowledge you have gained from the paragraphs above, draw up a two-column table and list the strengths and limitations of secondary data. Compare your table with that of another sociology student to see if you have highlighted similar factors.

Quantitative data

Quantitative data take the form of numbers, statistics and so on. Emphasis is placed on the quantity (amount) of the information rather than its quality (depth/detail) so that patterns and trends and/or correlations can be established and generalizations made. Generally, the more structured the process of data collection, the more likely it is that the data will be quantitative. Quantitative data are generally favoured by structuralists and positivists (see Chapter 3) who are interested in objective, systematic, macro-level (large-scale) analysis.

Quantitative data tend to be reliable because they are more a reflection of fact than an expression of opinion – although this point is controversial and will be discussed below in the section on the nature of social facts. To recap, research that is reliable will produce similar results if replicated. If research is structured and the data collected are in numerical or statistical form, there is little scope for deviation from one investigation to the next. For example, if you are asked 'What is your age?' in a questionnaire and you select the appropriate age band (such as 16–18), if the research is replicated a few weeks later the likelihood is that you will give the same response (unless you lied originally, or have just had your nineteenth birthday!).

In contrast, if you are asked a less specific question, for example, 'What does it feel like to be a teenager?', your response will be less structured and what you say may be dependent upon how you are feeling at the time. In this case, if the research is replicated a few weeks later you may respond differently, perhaps because your opinion has changed or because you cannot remember what you said originally. Such questioning will produce a response that is low in reliability but high in validity (truth) as it generates qualitative data (see below).

Ⓔ

Exercise 6.9

This exercise is designed to help you to evaluate the usefulness of quantitative data. Apply the knowledge you have acquired from the above paragraphs to fill in the gaps in the following passage.

Quantitative data are generally favoured by _____ and _____ , who aim to establish _____ and _____ , which help us to understand aspects of the social structure. While high on _____ , quantitative data are low on _____ These data are in _____ and form and so an in-depth picture is not really presented. Quantitative data are most likely to be used in the following circumstances to investigate the following issues: _____ .

Qualitative data

Qualitative data take the form of commentaries, transcripts, dialogues, text and so on. Emphasis is placed on the quality (depth/detail) of the information rather than quantity (amount) so that a detailed picture can be obtained. Generally, the less structured the process of data collection, the more likely it is that the data will be qualitative. Qualitative data are generally favoured by anti-positivists and action theorists (see Chapter 3), who are interested subjective, meaningful, micro-level (small-scale) analysis.

Qualitative data are high on validity because they contain detailed, in-depth information on unique cases. For this reason they are low on reliability. If qualitative research is replicated, even in comparable circumstances, it is unlikely that similar results will be obtained. This is because the information is based more on opinion than fact and responses are prone to individual variation, whereas facts are less so. Again, however, this line of thinking is controversial and will be investigated further in the section on the 'nature of social facts'.

Link Exercise 6.2

Reproduced here is a questionnaire on drinking habits. It is designed to collect quantitative information and is structured so that all responses fall into certain categories for ease of analysis. Each category has a code (for example, 1/1 means question 1, response 1), which reduces answers to numerical values for analysis by computer.

Read the questionnaire carefully and, using your knowledge of qualitative data, complete the tasks that follow. You should read the section on questionnaire design in Chapter 7 before you begin.

Drink – what do YOU think?

(Please tick appropriate answer)

1. What is your age?

(1/1) under 16 years	(1/5) 26–30 years
(1/2) 16–18 years	(1/6) 31–40 years
(1/3) 19–21 years	(1/7) 41–50 years
(1/4) 22–25 years	(1/8) 50–60 years

2. How often do you have a drink?

(2/1) more than once a day	(2/4) less
(2/2) once a day	(2/5) rarely
(2/3) three times a week	(2/6) never

3. What do you drink?

(3/1) Bacardi	(3/4) Snakebite
(3/2) Rum and Black	(3/5) Hooper's Hooch
(3/3) Pernod	(3/6) Something else

4. Tick the sentence you most agree with.

    (4/1) Drinking helps me to unwind.
    (4/2) Drinking makes me more confident.
    (4/3) I only drink because my friends do.
    (4/4) When I'm stressed I crave a drink.
    (4/5) I don't like drinking; it makes me depressed.
    (4/6) I think I drink too much and this worries me.

1. Identify as many flaws in the design of this questionnaire as you can. What modifications would you make to correct them?
2. Why would the quantitative data obtained from the questionnaire be of limited use?
3. Are there any questions that would be worth retaining if a less structured approach to data collection were adopted? Justify your answer.

Exercise 6.10

Write your own evaluation of qualitative data. You will need to draw on the knowledge you have acquired from the text above. It may be helpful to use the evaluation paragraph on quantitative data as a guide to structuring your work. When you have finished, compare your evaluation with that of at least one other sociology student. To what extent do they agree?

TRIANGULATION OR METHODOLOGICAL PLURALISM

Sociologists are often pragmatic in their approach to their choice of research methods. They will choose the methods for which they have the time, resources and people at their disposal to successfully complete a project or piece of research. This may involve choosing methods that span the quantitative/qualitative divide or primary/secondary divide. Other sociologists might choose a variety of methods to overcome the weaknesses inherent in using one main method, whether quantitative or qualitative. Some sociologists may wish to draw on the theoretical traditions which give precedence to structural and action explanations of society and their methodological decisions will reflect this diversity.

SELECTING RESEARCH PARTICIPANTS

Concepts

Sampling

Sampling refers to the selection of people to take part in research. Clearly researchers have to be selective. They cannot possibly include everyone in their research and it may not be appropriate to do so. It would be very expensive and time-consuming and the data would be unmanageable. Because of this, sociologists use a range of techniques to assemble individuals to take part in their studies.

Population

The term 'research population' is used to refer to all members of the group of interest to the researcher. For example, if a sociologist is interested in researching women's experiences of the labour market, the research population will consist of all women who work. However, it is clear that this group would be too big for the researcher to incorporate into his or her study, so the researcher selects a smaller group of individuals from this larger target group.

Sample

'Sample' is the term used to refer to the smaller group of individuals selected from the target population for the purpose of the study. However, as Coolican (1994) notes, a sample might not consist of people. For example, a biologist might be interested in studying the quality of cabbages in one field. In this case a number of cabbages would be chosen to form the research sample, and all the cabbages in the field would comprise the research population.

Sampling frame

For sampling to be representative (that is, for it to mirror the target population) it is necessary to obtain or develop a comprehensive list of the individuals who make up the target population. This list is known as the sampling frame. The sampling frame gives some structure to the sampling process. This is because only individuals on that list are relevant to the research and hence form a logical group from which to select the sample. For a sampling frame to be accurate it must include all the potential members of the target population. If the list is incomplete or inaccurate, the sample may not reflect the target population.

Sample size

It is important for the researcher to give careful consideration to the size of the sample to be used in the study. Small samples may lead to biased results because there is a greater chance of disproportionate representation. If generalizations are made from the research findings a misleading picture may be given. Larger sample sizes can reduce the chance of sampling bias and the findings are likely to be more accurate. However, very large samples are rarely used, owing to time and financial constraints. Some would argue against very large samples because they can sometimes obscure subtle but specific effects, and may also disguise weaknesses in the design of the experiment (see Coolican, 1994, for a discussion of this).

Professional sociologists vary their sample size according to the purpose of their research. If generalizations are to be made, a minimum sample of 200 is desirable. For A level coursework, it is likely that students will use a sample of between 30 and 40. With a sample any smaller than this it will be difficult to generalize; with a larger one the research will no longer be cost- and time-effective.

Types of sampling

Systematic versus random sampling

Before selecting their samples, researchers must decide which type of sampling they will use. The main distinction is between systematic and random sampling. Systematic sampling involves employing a specific technique to structure or 'engineer' the selection in order to meet specific, predetermined criteria or expectations. Random sampling involves employing a technique to ensure that everyone in the target population has a fair and equal chance of being selected. Both types of sampling are considered below.

Random sampling

Social researchers use a range of sampling techniques to choose an appropriate group for their research. Statistically, the most accurate is a random sample. This is defined as a sample in which all members of the population have an equal chance of being selected. This sounds easy but in reality it is very hard to arrive at a truly random sample. The larger the target group to be studied, the harder it becomes. The researcher needs to find a way to select a sample so that any choice made is unpredictable in terms of any preceding sequence of events. Researchers cannot rely on volunteers because this erodes the 'unpredictable' nature of random sampling; there would be systematic inclusion of those who were willing to put themselves forward.

Techniques for random sampling

Manual selection – This is well demonstrated by the system used to select the numbers in National Lottery draws. Set numbers are placed into a container, shuffled and picked out. Crucially, all the numbers are invisible to the selector and there is no way of predicting which will be chosen. All that is certain is that, statistically at least, all the numbers have a fair and equal chance of being chosen. Other examples of this technique include numbers out of a hat, numbered bingo balls selected by a blast of air and so on.

Random-number tables – This involves using a set of random-number tables to select a sample. Because the numbers are generated at random, it is possible to move horizontally or vertically along the lines of the tables to pick a series of numbers. Members of the target population are allocated a number from those represented on the random number tables. Those whose numbers are chosen form the research sample.

Computer-generated samples – The names of the individuals in the target population are typed into the computer and the random number program is used to generate a random list of individuals to make up the research sample.

Non-random techniques

Many sampling techniques are not random in that not everyone has an equal chance of being chosen. Instead, sampling is structured such that certain individuals have a greater chance of being selected than others. This might be because they possess characteristics or qualities of interest to the researcher. Alternatively the sample might be designed to mirror distinct groups present in the research population. Individuals might also be chosen out of convenience. In such cases it is likely that individuals who have had contact with the researcher or are known to individuals previously selected to form part of the sample have more chance of being chosen than non-contacts.

Quota sampling – This involves identifying specific qualities or characteristics in the target population and classifying them into categories. A sample is then drawn that consists of a specified number of subjects for each category, in roughly the same proportions as they occur in the population. Commonly used by market researchers, the technique involves ascertaining which categories individuals fit and obtaining data from them. Data collection stops when all the information required has been collected from the specified number of individuals, for example, 10 men, 10 women, 10 boys, 10 girls and so on.

Stratified sampling – This is a special kind of sampling where the target population is divided into strata or layers, for example, according to social class, age or family income. A number of people from each layer are separately chosen to represent their stratum in the study. This ensures that all important groups are represented independently. This can increase precision and reduce time, effort and cost by allowing smaller sample sizes. For example, poverty is known to be most common among the elderly, the unemployed and single-parent families, so research on the effects of poverty might well sample each of these three strata separately as part of a survey of poverty in the population as a whole, which would permit the total sample size to be reduced because the investigator would know that the groups most affected by poverty are guaranteed inclusion (Abercrombie *et al.*, 1984).

Snowball sampling – This method is commonly used when the relevant research population is not easy to contact or identify. It involves asking existing contacts to tell their friends about the study and asking them to get in touch with the researcher. The technique is commonly used when the target population is secretive about group membership for legal or moral reasons. Thus snowball sampling might be used to contact drug users, or people who are members of sexual or religious minorities.

Convenience or desirability sampling – In practice, many researchers and almost all students doing research use convenience or desirability sampling, which involves taking a sample from the people closest to hand. Although criticized as unrepresentative, it is a quick and convenient way of generating research participants.

Self-selecting samples – Self-selecting samples are often used in university research departments. A general request is made for volunteers to take part in a research project, for example, by pinning a card on a noticeboard. Those who volunteer are termed a 'self-selecting' sample as they have personally decided to put themselves forward for the research and the sociologist has had little control over the process. The technique is non-random because not everyone has a fair and equal chance of being included in the sample. Only those who see or hear about the card will consider becoming involved.

Exercise 6.11

Copy and complete the accompanying table and summarize the relative merits of the different sampling techniques. Some examples are given to help you get started. Refer to a sociology textbook if you get stuck.

Relative merits of the different sampling techniques

Technique	Advantages	Disadvantages
Random	Least likely to produce biased sample.	
Quota		May produce unrepresentative sample as the quota could be filled by similar people, e.g. a group of adolescent girls out shopping together could fill a quota target of 10 young women.

Stratified		It is complex and time-consuming to identify strata and sample the various subgroups of the target population.
Snowball	Can allow contact with people who cannot be met through conventional means.	
Convenience		
Self-selecting		

THE NATURE OF SOCIAL FACTS

Background to the debate

There is some controversy in sociology about the legitimacy of treating quantitative data as 'fact'. The debate stems from the writings of Emile Durkheim. Durkheim is regarded by many as a founding father of positivism (see Chapter 2), although critics argue that this misrepresents his work and that he was in fact a realist.

Durkheim is not unique or unusual in his reliance on and faith in 'social facts'. As Tomas Boronski (1987) highlights in *The Sociology of Knowledge*, 'to a great extent, the knowledge and image we hold of modern industrial Britain are the result of a vast amount of statistical information we come across in the media and official reports produced by the government'. Much of our conception of 'reality' is in fact constructed for us, because the data upon which our image is based are a product of the actions and interpretations of those who collect and compile the data.

Item E

The Use and Abuse of Statistics

Each year the government produces the 'SATs' statistics for every maintained school in England and Wales. These are the results of the tests that are taken by every schoolchild at certain points in their school career. The purpose of the publication is to provide parents with information about how a school is doing, so that they can make informed choices when looking at schools to send their children to. One of the unintended conse-quences of the publication of these statistics is that the newspapers tend to focus on the 'best and worst' dimension of the figures, identifying which are the 'best' and the 'worst' schools in England and Wales. For those named and shamed as the 'worst' the effects can be devastating, with the loss of pupils and income, so that they go into a spiral of decline.

Exercise 6.12

This exercise will enable you to develop your skills of critical analysis and inves-tigate the validity of treating data as social fact. Read Item E and answer the following questions.

1. The government publishes SATs results for all schools on its Department for Children Schools and Families website (www.dcsf.gov.uk). Find out from the website which are top- and bottom-performing schools in the current year.
2. Give some reasons why the government publishes results for schools on its website.
3. To what extent to you agree that the SAT statistics represent 'fact'? (Hint: Is there any way that they could be ambiguous – that is, open to interpreta-tion? How confident would you be in making inferences or assumptions or generalizing from such data?)

Traditional objections to the 'social fact' concept

To treat data as a social fact involves a degree of risk. Phenomenologists (see Chapter 2) argue that it is completely inappropriate to do so because data collected by humans are inevitably exposed to subjective interpretation. The researcher will influence the way in which the data are both collected and interpreted. This point led Gouldner to argue in his 'Anti-Minotaur: The Myth of a Value Free Sociology' (Gouldner, 1973) that just as the bull and the man comprising the mythical minotaur cannot be separated, so facts and values cannot be separated in sociological research. By this he means that data collected in sociological research are not objective facts, as they have been exposed to subjective influences. They simply masquerade as objec-tive fact.

As mentioned earlier, Durkheim is not the only sociologist to have been 'duped' by belief in the existence of social facts. Remember Boronski's point that statistics pervade our everyday lives? Much of what receives attention in the political arena and subsequently in the mass media does so because of knee-jerk reactions to statistical data.

Item F

Single Parents

Today, public concern about single parenthood revolves around notions of the social, economic and moral 'costs' of the growing number of single parents. In 1981 there were 91,000 births outside marriage in Britain. By 1991 that figure had risen to 236,000. By the late 1990s, there was a full-blown moral panic about the rate of teenage motherhood in particular, with the number of live births to women under 20 reaching over 45,000 in 2004.

More than this, rising single and young parenthood has been associated in public and academic debate with rising levels of crime and disorder, educational problems, and the general fraying of society.

The popular image of children in such families being born largely to unmarried, 'feckless' teenage mums is not supported by the facts. Around 50 per cent of single parents are divorced and only one-third have never married; only around 5 per cent of single parents are female teenagers. Furthermore, ONS figures show that single parenthood was higher in the early 1970s, the perceived golden era of the nuclear family, than it was in the early years of 2000s. Social scientists such as Norman Dennis and Professor A. H. Halsey have argued that the absence of the responsible father figure almost inevitably 'damages' children. Halsey contends that: 'All serious studies show that, on average, the children of two parents do better educationally, physically, emotionally, psychologically and socially than do the children of single or conflicting parents.' Others take a different view. Sue Slipman of the National Council for One Parent Families argues that rising single parenthood suggests that '[W]omen have found they can survive without men and they are choosing to do so because what they want is a suitable relationship not a breadwinner.' Duncan (2006) argues that his and other qualitative research actually demonstrates the positive outcomes for young single parents, particularly mothers, who used their situation as a turning-point in their lives which 'spurred' them into education or employment. He goes on to report that the negative policy implications of single parenthood and the media reflection of it as a 'calamity' is misplaced.

(Adapted from John Williams, 'In Focus – Single Parents', *Sociology Review* 4(4), 1995; Simon Duncan, 'What's the Problem with Teenage Parents?', *Sociology Review* 16(1), 2006)

(E)

Exercise 6.13

Read Item F, which analyses the 'single parent' phenomenon and suggests that at least some of the 'problem' could be due to the faulty interpretation of statistics rather than being 'a growing social ill'.

This article sheds doubt on the validity of generalizing from statistical data, and in doing so it draws attention to two prominent social scientists, Norman Dennis and A. H. Halsey, who appear oblivious to the risk involved in drawing conclusions from data such as those provided by the OPCS.

Write a critical evaluation of Dennis and Halsey's argument, drawing upon your knowledge of the limitations of treating data as social fact. You could do this in the form of a letter to one of the sociologists or in a more conventional format, as would be appropriate for a piece of written work or an examination answer.

Data as social construction

In the light of arguments about the demise of positivism and the rise of the antipositivist paradigm (that is, collection of ideas, way of thinking – see Chapters 3 and 10) it is becoming more common for data to be viewed as social constructions rather than social facts. This line of thinking stems from the phenomenological argument by Peter Berger and Thomas Luckmann that all knowledge in society is created by the meanings and definitions of reality held by its people. Shared knowledge differs from society to society and culture to culture as it reflects a socially derived 'universe of meaning' (common ideas about how the world should be understood). Tomas Boronski (1987) develops this argument, suggesting that the construction of knowledge is an important source of power:

> Collecting social statistics . . . is not merely an academic exercise, neither are they read out of pure interest. They are the raw materials which governments use to build their policies, and without them governments would be unable to make decisions on questions such as how many schools to build or how many doctors to train. On the basis of existing data policy makers are able to make projections about the future needs of society.

Boronski describes how social statistics are a source of power for those who control them. For example, he highlights that by withholding information or releasing it selectively, governments are able to confound their opponents and influence the population's perception of the country's social and economic performance. Boronski goes on to argue that because governments control the agencies responsible for data collection, for example, the Government Statistical Service in Britain, they are also able to influence the way in which official statistics are gathered.

The above lends support to the idea that statistics should be treated with caution. This is further strengthened by Irvine *et al.*'s (1979) account of how government statisticians are involved in the social construction of knowledge (see Exercise 6.14):

> The methods and concepts developed and used for official statistics are shaped by the sorts of policies powerful people in the state wish to consider and by the concerns which preoccupy them. These concerns determine, at least partly, which phenomena are to be investigated as 'social problems' and which are neglected.

Judging by the above, it would appear that any information produced by government statisticians is not an objective reflection of reality but a subjective interpretation of events. This raises the question of whether official statistics can ever be regarded as neutral, or whether they reflect a biased (one-sided/incomplete) picture of events. This has far-reaching implications for sociologists who base their understanding of broad social issues such as employment, unemployment, housing, divorce, crime, poverty, health and welfare, educational achievement, politics, homelessness and so on on official statistics.

Item G

The Gender Pay Gap

In 1975 the Equal Pay Act came into operation with the purpose of preventing employers paying women less than men for work of the same value. At the time women's full-time earnings were roughly 30 per cent of men's. By 2003 the gap had narrowed to 18 per cent. For the tax year 2002/3 annual average full-time earnings for employees were £25,170 with men earning £28,065 and women earning £20,314.

The headline figure of 18 per cent does not however reveal a true picture of the earnings differential. The figures are based on full-time earnings, and do not take account of the longer hours and overtime worked by men. The average *weekly* earning of full-time employees in 2003 for women were £395 and for men £525 – women were earning 75.4 per cent of men's earnings.

Exercise 6.14

Ⓐ 1. Look at the Equal Opportunities Commission website (www.eoc.org.uk) and find out the current situation with regard to the incomes of men and women.
Ⓐ 2. What are the implications for women of working part-time besides the lower income?
Ⓔ 3. What other ways could there be to look at earnings? How might results differ when looking at earnings over a lifetime?
Ⓔ 4. In general terms what problems do the statistics on income reveal?

Contemporary thinking on the nature of social facts

New developments in sociological thinking have added an interesting dimension to the debate on the nature of social facts. For example, postmodernism (see Chapter 4) highlights the demise of the metanarrative and acceptance of the relativity and social construction of knowledge. Specifically, in opposing the modernist assumptions about the existence and desirability of objective, valid knowledge, the source of such knowledge (systematic, rigorous, impartial research) and the ability to generalize from structure to whole society, postmodernism would appear to provide support for the phenomenological claim that knowledge is simply the product of shared 'universes of meaning'.

Central to postmodernist thinking is the concept of 'deconstruction', defined by Phil Brown (1996), as 'a particular type of analysis which is designed to reveal the contradictions and speculative characteristics inherent in the issue under consideration'. Deconstruction of 'social facts' and, more broadly, modern social theory in general, shows that everything is based on uncertain assumptions. This leads to the conclusion that any production of demonstrably valid knowledge is impossible. No objective truth exists: 'what is truth on one side of the Pyrenees can be falsehood on the other' (Pascal, cited in Jones, 1993). Instead, multiple versions of reality compete for sociologists' attention. Pessimistically, it is suggested that this will lead to the end of sociology. As Brown (1996) highlights: '[B]ecause there is no objective knowledge, there can be no rational basis for intervention. Knowledge cannot liberate, subject-centredness is undermined and the death of the subject is proclaimed.'

Boronski's argument about the power of statistics is affirmed by postmodernists. However, instead of knowledge having the power to shape our *interpretation* of reality, it is seen as shaping *absolute reality*. Postmodernists propose that rather than people producing knowledge, knowledge produces people because it shapes our self-concept or identity, our thoughts and actions. To accept the existence of the grand theory or macro-sociology is to be duped by the 'metanarrative' (a critical term used by postimpressionists for large-scale theories that falsely adopt the status of truth).

As a result of the impact of postmodernism the debate on the nature of social facts is becoming increasingly cohesive. There are clear links between postmodernism and phenomenology, for example, as both see reality as socially constructed. Interestingly, while postmodernists reject the metanarrative of capitalism proposed by Marx, they should perhaps acknowledge that in his writings on religion he recognized the social construction of religious knowledge.

Exam focus: structured questions

The following exercise gives you the opportunity to attempt an exam-type question. Read Items H and I carefully before you begin to write. To answer the questions you may need to refer to information presented earlier in the chapter. (Hint: For questions 3 and 4 it is a good idea to plan your answers carefully before you begin to write. This will ensure that your response is well structured and the information you present is relevant to the question being asked. It is also important to apportion your time so that you spend longer on questions that require a more detailed response.)

1. What is meant by the term 'sample'?
2. What is the difference between a random and a non-random sample?
3. Describe and evaluate the two types of data that are most likely to be collected by the research methods featured in the Items.
4. Drawing on information contained in the items and elsewhere, evaluate the legitimacy of treating data as social 'facts'. (20 marks)

Item H

Social Surveys

A social survey is carried out at a particular moment in time and therefore is not conducive to the study of social change. Even where repeated surveys on the same subject are carried out (such as the Census), the amount of information about social change collected is limited. For example, unless exactly the same questions are asked every 10 years, then the data will not be directly comparable. Surveys might ask questions about the past to try and capture some sense of social change, but unless the questions are directly factual (number of children, dates of birth and so on) the answers are reliant on memory, which is tricky for establishing reliability. What can be established by repeated surveys are data about social change at the higher social levels of the population as a whole or in particular social groups.

Item I

Discussing Experience

When investigating personal or sensitive issues, the quality of the data gathered is of utmost importance. Data gathered through one-off events like a questionnaire are unlikely to gain the depth of information that would illuminate the issue. The first difficulty for the researcher is in choosing a sample which is representative of the group under study as a whole. Trust has to be established between researcher and researched when sensitive issues are being aired, and this takes time and effort on behalf of the researcher. The more time the interviewee is willing to give to the researcher, the more likely it is that illuminating material will be gathered. There is, however, a problem of analysing such in-depth data is that the choice of material to be presented is at the discretion of the researcher, and their own biases may influence how they choose to present the views of the interviewee.

Important concepts

reliability • validity • representativeness • standardization • objectivity • subjectivity • qualitative • quantitative • methodological pluralism • triangulation • sampling techniques • random/non-random

Critical thinking

- How far do you agree that the distinction between the gathering of quantitative and qualitative data has been superseded by the notion of structuration and feminist research?
- Can sociology ever be objective?
- Is there an argument for always making use of secondary as well as primary data?

Chapter 7

Research Techniques

By the end of this chapter you should be able to:

- identify the research techniques most commonly used by sociologists and give a definition of each
- give examples of research studies using each technique and understand the rationale behind the choice of method in each case
- pinpoint the advantages and disadvantages of each technique
- evaluate the relative merits of research techniques
- distinguish between experimental and non-experimental techniques
- distinguish between and give examples of quantitative and qualitative techniques

INTRODUCTION

In order to understand sociological research that has been conducted by others or undertake your own projects, it is important to have a working knowledge of the range of techniques available to sociologists, the rationale behind the choice of method and the relative merits of research techniques. This chapter outlines some of the most commonly used research methods, giving definitions and examples of each. It also includes some interpretation and application exercises to enable you to test your understanding of the various methods. You are encouraged to analyse the advantages and disadvantages of each method and evaluate their relative merits. Some attention is given to contemporary trends in the use of research techniques, although this theme is developed further in Chapter 8. This chapter starts by considering the distinction between experimental and non-experimental methods and then moves on to consider the nature of quantitative and qualitative methods.

THE SCIENTIFIC METHOD

Use of the scientific method in sociology is advocated by positivists (see Chapter 3 for a review of the rationale behind its use), although many critics are skeptical about its validity in sociological research. The controversy over its usefulness is dealt with in Chapter 10. For now, attention will focus on the nature of scientific methodology.

The nature of scientific methodology

There is a common consensus that to be termed 'scientific', methodology should be characterized by the key elements that define science (see Chapter 10 for a fuller discussion of sociology and science).

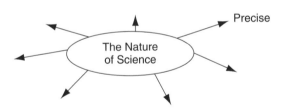

Exercise 7.1

Using your knowledge of science and scientific methodology, think of as many words associated with science as you can and record them on a diagram copied from the one here. Use these words to compose a clear definition of science. When you have finished, check your definition against the one presented in the text below and assess the extent to which the two agree.

Precise

The Nature
of Science

Science is a systematic, rigorous, controlled discipline aimed at understanding, gathering knowledge about and predicting occurrences within the natural world. If a research method has these characteristics it can been deemed 'scientific'. The purest example of the scientific method is the experiment.

Characteristics of an experiment

The term 'experiment' has a specific meaning for social scientists. It refers to a process characterized by systematic, precise, logical research under controlled conditions (normally in a laboratory environment), where the primary research aim is to manipulate an independent variable (a factor that stands alone) and precisely measure the associated effect on a different but dependent variable (a factor that is hypothetically related). Experiments are regarded as objective and replicable (see Chapter 6 for a review of these concepts), and thus are highly reliable but low on ecological validity (that is, the findings don't necessarily translate to a 'real-world setting', and thus might not reflect the truth).

Types of experiment

There are three main types of experiment: laboratory, field and natural. Each of these will be considered in turn.

Laboratory experiments

As the name suggests, the term 'laboratory experiment' is applied to research that adopts the characteristics of an experiment and takes place in the unique, controlled, artificial environment of the science laboratory.

The laboratory experiment is not often used by sociologists as it is regarded as inappropriate to study social life in isolation – that is, within the confines of an artificial laboratory setting. Instead sociologists, especially positivists, are more likely to test hypotheses via comparative research. Experimentation is more likely to be used by psychologists in order to test predictions precisely and develop their understanding of human behaviour.

Item A presents a now infamous example of experimentation in social research. It was conducted by an American social psychologist, Milgram (1974), who was interested in obedience and wanted to test ideas about the extent to which obedience is related to the power and status of the individuals giving and receiving commands/instructions (see Exercise 7.2). It is rare for social psychologists to resort to laboratory experimentation to develop theories as they are 'concerned with those aspects of human behaviour which involve people and their relationships with other people, groups, institutions and society as a whole' (Flanagan, 1994). Social psychology therefore has much in common with interpretive sociology.

Item A

Laboratory Experimentation – Milgram

The laboratory experiment conducted by Milgram is one of the most-cited examples of this kind of research. Milgram was interested in how far people would go in obeying an authority figure, in his case, a scientist conducting an experiment. Test subjects were told that the scientist was investigating the effects of punishment on learning and when a confederate answered any question wrongly, the test subject was required to administer an electric shock to the confederate, who then pretended to be affected by the shock. A majority of the test subjects continued to administer 'shocks' to the confederate even when the equipment indicated that the electricity was set at a dangerous level. The conclusion was that many people were prepared to carry out the orders of an authority figure, even if there was a potential risk of death, as long as the authority figure was seen as legitimate.

Exercise 7.2

Read Item A and answer the following questions.

1. In your opinion, what specific advantages did Milgram gain from using the laboratory method for this piece of research?
2. To what extent would the above piece of research fit in with positivist thinking?
3. Why would the majority of sociologists object to the use of such a technique?

Link Exercise 7.1

Read the section 'Ethics' in Chapter 9 and write a critical evaluation of Milgram's research (Item A), which has been heavily criticized on ethical (moral) grounds.

1. What aspects could be regarded as immoral?
2. Do the benefits gained in terms of the findings of the research outweigh the ethical costs?

You should present your response in the style of a formal letter to the APA (American Psychological Association), the professional organization responsible for regulating the conduct of psychologists. For authenticity, the address of the APA is as follows:

American Psychological Association
1200 Seventeenth Street N.W.
Washington, DC 200036
USA

ⓀⓊ
ⒾⒶ

Exercise 7.3

Apply the knowledge you have acquired so far to complete the following description of laboratory experiments.

Laboratory experiments are seen as desirable as they enable research to be p_____ y c_____ d in order that c_____ and e_____ t relationships can be established. Normally, they involve the m_____ n of an i_____ t variable and sensitive measurement of the subsequent change in the d_____ t variable. While p_____ s would advocate the use of s_____ c m_____ d, l_____ y e_____ s are seldom used by s_____ s as it is seen as inappropriate to study human behaviour outside its n_____ l e_____ t. Instead, they are more likely to be favoured by p_____ s, who are interested in establishing the f_____ s or l_____ s that underlie h_____ n b_____ r.

 Even in p_____, the use of l_____ e_____ is becoming less popular, owing to the c_____ y surrounding a now infamous piece of research by S_____ y M_____ m in 19_____, which raised questions about the e_____ s of l_____ y e_____ n. If they are used today, it is most likely to be by c_____ e p_____ s, because such researchers are largely dependent for their k_____ e upon testing h_____ s drawn from h_____ l m_____ s which attempt to account for the i_____ l m_____ l p_____ s responsible for h_____ m f_____ g invisible to the human eye.

Field experiments

The term 'field experiment' refers to research conducted outside the confines of the laboratory in a natural setting but still contains the element that makes the experiment unique – that is, manipulation of an independent variable in order to assess the subsequent change in a hypothetically related (dependent) variable. By taking the experiment outside the laboratory, researchers reduce the artificiality of the research setting and consequently increase the ecological validity of the research (the application of research findings to everyday life). They are able to test hypotheses in a 'real world' that is far more appropriate to their subject matter. This takes us back to a point made earlier in the chapter, namely that sociologists seldom conduct laboratory experiments because they deem it inappropriate to study social life in isolation.

 Field experiments do have drawbacks, however. The precision that is possible in the controlled environment of the laboratory is less likely to be attained in a real-world setting. Many factors can interfere with the research and affect both the validity and the reliability of the findings. For example, 'confounding' can occur. This means that the results of the research may be due not to the manipulation of the independent variable by the researcher but to some unintentional, unaccounted-for factor of which the researcher may not be aware. This can lead to ambiguous results and misleading conclusions. For this reason field studies are difficult to replicate – because the researcher has no control over environmental factors it is unlikely that similar results will be obtained even if the research is conducted in 'comparable' circumstances.

Item B

Pygmalion in the Classroom

A classic example of a field experiment is Rosenthal and Jacobson's (1968) study of teacher expectation entitled 'Pygmalion in the Classroom'. Via earlier research on laboratory rats, they developed a theory that quality of learning was dependent upon the beliefs of the person training. They extended this to a real-life setting, visiting an American elementary (primary) school, claiming to have devised a new test which could predict which pupils would 'bloom' academically during the course of the next year. The children were IQ-tested and a random sample (see Chapter 6) were targeted by the researchers as likely to 'spurt'. Teachers were informed, by 'accidentally overhearing' a conversation between the experimenters.

Eight months later the children were tested again using the same IQ test. The 20 per cent singled out were known as the experimental group and the remaining 80 per cent the control group – that is, a group which is used for comparison with an experimental group. When Rosenthal and Jacobson analysed the scores of the retested children, they found marked differences in performance between the experimental group and the control group. The children in the experimental group had improved considerably and this was taken as evidence that teacher expectations could directly influence pupil performance. They called this phenomena [sic] the self-fulfilling prophecy: the pupils seemed to have done better because the experimenters had 'predicted' they would.

(Adapted from P. Banyard and N. Hayes, *Psychology – Theory and Applications*. London: Chapman & Hall, 1994.)

Read Item B, which summarizes another well-known experiment, and answer the following questions. This should help you to develop your understanding of field experiments.

(I)(A) 1. What were the 'independent' variable and 'dependent' variable in this study?
(I)(A) 2. How could the experiment have been 'confounded' – that is, adversely
(An)   affected by unknown/unintended effects?
(I)(A) 3. What ethical criticisms could be directed at this study? (Hint: It may be helpful
(An)   to look at the section on Ethics in Chapter 9.)
(An)(E) 4. If you had an interest in the sociology of education, particularly the 'self-
       fulfilling prophecy', and were tempted to replicate this research, what
       considerations might shape your decision?

Natural experiments

If someone asked the question 'When is an experiment not an experiment?', the probable answer would be, 'When it's a natural experiment'! Having learned that the factor that makes an experiment unique is manipulation of the independent variable in order to assess its impact on a hypothetically associated (dependent) variable, and that this manipulation is done by the researcher, we now come to a third type of experiment, which would appear to contradict this!

Natural experiments involve the study of events (independent variables) that have significantly changed crucial factors (dependent variables). In this case the independent variable is not deliberately manipulated by the researcher. Instead a change occurs in society, normally as a result of a natural, political, social or economic event and the researcher simply treats it as an independent variable and studies it. By exploring the outcome of the change, it is possible to develop conclusions about the cause.

As Banyard and Hayes (1994) point out, a classic example of a natural experiment occurred as a result of the partition of Germany after the Second World War. Because of the partition into East and West Germany the education system, which had previously been unified, had to adapt to two entirely different economic systems and social structures. It was therefore possible for educationalists to study the differences between the two education systems in terms of their economic and social contexts, knowing that the prior variables had been controlled. The reunification of Germany may offer a similar, albeit reversed, opportunity in the long term.

Natural experiments are becoming more commonly used to study the implications of policy decisions. For example, much attention has been given in recent years to the problems posed by HIV and how to prevent further infection. Some police forces have changed their policy towards drug use to turn a blind eye to the selling of needles and syringes. Pitts and Phillips (1991) studied the effects of this action by investigating the patterns of sharing injection equipment – a crucial factor in the spread of HIV. They found that the police's new pragmatic approach had led to the development of 'safe houses' where drug-taking was less dangerous because clean equipment was readily available, and this made sharing less likely. The research was valuable in highlighting the impact of the new policing approach to a long-established social problem, and it provided valuable feedback to validate policy changes.

Because they offer the highest degree of ecological validity of all the experimental techniques, natural experiments are the ones most likely to be used by sociologists. Social life can be studied, largely uninterrupted, in its natural setting, which means the research is likely to present a picture of the truth rather than an artificial, clinical version of events. Natural experiments can also be regarded as reasonably objective because the independent variable is not directly manipulated by the researcher but changes as the result of natural circumstances (see above), so there is little opportunity for the researcher to interfere with the course of events. While the choice of which topic to study involves a subjective element, beyond this the research should, at least theoretically, be 'value-free' (see Chapter 6).

The experimental method in sociology – an evaluation

Strengths

1. Experiments are precise and enable cause-and-effect relationships to be systematically studied.
2. Predictions can be made and these can be tested against reality. Quantitative data can be gathered. This enables generalizations to be made from sample to population.
3. Positivists advocate the use of experiments as part of the scientific method because they regard science as the key to progress. The use of scientific techniques can enable us to uncover the patterns that govern human behaviour and thus develop social laws.

Disadvantages

1. Experiments are artificial and are not appropriate for the study of human beings, as life cannot be viewed in isolation. Human behaviour is the product of interaction between humankind and the environment and should be studied as such.
2. We cannot necessarily generalize from experimental findings. The findings might be more a product of the experimental process (for example, experimenter expectancy, demand characteristics, and so on) than evidence of a real relationship.
3. Anti-positivists would dismiss the use of experiments and scientific methodology in sociology. They would argue that humans are unique and should be investigated via in-depth qualitative methods that are sensitive to the individual differences between people.

NON-EXPERIMENTAL METHODS: QUANTITATIVE METHODS

Social surveys

Social surveys are large-scale pieces of sociological research that normally involve a combination of research techniques, although the primary vehicle for data collection is usually the structured questionnaire. This can be administered via the post or face-to-face in the form of a structured interview. Social surveys are aimed at investigating societal patterns and trends at the macro level.

Social survey data can have implications for social policy. For example, feedback from the British Crime Survey, a large-scale study of victims of crime conducted by the Home Office, could lead to the development of new policies on law and order. Similarly the massive amount of data collected from national social surveys such as the Census (the 10-yearly questionnaire that each household in Britain must complete by law) can provide the government with vital information to shape social reform. For example, the data obtained on health from the 1991 Census, which highlighted the relationship between low income and illness, could provide the basis for tax concessions to those opting for private medicine within the NHS to fund the increased demand on the NHS.

Several sociologists have attempted to use social surveys as a primary research technique, although their research has been relatively small-scale compared with the massive undertaking of the census. For example, Peter Willmott (1987) used a small-scale social survey to investigate the role of friends, neighbours and relatives in the lives of people from different social classes. The survey largely produced quantitative data, drawn from structured interviews (following a questionnaire format), which were then analysed for statistical significance. Some qualitative data were collected via a section on the 'meaning of friendship' to increase the validity of the research.

Rose and Gershuny (1995) describe the benefits of social surveys, arguing that they are 'a central technique of social investigation', and in particular that they help us to understand processes over time. They especially highlight the worth of regular or repeated cross-sectional surveys – that is, those which explore social phenomena at various points in time as a source of secondary data for sociologists investigating social change.

One such is the General Household Survey, where in consecutive years the same questions are put to different samples of the population. However this only enables macro-level (general-trend) analysis because the same individuals are not used from year to year. Micro- or individual-level comparisons are not possible. To overcome the limitations of such research, Rose and Gershuny (1995) suggest that sociologists should turn their attention to longitudinal social surveys, which collect data from the same individuals at different points in their life.

Cohort studies (where a sample is followed over a period of years via regular monitoring and data collection) could be the most accessible and useful source of longitudinal secondary data. Examples include the National Child Development Study, which has been following a group of individuals from their birth in 1958, and, more recently, the British Households Population Survey (BHPS) of 10,000 individuals drawn from representative households across Britain. The latter have been interviewed annually throughout the 1990s by the Economic and Social Research Council and the University of Essex.

Exercise 7.5

In their review of social surveys Rose and Gershuny (1995) list the many advantages of using longitudinal data. Draw up a two-column table and write down as many as you can think of under the heading 'Advantages'. In the second column (headed 'Benefits') explain why each one is beneficial to researchers.

Globalization and research

In recent years globalization (see Chapter 5) has greatly increased the scope of sociological research. Increasingly compatible information technology has made it easier for researchers to tap into international and global data and to conduct research at such levels. It is recognized that it is no longer appropriate to study phenomena at the national level when the nation-state is now part of the global community rather than an isolated, insular society. For example, Giddens (1995) highlights the impact of globalization on personal experiences: events in distant places can now have a direct consequence on our daily lives. Social surveys enable us to understand the worldwide economic climate and culture that have emerged with the demise of national boundaries.

Social surveys – an evaluation

Strengths

1. Social surveys facilitate the collection of quantitative (and to a lesser extent qualitative) data on a large scale at the macro level. This data can be assessed for patterns and trends to aid our understanding of what shapes human behaviour.
2. Social surveys produce data that would be deemed reliable by positivists and can be used to extend generalizations or inferences from a research sample to the wider population. This enables local, regional, national, international and, increasingly, global comparisons to be made between data sets.
3. The longitudinal nature of some social surveys means that sociologists can study social change over time, in terms of both its causes and its consequences for society and its members.
4. Certain social surveys, namely cohort studies, enable us not only to study social phenomena and social change at the general or societal level, but at the individual level and over time (the evolutionary view).

Disadvantages

1. Social surveys rely heavily on quantitative data and the treating of such data as 'social facts'. This approach has received heavy criticism from anti-positivists. Reliance on data from questionnaires is also controversial, as questionnaires are not without limitations.
2. Owing to the expense involved in conducting large-scale, survey-style research, sociologists are more likely to rely on secondary data from previous social surveys. Hence their interpretation of reality depends largely on someone else's data. Even if they adopt a critical stance, they could be misled by ambiguous data.
3. Anti-positivists argue that it is inappropriate to adopt large-scale, macro-level research methods to study humans. Instead they advocate the use of small-scale, microlevel methods that embrace the uniqueness of individuals.

Questionnaires

Questionnaires present a series of questions as a vehicle for data collection. There are several types of questionnaire, varying in the degree to which they are structured (that is, structured, semistructured, unstructured). Examples include postal questionnaires, which are sent out by the researcher and returned after completion, and face-to-face questionnaires, which are completed by the researcher in the presence of the respondent. Questionnaires can also be given out to individuals in person and collected after completion. In this case it is not unusual for the researcher to supervise the completion, although sometimes it is advantageous to do so – for example, to clarify ambiguities and so on.

Questionnaires tend to be administered to a research sample so that generalizations and inferences can be made with regard to the wider population. Because of this, sample selection is an important factor in questionnaire style research. It is normally seen as desirable to select a sample through a precise logical process. Five main sampling techniques are available to researchers (see Chapter 6), namely random, opportunity, quota, stratified and snowball sampling. Occasionally researchers ask for volunteers to take part in the research, and these are termed a 'self-selecting' sample.

Many sociologists have used questionnaires in their research. For example, Young and Willmott (1961), in their classic study of family life in London, used questionnaires to investigate family networks and explore how community, economy and family are intimately interwoven. In this case the data collection took the form of structured interviews and the questionnaires were administered to respondents by a member of the research team. O'Brien and Jones (1996) used a similar method for their follow-up research on the extent to which working-class family life had changed since Young and Willmott's research more than three decades earlier.

Questionnaires continue to be an important technique for investigating public opinion on social phenomena. One example is Morrison's (1994) research on the reporting of war. As part of a large study of the Gulf War, Morrison, research director at the Institute of Communication Studies, University of Leeds, set out to examine television viewers' perception of the images of the war. He looked particularly at how they judged the television scenes of death and injury after the air attack on the al-Amiriya shelter in Baghdad in 1991. Also included in the exercise was an investigation into how children judged the war and whether, as reported at the time, it caused them anxiety.

Item C

From the Falklands to the Gulf – Doing Sociology and Reporting War

Ten adult group discussions were convened, split for age, class and sex, spread geographically between the north, Midlands and south of England. They were shown news footage of the strike on the shelter from the late evening news bulletins of the BBC, ITN and the French channel TF1. Viewers were also shown news footage [from] WTN, that went into the ITN newsroom, but which was not broadcast because it was considered too horrific. The WTN footage showed close-up pictures of cindered bodies.

One cannot generalize from group discussions to the population as a whole, but along with the group discussions we conducted a national survey. This was based on an initial random sample location of 88 enumeration (numbered) districts and within each sample point quotas were set for age, sex and social grade, all interlocked so as to ensure that the population was represented accurately. Over 1,000 adults were interviewed, at home, for an average of 55 minutes.

We conducted 4 group discussions, 2 in the north, 2 in the south of England, with boys and girls aged 10–12 and 13–15. We also included 212 children aged between 9 and 15 in our national survey. These were drawn from the same sample as the main adult sample, with quotas set for age and sex. This questionnaire was much shorter than the one the adults answered, lasting only 10–15 minutes.

(*Source*: David Morrison, 'From the Falklands to the Gulf – Doing Sociology and Reporting War', *Sociology Review* 3 (3), 1994)

Exercise 7.6

This exercise will enable you to explore Morrison's research in more detail. Read Item C and answer the following questions.

(K)(U)
(I)(A)
(An)(E)

1. Why was it important to split the sample according to age, class, sex and geographical region?
2. To what extent do you agree that the news footage of the airstrike shown in the main evening news bulletins on BBC1, ITN and TF1 was representative of media reporting of that event?

(An)

3. What ethical issues are raised by the showing the WTN footage? Why should Morrison be aware of this?

4. Why did Morrison argue 'one cannot generalize from group discussions to the population as a whole'?

5. To what extent would you agree that an 'initial random location sample' was the most effective way of selecting respondents to take part in this research?

6. What disadvantages stem from questionnaire completion via structured interviews conducted in adults' homes?

7. Why do you think the 10–12 and 13–15 age categories were selected for the group discussion on the impact on children of the coverage of the Gulf War?

8. What advantages would come from drawing the second group of child respondents (9–15 years) from the same household as the main adult sample?

9. Why was quota sampling used here?

10. What advantages and disadvantages would arise from giving the children a shorter questionnaire?

Questionnaire construction

When commenting on the advantages of questionnaires, it is often suggested that they are a quick, easy and effective means of data collection. While this may be true relative to more lengthy techniques such as the interview, observation and so on, it is somewhat misleading because the process is only quick once the questionnaire is in existence.

Questionnaires normally need to be designed and constructed with specific research purposes in mind, and this can be a painstaking operation requiring considerable expertise and skill. Often, once a draft questionnaire is produced a pilot trial is undertaken to enable researchers to test the questionnaire. This again can take time, especially if the postal method is used, as this is notorious for low response rates (10–15 per cent) and delays in the completed questinnaires being returned.

Questionnaires can be structured in format – that is, have a series of boxes to tick for the range of answers available. This format is popular with those wishing to obtain quantitative data that is high on reliability (see Chapter 6). The two are related because the more structured the questionnaire, the more limited the variation in response. Theoretically, at least, there should be little variation between initial completion and any replication. Structured questionnaires with precoded responses are commonly favoured by those wishing to analyse their data via a series of statistical packages for the social sciences now available for most computer systems, for example, Logistix, PASW-X, PASW-PC, Excel and so on.

Semistructured questionnaires involve a combination of predetermined response options and some free-response or open-ended questions. This enables respondents occasionally to express themselves without the constraint of predetermined answers. This can increase the validity of the questionnaire, because if individuals have the opportunity for free expression the data are more likely to present a valid picture. Incorporating free-response sections can make the questionnaire harder to analyse by computer because qualitative data need to be processed alongside quantitative. Increasingly, however, computer content analysis packages are being developed, although they may still prove time-consuming because the data have to be input before the analysis can begin.

Although some sociological research texts highlight the existence of a third questionnaire format – that is, unstructured – it is hard to imagine how such a format could meet the above-mentioned definition of a questionnaire – that is, a series of questions that provide the vehicle for data collection. Unless these questions are presented in a haphazard way to make the application of the unstructured label legitimate, terming questionnaires 'unstructured' could be problematic. Perhaps the closest some questionnaires get to an unstructured format is when a series of very open-ended questions are presented and considerable space is allowed for personal reflection. It is highly unlikely that this approach would be favoured, however, because positivists could not obtain the reliable data they want and anti-positivists would regard other methods (for example, interviews, observation) as more suitable for the study of the uniqueness of humanity.

Much has been written about the process of questionnaire construction. De Vaus (1986) suggests that researchers should follow a series of logical steps, giving consideration to the following:

- Carefully select areas of interest to ensure that all relevant questions are asked at the time – it is difficult to go back to collect additional information if this is later discovered to be necessary.
- Word the questions so that they are clear, unambiguous and useful – the language used should be simple, short, free from bias, not leading (prompting a certain response) and so on.
- Select the question type – open, where the respondents formulate their own answers, or closed, in which a number of alternative answers are provided, from which the respondents select one or more.
- Evaluate the questions – once the initial questions have been developed each must be rigorously evaluated via pilot testing before being included in the final questionnaire.

■ Questionnaire layout – there are six key areas: answering procedures, contingency questions, instructions, use of space, order of questions, and setting up for coding.

De Vaus stresses that a questionnaire should be the product of the research problem, the theory, the method of administration and the methods of data analysis. Good questionnaires do not just happen; they involve careful thinking, numerous drafts, thorough evaluation and extensive testing.

ⓤ
ⓐ

Exercise 7.7

This exercise will enable you to interpret and apply the information on questionnaire construction outlined above. Read the following questionnaire on 'lifestyle' and complete the tasks that follow.

Questionnaire on Lifestyle

For my mini-research project, I'm doing a study on the way people live. I'm a bit nosy really and it seems a good way to get to know people a bit. Thanks for filling it in for me!

1. What is your name and how much do you earn?

   _____

   (Write on the line.)

2. How old are you?

0–10 years	26–45 years
11–13 years	46–50 years
14–25 years	51–76 years

   (Tick one category only.)

3. Where do you live?

   _____

   (Write on the line.)

4. How would you describe your lifestyle?

Comfortable	___
Uncomfortable	___
Don't know	___
Not as good as you'd like	___
All right considering	___

   (Tick one category unless you're not sure.)

5. What do you do in your spare time?

    Go out   ___
    Stay in   ___
    Stay in then go out later?   ___
    Only go out at weekends   ___
    Other (please state)   ___

6. Are you happy with your life?

    Yes   ___
    No   ___

    (Tick one category.)

7. Do you have many friends?

    Yes   ___ Go to question 9
    No   ___ Go to question 8

    (Tick one category.)

8. How does your lack of friends affect your lifestyle?

    _____

    (Write on line.)

9. Are you popular because of your lifestyle or is your lifestyle a product of your popularity?

    _____
    _____
    _____

    (Write a lot here because my teacher said my study would be more valid if I got some comments.)

10. How would your lifestyle be different if you had more money, more friends, more time, less strict parents etc.?

    _____
    _____
    _____

THANKS FOR FILLING THIS IN,
MY SOCIOLOGY CLASS WILL BE INTERESTED TO READ IT!

1. Using the information provided above on good practice in questionnaire construction, find as many design factors in the questionnaire as you can that contradict (go against) the advice of De Vaus.
2. Redraft the questionnaire in semistructured format (that is, using a combination of closed and open-ended questions to increase its value as a way of collecting data). Restrict yourself to a maximum of 10 questions.
3. Compare your questionnaire with that of at least one other sociology student. Evaluate which redrafted questionnaire appears most useful and why? What design factors does it adopt? What do they 'add' to the original?

Questionnaires – an evaluation

Strengths

1. Questionnaires can reach a large sample of people and produce large amounts of data relatively quickly. Once well designed, the administration of questionnaires should be reasonably easy.
2. As they mainly collect quantitative data, questionnaires are favoured by positivists. They enable databases to be developed that facilitate generalization from sample to population.
3. If data are obtained in structured, often precoded, format it is easy to analyse both manually and by computer. Even when free-response sections are included, questionnaires are still useful as the document provides a permanent record of the respondents' comments. These can also be analysed with the help of computer programmes.

Disadvantages

1. Although questionnaires can potentially cover a wide area and reach a large sample, there is no guarantee that they will be completed. Postal questionnaires have a low response rate.
2. You cannot always be sure that the answers are reliable or valid. For example, the unsupervised group completion of questionnaires may mean that a 'group effect' operates – that is, people fill it in together and all express the same views. Supervised completion may lead to a 'desirability effect' – that is, people give the answers they think they should because they want to please the researcher or feel pressured by his or her presence.
3. Anti-positivists would argue that any form of questionnaire, by its very nature, involves forcing people's responses into preset categories, which invalidates them. If a questionnaire has to be used at all, they would probably advocate face-to-face completion – that is, via structured interviews, but in this context the use of the term 'questionnaire' becomes somewhat ambiguous and misleading.

NON-EXPERIMENTAL METHODS: QUALITATIVE METHODS

Interviews

The term 'interview' describes a research process whereby the researcher and the participant converse, normally face-to-face, although sometimes over the telephone, and increasingly, due to technological advances, via video and satellite links.

Interviews enable researchers to collect qualitative data that is regarded as high in validity but low in reliability. Owing to the time consuming nature of interviews it is likely that if a sampling technique is used at all, the sample selected will be relatively small compared with the number involved in questionnaires and social surveys. For this reason we cannot assume that the interviews will be highly representative and we should be cautious when attempting to make generalizations. Interviews are regarded as a micro-level technique and are favoured by anti-positivists who want to collect in-depth information that reflects the uniqueness of the interviewees' insights.

Feminist researchers like Ann Oakley (1981) and Helen Roberts (1991) have argued that there should be a feminist approach to interviewing which is different from the masculinist paradigm outlined in traditional methodology textbooks. Oakley argues that the notion of interviewing that advocates 'objectivity', 'neutrality', 'detachment' is a culturally, positivistically constructed approach which does not get at the true picture of life that should be under investigation. Indeed some areas of social life which are very sensitive to research, like domestic violence, childbirth, housework and conjugal roles cannot be approached from the traditional perspective. Oakley found that her respondents frequently wanted to ask questions as well as answer them, so she adopted an open and honest response and collaborative relationships developed as a consequence. Oakley felt that by making sure she did not exploit the women she was interviewing her research was more valid, ethical and caring. Most of her women respondents said that they had been affected by being interviewed mainly in a positive way that had enabled them to reflect upon their experiences.

(An)(E)

Exercise 7.8

Write down a list of arguments for and against the view that Oakley is putting forward. Try to use methodological terms such as 'representativeness', 'validity', 'reliability', 'ethics', 'objectivity', 'neutrality' and so on to explain whether your argument agrees or disagrees with the feminist view.

Interviews can vary in their degree of structure. For example, structured interviews (sometimes known as 'formal' interviews) involve a series of questions devised in advance. Such techniques make the interview process more economical timewise, and can increase the reliability of the data by imposing restrictions on the scope for variation in the responses to the questions. Replication of structured interviews is relatively easy. Also, a team of interviewers can be used to collect the data because a previously agreed, precise schedule can be followed by a group of individuals. This increases the 'standardization' of data collection (see Chapter 6).

This format is especially useful if the interviewers have limited expertise in interviewing. However it does require the researchers to be well informed about the research topic/issue. Also, there is little opportunity for probing, clarification or exploring issues not considered or known of by the researcher.

Semistructured interviews are often favoured because of their less rigid format. Normally a list of areas for investigation is drawn upon in advance, but this merely serves as a guide for the interviewer rather than a precise schedule. Semistructured interviews require more skill as they are often conducted in the style of a conversation, and if interviewers wish to promote a 'natural' feel to the interview they must be able to adapt their line of questioning in response to the comments of the interviewees. Semistructured interviews tend to produce more valid data than structured interviews because there is scope for reflection, probing and clarification of ambiguity. However, there is still a small chance that the prepared headings may not encompass all possibilities or salient issues. It is also far harder to replicate semistructured interviews as there may be no record of the all-important 'trigger' questions that lead to interviewees opening up to the interviewer.

Unstructured interviews (sometimes known as 'informal' interviews) require a great deal of skill. The interviewer does not rely on predetermined issue headings, but simply works from a broad starting-point and attempts to gather data that is as valid as possible. This approach probably offers the greatest insight into the uniqueness of human attitudes and behaviour, but it can be very time-consuming and is almost impossible to replicate. While anti-positivists would regard such an approach as desirable, it is likely that practical factors will intervene (see Chapter 9), and therefore unstructured interviews are less commonly used in sociological research than their more 'ergonomic' alternatives (structured, semistructured).

The interview continues to be an important research technique for sociologists. Denscombe (1991) highlights its use in the study of part-time and flexible working patterns. A large study conducted on behalf on the Economic and Social Research Council (ESRC), entitled 'Social Change and Economic Life', set out to test the prediction that the 1980s would see a huge growth in the so-called 'peripheral' sector of the workforce: part-time workers, casual workers, people on short-term contracts and people working through agencies. The study involved interviews with 6,000 people in six contrasting localities: Aberdeen, Kirkaldy, Rochdale, Coventry, Northampton and Swindon. It combined surveys of employers, individuals and households with a range of intensive case-studies and covered a range of issues. It was found that although working patterns had changed, the proportion of workers who could genuinely be regarded as 'peripheral' at the end of the decade was no more than 3 per cent. Although the number of part-time workers had increased, far from being on the sidelines of the labour force, they had become part of the mainstream of employees and had a fair degree of continuity in employment.

Item D

Religion and Gender

In order to examine the experiences and attitudes of second-generation Asian Muslim women in Britain I carried out research in Coventry and Bradford. Thirty semi-structured interviews were obtained from both men and women in these areas. All of the informants (15 men and 15 women) were aged between 18 and 30 years. The choice of informants was made to try to obtain a broad cross-section of people in terms of age, gender, marital status, education and occupation. Informants were gained from youth centres, Muslim community centres and contacts within the two communities

(*Source*: Charlotte Butler, 'Religion and Gender – Young Muslim Women in Britain', *Sociology Review* 4(3), 1995)

Exercise 7.9

This exercise will enable you to explore an example of the use of interviews in sociological research. Read Item D and answer the following questions.

1. Given that the research in Item D aimed to examine the experiences and attitudes of young Muslim women, why were 50 per cent of the sample men?
2. Why did the age span of the sample fit the research criterion of 'second-generation'?
3. To what extent would semistructured interviews be beneficial in research such as this?
4. When choosing participants, why did Butler 'try to obtain a broad cross-section of people'?
5. How might the way in which Butler obtained her sample have affected the representativeness of the research?

The examples above demonstrate the value of interviews in sociological research and reveal the emergence of an interesting trend – the use of interviews in conjunction with other research techniques, for example, questionnaires. If they are not used as the principal research technique or vehicle for data collection, it is quite common for them to be used as a subsidiary technique to counteract the low validity of questionnaires. Similarly, questionnaires can be used to counteract the low reliability of interviews and assess the representativeness of interview data. When two or more techniques are used as a complementary strategy, this is termed 'methodological pluralism' or 'triangulation'. This approach will be covered in Chapter 9.

Devising and conducting interviews

As with questionnaires, those who are not familiar with research methods often believe mistakenly that interviews are a relatively easy way of collecting data, that they require little preparation as the data are easily obtained (the interviewee is present). We have already seen that this is not true. Good interviewers require a great deal of knowledge about the research topic under consideration, foresight to select appropriate questions and considerable expertise in conducting interviews to ensure that maximum benefit is gained from the time spent.

In the words of Dennison and Kirk (1990), 'most of what we learn comes from doing'. Thus it logically follows that it is easier to appreciate the difficulties involved with interviews if you have attempted to design and conduct one. Exercise 7.10 requires you to do so, and this should increase your understanding of the principles and pitfalls of the interview technique.

Exercise 7.10

This exercise is designed to demonstrate some of the practical considerations involved in designing and conducting interviews. It will give you the opportunity to compare the relative merits of structured and semistructured interviews and to gain an appreciation of difference between interviewing on factual/biographical issues versus 'sensitive' issues.

1. Select a topic from the following list. You will notice that some are biographical/factual and some are 'sensitive' in nature.

   - School/work.
   - Family.
   - Friendships.
   - Hopes/ambitions.

- Fears/worries.
- Regrets/disappointments.
- Personal beliefs/morality.

2. Spend 10 minutes preparing a mini-interview to investigate a single interviewee's opinions on this issue. In order to do this effectively you will have to consider design issues as this will affect what you do and how you do it. For example, will you use a structured (formal) format? If so, why? What will be the benefits over other interview styles? Or will you use an unstructured (informal) format? How might this alter the data you obtain?
3. Conduct a 5-minute mini-interview with a 'volunteer'. In order to make the process more authentic, try not to use a close friend.
4. Afterwards, 'debrief' the participant – that is, tell her or him that the purpose of the interview was to gain experience of conducting an interview, and reassure the interviewee that all responses will be treated with the strictest confidence. This is good practice in ethical terms (see the section 'Ethics' in Chapter 9).
5. Evaluate the design/format and conduct of the interview and assess the quality and quantity of the data you have obtained. Use the following questions to guide you.

Design/format

- Was the interview well thought out?
- Did the questions follow a logical sequence?
- Was the language clear?
- Were any important questions omitted?

Conduct

- How confident were you when conducting the interview?
- What degree of rapport did you achieve with the interviewee?
- To what extent did the interview go as expected?

Data obtained

- How satisfied are you with the *quantity* (amount) of information obtained?
- How satisfied are you with the *quality* (depth/detail) of information obtained?

Interviews – an evaluation

Strengths

1. Interviews are useful for obtaining in-depth or detailed data that is high on validity. This is partly because the data is collected via personal contact

with the people being researched, allowing a rapport to develop that enables the researcher to obtain information that would otherwise remain unknown.

2. In some cases interviews are the only possible way in which the researcher can collect data. For example, when Dobash and Dobash (1980) conducted their study of wife-battering it would clearly have been inappropriate to send a questionnaire to the homes of suspected victims of abuse.

3. Interviews can be used to complement more quantitative methods – for example, questionnaires – and this compensates for low validity. It is quite common for interview data to be collected as part of more macro-level research initiatives to add dimension/perspective to the research data.

4. Feminists, such as Ann Oakley (1980, 2005), have argued that if researchers use the interview techniques in an empathetic manner and not assume a position of authority over the respondent then the material they produce will be fuller, richer and more detailed. In her research into childbirth, motherhood and housework Oakley tried to develop a rapport with her interviewees and often became friends with them. Oakley wanted to break down the notion of the 'objective, value-free' researcher.

Disadvantages

1. Interviews are very time-consuming and costly. Conducting them requires great skill and once the data are collected they can take months to analyse. Even if tape-recorders are used, transcribing data can take ages.

2. Because of the time involved it is likely that a team of interviewers will be employed, and this brings its own difficulties. Unless the interview schedule is very well structured it is difficult to achieve a high degree of standardization. Conversely, if the interview schedule is highly structured the validity of the data will decrease because the prearranged format will limit the potential for individual variation in response.

3. Positivists would question the appropriateness of a technique that invites rapport/contact with those making up the research sample. They would regard this as a threat to the 'objective' nature of the research (see Chapter 6), arguing that researchers cannot hope to be 'value-free' when analysing their findings if they have forged relationships with the interviewees. Subjectivity will cloud their interpretation of results, especially if the interviewers have developed sympathies with the interviewees. This may well occur when interviews involve 'shared' experiences between

interviewer and interviewee, for example, when the interviewee discloses information not previously expressed – abuse, marital discord, infidelity and so on.

Observation

In its broadest sense, observation refers to the act of physically watching events, although when used in sociology it generally involves the added dimension of recording what is seen. Such recording can be systematic, involving some form of quantitative process, for example, a prestructured coding sheet. However, it is not uncommon for researchers to document data in a qualitative way, for example via notes in a research log or diary.

Observation can occur in a laboratory environment as part of the data collection phase of an experiment. However, it is more commonly used as a technique for studying human behaviour and events as they would normally occur in a natural environment. For this reason the technique is seen as high on validity, as access to qualitative data can provide an in-depth picture of the situation under study.

There are many observational techniques available to the researcher. A distinction is made between overt (open) and covert (hidden) observation, and between the participant (direct) and non-participant (indirect), methods. Any possible combination of these techniques can be included, depending on the research aim. For example, if a researcher decides to observe a group from within – that is, to join in with what is going on, she or he can be open about it and ask the group if they mind being studied (overt observation) or they can keep their purpose a secret (covert observation). Similarly researchers can observe without participating and still decide whether or not to conceal their identity.

Each type of observation has its relative merits. The greatest questionmark probably hangs over the ethical dilemma involved in covert observation. Sociologists have a moral responsibility to abide by certain guidelines when conducting their research (see Chapter 9) and this makes failure to gain consent ethically questionable. If consent is not obtained, sociological research can breach ethical guidelines on invasion of privacy and right to withdraw.

Such difficulties have to be traded off against the limitations of overt observation. If a researcher reveals his or her true identity, it may alter the course of the events being studied (see Calvey 2000). A 'desirability effect' may operate, whereby participants act in certain ways to please the researcher. Alternatively, 'demand characteristics' may emerge, whereby the researcher unconsciously communicates expectations about behaviour to the group under study, who then intentionally or unintentionally internalize these expectations and act accordingly. If the researcher's presence alters the natural course of events or behaviour, this obviously negates the validity of the research. The observation does not produce a picture of the truth but a distorted version of reality.

Such a justification was presented by Humphreys (1970) in *Tearoom Trade*, his highly controversial study of homosexuality in men's public toilets in the United States in the late 1960s. Humphreys engaged in participant observation (he adopted the role of 'watch queen' or voyeur) because he claimed it was 'least likely to distort the real world...there is only one way to watch highly discreditable behaviour and that is to pretend to be in the same boat as those engaging in it'. Humphreys also insists that a valid picture of events could not have been obtained had he revealed his identity: 'How "normal" could that activity be? How could the researcher separate the show and the cover from standard procedures of the encounter?'

So while ethical guidelines suggest that it is morally wrong for a researcher deliberately to deceive the subjects of research, Humphreys defends his conduct. He argues that the primary aim of the research scientist should be to 'prevent harm to his respondents', and suggests that as he endeavoured to do so and to protect the identity of the subjects, his research was ethically justified. Interestingly though, he does draw attention to the ambiguity surrounding the word 'protection', by stating: 'We are not, however, protecting a harassed population of deviants by refusing to look at them' (ibid.). This in turn raises an important general issue about the arbitrary or relative nature of defining what is 'ethical'.

Even when researchers are open about their purpose the choice of participant or non-participant observation is not without problems. For example, the very presence of the researcher will inevitably change the nature of group interaction. Imagine you are chatting with friends and someone else joins the group – the group dynamics are inevitably altered. Now imagine that that person asks whether he or she can join you in order to conduct an observation. Imagine further that he or she states that the observation will be on the ethnography of informal groups, and that his or her specific interest is turn-taking in conversation!

With each disclosure the group dynamics will be affected proportionally. To allow someone to join your group is one thing, to allow them to observe you is another. It makes the situation somewhat artificial (people are not used to people joining in for the purpose of 'spying' on them!). Knowing that the researcher's aim is the systematic study of you as an 'informal' group further increases the artificiality of the situation because a value judgement has been applied – that is, you have been regarded and classified or labelled as an 'informal group' – and hence your self-awareness will increase. Some researchers, famously Whyte (1993) but also Patrick (1981), partially revealed their intentions to the 'leader' of the gang who then afforded them some protection when other gang members became too inquisitive. 'Doc' in Whyte's study and 'Tim' in Patrick's were at some times pivotal in maintaining the 'cover' of the respective researchers and thus enabling them to achieve a depth of knowledge which otherwise would not have been possible. Finally, knowledge of the specific area of study will further exaggerate this self-awareness. Turn-taking in conversation will no longer be an unconscious reflex, but a controlled response. You will all be self-conscious and any interaction observed is more likely to be a product of demand characteristics than a natural (innate) or socially conditioned (learned) exchange.

The above example demonstrates the methodological and ethical implications involved when choosing an observation method in terms of the quality of data obtained and the effect upon participants. Another important factor is the effect that choice of method has upon the researcher. Any observational study will inevitably lead to subjective involvement with the group being studied. This could be both beneficial and harmful. On the positive side, the researcher will have the opportunity to develop the empathy so desired by anti-positivists. Personal involvement can be tremendously rewarding. For example Eileen Barker (1984), when relating her experience of participant observation of the Moonies (a religious group), said; 'I usually found my time with the movement interesting, and grew genuinely fond of several individual Moonies.' On the negative side, personal involvement can place the researcher at risk. For example, in his classic study *Glasgow Gang Observed* James Patrick (1981) describes the difficulty involved in studying, at close hand, a violent group in a volatile community:

> I have deliberately allowed some years to pass between the completion of the fieldwork and publication. The main reasons for the delay have been my interest in self-preservation, my desire to protect the members of the gang, and my fear of exacerbating the gang situation in Glasgow which was receiving nationwide attention in 1968 and 1969. Reasons of personal safety also dictate the use of a pseudonym.

Given the controversy surrounding observation as a technique, it is interesting that it continues to be widely used in sociology. Despite the considerable cost and time involved in obtaining data via observation, researchers recognize its worth in uncovering information that could not be gained by other methods. Sim (1994) used observation to investigate the Amish, a distinct religious community (direct descendants of the Swiss Anabaptists) living in the flat lands of central USA and characterized by persistence of custom and slowness to change. Sim was particularly interested in investigating the reality behind the myth of Amish separatism – that is, the reality behind the stereotype: 'In both academic and popular mind the Amish are a group who have as a central goal the maintenance of their unique identity by preserving their distance from mainstream society.'

Williams *et al.*'s (1984) research into football violence highlights the problems of gaining acceptance into a group and how 'hanging around' with the group was part of observation. Like Patrick he was also aware that the pressure to participate in the hooliganism and wider street crime was intense but could also have compromised his position as a researcher.

Item E

Researching the Amish Community

In my research in North East Ohio, the area with the largest population of Amish in the USA, I had the opportunity to observe Amish interaction with the wider community at first hand...

In Kidron, Wayne County, is Lehman's Hardware. This is a large retail store that has been serving the Amish community for decades. It deals in goods which are needed for the Amish lifestyle, such as wood stoves, kerosene lamps, hand-cranked wringers and a variety of tools no longer in common usage outside the Amish community. The store is frequented by numbers of the community with some regularity, especially on the days when auctions are being held in Kidron. Yet Lehman's is more than just a hardware store for the

Amish and non-Amish population of Kidron – it is also a tourist attraction; Lehman's produces its own glossy pamphlets aimed at encouraging the tourist trade, as well as being listed in the Wayne county guide for visitors. Emphasized in the advertising is its long service to the Amish and the fact that they still do business with them...

Lehman's is as much a tourist store as it is a hardware store. Yet the Amish do still shop there. Perhaps they have no other choice, but the Amish I observed were still on friendly terms with the staff. It seemed that if they were not happy with their position as a tourist attraction, they had at least attempted to come to terms with it...

(Adapted from Allan Sim, 'Did You See "Witness"? The Myth of Amish Separatism', *Sociology Review* 3(3), 1994)

Read Item E and answer the following questions.

①Ⓐ 1. Given the reason for Sim's research (to explore the myth of Amish separatism), why was it useful to adopt observation as a technique?
Ⓔ 2. What advantages would using observation in this case have over other methods?
Ⓔ 3. What benefits might have come from using covert participant observation for this piece of research?
ⒶⓃⒺ 4. Why would it have been difficult for Sim to adopt that method?
Ⓔ 5. How would positivists attack the reliability and representativeness of Sim's research?
Ⓔ 6. How might he defend the usefulness of his research findings?

Designing and conducting an observation

Like interviews, observations require careful, preparation. Researchers must decide on the method they will adopt – overt, covert, participant or non-participant – and must gain access (entry) to the research situation. If method adopted is covert, the researcher may have to spend months gaining entry to the group and earning their trust.

Researchers must enter the research situation with preconceived ideas about what they will observe or a specific hypothesis to test. This can make the observation process more economical because the researchers will pay attention only to the information in which they are specifically interested. However it can also mean that they ignore or miss information that emerges naturally and might add to the validity of the data being collected.

Sometimes researchers enter the 'field' with no preconceptions and simply spend some time gaining a feel for the group. This can lead to a hypothesis being formulated or simply to the collection of unstructured information that provides insight but has no specific focus. Such an approach can be advantageous because it reduces the likelihood of missing interesting information.

Alternatively it can mean that the research is much more time-consuming and less ergonomic (maximum productivity for minimum effort). This is because the researcher collects data without an underlying logic or rationale, so it is far harder to judge when enough information has been collected and to retreat from the research situation. Unstructured information is especially hard to analyse compared with structured information.

This brings us to the issue of how the data is collected. Normally, when researchers have preconceived ideas about the topics to be researched they devise a coding sheet to quantify what they observe. Although this is usually supplemented by some form of research log or diary for the recording of more qualitative information, it does mean that the information is relatively easy to interpret and analyse, especially with the help of a computer.

If researchers devise their hypothesis 'in the field', or simply record their impressions of what they observe in an informal way, it is likely that the information will be far more qualitative in nature. This will make it higher in validity but harder to interpret because they will have to rely on manual or computer content analysis. Both techniques are very time-consuming and the results, while valid, are not necessarily reliable or representative.

The best way for you to gain an appreciation of the advantages and drawbacks of observation as a research technique is to design and conduct one, as in Exercise 7.11.

Ⓐ
Ⓔ

Exercise 7.12

A number of studies on aggressive behaviour among preschool children have tended to find that aggressive acts are more frequent among boys than girls (for example, Bardwick, 1992; Maccoby and Jacklin, 1974). Such research is normally conducted via direct observation of free play. The research is interesting because it makes a distinction between physical aggression and verbal aggression – boys demonstrate more of the former and girls more of the latter.

You can test these ideas by conducting a simple observation study in a children's playground or park, as follows.

1. Decide what type of data (that is, quantitative or qualitative) you will collect and how you will record them (that is, on a prepared data coding sheet or in a notebook – if you plan to use a record sheet, you will need to design it in advance).
2. Spend approximately 10 minutes in your chosen location and observe children engaging in free (that is, unstructured) play. Record any gender differences in aggressive acts. (Note: You will need to obtain the parents' or teachers' consent to observe the children.)
3. Analyse your data. To what extent does it mirror previous research findings?
4. Evaluate your observation study:

   (a) How effective was your observation method?
   (b) How useful are your findings?
   (c) What modifications would you make if you were to conduct similar research in the future?

Observations – an evaluation

Strengths

1. Observations provide a detailed, in-depth insight into naturally occurring events or behaviours. For this reason it is assumed they are more likely to produce valid data as there has been less opportunity for artificiality to creep in.
2. Observations enable the meanings behind actions to be revealed. For this reason they are favoured by anti-positivists, who argue that the primary purpose of research should be to portray the world in terms of social actors' values and norms.
3. As research is small-scale, it normally requires only a single researcher. This is particularly important given the huge demands placed on individuals conducting such research. For example, Eileen Barker's (1984) research on the Moonies involved a personal commitment lasting 6 years.

Disadvantages

1. Anti-positivists would criticize observation for being unreliable and unrepresentative. Observational research is small-scale and often lacks social and historical setting.
2. It has been recognized that the mere presence of researchers invalidates the research regardless of whether they are 'open' or 'closed' about their identity or purpose.
3. Involvement with groups through observation leads inevitably to allegations about the degree of subjectivity involved in interpreting findings.
4. Observational research raises ethical and practical questions. It can involve breaching the principles that have been devised to protect the subjects of study and can put the researcher at considerable risk of physical harm or personal discomfort or difficulty.

Ⓚ Ⓤ
Ⓘ Ⓐ

Exercise 7.13

This exercise requires you to review material covered in this chapter to ensure you have a clear understanding of the differences between quantitative and qualitative research techniques. Copy and complete a larger version of the accompanying table to summarize the relative merits of non-experimental research methods.

Non-experimental methods – summary of the relative merits of quantitative and qualitative methods

Technique	Definition	Key study	Advantages	Disadvantages
Quantitative methods: Social surveys Questionnaires				
Qualitative methods: Interviews Observations				

EVALUATION OF QUANTITATIVE VERSUS QUALITATIVE METHODS

Exam focus: writing an essay

Using the above table and the hints provided at the end of Chapter 2 and below, answer the following question:

Compare and contrast the use of quantitative and qualitative research methods in sociological research. (25 marks)

The following will help you to structure your answer.

Introduction

How do the quantitative and qualitative methods differ? Provide a brief definition/description of each.

Main body

(a) Most common use of quantitative methods – provide examples of research projects/key studies/supportive evidence.
(b) Most common use of qualitative methods – provide examples of research projects/key studies/supportive evidence.

Evaluation/conclusion

(a) Explicit appraisal of relative merits of each type of method – strengths/limitations.
(b) Consideration of contemporary developments – now that methods that can be seen as both quantitative and qualitative are becoming more popular, what impact might this have upon sociological research in the future?

Important concepts
the scientific method • experimental/non-experimental methods • interviews • questionnaires • observation • ethics • feminist methodology

---

Critical thinking

- Has the feminist critique of conventional sociological methods rendered quantitative 'scientific' research redundant?
- Can quantitative and qualitative research and data be seen as mutually exclusive?
- How far do ethical considerations and the importance of gaining permission from respondents in research mean that many research techniques are no longer appropriate?

Chapter 8

Contemporary Trends in the Use of Research Techniques

By the end of this chapter you should be able to:

- recognize contemporary research methods that are gaining popularity due to recent developments in sociological thinking
- identify and evaluate examples of studies that use such techniques
- consider the relative merits of the various techniques and understand how they can be used alongside the existing methodology
- understand the contribution that information and communication technology is making to sociological research and how use of virtual on-line environments generates new methods of research

INTRODUCTION

This chapter gives an overview of contemporary trends in the use of research techniques, acknowledging new developments in sociological theory that have inevitably led to changes in research methodology. A starting-point for this exploration is that Payne *et al.* (2004) found that only 5 per cent of papers published in sociology journals used quantitative analysis. Consideration is given to the increasing use of methods that can be regarded as both quantitative and qualitative, the rise of comparative research in response to globalization, the forward march of less-known techniques and the impact of information and communication technology on sociological research.

QUANTITATIVE AND QUALITATIVE METHODS

Case-studies

The term 'case-study' refers to a detailed investigation of a single research area – for example, an individual, a geographical region, a group, an organization, a community, a nation or a social phenomenon. Case-studies are both quantitative and qualitative because they are normally based on both statistical data and more in-depth or detailed information drawn from a variety of sources.

In a review of the uses and limitations of case-studies in sociology, Platt (1993) highlights the ambiguity surrounding the use of the term case-study. She argues that, in particular, the term has been associated with qualitative methods, with older writers having life histories in mind while more recent writers think first of participant observation. To ease the confusion Platt (ibid.) suggests that a simple definition of case-study be adopted:

> Our definition of a case study is, then, one in which there may be only one case or may be more, but the crucial feature is that the individuality of each case is retained, and the numbers of cases which fall into any category are not treated as important. The cases in question may be individual people, small groups, organisations, communities, nations or events. Case-studies may stand alone, or may be used as one part of a larger research enterprise which also draws upon other types of work; in the latter case, the function of the case-study depends on its role in the larger enterprise.

Exercise 8.1

1. Read the following list of research studies and, in the light of Platt's definition, decide:

   (a) Which ones could be termed case-studies?
   (b) Which ones could not?
   (c) Are there any which are difficult to classify? Why?

Research studies

- An in-depth investigation into a schizophrenic person's experience of mental illness.
- Attendance at the most popular preserved steam railways – a statistical analysis.
- A project on fish stocks, by sea area and selected species.
- Television viewing and social class.

- The sociological significance of the Ford Capri in British youth culture.
- From Croydon to Crawley – an insight into the development of the A23 road link.
- Roman Catholics' attitude towards contraception and abortion.
- 'Neckin' in Newbiggin' – an historical study of the mating habits of Geordie teenagers.

Ⓐ 2. Record your answers in an extended version of the table here. Some examples are provided to help you get started.

Case-studies	Not case-studies
Schizophrenic's experience of mental illness	Attendance at the most popular preserved steam railways – a statistical analysis

Difficult to classify why?
'Neckin' in Newbiggin' – a historical study of the mating habits of Geordie teenagers: could be based on information drawn from a variety of general sources rather than a single in-depth study.

Until relatively recently, case-studies were not really regarded as a central research method. In part, this could have been because they do not involve a representative sample and are difficult to generalize from. Positivists would strongly criticize case-studies because of these limitations.

However, case-studies have enjoyed a revival and are becoming a much more commonly used research technique. Platt (1993) suggests that this may be because researchers are now realizing that it is foolish to dismiss case-studies outright simply because they do not live up to the requirements of the 'ideal' study. Instead, more consideration is being given to the aim of research when choosing methods. Researchers are realizing that because different studies have different aims, different methods will be appropriate. If the aim is to produce a thorough overview of individuals, groups, events and so on that combines both qualitative (statistical, numerical) and quantitative (in-depth, detailed) information, then the case-study may well be the perfect choice.

Platt investigates the use of the case-study in sociological research and suggests that it offers a number of benefits to empirical researchers (see Exercise 8.2). First, intensive case-studies can throw light on the distinctive features of influential historical figures (for example, Charles Darwin, Mahatma Gandhi) as well as many wider issues – for example, unique historical events such as the rise of capitalism. Platt also suggests that comparative research enables researchers systematically to study events such as this. This involves comparing several capitalist countries in order to identify common features, although such data will inevitably be less detailed and less useful than an in-depth investigation of one country.

Platt argues that even when the case being studied is atypical or 'deviant', it can tell us much about existing theories:

> A deviant case is one which does not fit the existing theory or empirical generalisations – or at least appears not to do so. If a case is truly deviant even on closer examination, this refutes the generalisation or means that it must be modified. If it turns out not to be deviant really, this gives stronger confirmation to the generalisation than it had before. (Ibid.)

Hobbs and Dunningham (1998) used their case-study of individuals involved in loose-knit local networks of organized crime in a northern town to hypothesize about the changing nature of local and international criminal networks. Their research shows how criminals begin their 'career' locally and, much like a legitimate business would, look constantly for opportunities to expand and develop their profits. Sometimes this can involve linking with global networks such as drug-smuggling or even emigrating. Similarly, Plummer (1995) has used individual case-studies to illustrate 'newly emerging narratives' about such sexual issues such as 'coming out' as a gay person, rape stories and recovery stories of those who have suffered abuse.

Platt also highlights the usefulness of large-scale case-studies in sociological research, suggesting that this technique can be at least as valuable as large-scale quantitative work, if not more so. It enables researchers to investigate how and why numerical minorities behave differently from the majority of those included in the study.

Many sociologists have used case-studies in their research. For example, Goldthorpe *et al.*'s (1969) *Affluent Worker* study on manual workers' attitudes towards politics, work and relationships in a test of embourgeoisement would fall within Platt's definition of a case-study. Gallie's (1978) study of industrial relations and work attitudes at two oil refineries in France and two in Britain is another example. In addition, although Willis (1977) used a wide variety of research methods (participant observation, group discussion, informal interviews, diaries and so on) in his study of a school in England in the 1970s, it could be interpreted as a case-study owing to its focus on the experience of schooling from the perspective of a small group of 12 working-class boys known as the 'lads'.

(E) 1. Draw up a two-column table and list of the advantages and disadvantages of case-studies. Use this to write an evaluation of their usefulness as a research technique.

(E) 2. Compare your ideas with those listed below. How good are your evaluation skills?

Case-studies – an evaluation

Strengths

1. Case-studies provide an in-depth, detailed insight into specific, unique cases and reveal information that is often overlooked with larger-scale research techniques (for example, information about minority cases and atypical or diverse groups).
2. Although qualitative data does not necessarily guarantee validity, the use of raw interview transcripts and observation notes in case-studies can mean that they are reasonably valid.
3. As case-studies often involve quantitative data too, the reliability of the research should be reasonable, although it must be accepted that such data may be quite small-scale.
4. Case-studies provide a reasonably sensitive research method for issues not previously studied or which are difficult to study. They provide a comprehensive insight into areas that may not have been well known or clearly understood prior to the study.

Disadvantages

1. Questions have been raised about the representativeness of case-studies. It has been argued that a single case cannot provide representative data. However, this is controversial. The researcher will claim it is representative of the group being studied. Critics will argue that it is not representative as it does not mirror wider society. The main reason for this is that sampling to select a research group has not taken place.
2. The debate on representativeness has implications for generalization. It is argued that one important weakness of case-studies is that generalizations cannot be made because they are not representative. Platt (1993) defends case-studies in this respect, arguing that just because a representative sample is not drawn at the start of research, this does not mean

that generalizations cannot be made. For example, many surveys have drawn excellent random samples from one large town, which makes the research a case-study of that town, irrespective of whether or not it is intended as such. So Platt argues that if ambiguities in sampling mean that we cannot generalize from a representative sample, we cannot really condemn case-studies for lacking generalizability. Platt goes on to suggest that much sociological research makes false generalizations, whereas one strength of case-studies is that they make no claims to generalizability.

3. If there is only one case or just a few of them it is too easy to find a theoretical interpretation that will fit. Many interpretations could be devised that are compatible with such limited data, so any interpretation put forward cannot be treated as valid even for the cases in question. Platt (ibid.) responds to this by arguing that if there are rich and detailed data on many aspects of the case(s), it may be more of a challenge to find an interpretation that fits all the information than it would be to find a more superficial generalization for a larger number of cases. Moreover, if a prediction about a single case is confirmed, the theory has survived a very severe test because it is very unlikely that such a result could have come about by chance.

Documentary and content analysis

Documentary and content analysis refers to the secondary analysis of published or unpublished information and/or data. A common error is to assume that documents and contents are qualitative in nature, but in reality documents are likely to include numerical data and other quantitative information. Examples of qualitative documents include written diaries, journals, personal records, newspapers, books and so on, but content analysis can also be performed on the products of the mass media, including video footage, advertisements and so on.

Examples of quantitative documents include *Social Trends* data, produced annually by the Government Statistical Service in document format, bound versions of official statistics – such as the Home Office Statistical Bulletin – official crime statistics, United Nations Population Fund data on world population growth and so on. With the rise of new technology, rather than such data being made available in printed form, they are increasingly being made available on CD-ROM or the internet. There are a number of statistical websites that are freely accessible containing a massive range of official data from annual patterns of examination results through trends in living arrangements to data about population composition. See the following websites for useful information: www.nationalstatistics.gov.uk and www.issp.org/

Content analysis

Content analysis can be a quantitative and/or qualitative method often associated with the study of the media, although it is also used to research such areas as children's books (Lobban, 1974), teenage girls' magazines (McRobbie, 1996), newspapers and TV new coverage (GMUG, 1970s, 1980s, 1990s, 2000s). The quantitative method usually involves defining a set of categories and then classifying the material in terms of the frequency of appearance. Qualitative content analysis can involve a selection of categories or criteria used to carry out an analysis of the 'under-the-surface' meanings of those categories or criteria. Semiology – the study of signs or signifiers in all forms of communication – can be carried out to investigate both the face-value understanding of the image or text (denotative code) and the underlying, under-the-surface context of what is being displayed (connotative code).

Pawson (1995) identifies four main types of content analysis:

- *Formal* – This involves a systematic sample of features or texts which are then counted.
- *Thematic* – Choice of a specific area to decode the underlying intentions of the authors.
- *Textual* – Examining of the use of language and particular categories of words alongside visual images to create an effect.
- *Audience analysis* – Focus on the response of the audience to the massages, images and language to check the researcher's interpretation alongside that of the audience.

The Glasgow University Media Group (GUMG) is well known for its wide range of content analysis of the media. Beginning with the agenda-setting techniques of TV news reporting of industrial relations and news bias generally in the 1970s, the reporting of war news in the 1980s and then, in the 1990s, their change of emphasis to look at the impact of the media on the audience using group discussions and activities, GUMG work has been used to test the cultural hegemony argument alongside some elements of Marxist theory. Their research has been shown how the media can be systemically biased in favour of views of dominant groups in society. However, in *Seeing and Believing* (Philo, 1990) they show, like Stuart Hall, that audiences do not always accept or believe what they have been told. Philo and Miller (2002) have combined a variety of different approaches to the study of the media – looking at the presentation of content, how the audience interpret and respond to it, and also how the wider social and political contexts of the messages are created; this has been termed the 'circuit of communication'. A historical context is also used in their research into the Israeli–Palestinian conflict (Philo and Berry, 2006) and an analysis of the ways reporting and coverage of the conflict relates to and is based around the beliefs, understanding and attitudes of the TV audience (Philo and Berry, 2004). Berry and Philo found:

> There is a preponderance of official 'Israeli perspectives', particularly on BBC 1, where Israelis were interviewed or reported over twice as much as Palestinians. On top of this, US politicians who support Israel were very strongly featured. They appeared more than politicians from any other country and twice as much as those from Britain. (pp. 196–7)

The treatment of various social groups in the media has been the subject of much research. Studies of the representation of gender, age, ethnicity, sexuality, disability and social class in the media have shown a consistent bias against and stereotyping of women, younger and older people, the disabled, homosexuals, black people and the working class over a considerable period of time (Broadcasting Standards Commission, 1999). (See Exercise 8.3.)

Exercise 8.3

Choose one category from gender, age, sexuality, ethnicity, social class or disability. Draw up a grid with as many stereotypes of the group as you can think of. Choose a TV genre such as soaps, drama, documentary, adverts and so on and watch your chosen genre on TV over a period of days with your grid in front of you. Note down the number of times a stereotype appears. At the end of the period of time you have chosen, add up the scores from your grid and write a short summary and evaluate your findings. You may encounter more positive portrayals of certain groups such as homosexuals. What does this tell us about representation in the media?

Alternatively you could develop a more qualitative (denotative/connotative) approach and choose a particular programme or character(s) being portrayed and carry out a semiological analysis of their portrayal.

(See Link Exercise 8.1 below to help you organize your grid.)

Content analysis can be recorded in computer databases and only relevant information need ever make it into print. This is a particularly interesting development for sociologists as it enables rapid global comparisons to be made between nations. Increasingly, technological innovation is streamlining data analysis to the point where the contents of massive databases can be sifted at the touch of a button.

Hence the potential of documentary and content analysis in sociology is growing rapidly. Sociology students have no doubt been able to benefit from this new technology, as more and more educational institutions will link up with sociological resources throughout the world and have instant access to contemporary and classic sociological studies, ICT facilities and statistical programming packages such as PASW (formerly known as SPSS).

Research diaries

Dyson (1995) highlights the role that research diaries can play in the research process. He argues that keeping a research diary can have enormous potential 'beyond its central role in a multi-method piece of fieldwork anchored by the method of data collection'. Dyson suggests that all research has a social context and that researchers' place in this context (including of course their role in contributing to the creation of the social context) should be thought about critically. Since access to research situations usually has to be negotiated in some form or other, and to the extent that research subjects are not passive 'respondents' but actively try to create the terms and conditions of their participation, then the research process is always far more extensive than the data collection itself.

Item A

Keeping a Research Diary

The usefulness of research diaries goes beyond keeping a factual account of contacts and dates. It is part of a process of self-reflection by the researcher about their role in the research. All research exhibits power relationships, and the mutual roles of researcher and researched are negotiated rather than given. This negotiation can be recorded in the research diary and is important in fixing the context of the research, which is always much more than the mere collection of relevant data. Diaries can contribute to the triangulation of data.

Exercise 8.4

Read Item A and answer the following questions.

(I)(A) 1. What do you think Item A means when it says that 'All research exhibits power relationships'?

(I)(A) 2. What do you think is meant by the term 'triangulation'? (Hint: If you are unsure, see the section on 'methodological pluralism' at the end of Chapter 9.)

(U)(A) (E) 3. Why is it important for researchers to be aware of the negotiation of roles in research?

(An)(E) 4. Why might it be useful to keep a research diary, beyond the reasons given in the Item?

Dyson has demonstrated several advantages of keeping a research diary as a record of primary research. Research diaries also provide secondary data to other sociologists wishing to find out about the way the research was conducted – that is, the research process. This background knowledge could be important in ensuring that any research findings are viewed in the appropriate context. Some researchers may wish systematically to analyse the research process in order to evaluate the methodology of the research or uncover the basic features of the research so that it can be replicated or modified. Research diaries clearly have many practical applications for sociologists and sociology students alike.

While documentary and content analysis has become increasingly sophisticated and methodologically more diverse since the work of Glenys Lobban, the basic principles of quantifying content and analysing data can still be applied to shed valuable light on new areas of sociology. For example, documentary and content analysis can be used to investigate the truth behind postmodern thinking on the media and popular culture. The following exercise is designed to enable you to do this.

Item B

Postmodernism, Popular Culture and the Mass Media

Chapter 4 highlighted the thinking behind postmodernism and gave examples of post-modernist analysis. One important issue within this perspective is the claim that the media are responsible for consumerism. It is argued that in a postmodern world, people consume images and signs for their own sake – that is, we now buy the packaging and design of goods rather than the goods themselves. Advertising is no longer about promoting the quality or usefulness of a product. Instead the product features less and less directly, and the emphasis is on the style and look of the ad, its clever quotations from popular culture and art, mini-sagas and joking quips at the expense of advertising itself. Strinati (1992) sums this up with the following example: 'Once Guinness was good for us. Now all we see is an actor drinking a glass without any positive suggestions as to why we should drink it too.'

Link Exercise 8.1

This exercise will provide you with another experience of conducting content analysis. It will also enable you to test the validity of the postmodernist ideas on popular culture explored in this book. Read Item B and carry out the following task.

Using either a selection of magazines or a video recording of television advertisements, attempt content analysis of media output to test the claim that advertising today concentrates more on form (style, image and so on) than function (usefulness, quality and so on). To do this effectively you will need to consider the following issues: Use the material above on quantitative/qualitative content analysis as a guide and the grids below to help you.

1. Which *medium* will you analyse, for example, teenage magazines, TV?
2. How will this affect the type of data obtained?
3. How much *content* will be needed?
4. How will you *classify* the adverts – function, form, 50/50?
5. What happens if two different adverts appear for the same product – will you classify each separately?
6. How will you *record* your data? (Hint: You will probably need to devise a summary chart like the one here.)

Content analysis – data record

Nature of advert

Brand/product	Function	Form	50/50	Notes
Guinness – stout				Man drinking – no justification.
Dettol – detergent				Man cleaning work surface in kitchen.
Nike – trainers				Basketball game but close up on slogan 'Just do it'.

7. How will you *analyse* your data? (Hint: You could produce descriptive statistics such as percentages and present them in a table like the one below.)

Content analysis – data breakdown

No. of adverts	% function	% form	% 50/50	Support for Strinati?	
				Yes.	☐
				No.	☐
				Hard to tell.	☐

8. How will you interpret your findings? (Hint: You might aim to identify trends, for example, some products are more likely to be promoted by function, such as detergents, while some are more likely to be promoted by form, such as clothing.)

Documentary and content analysis – an evaluation

Strengths

1. Documentary and content analysis encourages researchers not to take information at face value, but to adopt a critical stance when interpreting data.
2. Sometimes it is the only way systematically to deconstruct sociological knowledge and test hypotheses about the way that reality is constructed.
3. Analysing the content of some documents may be the only way to gain access to information. There are many areas in sociology where our knowledge is restricted to data contained in documents. It is important that this information is considered systematically in order that our impressions and inferences are as objective as possible.

Disadvantages

1. The success of documentary and content analysis is largely dependent upon the quality of the data available. If the data are incomplete or of poor quality, any analysis will be partial.
2. The methods can be time-consuming and require considerable skill of analysis and interpretation.For example, to interpret statistical databases

requires a degree of mathematical competence and, increasingly, computer literacy. To interpret more qualitative information requires focused analytical skills.

3. Any conclusions drawn will be only as valuable as the initial data. For example, the 'social facts' argument (see Chapter 6) must be considered when interpreting quantitative documents. The debate on subjective interpretation of events creeps into the analysis of more qualitative documents.

ETHNOGRAPHIC RESEARCH

Ethnographic research is a way of doing research that for all practical purposes began with the work of Western social anthropologists studying non-Western societies in the early years of this century (Hammersley, 1992). It developed from the work of Bronislaw Malinowski, who devised a new approach to anthropology involving the study of individuals at close range. In order to document their lives 'from the native point of view', Malinowski lived with the people he was studying. His work became very influential and led to the development of a new trend in social and cultural anthropology – first-hand contact with other cultures.

Hammersley (1992) documents the subsequent rise of ethnographic research in sociology. One famous example of the approach is from the Chicago School's work on the ecology of crime and deviance. A comprehensive review of this approach can be found in Lawson and Heaton (1999), but in summary the Sociology Department of the University of Chicago proposed a theory linking crime to such issues as urban development patterns, loss of community and high population turnover. With the demise of the Chicago School the popularity of ethnography declined, but in recent times it has re-emerged as a practical and imaginative research technique.

Exercise 8.5

While it is difficult to define ethnographic research precisely, Hammersley (1992) identifies a number of important characteristics. This exercise is designed to highlight the main features of ethnography and enable you to evaluate its relative merits. Copy the table here. Read the outline of the main features, then think about and complete the advantages and disadvantages columns.

Characteristics of ethnographic research

Distinctive features	Advantages	Disadvantages
The study of one or a small number of cases, often over a lengthy period of time (certainly days, perhaps even years)		
The adoption of a wide initial focus (that is, a general idea) at the outset of research, rather than the testing of narrowly defined hypotheses.		
A range of types of data are employed, not just one: observational and/or interview data are usually the main source but use can be made of documents, official statistics or questionnaire data.		
There is minimal prestructuring of the data collected. Instead detailed field notes are written, documented events in qualitative rather than quantitative form. Audio and video data can also be used.		
Analysis generally takes the form of verbal descriptions and explanations, with quantification and statistical analysis taking a subordinate role at most.		

(Adapted from Hammersley, 1992)

Hammersley (1992) argues that ethnography is based on distinctive assumptions about the nature of the social world and how it should be studied:

- *Naturalism* – The idea that social research should be aimed at understanding naturally occurring human behaviour.
- *Understanding* – Recognition that human actions differ from the behaviour of physical objects because they involve the interpretation of stimuli and the construction of responses. This implies that if we are to explain human behaviour effectively, we must gain an understanding of the cultural perspectives or distinctive world views upon which they are based.
- *Discovery* – 'Research is seen as devoted to exploring the nature of social phenomena, towards discovering their character, rather than being limited to the testing of explicit hypotheses. It is argued that if one approaches a phenomena [*sic*] with a set of hypotheses to test one may fail to discover

the true nature of the phenomena, being blinded by the assumptions built into the hypotheses.' (Ibid.)

One area of social life that Hammersley highlights to demonstrate the large body of ethnographic studies that have accumulated in recent years is police work. Ethnographic studies of police work have been carried out in many different geographical areas (inner city, suburban, rural), covering various types of policing (constables on the beat or in their cars, detective work, specialized squads and so on) and using a variety of research strategies. Sometimes the studies have been done by the police officers themselves, covertly or overtly; but more often than they have been conducted by outsiders who have negotiated access for the purposes of research. According to Hammersley (1992), the aim of this research has been to

> map the various facets of police work and how these vary between places and over time. Equally, there have been attempts to explain both the constant and the variable features of policing, and to understand its role in modern societies.

Although ethnographic research has enjoyed a revival in recent years, it would be wrong to assume that it is accepted by all researchers as a legitimate and desirable technique. While it is recognized that such research can overcome some of the limitations of the more conventional approaches, it is still criticized. Certain sociologists have paid attention to the biased nature of ethnography, most notably feminists, who have argued that ethnography must be transformed into a collaborative process where the distinction between researcher and the researched has to be removed if it is to serve the goals of feminism.

However, criticisms about lack of objectivity have been weakened by recent philosophical trends (poststructuralism, postmodernism and so on – see Chapter 4), as these throw doubt on the very possibility of a true, objective representation of the social world:

> These philosophies emphasize that all views are constructions and reflect the socio-historical circumstances and interests of the person producing it. There is no 'God's eye view' which stands above the social world: ethnographers are necessarily part of the world they describe and their descriptions are structured by their place in that world. Furthermore, it is suggested, the claim to be able to produce an objective, neutral account of social reality effectively serves as a device by which voices from some

social locations –usually those of white, middle-class, Western males - seek dominance over those of others. (Ibid., pp. 21–2).

In response to these points, researchers have taken a more measured approach to ethnographic study based within a broader critical perspective towards sociological research, largely informed by feminism. The 'critical social research' perspective argues for the acceptance that knowledge or truth cannot just be discovered through study. Knowledge cannot be separated from values and attitudes, and therefore researchers are affected by those values and attitudes in their choice of topic and the ways they conduct their research. They argue that 'commonsense, taken-for-granted' values must be viewed critically to find out what lies under the surface, after which research can take place which may generate new knowledge (Harvey, 1990). Feminists like Oakley used this approach to show how housework, childcare, childbirth and motherhood had all been viewed in sociology from a male-dominated commonsense perspective that devalued women's work and women's role in society generally and saw what women do as unimportant or secondary. Other research adopting this approach has focused on oppressed groups or oppressive structures in society – Westwood's (1984) study of Asian and white female factory workers and Mac an Ghaill's (1994) study of the development of masculinity in young homosexual and heterosexual males are two examples.

Cyberethnography

Cyberethnography is defined as the study of online interaction (Gajjala, 1997). It can be used in chatrooms, via bulletin boards, emailing lists, mobile phones and virtual learning environments (VLEs).

With the increasing use of the internet for work, education, leisure and communication as a 'virtual culture', and as we all become networked into an increasingly global communication web, it makes sense to study these new forms of interaction sociologically in the society in which we live. Indeed, Wellman and Haythornthwaite (2002) argue that the internet is now so integral to our lives that it is embedded in everyday life. Cyberethnography is therefore growing as a means to research the study of online interaction, communication and communities. However there is some debate about the nature of 'community' and whether there are similarities/differences between online/virtual communities and physical communities. (Ward, 1999). The notion of community then has implications for the study of online networks – with the ethical issues of traditional ethnography being reproduced in the discussions about and implementation of cyberethnography. Ward argues that cyberethnography can be used as a method in its own right but also as a supplement to conventional methods such as interviewing and observation but basically it is a means to be become involved in internet culture as a participant and an observer. Ward used semistructured interviews in cyberethnography of two feminist online communities, modifying the interview process to match the facilities available on the websites and enabling the participants to take the 'lead role' in establishing the nature of their group.

Fay (2007) reviews the development of cyberethnography and concludes that there is little to gain from retaining a binary view of the 'real' and the 'virtual' community. Rather, online communities both share many characteristics with real ones, but also have some distinctive aspects from them. Virtual communities inhabit the real world, in the sense that there are social, political and economic contexts for those who participate, that enable and limit the practices of such communities. On the most basic level, having no access to virtual technologies will prevent participation. Such access is structured, with many parts of the developing world having much less access than the developed world. In addition, Urry (2003) argues that there is a relationship between face-to-face meetings and online meetings, in that where both occur within a network, stronger emotional bonds emerge that have the effect of increasing the commitment of participants to sustain the community in the virtual world.

Whereas much cyberethnography has concentrated on academic online communities, for example those that arise from conferences or a shared academic interest, the emergence of social networking technology, as exemplified by MySpace or Facebook, provides a further area on research. The importance of these social networking sites is demonstrated by the millions of users, with over half of American 12-to-17-year-olds being on them (Lenhart *et al.*, 2007). Fontes and O'Mahony (2008) have used in-depth semistructured interviews to explore the use of social networking sites such as MSN using instant messaging. Their research is also based on exploratory online ethnography to investigate the little-known area of social networking. They are aware however of problems such as representation in sampling and validity of material from respondents as well as the limitations of remote or 'virtual' forms of communication in this type of research.

Rybas and Gajjala (2007) suggest that one of the key differences between ethnographic and cyberethnographic research is the relationship between the researcher and the researched. While traditional ethnography calls for immersion in a culture in order to understand it, they argue that there is a stage in cyberethnography that makes this process different. In order to participate in an online community, the researcher has to produce an online self. This is done through typing and image manipulation – 'typing oneself into being'.

Other participants are also constructing their 'selves' through the act of typing and therefore both researcher and researched exist as double subjects, the one doing the typing and the one that is typed. It is not therefore that a researcher is immersed in a culture, but that the constructed researcher is an active creator of the culture. This raises questions of bias and influence that are difficult to overcome.

Another area of difficulty is that traditional methods of social network analysis are not easily applied to cybercommunities, where the boundaries of the community are unclear and constantly shifting. Nor is it easy to assess the strength of ties between participants in an online community, as interaction does not necessarily mean attachment in such virtual spaces (see Schlager *et al.*, 2009). The automated collection of interactions enabled by the technology could provide a sociogram of the patterns of actions in an online community, but do not tell the researcher anything about the meaningfulness of such interactions to the participants. Research has found that cyber communities fostered weak ties, and while this was fine for information flows, for more focused activity and development of participants, they did not assist the emergence of the 'social capital' that was the object of such communities (for example teachers).

Moreover, traditional methods of data collection, both quantitative and qualitative, have limited application in online networks. Even small groups of participants are constantly changing, interacting and withdrawing seemingly randomly, making investigation difficult. On the other hand there are large data sets of use available that need a great deal of time and expertise in large-scale quantitative analysis, to the extent that makes them difficult to analyse. Schlager *et al.* (2009) therefore argue that new software tools need to be developed that would allow the capture not only of the products of interaction (this is what is analysed at the moment) but also the processes (much more difficult to get a view of) whereby the products emerge. In developing new software, designers need to take account not just of frequency counts but of establishing the meaning of interaction and the utility of the network to participants. One idea would be to analyse the 'uptake' of network artifacts (ideas, resources and so on), not just by those involved in directly producing them but also by other members of the network. On the other hand, Jankowski *et al.* (2004) argue that most research into the internet and online communities uses modifications of existing techniques, such as electronic questionnaires, rather than developing new, ever more technological methods. Nevertheless, new strategies are developing, including mapping exercises (of internet use), hyperlink analyses and interactive electronic interviews (contemporaneous or time-stretched) (see Hine, 2005).

Ethnographic research – an evaluation

Strengths

1. Owing to its wide initial focus, ethnographic research could be said to produce varied data that do not reflect the actions and interpretations (predetermined hypotheses) of the researcher. Thus, it would be supported by interpretive sociologists.
2. The range of data collection techniques (methodological pluralism) should mean that the research is relatively high on validity and reliability.
3. Because ethnographic research uses both quantitative and qualitative data, it provides a good example of how the two methods can be integrated successfully in sociological research.
4. Cyberethnography could complement traditional ethnographic research by providing an additional means to explore and understand social processes in text-based virtual space.

Disadvantages

1. Positivists would criticize ethnographical research for lacking specific hypotheses. Without this, in their view, research lacks scientific credibility.
2. They would also argue that it is difficult for researchers to be objective if at the outset they are unsure about which issue will be studied. Any direction the research takes will be due to subjective interpretation and may be unethical.
3. The absence of a specific hypothesis also has funding implications, as it is far harder to secure funding for research that is not directed at a specific, quantifiable (measurable) issue. Most funding councils would not regard discovery-style research as cost-effective.
4. Owing to the loose initial focus, ethnographic research can be very time-consuming. It may take many months of research to arrive at a suitable focus and many unnecessary data may be collected during this time.
5. Collating of data obtained through a variety of methods may be logistically difficult. It is far harder to present coherent findings when there is no central theme (research hypothesis/aim) to pull the research together.
6. Cyberethnography in particular could misrepresent the communities being studied because of the cultural assumptions relied upon by the researcher in studying online groups.

COMPARATIVE AND LONGITUDINAL RESEARCH

Comparative research, as its name suggests, involves making comparisons between individuals, groups or sections of society. These comparisons can take the form of cross-sectional studies that compare different groups at one distinct point in time. Taylor's (1994) research on firearms is an example of such research. Taylor compares patterns of private gun usage in two capitalist countries – Britain and the United States – in a attempt to establish whether the current 'moral panic' (social outcry) in Britain about firearms is justified. However this research could just as easily be termed 'cross-cultural', as it compares countries with distinct cultural patterns.

Sheehy's (1974) study of the predictable crises of adult life, *Passages*, is another example of cross-sectional research. Sheehy compared the experiences of individuals at various stages of adult life to investigate whether distinct developmental stages could be identified. Instead of undertaking a longitudinal study of adulthood, Sheehy attempted to capture several groups, of different ages at one specific point, the general goal being to map developmental stages.

Item C

Passages

My own work progressed in stages. It began with an innocent's excitement...which was quickly followed by panic. Suppose ten people took what I said seriously? Most of us don't influence ten strangers in our lives. The responsibility was awesome. I became a grind: reading psychiatry, psychology, biographies, novels, longitudinal studies and bloody dull statistical printouts. I was a million laughs at dinner parties, so I stopped going, or shut up and passed the pistachio nuts...

In all I collected 115 life stories. Many of the couples I saw together, after first reconstructing their biographies separately. Those sessions supplied a fascinating complexity and threw a good deal of light onto individual psychology.

The people I chose to study belonged to America's 'pacesetter group' – healthy, motivated people who either began in or have entered the middle class, though some began in poverty, even ghettos. I chose this group for several reasons...

The people in this book range in age from 18 to 55. The men include lawyers, doctors, chief executives and middle managers, ministers, professors, politicians, and students, as well as men in the arts, the media, the sciences, and those who run their own small businesses. I sought out top achieving women as well and also followed the steps of many traditional nurturing women.

> Almost all of the people I interviewed asked to remain anonymous ...
> Although many of the respondents were raised in small towns, the urban centres to which they have gravitated include New York, Los Angeles, Washington, San Francisco, Chicago, Detroit, Boston, New Haven, and Dayton, Ohio, the city considered by posters as the home of the average American couple.
>
> (Adapted from Gail Sheehy, *Passages: Predictable Crises of Adult Life*. London: Bantam Books, 1974)

Exercise 8.6

This exercise will enable you to explore how Sheehy conducted her research. Read Item C and answer the following questions.

1. Why was Sheehy ethically right to regard her responsibility as 'awesome'?
2. What benefits could have been gained from Sheehy's reading of published material?
3. Are data from life stories likely to be higher on reliability or validity? Why?
4. To what extent was Sheehy's sample representative? Give reasons for your answer.
5. What might be the drawbacks of focusing on 'America's pacesetter group'?
6. Despite this, Sheehy claims to have chosen the group for several reasons. Suggest two possible reasons.
7. If the people in a study wish to remain anonymous, what steps can a researcher take to prevent them from being identified?
8. Evaluate the relative merits of drawing at least some of the sample from a city considered by pollsters as the home of the average American couple?

Cross-cultural studies aim to enhance our understanding of human behaviour in societies by investigating the distinctive features of different cultures. A classic example of this approach is provided by the anthropologist Margaret Mead (1935), who in the 1920s and 1930s conducted a series of studies on islands in the Pacific to determine whether gender roles are universal or the product of culture. She suggested that if gender roles are the product of cultural factors it should be easy to identify cultural variation in behaviour between different societies throughout the world. Her research (documented in all major sociology textbooks) suggests there is evidence to support this assumption and that gender roles are 'socially constructed' (shaped by social norms and expectations) rather than biologically determined (shaped by nature). The significance of this finding speaks volumes for the value of cross-cultural comparative research.

Normally, comparative research aims to establish the degree of similarity or difference between data sets or to uncover patterns and trends in data. For this reason, such research is often favoured by structuralists who are interested in the underlying factors that govern human society. A classic example of comparative research is Durkheim's (1897/1951) study of suicide. Durkheim compared the suicide rates in nine European countries in an attempt to reveal common factors that might explain suicide (see the section on positivism in Chapter 3).

Partly because Durkheim's research was heavily criticized and partly because of the rise of antipositivism and interpretive sociology in the 1950s, the structuralist form of comparative research declined in popularity. For example, action theorists emphasized the uniqueness of human behaviour and therefore regarded large-scale, macro-level comparisons of human beings as inappropriate. However, comparative research retained its status among staunch positivists and many university sociology departments continued to rely on comparative methods to aid their understanding of macro issues. In particular, much research on social stratification and social mobility adopted a comparative stance when assessing objective and subjective social class and social mobility issues.

More recently, factors such as globalization and the rise of new technology have led to comparative research enjoying a revival. Its value is being recognized increasingly in terms of making global comparisons between nations, as sociologists acknowledge that the societal characteristics of single nations can no longer be viewed in isolation, but rather should be viewed as being affected by, if not the result of, global forces (see Exercise 8.7).

Cherrington (1993) provides an example of the role that comparative research can play in increasing our understanding of crime and deviance. Her research concentrates on the growing drugs problem in China, as identified by the Chinese authorities. Owing to the lack of reliable data and in-depth studies it is difficult to draw conclusions about the extent and nature of the current problem, although Cherrington demonstrates how British sociological theory and research can be usefully applied to aid understanding of drug abuse in China – a country with different social, cultural and political norms:

This involves drawing comparisons between both societies and considering how the reactions of the respective authorities affected the subsequent developments. This attempt to understand the situation in China can lead to a reconsideration of what is happening within the British context. (Ibid.)

Another example of comparative research is that by Stockman *et al.* (1992), who investigated the impact of industrialization upon societies. They were particularly interested in whether industrialization causes societies to 'converge' (that is, increasingly resemble each other in their institutional patterns) or 'diverge' (develop alternative responses to similar dilemmas of social organization and become increasingly different).

Stockman *et al.* focused on one aspect of the industrialization process that might be assumed to be universal among women – the separation of home from work and the changing role of women – that is, from participants in the household economy in pre-industrial times (cottage industry) to participants in solely the domestic sphere. Stockman *et al.* predicted that if the 'convergence' thesis was accurate, then this pattern should be universal (occur throughout the world).

Item D

Women's Work

The data on China and Japan derive from the Working Women's Family Life Survey, a project carried out jointly by the Institute of Sociology of the Chinese Academy of Social Sciences in Beijing and by the Japanese Institute of Youth in Tokyo. Women with children attending nurseries, kindergartens and childcare centres in three major Chinese cities and in urban areas in Japan were questioned in 1987. There were 2,070 women in the Chinese sample and 1,865 in the Japanese.

In order to provide roughly comparable data for Britain, we have drawn on some findings from the ESRC Social Change and Economic Life Initiative. This research involved interviews with 1,000 respondents in each of six medium size British urban labour markets in 1986 and 1987. The data used in this article derive from a sub sample of 466 respondents who were female, married, employed and who had children of school or pre-school age. These data are supplemented with material from the Women and Employment survey carried out by OPCS in 1980 (Martin and Roberts, 1984).

(*Source*: Norman Stockman, Norman Bonney and Sheng Xuewen, 'Women's Work in China, Japan and Great Britain', *Sociology Review* 2(1), 1992)

Read Item D and answer the following questions.

(K)(U) 1. Give two possible reasons why the researchers used data from the
(I)(A)   Chinese Institute of Sociology (Beijing) and the Japanese Institute of Youth
          (Tokyo).
(An)(E) 2. Why was it important that the Chinese sample was drawn from three major
(K)(U)   cities and the Japanese samples from urban areas?
(I)   3. How many women were involved in the study in total?
(An)(E) 4. To what extent would you agree with the researchers' claim that the
           data for Britain were 'roughly comparable'? (Hint: look at the sample
           size, the size of the urban areas selected, the characteristics of the sam-
           ple and so on – how similar are these to the Chinese and Japanese
           samples?)
(An)(E) 5. Why might it have been risky to supplement the research data with mate-
           rial from the Women and Employment survey carried out by OPCS in
           1980?

While Stockman *et al.*'s research is an interesting example of how comparative research can be used to reveal the similarities and differences between
societies, they quite rightly conclude that it provides only a preliminary comparison of the allocation of household members to paid and domestic work in
three countries and cannot be conclusive.

Given the rise of global sociology, it is likely that comparative research
will become more and more popular. There is considerable scope for data
collection owing to the range of comparisons that can be made – that is,
cross-sectional, cross-cultural and longitudinal. Developments in information
technology will make comparative research easier. Rather than researchers
spending long periods of time manually collecting and sorting data, it will
be possible to scan data and select variables or even countries, continents or
nations to compare in a matter of seconds.

The type of comparative research that is most useful to global sociologists
is cross-cultural study – that is, the juxtaposing of the distinctive features of
different cultures or societies. Such comparisons enable small-scale tests of the
globalization hypothesis to be conducted. For example, if it is true that globalization is occurring, one would assume that the events described above could
be identified and their effects in various countries monitored. Giddens's suggestion that globalization can produce a 'diversity of local reactions' (geographical
variation in impact) could also be explored.

Another type of comparative research is the longitudinal study. Longitudinal research is conducted over a period of time, usually involving the same or a similar sample of people and using interviews and/or questionnaires to gather the data. First used in the USA to measure changes in public attitudes by asking a 'panel' or sample of people over a period of time, the researchers thought they could be reasonably sure that any changes in attitude were not a result of the make-up of the panel.

Perhaps the most famous longitudinal study to date in the UK in sociology is *The Home and the School* by J. W. B. Douglas (1964). Douglas examined the primary educational career (up to the age of 11) of 5,362 British children born in the first week of March 1946. In a second book, *All our Futures* (1968), he followed 4,720 of the original sample through secondary school until they reached 16 1/2 in 1962.

Douglas investigated a range of education-related issues, such as social background, educational performance and parental attitudes towards education, and drew conclusions about which factors are conducive to educational 'success or failure'. This study has since been heavily criticized, mainly for drawing inappropriate and unfounded conclusions. However, at the time it both provided a valuable insight into children's experience of education and became a major catalyst for research into the impact that events in early childhood can have upon subsequent educational performance. In 2008 the government decided to invest heavily in this social research by bringing it up-to-date. Children born in one week in 1946, 1958, 1970, 2000 and 2012 are being studied. In August 2008 interviewers set out to question again the 17,000 people born in one week in 1958. The comparison with those born in 1946 and 1970 has already revealed the connection between smoking in pregnancy and low birth weight. Two-thirds of the 1958ers left school at age 16, showing lifelong disadvantage as a result (although others gained qualifications later in life). The social mobility of the 1958s was revealed as a result of the demand for more white-collar workers. However, as Polly Toynbee (2008) has pointed out there was no research conducted between 1970 and 2000 – a period of mainly Conservative rule.

Another example of ongoing longitudinal research is the British Household Panel Survey conducted by researchers at the University of Essex. Periodic interviews take place with a very large sample of 10,000 people drawn from 5,500 households to provide data on social change in family life. Many other studies have used this research as secondary data.

An influential study on social mobility was based upon two longitudinal pieces of research (Blandon *et al.*, 2005) – the National Child Development Study (1958) and the Birth Cohort Study (1970) – and found that income mobility appears to fall between these two dates. However, this research excluded all women, single people and the unemployed as well as a significantly smaller cohort than the original studies.

Comparative research – an evaluation

Exercise 8.8

This exercise requires you to identify the main features of comparative research and to consider the advantages and disadvantages. Copy and complete a larger version of the accompanying summary table. In order to add to the advantages and disadvantages boxes you may need to reread the above section and consider the relative merits of the examples outlined.

Distinctive features of comparative research

1. Comparative research involves _____
2. Research can be one of three types: _____
3. Comparative research is favoured by _____
4. It has increased in popularity as a result of _____

Advantages	Disadvantages
1. It enables the similarities and differences between groups to be revealed, which can help to increase our understanding of human behaviour.	1. It often involves making comparisons between groups with more differences than similarities. Thus any findings will be of limited use.

Longitudinal research – an evaluation

Strengths

1. Rather than give a snapshot, longitudinal sociological research can provide us with data collected over an extended period of time and therefore reveal trends, patterns and changes.
2. Relatively large samples can be used making the research more representative and valid. The research can be replicated and the same people contacted again and again.
3. Quantitative longitudinal research can often examine a large number of variables and therefore be very detailed.

Disadvantages

1. The original sample size may be considerably reduced over time as people drop out, die, move location and simply fail to respond (attrition rate), thus making the sample size less representative and the results distorted.
2. The predominant use of questionnaires and interviews in longitudinal research has its limitations in terms of gaining in-depth data. (See earlier criticisms of the use of these methods.)
3. They can be costly in terms of researcher's time and analysis of results.
4. The respondents may change their behaviour because they are aware that they are being studied.

QUANTITATIVE AND QUALITATIVE METHODS – AN EVALUATION

Link Exercise 8.2

So far this chapter has concerned itself with methods that could be considered both quantitative and qualitative. This provides a contrast with the approaches considered in Chapter 7, where techniques were identified as distinctly quantitative or qualitative. Copy and complete a more spacious version of the summary table here in order to review the material covered in this chapter and compare it with that covered in Chapter 7. A clear knowledge and understanding of the similarities and differences between the various techniques will be invaluable to you when answering an exam question on quantitative versus qualitative methods, such as the one featured in the exam focus section at the end of Chapter 7.

Non-experimental methods – a summary of the relative merits of quantitative and qualitative methods

Technique	Definitions	Key studies	Advantages	Disadvantages
Case-studies				
Documentary and content analysis				
Ethnographic studies				
Comparative research				
Longitudinal research				
Visual Methodologies				
Focus groups				

THE FORWARD MARCH OF LESS-KNOWN TECHNIQUES

Human documentary sources

Until relatively recently, a range of research techniques falling under the general category of human documentary sources (for example, autobiographical accounts, letters, diaries, oral histories and life histories) were largely ignored by sociologists. Hitchcock and Hughes (1995) argue that while these sources of information have been collected and used by social scientists for a number of years they have remained very much the 'underside' of sociology (Plummer, 1983).

In a review of the human documentary tradition, Hitchcock and Hughes (1995) explore the nature and significance of these sources of data and some of the methodological and theoretical issues underpinning their use. They argue that researchers turn to human documentary sources in an attempt to investigate experiences of events and situations from the individual's or group's point of view. The emphasis is on empathy, and thus the approach has much in common with the type of sociology advocated by Weber and the interpretive sociologists (see Chapter 2 for a review of these ideas). Plummer (2001) has used life histories as part of research into homosexuality and argues that all documents – including photos, letters, diaries, memos, memoirs, notes, graffiti, music – are rich sources of data for sociologists. The approach is also popular among those feminists who seek to redress the malestream balance of sociology by studying issues from the perspective of women, the basis of such research being the recognition that women's perceptions are different from men's. Indeed for some feminists (Stanley and Wise, 1990) the only point in research is to begin from the standpoint of the experiences of the participants and derive theoretical understanding from it. They justify this claim by arguing that the dominant epistemology in sociology has usually been white, middle-class, heterosexual men's.

(An)(E)

Exercise 8.9

This exercise introduces the human documentary techniques and enables you to consider the relative merits of each. Definitions of each approach are provided. Your task is to use these definitions to help you identify one advantage and one disadvantage of each approach.

Summary of human documentary sources

Source	Definition	Advantage	Disadvantage
Autobiographies/ life history	The recollection of the trajectory of an individual's life by the individual himself or herself. It may be focused on specific aspects of experience or a more 'stream of consciousness' remembering.		
Oral/life histories	A researcher interviewing a respondent about his or her past, including attitudes as well as actions. The researcher may use prompts to keep the respondent focused on the issue at stake.		
Letters and correspondence	Written data, produced by an individual in real time, and directed to another or others.		

In evaluating the relative merits of human documentary sources, Hitchcock and Hughes highlight the fact that despite their 'obvious potential', sociologists are often suspicious of them. Even with the rise of the anti-positivist paradigm (see Chapter 10), many sociologists are reluctant to embrace techniques that produce data of questionable representativeness and reliability, regardless of high validity. Hence, it would appear that there is little place for the personal in sociology.

However, Hitchcock and Hughes challenge this assertion. They suggest that the impact of postmodernist philosophy, feminism and the rise of ethnography all bode well for the human documentary tradition. Sociologists embracing contemporary thinking have started to look towards methods that emphasize personal perspectives and stress the necessity of understanding subjective and interpretative processes when explaining social life. This stems at least in part from acknowledgement of the demise of the metanarrative – that is, the all-encompassing explanation of social phenomena.

The value or otherwise of human documentary sources has prompted a lively debate. Positivists reject research in the human documentary tradition, regarding it as lacking rigour and systematic methodology. Data drawn from life histories, oral histories, letters and correspondence inevitably involve an element of subjective interpretation – that is, the researcher assesses the information from a personal perspective. Also, the researcher has little control over the knowledge gathered – much of it originates from one individual and is designed for consumption by a third party. The researcher can work only with the data available. Finally, if science is defined as 'aimed at gathering knowledge about and predicting occurrences within the natural world' (see Chapter 7 for a full definition), positivists would dismiss human documentary research as not meeting these criteria. Research in the human documentary tradition does not aim to make predictions; instead it attempts to 'investigate experiences of events and situations from an individual's or group's point of view' (Hitchcock and Hughes, 1995).

This fundamental disagreement has prompted Hitchcock and Hughes to explore whether the perceived lack of scientific credibility amounts to a legitimate criticism of research in the human documentary tradition. They suggest that no research is concerned solely with scientific method. Instead, researchers are concerned with the 'art' of their world as much as, or more than, the 'science' of their endeavours. For example, developments in life history research raise important questions about the nature and form of cultural representations. They quotes Mills (1949) in suggesting that such representations form part of meaningful scientific analysis of the interface between individual and society, between individual life history and social structure and, inevitably, between private issues and public troubles. If this is the case, then a research method that explores the interplay between aspects of society and their role in the creation of social reality is particularly useful.

To defend the human documentary tradition further, it is likely that in the light of contemporary developments in sociological thinking, research that explores cultural representations will play a more central role in sociology. Research has already explored such issues as postmodernism and popular culture – for example, the erosion of collective and personal identity, globalization (the development and personal impact of global culture and economy), fundamentalism (the emergence of a world view highlighting the essential truths of traditional faiths and applying them with fervour to the twentieth century), cosmopolitanism (the coexistence of a variety of cultures, ethnic groups and social movements) and so on.

It is perhaps not surprising that Hitchcock and Hughes (1995) foresee a healthy future for human documentary sources in sociology:

> An interest in biography and individual life histories forms part of an emerging sociological discourse concerned with writing and analysing lives ... In

collecting and encountering life stories we are, after all, encountering and rediscovering our own selves.

Furthermore, alongside the development of new methods which stem from the postmodern critique of conventional methods such as interviews, insight from that perspective could also be used to improve upon conventional methods. Alvesson (2002) believes that if researchers are aware of the ways in which dominant discourses can influence the interview process they can refine their interview techniques to take account of the views of the interviewee. Similarly the interviewer can be sensitive to the views, opinions, attitudes and values of the interviewee and, as Ann Oakley (2005) has discussed widely, make sure that an unequal power relationship is not formed along the lines of gender, ethnicity, age, disability or social class.

Human documentary sources – an evaluation

Exercise 8.10

Use the information contained in this section to complete a two-column table listing at least three advantages and three disadvantages of human documentary sources. Beneath your table, write an assessment of these to arrive at a balanced evaluation.

Contemporary qualitative analysis

In their review of qualitative analysis, Banyard and Hayes (1994) highlight a whole range of techniques that have increased in popularity over the last few years. These include crowd analysis (studying the ritualized behaviour of individuals in a crowd setting), protocol analysis (identifying the steps involved in particular types of cognitive – that is, mental, processes; see Sloboda, 1985), thematic qualitative analysis (interpreting the outcomes of decision-making against a series of pre-established thematic criteria; see Hayes, 1991), conversational analysis (see Billig, 1990) and q-methodology (factor analysis of individual accounts, preferences, judgements, identity and so on; see Stephenson, 1981; Stainton-Rogers, 1991).

The techniques noted above developed within psychology, but influential sociologists are increasingly recognizing the value of developing new qualitative interests. For example, exploring the new sociology of self (see Chapter 5) appears to be more in keeping with the qualitative methods highlighted by Banyard and Hayes than the quantitative methods that are regarded as so integral to the sociology of 'modernity'.

What this means is that the focus of sociology is changing and that the issues now regarded as important to understand demand new methods. While the quest for macro understanding of global issues is central to new sociological theory, Giddens (1994) stresses the implications globalization has for culture and for individuals. For example, he talks of global issues having a 'diversity of local reactions' – that is, affecting communities in varied but important ways.

In addition, as part of structuration theory (see Chapter 5), Giddens (1992) identifies 'reflexivity' as a critical aspect of the modern self. By this he means the process of thinking about what we are doing, making decisions and making choices. What makes this so interesting in the late-modern world is that the certainties of the past no longer exist. The demise of the metanarrative means that social practices cannot be founded on the past – that is, individuals can no longer base their behaviour on tradition; instead everything must be justified in the light of new information. So presumably, if sociologists cannot rely on the metanarrative as the basis for explaining human motivation/behaviour because it no longer exists, they must turn their attention to the role of reflexivity (interpretation) in determining or contributing to human action. This may lead to increased use of qualitative methods aimed at exploring interactions at a micro level in order to develop our understanding of reflexivity as a social process. Two approaches to research which have emerged from the development of more reflective thinking in sociology, and particularly the desire to understand and explain the world from the perspective of those being studied, are the use of visual methods such as video, film, photography and the internet, and the use of focus groups.

VISUAL METHODOLOGIES AS RESEARCH TECHNIQUES

In recent years, visual methods such as the use and analysis of photographs, video images, film, illustrations, advertising, TV and the internet have been used by some sociologists (Sweetman and Knowles, 2006; Hillyard, 2007), both to complement the use of traditional qualitative methodologies such as interviews and also as research tools in their own right. This is to some extent a reflection of the modern world which is characterized by the constant bombardment of visual images and messages from a wide variety of sources – TV, internet, magazines, videos, DVDs, play stations and so on, but also by the wider use of digital technology in cameras and mobile phones as they become cheaper, more accessible and in frequent use.

There are three broad approaches to the use of visual images in sociology. The realist approach sees photographs and videos as a form of evidence that can be collected like any other data for analysis by the sociologist. Associated with poststructuralism, images can also be viewed as a feature of the social construction of society and in particular with the disciplining of the body. For example, one of the early uses of photography was to take images of criminals, so that a record of their features could be kept for future investigation. The last approach is drawn from semiology and is where images are treated as texts to be read for their deeper ideological or social significance (see Knowles and Sweetman, 2004).

Hillyard (2007), for example, asked the subjects of a study in rural sociology to provide a photographic record or account of their lives to ensure that the perspective and interpretation of the images are from a subjective standpoint rather than an imposed interpretation which may occur if photographs are taken by a researcher. Hillyard points out how the complexity of the life of a gamekeeper is shown in the pictures taken where social contacts are an important part of his working life. Even with a picture which seems relatively uncomplicated to an untrained eye – like a photo of a field – there are subtle elements that need to be explained, such as the way in which different parts of the 'maize plot' are managed to ensure game bird feeding is provided and habitat maintained. The section beyond the 'maize plot' is maintained for shooting the birds and ensuring they achieve sufficient height to be shot. Hillyard points out the importance of analysing the photographs with knowledge of the role of the gamekeeper to move beyond a 'face-value' interpretation to a more sophisticated account with the subject's perspective in mind.

Shaw and Mizen (2007) have argued that the origins of photography and sociology 'have similar starting points' in that they shared the wish to objectively document society and societal development and to improve social conditions for the underprivileged and poor, but have been 'notably disconnected'. However, Goffman as far back as 1979 used photographs to analyse how power relations underpinned the portrayal of men's and women's roles in gender advertisements. Other researches into images in children's books (Lobban, 1974), teenage magazines (McRobbie, 1996) and science textbooks are familiar to sociology students, although these tend to be more content-analysis-driven and involved counting the number of times a particular image was used in an empirical, quantitative approach. More recently sociologists have used images, photographs, video diaries and so on to research and document areas of social life, such as rural life (Hillyard, 2007) and body adornment and modification (Sweetman, 2000), that have been under-researched to try to understand social life as seen from the participant's perspective.

Harper (1998) used photographs of the subject's world taken by the researcher as part of a 'photo-elicitation interview' but realized that the 'cultural information' in the photograph is unknown to the photographer.

This highlights one of the issues of such methods, namely that the cultural significance of the image can be lost, misunderstood or misinterpreted. Shaw and Mizen (2007) argue however that the photograph as an external narrative can be used as part of qualitative research to provide the richness and depth that is the quest of such a research. The significance and context of photographs can tell us much about the social worlds we inhabit and about how social reality is constructed historically and culturally. 'Re-photography' – taking images of the same subject(s) separated by time – can provide this understanding of social change.

Rose (2001) states that the meanings attached to an image are constructed at three sites, first at the production stage of the image, second the image itself and third the audience who view the image. None of these 'sites' is neutral – all are bound and influenced by cultural significance, social practices and power relations, and all of these are used to interpret the meaning and message behind an image or picture. Feminists have long held the view that common images of women help to construct patterns of masculinity and femininity which present men as dominant and women as subservient.

Gauntlett (2007) uses visual methodology in a different way in developing an approach to study based on 'visual culture'. As part of research into the place of popular media in people's lives, he has asked participants in research to produce visual material as ways to explore the meaning of their relationships with various forms of media. Participants may be asked to think and build a metaphor initially and then go on to explore that metaphor in relation to their identity. Gauntlett believes that because we are surrounded by a visual culture it makes sense to incorporate visual methods into social research rather than using a one-dimensional approach such as a questionnaire or interview. Seeking alternatives to interviews and focus groups, Gauntlett has undertaken some innovative projects. His research regarding what identity means to people themselves has shown that, rather than the 'fragmented postmodern' identities talked about in academic circles, his respondents demonstrated remarkable coherence, clarity and distinctiveness. Other projects have involved children producing videos to explore their understanding of the environment; to explore young men's ideas of masculinity they produced designs for magazine covers; and to investigate teenagers' aspirations they drew pictures of celebrities and media stars they admired.

While visual methodologies are beginning to provide a rich and diverse picture of the world in sociological research it must be borne in mind that visual images like the written or spoken word of more traditional methods are open to interpretation and mis-interpretation. Images are, by their nature 'polysemic' – that is open to a number of different readings. In addition, there are other difficulties associated with visual methodologies, including the ownership of copyright, the right of confidentiality and anonymity if personal images are used, and the selection of specific images from many to support points made. In defence of visual methods Pink (2001) argues that the same criticisms can be levelled at written forms of sociological evidence and that, as we inhabit an image-rich society with high levels of visual literacy, the analysis of images should be a key concern for sociologists. Now refer back to Link Exercise 8.2.

Exercise 8.11

1. Choose a picture which interests you and write down all the key points about the image and what it means to you. Give the picture to a group of friends and ask them to do the same. Compare your results and discuss the similarities and particularly any differences that have emerged.
   Try to imagine that you have no idea what the image is. Treat it as 'anthropologically strange', in other words from a world or culture different from your own, and decide how you would make sense of it.
2. Think of some ideas for research projects in which you could incorporate examples of creative visual materials such as videos, collages, drawing or Lego-building produced by your respondents as part of the investigation. Which areas of sociology would lend themselves well to such an approach?

Visual methods – an evaluation

Strengths

- Visual images can provide an additional qualitative dimension to a research project.
- Rather than being passive respondents, the participants in research can have a more active role in the research process, particularly if the approach asks for their visual input.
- The visual images can be provided by the subjects of the research to illuminate their perspective, lifestyle, identity working life, culture and so on.
- It may be possible to use photographs to make comparisons over time.

Disadvantages

- Visual accounts are also open to interpretation and there is a danger of misunderstanding.

▦ The cultural significance of images makes them difficult to use in contexts other than the one in which the research is taking place. They can also become out-of-date very quickly.

Focus groups

Group interviews with focus groups have had a tradition in market research since the 1950s and in media research more recently, but have been increasingly used in sociology and health and nursing research. Focus groups have been used to explore a range of health and medical issues and topics which may be difficult to study using conventional interviews or questionnaires. Their aim is to collect and analyse data from 'hard-to-reach' groups, including diverse ethnic groups. Using focus groups usually involves the collection of qualitative data about a topic through the use of group discussions (Morgan, 1998). According to Culley *et al.* (2008) groups are comprised of a relatively small purposive sample of about 6 to 10 people who take part in a 'guided discussion' generated by a researcher who does not take part but asks questions. Such discussions can provide a rich, detailed picture of the participants' lives and experiences. In their research Culley *et al.* explored a topic – childlessness in the British Asian community – which would be difficult to study conventionally as it is sensitive and often not well understood. Using focus groups, she argued, put the participants at ease and allowed for their opinions and beliefs to be explored in a way that one-to-one research would not. Now refer back to Link Exercise 8.2.

Focus groups – an evaluation

Strengths

▦ It is possible to gather information from diverse or hard-to-reach groups.
▦ Information is given from the perspective of the participants in the group.
▦ The material is likely to be high in validity.

Disadvantages

▦ Misunderstandings could occur if the researcher is not fully aware of cultural norms or the language of the group.
▦ Recording, transcribing and analysing the data can be time-consuming, and it may also be difficult to distinguish who said what in a group discussion.
▦ Getting focus groups together in the first place may be difficult.
▦ Ensuring views are genuine and not influenced by others in the group may be an issue that may thus affect validity.

▪ It would be difficult to replicate a study based on the use of focus groups.

▪ The groups may not be representative.

The forward march of less-known techniques – an evaluation

Strengths

1. New and less-well-known techniques can bring a fresh approach to old debates.
2. New methods offer alternatives to the traditional scientific method. As they increase in popularity, non-scientific methods may gain more credibility.
3. New methods broaden the sociological imagination – reflexivity can become an integral part of sociological methodology.
4. Individuals, groups and issues previously little studied in sociology (for example, cultural groups, women, ethnic minorities, criminals and so on) may achieve more attention as new, more appropriate methods are developed.

Disadvantages

1. The development of more and more research methods could be interpreted as internal fragmentation of sociology – in other words, if the discipline is so cohesive why does it have to keep reinventing its methodology?
2. The less-known techniques could be regarded as trendy fads that are less credible than the more established methods. This may have funding implications.
3. Separatists within the disciplines (sociology and psychology) may be against methodological collaboration, seeing it as devaluing their subject specialism.

THE IMPACT OF INFORMATION TECHNOLOGY ON SOCIOLOGICAL RESEARCH

The considerable benefits to be had from information and communication technology (ICT) are discussed above. Not only can sociologists benefit from ICT when conducting research and presenting and analysing data; ICT has also added a new dimension to the study of the social world. As noted above, there are statistical packages specifically designed for social scientists such as PASW formerly known as SPSS, which is widely available in university departments.

The development of ICT has raised a number of new research issues for sociologists. For example, the existence and rapid expansion of the internet has provided a vast global communication system, and this cannot fail to change the nature of social, political and economic relations. Potential research projects could include exploring the role of the internet in linking transworld education projects. A recent example of such work is collaborative work between a Welsh primary school and an Australian elementary school to explore the implications of the ecological disaster off the south-west coast of Britain (*Western Mail*, July 1996).

Not surprisingly, there has been rapid growth in the number of publications designed to help sociologists to understand the scope of ICT and utilize it fully in sociological research and practice. For example, Blank *et al.* (1992) consider the role of new technology in sociology, Lee (1995) gives practical advice on ICT for social scientists, and Lawson (1993) puts the use of ICT within the broader context of new strategies in social research. What is clear, from these and other publications, is that sociologists cannot afford to ignore the edge that ICT can give them in their research. Reading any of the above texts will provide a comprehensive insight into the extent to which the practice of sociology can be enhanced by high technology.

Competency in the use of ICT is now part of the Key Skills in schools and colleges. Students are expected to develop. Indeed the primary school curriculum has a number of areas where children are expected to understand and be able to use computers, interactive whiteboards and VLEs in their work, and ICT is commonplace in secondary school, colleges and universities today.

Teachers are now expected to keep abreast of current developments in ICT within their discipline and are tested for their competency during their teacher training course, so at some point on your course you should expect to have contact with information technology in the form of word processing, databases, use of the internet, your virtual learning environment (VLE – Moodle and Blackboard) and graphics packages like Excel. Even wikis, blogs and podcasts are being incorporated into mainstream teaching and learning in schools, colleges and universities.

Item E

Just for the Taste of it? A Study of the Impact of Postmodernism on Drinking Habits

Context – Do people drink alcopops for the taste or for the image? (Rationale/context – Is consumption driven by image above substance? – The impact of postmodernism on patterns of consumption.)

Method – My data were collected from people who regularly drank alcopops. I went to three pubs and asked people who had ordered alcopops why they had. I made up categories to make it easy to analyse the data. If people gave two reasons, I recorded their first one. The results are shown below.

Results:

Why drink alcopops?

	Reason	No of people
1.	Taste better	33
2.	Cost less	19
3.	Trend value/image	13
4.	Pressure from friends	13
	Total	114

Breakdown of reasons by pub

	Flying Frisbee	Flag & Fishwife	Dog & Doughnut	Total
1.	12	15	6	33
2.	8	5	6	19
3.	40	6	3	49
4.	10	2	1	13
Total	70	28	16	114

   'Flying Frisbee'   'Flag & Fishwife'   'Dog & Doughnut'

Figure 8.1 Alcopops consumption: pie chart of percentages of people with reasons given, by pub

Calculation

	Each choice in percentage terms	Pie chart degree calculations
FF		
1.	$12/70 \times 100/1 = 17.1\%$	$17.1 \times 360/100 = 63.36$ (63°)
2.	$8/70 \times 100/1 = 11.4\%$	$11.4 \times 360/100 = 41.04$ (41°)
3.	$40/70 \times 100/1 = 57.2\%$	$57.2 \times 360/100 = 205.92$ (205°)
4.	$10/70 \times 100/1 = 14.3\%$	$14.3 \times 360/100 = 51.48$ (51°)
F&F		
1.	53.6%	192.96 (193°)
2.	17.9%	64.44 (64°)
3.	21.4%	77.04 (77°)
4.	7.1%	25.56 (26°)
D&D		
1.	37.5%	135
2.	37.5%	135
3.	18.75%	67.5
4.	6.25%	22.5

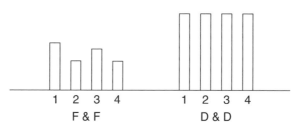

Figure 8.2 Alcopops consumption: bar chart of reasons given, by pub

Exercise 8.12

This exercise encourages you to identify weaknesses in presenting data and devise strategies to improve the presentation of data. Item F presents the results section of a fictitious sociology project. Read the item carefully and in pairs complete the following tasks.

1. Discuss the strengths and limitations of the data presentation.
2. Identify errors made in presenting this information.
3. Suggest how each error could be corrected to improve the overall quality of the work.

Statistical software for the social sciences

Increasingly, IT packages are also used to analyse the results of mainly quantitative research in sociology. PASW is a common and popular example. It is a computer software package designed to store, retrieve and analyse quantitative or numerical data. The software allows the researcher to create data sets arranged in the form of variables and to test the strength of the relationship between these variables. For example, if we construct a simple two-variable data set comprising gender and voting intentions based upon respondents replies to a questionnaire, PASW will allow us to accurately determine the degree to which gender is a factor in party support. The package incorporates bivariate (two-variable) functions as in the example above and a more sophisticated multivariate capacity.

Using content analysis

Glenys Lobban's (1974) study of sex role stereotyping in children's books provides a classic example of content analysis. The following exercise is based on a replication of this study, carried out in February and March 1992 by three groups of BTEC national social care students at Park Lane College of Further Education in Leeds.

Item F

'Dragons, Dinner Ladies and Ferrets': Sex Roles in Children's Books

Background – Prior to carrying out the research topic, we had looked at the sociology of education and in particular at gender issues within education. The work of Glenys Lobban on sex roles in reading schemes was referred to, and this current piece of research stemmed from her ideas. She pointed out that reading schemes are influential 'because they are usually the child's first introduction to the written word'. I felt that now that so many children go to nursery school or playgroup, it would be interesting to go one step further back and analyse the male and female roles portrayed in some of the pre-school books currently available.

Method – The students were asked to bring in three pre-school books each. They were not to look for particularly sexist or non-sexist books, just books that they had at home, or had used on placement in a nursery, or books they would read in a playgroup. In total we therefore had 132 books. Clearly, there are thousands of books to choose from, and if one tried I'm sure 132 non-sexist books could be found, and the results would be totally different. However, I have done this exercise on several other occasions with similar general results. The main points stand out clearly every time and indicate a very unequal balance between the sexes in pre-school books.

(*Source*: L. Best, 'Dragons, Dinner Ladies and Ferrets: Sex Roles in Children's Books', *Sociology Review* 2(3), 1993)

Exercise 8.13

Read Item F and answer the following questions.

(K)(U) 1. Why do you think the students were told 'not to look for particularly sexist or non-sexist books'?

(E) 2. In your opinion, was an adequate number of books used for this content analysis? Give reasons to support your answer.

(K)(U) 3. Why might it be wise to treat the research findings with caution in the light of the following comment: 'I have done this exercise on several other occasions with similar general results'?

(An)(E) 4. What explanations would sociologists offer for the discovery of a 'very unequal balance between the sexes in pre-school books'?

The example in Item F above demonstrates how documentary and content analysis can be a useful means of testing hypotheses on aspects of society, but it can also serve other purposes for sociologists. For example, it can enable them to analyse how other sociologists have conducted their research, presuming that information about the research process has been documented in some other form, such as a research diary, a log or a journal. This is particularly useful if a researcher wishes to replicate the work of another researcher or wishes to evaluate the study's reliability and validity.

In order to benefit from IT in coursework it is important to learn how to produce graphics and analyse data before you start to write up your project. This will give you added confidence and, more crucially, save time. The following exercise should help you to get to grips with the IT facilities at your school or college.

Using PASW

PASW (Predictive Analytics Software) is a computer-based statistical package designed to store and analyse research data in a quantitative (numerical) form. Once research data are entered into PASW, the software can be used to summarize those data – in the form of percentages or bar charts, for example – and to test the relationship between variables, for example between gender and voting behaviour or between ethnicity and unemployment. PASW will also perform more complicated, sophisticated statistical analyses.

The following example and activity is designed to introduce you to PASW. In order to carry out the activity you will have to have access to a computer with the PASW software loaded into it at your school, college or university. The spreadsheet below contains information regarding the performance of one class of primary-school children, aged seven, in the national curriculum (Key Stage One) tests. For each child we are given their gender (male or female), their results in the English test (T+ = target or better; BT = below target) and their results in the Maths test (T+ = target or better; BT = below target). Thus, for example, child number 12 (column 1) is a female (column 2) who achieved below target in English (column 3) and target or better in Maths (column 4).

Column 1: Child	Column 2: Gender	Column 3: English	Column 4: Maths
1	Male	T+	T+
2	Male	T+	BT
3	Female	T+	T+
4	Male	T+	T+
5	Female	T+	T+
6	Female	T+	T+
7	Male	T+	T+
8	Female	BT	BT
9	Female	T+	T+
10	Male	T+	T+
11	Male	BT	BT
12	Female	BT	T+
13	Female	T+	BT
14	Male	T+	T+
15	Female	T+	T+
16	Male	BT	T+
17	Female	T+	T+
18	Female	T+	T+
19	Female	T+	BT
20	Female	T+	T+
21	Male	BT	BT
22	Female	T+	T+
23	Male	T+	T+
24	Male	BT	T+

Using this information, the exercise using PASW will cover the following:

1. Creating a data set – setting up the variables (gender, English results, Maths results) and entering the data into the computer.
2. Calculating frequencies.
3. Producing bar charts.
4. Producing tables (called 'crosstabs') that indicate the relationship between variables (for example the relationship between gender and achievement in English).

Creating a data set (1): setting up the variables

In order to enter data into PASW we first have to 'set up' the variables illustrated in the spreadsheet above. Our spreadsheet indicates three variables each with two possible values:

Variable 1 – Gender – either male or female.
Variable 2 – English – either target + or below target.
Variable 3 – Maths – either target + or below target.

To set up these variables we of course need to open the PASW programme. Open PASW either by double-clicking the PASW icon on the desktop or through the program menu. In the window that opens, highlight the 'type in new data' option and click 'OK'. You will now see the main PASW window on the screen (see Figure 8.3).

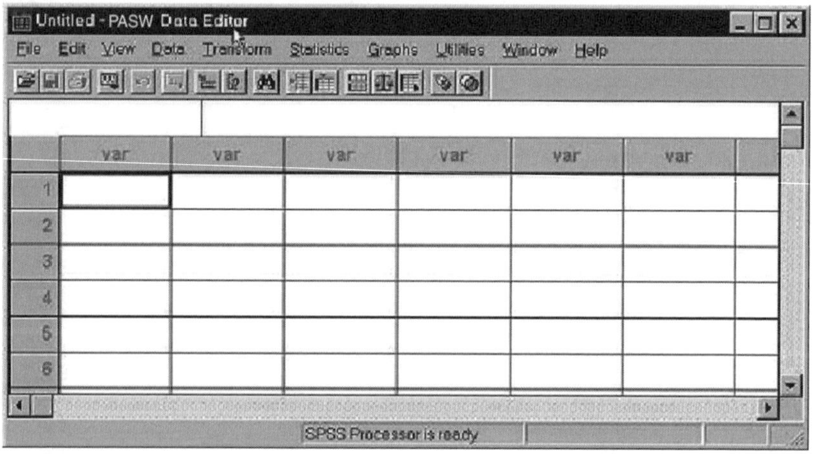

Figure 8.3 PASW: main window

Data view, variable view

Click the 'Variable View' tab. In the variable view window we can set up each of our three variables. Variables are listed in the first column, numbered 1,2,3,4 and so on. We will use only the first three of these rows as this is a three-variable data set. The other columns have various headings but only those labelled 'Name', 'Type' and 'Value' are important in this exercise:

Variable	Name	Type	Width	Decimals	Label	Values	etc.
1							
2							
3							
4							
etc.							

We will now set up our first variable, using row number 1 on the screen. Under 'Name' type in 'Gender'. In fact it is possible to give a variable any name you choose but it is always sensible to use relevant labels, particularly as others may read your work. Next, click on the cell under 'Type', highlight the 'String' option and click OK. Finally, click on the cell under 'Values'. A new dialogue box opens (Figure 8.4).

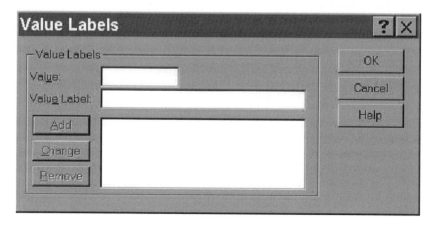

Figure 8.4   PASW: Value Labels dialogue box

As explained above, gender has two possible values, male and female. In the 'Value' text box type in '1' and in the 'Value Label' text box type in 'male'. Click ADD.

Next, type in '2' in the 'Value' text box and 'female' in the 'Value Label' text box. Click ADD then OK.

We have now completed our first variable, gender. The second and third variables, English and Maths, are set up in precisely the same way. For each, under the 'Values' heading, use value labels T+ (target or better) and BT (below target) with values 1 and 2 respectively. On completion click on the 'Data View' tab on the bottom left of the screen and you will see the main PASW window again but this time with the three variables registered:

	Gender	English	Maths	Var 4	etc.
1					
2					
3					
4					
etc					

Creating a data set (2): entering the data

We are now ready to type in our data from the spreadsheet on page 312 above. The first pupil, row 1, is a male who achieved target or better in both English and Maths. Type in the relevant values for each of these ('1' in each case) and the row will now appear as follows:

	Gender	English	Maths	Var 4	etc.
1	Male	T+	T+		
2					

We continue with this process until all 24 pupils have been entered. On completion it is advisable to save the information: click on 'File' and 'Save As' and give the data set a name and location so that it can be retrieved in the future.

Calculating frequencies

'Frequency' refers to the percentage or number of times a variable appears.

Along the top of the data-view window there are a number of options: File, Edit, View, Data, Transform, Analyse, Graphs, Utilities, Window, Help. To calculate the frequency (per cent) of a variable, click on 'Analyse'. A new menu opens – click on 'Descriptive Statistics' then 'Frequencies'. A dialogue box titled 'Frequencies' opens with the three variables listed in a box on the left, an arrow in the middle and a blank box on the right (Figure 8.5).

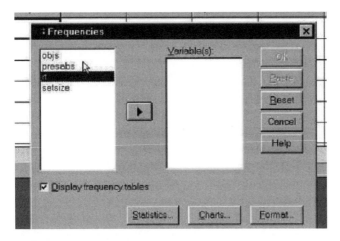

Figure 8.5 PASW: Frequencies dialogue box

For example, highlight the variable 'Gender' and move it to the right-hand side by clicking on the arrow. Click OK and you will be presented with a table that indicates both the numbers and percentages of males and females in the class:

	Gender	Frequency	%	Valid %	Cumulative %
Valid	Male	11	45.8	45.8	45.8
	Female	13	54.2	54.2	100.0
	Total	24	100.0	100.0	

You can repeat this exercise for the other variables in the same way.

Producing bar charts

Bar charts can be produced from the frequencies window illustrated above. Having moved a variable to the right-hand side select 'Charts'. Within the new window select 'Bar – PERCENTAGES' and click OK. A typical bar chart is shown in Figure 8.6.

Crosstabs

Crosstabs refer to tables that indicate the relationship between variables. From the data view screen select ANALYSE – DESCRIPTIVE STATITICS – CROSSTABS. You will be presented with a dialogue box (Figure 8.7).

The dialogue box in Figure 8.7 is for illustrative purposes, and displays a number of variables down the left-hand side. In our case there will be three variables listed: gender, English and Maths. Highlight the independent variable and move

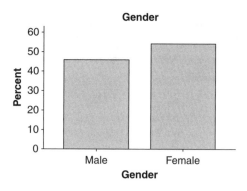

Figure 8.6 PASW: bar chart

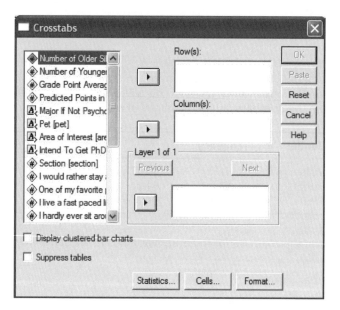

Figure 8.7 PASW: Crosstabs dialogue box

it to the Rows text box by selecting the relevant arrow. In the same way move
the dependant variable to the Columns text box. An independent variable is one
that can be used to explain a dependent variable. Here, gender can be used to
explain performance in English and in Maths. It is obvious that performance in
educational tests does not determine if one is male or female. Thus gender is
our independent variable and English and Maths are both dependent. You can
ignore the Layer text box for the purposes of this exercise. Select English first.
Next, click on the CELLS button and highlight the Row Percentages option, click
CONTINUE and then OK.

A table will appear in which the relative performance of girls and boys on the English test is presented. The table will allow you to judge the degree to which there is a relationship between gender and performance in English. You should then repeat the exercise for Maths.

PASW outputs such as frequencies, charts and crosstab tables can be easily imported into a word document by cutting and pasting. Remember also, if you are having difficulties the PASW software includes a useful tutorial. You can find this by selecting the 'Help' option at the top of the main data-view window.

Exercise 8.15

1. Find out:

   (a) What IT facilities are available at your school/college/university?
   (b) How can you learn how to use them? Who is responsible for ICT? Do they run training/'taster' courses?
   (c) What IT skills you are likely to require for your course – ask your teacher.

2. Use your knowledge to produce the following graphical representations of data on the computer. You may like to borrow some of these data to work with, or alternatively use the internet or a statistical website to obtain data on a topic that interests you: once you have established a data set, use PASW to work out the relationships between the variables and then produce the following charts to illustrate your findings.

   (a) A bar chart.
   (b) A line chart (or frequency polygon).
   (c) A pie chart.

(Hints: Make full use of appropriate labels to make it clear what is being shown. Keep your printouts in a safe place and make sure you have back-up copies on your memory stick. It may also be helpful to make a few notes on how you produced the graphs – the system used, the commands needed and so on – as well as any difficulties you faced and what you did to overcome them.)

Once you feel confident about using ICT, it might be valuable to practise your ICT skills by converting data from statistical tables (for example, from *Social Trends*) into graphics using Excel. If you pick your data wisely your time will be well spent. For example, updated information on the topics covered in your course will enhance the quality of your notes. This information can be filed in an appropriate place in your notes and referred to during revision. This will keep you on top of contemporary developments in the subject and impress the examiner. Remember Lawson's point, though: you must be able to *analyse* the tables you generate if you are to demonstrate fully your application, analysis and evaluation skills. Try to ensure that you download and store only *relevant* information in an accessible format that you understand and can interpret and apply confidently.

The impact of IT on sociological research – an evaluation

This section has highlighted some of the practical advantages that could be gained by using IT in sociological research. Theoretically, structuralists and macro-sociologists (see Chapter 3) would support the use of ICT. Remember, both advocate that society should be studied from as broad a starting-point as possible via quantitative methods, as this is the only way we can hope to uncover the social laws governing human behaviour. Action theorists and micro-sociologists would strong disagree with this view and would be against the increased use of ICT in sociology, particularly if this meant a move towards the use of more quantitative methods at the expense of qualitative ones.

Exercise 8.16

As well as theoretical opposition to the use of macro methods, a number of practical disadvantages might limit their use. Compile a list of drawbacks that might come from increased reliance on high technology in sociological research. Use the knowledge you have acquired from the last few chapters and the questions below to help you:

- Could sociology become stratified by access to IT facilities – that is, would those researchers with large research grants/private funding have greater access to state-of-the-art technology and thus be able to overshadow those undertaking less-well-funded research projects?
- Why would increased involvement with IT, especially as a vehicle for the expression of quantitative data, inevitably resurrect the old debate on the nature of social facts (see Chapter 6)?
- IT is being continually updated – what implications does this have for longitudinal research projects?

Exam focus: structured questions

The following exercise will enable you to revise, apply and evaluate the information presented in this chapter. Read Items G, H and I carefully and complete the questions that follow. If you need help with techniques for completing structured questions, look back at the hints provided at the end of Chapter 6 and 7.

Item G

Comparative Research

The comparisons that can be made in comparative research are at several different levels. Comparisons can be made between countries (macro comparisons) or within a country between groups or individuals in society. Often, because of the cost of this type of research, it is undertaken at one point in time, in a cross-sectional type study. Cross-cultural research is important in establishing the differences and similarities between countries. For example, the USA and the UK may seem to be similar on the surface, but cross-cultural research could establish substantial differences between them (or at least between substantial groups of the population within each country) over issues such as gun control.

Item H

Documentary Sources

In discussing research methods, the assumption is often made that 'active' strategies are the best way of achieving sociological data. Much has been written about the social survey, questionnaires, interviews and ethnographic techniques, but comparatively little about an immense source of data already available to the sociologist. Part of being human is the production of great swathes of human documents, generated as a matter of course during our lives. These human documentary sources (diaries, correspondence, autobiographies and so on) constitute a massive bank of information about human activity that is hardly mined at all by sociologists. Where they are used, it is often as an afterthought to research and they are not always seen as important as primary methods of research.

Item I

Combining Research Traditions

It is difficult to see quantitative and qualitative methods as mutually exclusive. Increasingly, sociologists are combining both approaches in single studies. As Bryman puts it:

> The rather partisan, either/or tenor of debate about quantitative and qualitative research may appear somewhat bizarre to an out-sider, for whom the obvious way forward is likely to be a fusion of the two approaches so that their respective strengths might be reaped.

Bryman points out that 'Most researchers rely primarily on a method associated with one or two research traditions, but buttress their findings with a method associated with the other tradition.' The practice of combining quantitative and qualitative research has a long history and is evident in the approach advocated by Weber.

(Adapted from M. Haralambos and M. Holborn, *Sociology: Themes and Perspectives*. London: Collins, 2004)

Questions

1. Give one advantage of a comparative approach to research. (Item G) (2 marks)
2. Give reasons why human documentary sources are not believed to be as important as 'active' methods. (Item H) (4 marks)
3. What do sociologists mean by 'methodological pluralism'? (Item I)? (4 marks)
4. Assess the relative merits of comparative and human documentary methods in sociology. (Items G and H) (20 marks)
5. Using evidence from the items and elsewhere, evaluate the usefulness of methodological pluralism in sociological research. (20 marks)

(Hint: Before answering questions (4) and (5), it may be helpful for you to read the section on methodological pluralism in Chapter 9)

Important concepts

the research process • documentary and content analysis •
case-studies • ethnographic research • comparative research •
visual methodologies • ICT and research • PASW

Critical thinking

- How far has methodological pluralism ended the division between the choice of quantitative and qualitative techniques?
- Do you agree that the increasing use of visual methods and ICT in sociology herald the future of the subject? Or is this a re-emergence of the quantitative/qualitative divide?
- Will the less-known sociological methods such as human documentary methods always remain very much peripheral to mainstream research?

Chapter 9

Choosing a Research Method

> By the end of this chapter, you should be able to:
>
> - recognize the range of influences that shape people's choice of research method
> - understand the influence that theoretical perspective may have upon choice of method
> - recognize practical constraints that may influence decisions about research design and subsequent choice of method
> - understand the importance of ethical and moral guidelines and recognize the impact they have upon research
> - recognize the rationale behind methodological pluralism, identify examples of studies using the approach and evaluate its usefulness in sociological inquiry
> - appreciate the interplay between all influences covered in the chapter and evaluate their relative importance

INTRODUCTION

When deciding how to approach research, sociologists are rarely free from constraint or bias. Inevitably, the process of decision-making involves giving preference to one method over another, and it gives research a subjective dimension. Furthermore, intentional bias occurs because researchers conduct their research in accordance with a certain theoretical perspective, philosophy or paradigm. Gouldner (1967) suggests that a certain amount of bias is inevitable as it is impossible to achieve value-freedom in humanity – people and their opinions/beliefs can never be separated.

Practical factors are also important in shaping choice of method. For example, research studies would not take place without finance from funding agencies, and inevitably this will affect the way research is conducted. As we shall see, the quest for funding has become increasingly important in recent years. While sociologists may still try to select the technique that best meets the needs of their research, the demand for a certain type of data from an external agency may limit the methods used in the study.

Increasingly sociologists are being required to consider the ethical implications of their research. The British Sociological Association lays down clear ethical guidelines for conducting sociological research which relate to sensitivity, the gaining of permission from respondents and ensuring that there are no negative consequences of research for those participating. (See below, pages 345ff., for a more detailed discussion on ethics.) You will find the guidelines on the British Sociological Association (BSA) website (www.britsoc.co.uk/equality/Statement+Ethical+Practice.htm), and those of the American Sociological Association (ASA) on theirs (www.asanet.org/cs/root/leftnav/ethics/code_of_ethics_table_of_contents).

This focus on good ethical practice is perhaps linked to initiatives such as the Citizen's Charter and the promotion of civil rights in party politics, and has led to far greater awareness of the need for sensitivity in the research process. Also, the numbers of sociology students who undertake research, whether on a small-scale basis at school or college (even though the coursework component no longer exists) or as part of an undergraduate degree programme, has increased, prompting the need for clear ethical research guidance.

The above issues demonstrate that choice of method is not straightforward, and in practice is likely to be a compromise between competing external influences and the researcher's theoretical or philosophical perspective. This chapter aims to explore such influences/processes via a number of research studies and practical exercises.

THEORETICAL CONSIDERATIONS

Chapters 2 and 3 gave you some idea of the way theoretical preference can shape research design, but, as shown above, it is unlikely that this will be the only influence – practical and ethical factors will also figure in the equation. However, for the sake of convenience this section will consider the effects of theoretical preference in isolation. The following exercise will help you to recap on the main ideas behind the various sociological perspectives and how these affect research design.

①Ⓐ

Link Exercise 9.1

Item A was devised by a newly qualified teacher, who was teaching theory and method (his least favourite topic) for the first time. He was a bit pushed for time as he had to mark 120 essays and had a football match the night before the lesson, so he scribbled a rough outline on the back of a shopping list and gave it to the school secretary to type. Unfortunately some of the words were a bit difficult to read, but knowing it was a rush job the secretary took a guess at what they were. After all, she was used to deciphering the messy writing of the deputy head.

1. Read the teacher's handout (Item A) carefully and see if you can spot what is wrong with it.
2. Mark correct information with a pencilled tick, incorrect information with a cross and draw arrows to indicate where information that is in the wrong column should be moved.
3. Draw up your own version of the summary table, with the errors corrected and the information reordered into a logical sequence. This should be useful for revision at a later date. (Now rub out your pencilled ticks, crosses and arrows!)

Your diagram should highlight how the basic distinction between structuralism and social action determines the way research is conducted. The main beliefs of each perspective lead logically to ideas about the way research should be conducted, the type of data required and which methods are best suited to obtaining this data. The methods featured in the summary chart are well-established forms of sociological inquiry.

Item A

Theory and Method – Who Believes What?

I am a structuralist	I am an action theorist
I see society as made up of relationships and exchanges between individuals.	My research focuses on social structure.
I am a positivist.	I believe we should study the meaning that individuals give to events because this is what combines to shape the nature of society.

This means I am positive that we should not treat sociology like science. Positivism means looking on the bright side of life and adopting an optimistic view of society.

My research focuses on social action.

I am influenced by the writings of Mead, Goffman, Schutz, Garfinkel and Weber.

My research aims to collect qualitative data so that I can capture in-depth, detailed, valid data about unique human behaviour.

I use primary and secondary data but find secondary data helpful in uncovering patterns and social trends which can be generalized to develop social laws.

I tend to use the following research methods: unstructured questionnaires, in-depth interviews, observation.

I see society as made up of influential institutions that combine to shape the lives of society's members.

I am an anti-pessimist.

This means I do not believe society should be studied in the same way as science, as humans have feelings and are more complex than the subject-matter of the natural sciences.

We should study social life at the micro, i.e. small-scale, level and try to develop an in-depth understanding of individual cases.

I am influenced by the writings of Comte, Durkheim, Marx, Engels and Weber.

I tend to use the following research methods: official statistics, structured questionnaires, surveys.

I use primary and secondary data, although primary is usually more useful to gain an insight into the meaning behind action.

The impact that theoretical factors have upon choice of method depends on what are regarded as research priorities or what forms of investigation are in favour at the time. This past century has seen the spotlight shift from interest in large-scale, macro methodology, inspired by structuralism, to small-scale, micro methodology inspired by interactionism. There are also significant examples of research by sociologists using a range of techniques drawn from both macro and micro methodologies.

It is easy to find past examples of research genres spawned by emergent ideas about how best to go about interpreting social life. For example, in the 1920s ecological sociology became increasingly popular. This involved a geographical emphasis being placed upon research – that is, it was assumed that environmental influences could provide an explanation of behaviour. The popularity of the ecological perspective at the University of Chicago led to a considerable amount of research being undertaken from a geographical angle, particularly when trying to explain patterns of crime. Although this was undoubtedly less cost-effective than the basic statistical approaches and represented a radical departure from the structuralist explanations offered by functionalists and Marxists, for a time there was much interest in the potential of ecological sociology, and research methodologies were developed to enable environmental and geographic influences on behaviour to be studied.

Similarly, in the 1960s increased interest in studying aspects of social interaction led to the development of research methods suited to quantifying the existing but unnoticed rules that govern human behaviour. Research in the United States included the study of turn-taking in conversation (conversational analysis) and exchanges in relationships (transactional analysis). Interest spread to British universities and similar types of research began in this country a decade later.

It is not difficult to find examples of sociological research where choice of method has been influenced by theoretical perspective. For example, the ongoing debate about suicide stems largely from disagreement about which perspective to adopt in the study of it, namely positivism or phenomenology (see the section in Chapter 6 on the nature of social facts).

Despite the fact that historical trends in the use of various research methodologies can be identified, it would be wrong to suggest that at certain points in time sociological research is dominated by the influence of a single perspective. Instead, it is more likely that certain research departments in universities will favour certain perspectives, and researchers joining a department will tend to adopt the perspectives used by the department or be sympathetic towards that perspective before joining. Thus, their research may reflect a preference for certain methodologies. This means that each year research publications reflect a whole range of perspectives and methodologies.

Given that the majority of sociological research is conducted within academic institutions, it is not surprising that the interests of the institution will affect the nature of the research and the methods used. Various sociology departments throughout the world have established their reputations by endorsing and developing various types of methodology for a diverse range of research projects. However, it would be wrong to assume that research institutions are dominated by adherence to a single theoretical perspective. Instead, it is likely that a department's methodological interests are applied in a range of research studies, although these are typically located within a broader conceptual framework.

For example, the Department of Sociology at the University of Surrey is known for its emphasis on research methodology and research training. It publicizes regular international workshops on theory and method (recent topics include qualitative analysis by computer, and the simulation of societies and social processes). The department pioneered the secondary analysis of large and complex data sets for sociological research, and recent methodological research has included work on the analysis of qualitative data, the development of methods based on social simulation and the study of ethnographic interviews.

As is typical in most contemporary research establishments, research is undertaken from both macro and micro perspectives. The department's research focuses on three interrelated strands:

- *Social differentiation* – Social divisions based on age and gender – for example, projects on women and employment, occupational pensions, health in later life and the sociology of reproduction and childhood; social divisions based on occupation and social class – for example, projects on the professions, the military and the police, and on race and ethnicity; social divisions resulting from the operation of key social institutions – for example, the criminal justice system.

- *Social change* – Research here comprises a combination of quantitative and qualitative approaches to key developments in social, political religious and cultural life. Recent projects have included studies of shifting European social, religious and cultural values, environmental understandings and transformations in European political systems. Current projects focus on the development of environmental life-cycle analyses and assessments, nationalism, changing technologies of work and the culture of jazz and blues musics.

- *Language and social interaction* – Research on spoken and written language in a variety of social settings, with a particular focus on the following: analysing the organization of verbal interaction in work settings in which people use computer and communications technology; developing computational models of patterns of verbal interaction, drawing on techniques from computational linguistics and sociological studies of everyday interaction; exploring the significance of discourse in scientific and social psychological processes.

Ⓐ
Exercise 9.1

The following projects have been undertaken by the Department of Sociology at the University of Surrey, UK. Using the information provided in the passages above to help you, sort the projects into the relevant research category. Record your answers in a three-column chart under the headings 'Social differentiation', 'Social change' and 'Language and social interaction'.

Research Projects

- 'Older Women's Working Lives' – Jay Ginn and Sara Arber.
- 'An Environmental and Social Life-Cycle Analysis of Coal and Waste as Fuels' – Martin O'Brien and Christian Heath.
- 'Modelling Talk in Context' – Andrew Fordham, Nigel Gilbert, Ian Hutchby and Robin Wooffitt.
- 'Social Impact Assessment: A "Post-Impact" Study of a Road Improvement Scheme' – Kate Burningham and Nigel Gilbert.
- 'Regional Analysis of Variation in Criminal Offending' – Alan Clarke and Nigel Fielding.
- 'The Politics of Spirituality' – Mike Hornsby-Smith.
- 'Popular Culture' – Colin Tipton.
- 'Women's Experience of Reproduction' – Hilary Thomas.

This section has focused on how theoretical factors can shape the choice of methodology and the nature of the research conducted. While it is valuable to understand the connection between theoretical preference and research practice, it is rare for choice of method to be based solely on theoretical considerations. Often sociologists' work is driven more by practical or ethical considerations than by theory, and it is quite normal for researchers to conduct research from a range of perspectives, depending on the interests of those commissioning or funding the research.

Now use the website of another university with a sociology department to find what their research interests and strengths are.

Theoretical considerations – an evaluation

Strengths

1. Identifying with a theoretical perspective gives researchers a framework for deciding how to conduct their research and which methods to use.
2. It provides a focus for data analysis – each theoretical perspective sees the purpose of social research differently, and so data will be analysed in these terms.
3. If theoretical preference shapes choice of method, this provides a logical link between sociological knowledge and practice.

Disadvantages

1. Research with a strong theoretical stance can be subjective and lead to biased interpretation.
2. Blinkered by a specific perspective, a researcher may reject appropriate/ suitable methods in favour of ones that are less valuable, simply because they are in keeping with the sociologist's philosophy.

3. Some perspectives/methods may be subject to funding restrictions as they are seen as not valuable or too small-scale to be useful.

PRACTICAL CONSIDERATIONS

This section will discuss a range of practical considerations, and examples and exercises are provided to help you understand how their influences operate. Many practical issues can affect choice of method, including:

- Topic to be studied – access.
- Research aim – type of data wanted, previous research.
- Resources – time, money, personnel.
- Funding – how much and by whom?
- The people being studied.

It is often difficult to assess the individual impact of these factors as they can combine to shape research. For the sake of convenience they will be considered separately, but it should be remembered that choice of method will rarely depend on a single factor.

Link Exercise 9.2

From the examples outlined in Chapters 7 and 8, identify and draw up a list of research studies where any of the above factors have influenced the choice of method used. Give full references for each study, using the reference section at the back of the book to help you (this will familiarize you with the correct format for presenting references in dissertations and research).

Topic to be studied

Sociologists must carefully consider the topic they are studying before deciding which research method(s) to use. Some topics lend themselves to a variety of methods, while others are very restrictive. Some topics can be studied by all sociologists, ranging from the GCSE student to the greatest academic. Other topics are much more complex and may require specific research methods or/and demand a high degree of expertise and credibility on the part of the researcher. Such topics will pose unique problems for researchers that limit their lines of inquiry.

Sensitive topics present many difficulties. Lee (1993) highlights a number of barriers to research in his book Doing Research on Sensitive Topics. First, the cultural inhibitions that exist within society can constrain research. Lee uses the taboo surrounding sex and death as an example of such constraints. Likewise Plummer (1981) found that he had to be extremely sensitive and aware of taboos in his research into homosexuality.

Second, Lee highlights the impact of 'forbidden research terrains'. This term describes areas of research that are institutionally identified as no-go zones. The concept was originally proposed by Fuller (1988), who set out to explore allegations of an anti-Cuban policy on the part of the US government, allegedly reflecting a range of economic, military and geopolitical interests aimed at isolating the island economically, politically and ideologically. However, the US government had created and maintained 'forbidden research terrains', making Fuller's research difficult to conduct and obscuring evidence of an anti-Cuban policy, Hence Fuller's choice of topic considerably limited her choice of methodology.

A third barrier to sensitive research is legal regulation. Research is subject to several legal constraints. For example, in some countries the conduct of researchers is regulated by the state. Researchers may face a legal requirement to ensure that those they research give their 'informed consent' – that is, explicit agreement to their participation based on knowledge of the nature and purpose of the research. Another topical issue concerns 'data protection', whereby regulations control the way in which information stored on computers or manual record systems is used. The implications of such constraints are discussed later in this chapter (see the discussion on ethical factors).

A fourth issue identified by Lee is termed 'chilling'. This occurs 'when researchers, anticipating hostile reactions from colleagues, are deterred from producing or disseminating research on a particular topic' (Lee, 1993, p. 34). Lee suggests that some social researchers, particularly in the United States, are constrained by the demand for 'political correctness' in academic life, and those who step outside the dominant left-leaning political consensus face marginalization, negative labelling or sanction. They also face hostility from colleagues, limited opportunities for publication, promotion or funding, and in extreme cases organized public protest against their research.

Exercise 9.2

In small groups, identify and list research areas that may attract hostility in these 'politically correct' times. How might researchers overcome these difficulties and justify their research?

The paragraphs above have considered how choice of methodology is limited by the sensitive nature of some research topics. As Lee (1993) highlights, one problem with researching sensitive topics is that there is no commonly agreed definition of what 'sensitive' constitutes. In sociological terms it is a 'relative' concept – that is dependent upon time, place, personal constructs, culture and so on. The following exercise will enable you to explore the difficulties arising from this and how researchers may try to deal with them.

Exercise 9.3

Consider the following list of research topics:

- Social phobia: fear of contact with others and/or social situations.
- Joyriding: stealing cars and driving them recklessly.
- Voting behaviour in Britain: how people use their right to vote.
- Child abuse: physical, sexual or emotional mistreatment of youth.
- Household expenditure: how money is spent in the home.

1. Write down those which you think are sensitive.
2. Suggest why these might be construed (regarded) as sensitive, and by whom.
3. Select one of the sensitive topics and using the text above to guide you:

   (a) Identify three problems that researchers might face when studying this topic.
   (b) Give one suggestion as to how researchers might attempt to overcome each of these three problems.

4. Choose one of the topics that you decided are not sensitive, and using your sociological knowledge and information contained in this book to guide you:

   (a) Identify one way in which this topic might constrain a researcher's choice of method.
   (b) Highlight one method that in your view could not be used to study this topic. Justify your answer.
   (c) Highlight your preference of method(s) for the study of this topic. Justify your answer.

As public awareness of sensitive issues has increased, so has interest in conducting research into them. Sociologists now face a dilemma. They must decide whether research that is seen by some as intrusive and lacking morality is justifiable. They must balance their desire to increase our understanding of previously unexplored aspects of the social world with the need for sensitivity. This should not deter them, however, as there is much to be gained from conducting research on sensitive topics.

Some would go as far as to suggest that sociologists have a responsibility to investigate such issues in order to enhance public understanding. As Sieber and Stanley (1988) succinctly put it:

> [S]ensitive research addresses some of society's most pressing social issues and policy questions. Although ignoring ethical issues in sensitive research is not a responsible approach to science, shying away from controversial topics simply because they are controversial, is also an avoidance of responsibility.

Similarly Lee and Renzetti (1990) state explicitly that just because sensitive topics raise complex issues and dilemmas for researchers, this does not imply that such topics should not be studied. Rather, researchers should proceed, but their work should be governed by self-regulation and adherence to the ethical guidelines produced by their professional bodies (see pp. 266–7).

Research aim

One obvious factor affecting choice of method is the purpose of the research – that is, what or whom is it actually for? This is clearly linked to the type of data required. For example, someone wishing to explore how patterns of church attendance have altered over time will logically turn to quantitative data. Similarly, someone wishing to investigate what religion means to individuals might be more inclined to use qualitative data.

One crucial issue that will shape choice of method is whether the researcher aims to identify and explore patterns and trends and to make generalizations, or whether he or she intends to provide a detailed insight into an individual case or situation. Sometimes researchers will not know the purpose of the research until they have gathered preliminary data, although this is rare nowadays as funding is normally tied to a specific research purpose.

Sometimes there will be demand for a topic to be researched but conflict about the expected findings. For example, in the aftermath of the Gulf War it emerged that there might be a link between certain illnesses being suffered by war veterans and the vaccines administered to them in preparation for the conflict. This led to heated public debate about whether a syndrome existed that could account for the symptoms being exhibited by some of those who served in the war. Public pressure mounted and calls were made for a public inquiry. As the campaign gained momentum, it became clear that those demanding research into the issue had different agendas, which may have affected the way in which the research was conducted. The following exercise will enable you to explore the implications of this.

Item B

Does Gulf War Syndrome Exist?

After the First and Second Gulf wars, concern was expressed about the exposure of soldiers in the course of the war to a number of different chemicals and toxins used in Allied munitions and injections given to soldiers to protect them against any chemical attack by Iraqi forces (see Lawson and Heaton, 2009, on state crime). It was argued that Gulf War Syndrome led to a number of birth defects in the children of soldiers exposed to such chemicals. The government was initially reluctant to hold any inquiry as to whether there was a connection between the incidence of defects among young babies born to military personnel who served in the Gulf and the toxins they were exposed to. Veterans of the conflict pushed hard for an inquiry and senior military personnel supported them. From the military's point of view, it was the 'not knowing' the effects of the use of such tactics that was paramount, while the families were more concerned about their existing and any future children. However, it is difficult to establish a causal connection between the two phenomena even if it could be shown that the incidence of defects was significantly higher than in the rest of the population.

Ⓐ
Ⓔ

Exercise 9.4

Read Item B and answer the following questions:

1. Both the military authorities and Gulf War veterans are pushing for an inquiry. Their motives for doing so are different. What are the motives of:

   (a) Gulf War veterans?
   (b) The military authorities?

2. What type of data would need to be collected to provide evidence that a 'syndrome' exists? Justify your answer.
3. How might research be organized to collect these data?
4. What type of data might help those families who are struggling to cope with the after-effects of the war? Justify your answer.
5. How might this information be collected?

The above example demonstrates how the same issue can be researched using different approaches, depending on the precise aim of the inquiry. Several sociologists have acknowledged in their published findings that they deliberately chose a certain research method to address a specific research question.

Padfield and Procter's (1996) study provides an example of this. The authors sought to explore the effect of interviewer's gender on the interviewing process in the light of increasing concern about this matter. Padfield and Procter conducted a series of interviews with a small group of young women to explore their experiences and aspirations with regard to work and family. Thirty-nine women were interviewed, 20 by Ian Procter and 19 by Mo Padfield. This allowed them to compare interviews conducted by a man with those conducted by a woman and investigate whether their respective genders had had an effect on the interviewing process.

Item C

The Effect of Interviewer's Gender or Ethnicity on the Interviewing Process: A Comparative Inquiry

Our research was conducted by semistructured interview in which we encouraged interviewees to speak freely in response to a carefully structured set of questions covering their work and household histories and their aspirations for the future with regard to both work and family formation. The interviews were shared ...

We are thus in a position to compare the interviews conducted by a man (Ian) and a woman (Mo) ... This is of interest because, although various claims are made about the effect of gender on the interviewing process, there is little empirically based comparative evidence to go on. Until recently most discussion of gender in field research was based on anecdote (Warren, 1988, p. 13). Much of this centred on what Warren calls the 'focal gender myth of field research' (1988, p. 64).

It is almost a truism of interview research, for example, that in most situations women will be able to achieve more 'rapport' with respondents because of their less-threatening quality, and better communication skills (1988, p. 44).

For many years this claim justified mainly male sociologists writing on the basis of interview material gleaned by often anonymous female interviewers. However, the myth proved to have a sting in its tail when taken up in more recent feminist discussion of research methods (Oakley, 1981; McKee and O'Brien, 1983). Rather than feminine 'rapport' being a convenient and taken for granted feature of interviewing, the much stronger claim was advanced that the interviewer's gender mattered and that male and female researchers would generate different kinds of 'knowledge'.

Other researchers such as Labov have found that the matching of the characteristics of the interviewer and interviewee in relation to ethnicity and age can have a marked impact upon the validity of the data gained.

(*Source*: M. Padfield and I. Procter, 'The Effect of Interviewer's Gender on the Interviewing Process: A Comparative Enquiry', *Sociology* 30(2), 1996; W. Labov (1973) 'The Logic of Nonstandard English', in N. Keddie (ed.) *Tinker. Tailor: The Myth of Cultural Deprivation*. Harmondsworth: Penguin.)

Exercise 9.5

Item C provides some details of Padfield and Procter's study. Read the item and complete the following questions. This should give you an insight into Procter and Padfield's rationale for conducting the research and how the research design reflected their aims.

1. What is a semistructured interview? (Hint: If unsure look at the section on interviews in Chapter 7).
2. Why was it important for the questions to be carefully structured in this research?
3. What was the authors' motive for exploring the chosen topic?
4. In your own words, explain what is meant by 'the focal gender myth of field research'.
5. According to Padfield and Procter, what was the sting in the tail of the myth?

As the above example demonstrates, the researcher may not need to choose a research method because in some cases it may be determined by the research aim. When considering the research aim itself, some consideration must also be given to the choices open to the researcher. In practice the research aim is often dictated by the external agencies that fund it and researchers will simply apply their skills to fulfil the research brief. This may involve choosing an appropriate method, or working with a method already defined by the research project.

Resources

Another factor affecting choice of research method is the availability of resources. One resource constraint is time. Some research methods are more time efficient than others and consequently will be favoured for research with a short time limit. Time is inevitably linked to money. For example, it is common knowledge that quantitative methods of data collection are expensive but analysis is relatively quick and economical. Although designing a vehicle for data collection may be time-consuming and require the expertise of several personnel, once this is in place the rest of the process should be labour efficient and wage bills low. In general once a large database has been established (via the encoding of information) computer analysis can be conducted by a few skilled individuals. The results can be interpreted quickly and reported succinctly. There is little need for a vast research team with large overhead costs.

Whereas quantitative methods tend to be seen as seen as quick and cheap, qualitative methods are regarded as more time-consuming. First, as the aim of the latter is to gather in-depth data to provide a realistic insight into events or situations, there may be a need to spend considerable time in the 'field' prior to commencing the research project. This can involve making useful contacts, learning the vocabulary, jargon or procedures associated with the group or simply developing empathy with those to be studied. For example, before undertaking her study of expectant mothers, *From Here to Maternity,* for a period of 6 months Oakley (1981) conducted observations in the maternity unit of a London hospital to gain grounding for her research. Similarly Langham (1991) spent time learning about the police force prior to starting her research on female recruitment and retention in the police force.

Second, in some cases the quality of the data produced will only be as good as the researchers' initial understanding of the groups they are studying. Qualitative methods rely on a degree of rapport developing between researcher and subject, and this cannot be rushed as otherwise any relationship that develops is likely to be superficial. It was for this reason that, for their classic study of domestic violence, Dobash and Dobash (1980) relied on the services of two female research assistants who spent many months in a refuge to conduct interviews with battered women.

Third, the need for in-depth data presents the researcher with two problems: recording the data will be a lengthy process, and meaningful analysis of the data will be difficult owing to the sheer amount of detail involved. If an attempt is to be made to quantify the data so that general patterns or trends can be discovered, a coding system will have to be devised to account for every possible variation in response. Even if the data is left in qualitative form it will have to be converted from a raw transcript into an accessible format.

This makes a considerable demand on time and labour power. For example, each of Oakley's tape-recorded interviews lasted approximately 2½ hours, and Dobash and Dobash's interviews took between 2 and 12 hours. To put this in context, if you can remember how long it took you as a child to transcribe (listen to and write down) the words of your favourite pop song so that you could sing along, you'll have a fair idea of the work involved in roughly three minutes of such work!

If a researcher works alone on a study, very little data can be gathered via qualitative methods unless the study stretches over a long period of time – for example, it took Barker (1984) 6 years to complete her in-depth study of a religious community. For this reason it is common for teams of researchers to collect quantitative data, although before the data collection starts they must standardize their approach to ensure that they are all interpreting and recording events in a uniform way. The importance of such an approach is demonstrated by Willmott (1987) in *Friendship Networks and Social Support*. Willmott used a team of five female researchers to collect data in his small-scale social survey of friendship and informal social support, and an important part of the research process was deciding how to measure ambiguous concepts such as friendship. Without agreement on this Willmott could not be sure that all his researchers were interpreting the data in the same way as he was. This could erode the benefit of employing individuals to speed up the research process.

Agreeing how key concepts will be quantified and ensuring that this interpretation is applied consistently throughout the research process can be time-consuming and costly, as it requires repeated liaison between the members of the research team. Anyone conducting research on a limited budget would not be able to coordinate such a complex data collection process and would probably be forced to adopt a more structured research method with less scope for misunderstanding and difficulties with interpretation.

Funding

Funding can dictate the methodology used. For example, a drug company funding research into the effectiveness or suitability of a drug treatment is likely to favour a methodology that is designed to collect quantitative data on recovery, remission, relapse and so on, as these are the types of statistic that will help with the marketing of the product. In contrast, those who are against drugs or are financially independent from clinical trials may be more interested in the qualitative effects of drug intervention – that is, the physical, social and psychological effects on the person undergoing treatment.

Sometimes it is less easy to identify the effects that funding has upon research but these can still be powerful. Sociological research can be funded from a variety of sources, including university research budgets, private companies, research councils and the public sector. Research funding is an emotive issue. For example, it could be argued that to conduct research is to exercise a fundamental human right to develop knowledge. Thus, in a democracy, all research is legitimate and should be supported. However, although this principle may be philosophically sound, financially it is less so. Research is expensive and can be conducted only if funding is secured. This can act to stratify potential research projects into those deemed worthy of funding and those deemed not.

Hence researchers cannot explore areas and issues of their choice without regard to the financial implications, and the harsh reality of financial constraints often sculpts their hypothesizing. Some researchers remain true to their academic or philosophical selves, actively seeking funding for the issues that they regard to be important. Some re-orientate their interests to secure funding, and in doing so compromise some of their interests and ideals for the opportunity to conduct research that may align itself with the interests they retain. Other researchers are largely value-free, operating as 'ministers without portfolio' and accepting research briefs shaped directly by the interests of commerce or the public sector. In such cases they act as consultants and apply their research skills to address the questions of the agency or client funding the research.

The first two types of researcher discussed above are more likely to be employed in a university setting, where it is still possible to retain links with pure research, and the third are more likely to be employed in a commercial setting such as market research, where the emphasis is largely upon applying research skills to answer commercial questions.

Those employed in a market research environment are less likely to be concerned with the impact that funding can have upon research, primarily because they have chosen to conduct research for commercial reasons. However, those employed in a university environment are more likely to be concerned with and affected by funding pressures. The funding of university research has become a very controversial subject in recent years. For example, Billig (1997) notes that structural changes have affected the type of research that is valued by society, and universities have been forced to respond to this. Billig discusses how the political circumstances of the 1980s affected the type of research conducted by university-based researchers. He suggests that the increased impact of conservatism, particularly with regard to its emphasis on market forces, forced universities to be seen as profit-making:

> The Universities, long suspected by Conservatives of being incubators of Socialism, were particular targets. They too were told to become entrepreneurial. Academics were to be useful members of society, contributing directly to the national goal of wealth creation. The government, which finances the main funding councils of research, has made it clear that research which aids the nation's profitability should be given priority. Sad to say, universities have accepted their new role as wealth-creators. Entrepreneurial professors are the order of the day. Academics compete to obtain research contracts. Funding is not sought in order to do research, but research is done in order to get funding. (Ibid., p. 8)

In response to political intervention, universities have been keen to promote their scientific leaning and raise the public profile of research whose value can be quantified in monetary terms. University research output has been increasingly policed by government arbiters and overseers have been put in place to grade this output. Hence every academic product can be assigned a commercial value. Funding is linked to grading and each published work has a financial value. The result of this, according to Billig, is that academics are under pressure to 'publish or be dammed'.

Such pressure has affected the way research is conducted. Social scientists, keen to earn lucrative contracts from their research, are promoting the scientific value of their discipline. Billig gives the example of psychology departments gravitating towards the use of IT and promoting their work from a human–machine interface perspective. Similarly, sociologists appear to be turning away from pure research, which is perceived as of limited practical value, in favour of applied studies to inform social policy and social and economic development. As a result the range of research studies is becoming more limited, and decisions as to whether or not certain research is worthy of funding are now based on evaluation of practical utility rather than academic worth.

Despite this, agencies associated with social research are keen to publicize their commitment to funding a variety of research projects, rather than simply those which fit a predetermined agenda. For example, their desire to clarify a misunderstanding over funding in 1996 led Professors Michael West and Charles Hulme of the Economic and Social Research Council to write an open letter to the academic journal *The Psychologist* (March 1996):

> We are members of the Economic and Social Research Council Research Grants Board which is responsible for the allocation of research funding in the social sciences of around £14.4 million annually.
>
> Recently, the ESRC has identified thematic priorities for research funding in the future in order to achieve a more strategic and directed approach to issues of scientific and applied social importance. However, one of the consequences of this appears to have been a misunderstanding that has developed on the part of some members of the scientific community who assumed that the ESRC no longer operates a responsive mode of funding, and that all research funding requests have to fit in with one of the thematic priorities identified.
>
> We wish to clarify and re-emphasise the fact that the Research Grants Board still operates in a purely responsive mode, so that none of its funding is allocated to any or all of the thematic research priorities identified.

In spite of the ESRC's promise to safeguard the development of the social sciences, it cannot be denied that research is now directly or indirectly influenced by funding. Faced with such pressures, researchers have to conduct research that is perceived to be of commercial value, and as a consequence may choose methods that reflect financial rather than theoretical considerations. Such a move is welcomed by those who argue that for too long researchers have been preoccupied with theorizing rather than practicality.

Educational research has attracted such criticism in recent years for focusing on theory at the expense of tackling the 'real issues' facing teachers. Alan Smithers, director of the Centre for Education and Employment Research at Brunel University, has lent support to this view by arguing that researchers have to become more rigorous if they are to continue to justify huge public expenditure. In an address delivered to the British Association's Annual Festival of Science at Leeds University, Smithers argued that too many researchers act like social scientists, exploring esoteric (mysterious/select) issues instead of addressing real issues of practical relevance. Smithers concluded that most educational research is not valued: 'despite receiving some £100 million in public funding each year, the results are largely ignored by everyone from politicians to class teachers' (cited in Barnard, 1997).

In small groups, discuss your opinion of Smithers's argument. To what extent do you agree that researchers should produce work of commercial rather than academic/theoretical value?

The impact that funding can have on research can be seen as both negative and positive. Those wishing to defend 'pure' research (that is, research that aims to broaden knowledge and understanding of the world rather than being motivated by practical or commercial aims) may regard the tightening of funding restrictions and the rise of cost effectiveness in the research department a disturbing trend. Research that is perceived to be of little financial value will be starved of funding. More cynically, research that is perceived to be subversive could be suppressed. However, those interested in promoting the practical applications of research may consider that increased financial restrictions and accountability are positive moves. Research will be conducted with definite aims and the findings will have a direct meaning for those in the world beyond the research department. Forcing universities to be cost-effective will bring them into the modern age of competition and financial viability, and their success in responding may determine their survival.

Personal characteristics of the researcher

It is not difficult to find examples of the interplay between the topic to be studied, the personal characteristics of the researcher and the choice of method in sociological research. Many topics can be studied only in certain ways by certain people possessing certain features, qualities or skills that gain them entry (access) to the research situation.

Griffiths's (1996) research into the social world of fruit machine playing demonstrates a number of ways in which the personal characteristics of the researcher can have a bearing on research. Griffiths explored the relative merits of participant versus non-participant observation in research fieldwork. In doing so he revealed how the personal characteristics of the researcher can have a bearing on which observation method is chosen.

Griffiths notes that anyone attempting to conduct observational research needs to have (1) knowledge of the people, culture and/or language being studied, and (2) the ability to pass as a 'native' member. Thus, personal characteristics such as the identity of the researcher are crucial in dictating whether such research is possible. He goes on to highlight how different observation methods make different demands on the researcher. For example, non-participant observation usually depends on the researcher not being known to the studied group, and in order for observers to blend into a research setting without altering the conditions they must be possess certain characteristics. In Griffiths' case, experience, age and sex were factors in the ability to remain undetected:

> [S]ince arcades are generally frequented by teenagers and young men, the general rule is that the older the researcher, the harder it will be to mingle in successfully. If the arcade is not too crowded, the only alternative is to be one of the 'punters'. (Ibid., p. 17)

Griffiths highlights how his personal characteristics enabled him to enrich his research by using a less-known observation method: 'self-ethnography' – that is, drawing on personal experience to enhance understanding of the topic under study. Griffiths used to be a regular fruit machine player, so he was in a position to analyse his own experiences. The value of this approach in providing raw research data is limited; rather its strength lies in being a source of hypotheses and theories about why people gamble. By drawing attention to the benefits that certain personal characteristics can bring to the research process, Griffiths does not imply that observational research should be conducted only by those with previous personal experience of the subject area. Instead he simply highlights how in some cases it may be beneficial for researchers to 'become their own subject' (ibid., p. 18).

The personal characteristics of the researcher can also have a detrimental effect on the research process in certain circumstances. For example, difficulties may arise if researchers have certain attitudes or beliefs that may compromise their ability to be objective (see p. 163) when conducting research. This issue received media attention when a well-known, controversial, right-wing academic, Dr James Tooley, was commissioned by Ofsted to conduct an inquiry into the practical value of publicly funded educational research. Ofsted stands for the Office for Standards in Education, and is a government-appointed organization of teachers and head teachers (usually retired) who inspect the quality of education in nurseries, children's services, schools and colleges nationally. They write reports and give grades to the organizations they inspect and these are published (for further information you can look at their website www.ofsted.gov.uk). Tooley's appointment attracted strong criticism from the representatives of the educational research community:

> While we would welcome any impartial inquiry into educational research we would also be very concerned that someone who is known to take a strong political position can have a biased perspective. The standards of fair inquiry must be upheld. (Michael Bassey, executive secretary of the British Educational Research Association, Annual Conference, York, 1997 – see Bassey, 1998)

A spokesman for Ofsted subsequently denied that Dr Tooley would allow his personal views to colour his research, but Tooley's own comments did little to silence the critics:

> We want to look at the value for money of current educational research ... how much of it actually feeds into schools and how much of it is for the rather incestuous benefit of the research community – to put it rather crudely. (Quoted in Budge, 1997)

Exercise 9.7

In small groups, discuss the following questions:

1. Why did educational researchers object to Dr Tooley's appointment?
2. What motives might Ofsted have had for making the appointment, given their knowledge of Tooley's 'right-wing' leanings?
3. To what extent do you agree that researchers had a right to be concerned about Tooley's appointment, under the circumstances?

The above discussion has highlighted how the personal characteristics of the researcher may have a bearing on the method chosen or the broader research process. Although it is unlikely that the personal characteristics of the researcher will be the most significant factor influencing the choice of research method, they will no doubt have a bearing upon what type of research is possible.

One thing worth bearing in mind is that simply because a researcher might share certain physiological characteristics (for example, age, race, gender) with the group being studied it does not necessarily mean that they will share the same insights. The reverse can also be true – that is, if differences between the researcher and the researched could benefit the research, leading to increased mutual understanding and respect. The relation between the personal characteristics of the researcher and those researched also has implications for issues such as objectivity and value freedom. For example, are researchers more likely to be objective if they are different from those being studied, or will their status as outsiders lead to a prejudicial or stereotypical interpretation of group behaviour? It is difficult to tell.

Rhodes (1994) has provided something of an insight into this through her study of the effects that race has on data elicited in interviews. She concludes that it would be wrong to assume that matching the personal characteristics of the interviewer and the interviewee will lead to more valid data being collected. Instead, she suggests that although a researcher with different personal characteristics from those of the respondent may access different information and arrive at a different interpretation and understanding, this can be equally valid.

Ethics

Until relatively recently, little attention was paid to the ethical considerations surrounding sociological research. If asked to 'critically evaluate the factors affecting a sociologist's choice of research method' in the 1980s, a typical student would probably have divided the discussion into theoretical and practical factors. If mentioned at all, ethical issues would have been given minimal attention.

There were several reasons why ethics played little part in sociological research and, more explicitly, choice of methodology, for example:

- Lack of awareness that researchers had a moral obligation to those being studied.
- Lack of legislation on the monitoring of ethical aspects of research.
- Society as a whole paying less attention to issues such as citizenship and empowerment (individual rights), resulting in faceless subjects who could be manipulated for the greater good of society as a whole.

In earlier decades, if any method was likely to be questioned on ethical grounds it was covert participant observation. This was due to the deception and betrayal involved in publicizing data collected from naive and unconsenting subjects. In the 1970s and 1980s works such as Humphreys' *Tearoom Trade* (1970) and Barker's *The Making of a Moonie* (1984) drew public attention to the intrusive nature of this research method and sociologists found themselves in the unenviable position of publicly defending themselves against the charge of being unethical.

Humphreys (1970) felt obliged to justify his research in order to challenge the criticism that it was unethical. In doing so he first provided a definition of 'unethical', arguing that research is unethical if researchers (1) misrepresent their identity or aims in order to acquire information, (2) breach confidentiality or (3) conduct research that is detrimental to the interests or welfare of the respondents. He then stated that, judged in accordance with his definition, his research was beyond reproach. Barker (1984) was less explicit about what constituted unethical behaviour in research terms, although she too vehemently defended her research, suggesting that it provided a unique insight into a group that was seen as threatening to society. Perhaps in this way her betrayal or exploitation of her sample (the few) was justified by the greater good it would bring to those in wider society (the many) who could potentially be duped or 'brainwashed' by the Moonies.

Research such as that by Humphreys and Barker undoubtedly heightened awareness of the ethical dimension of research. What followed was a concerted effort on the part of various professional bodies to draw up an explicit code of practice for those wishing to undertake sociological research. The ethical codes drafted by the American Sociological Association, the Association of Social Anthropologists of the Commonwealth and the Social Research Association provided the inspiration for the Statement of Ethical Practice and Guidelines for Good Professional Conduct issued by the British Sociological Association in 1992.

The BSA Statement of Ethical Practice

This document sets out a series of ethical obligations to guide the conduct of those engaging in sociological research. The guidelines are intended to 'inform member's ethical judgements rather than impose on them a set of external standards'. A number of key issues are covered within three main areas:

1. *Professional integrity* – Sociologists should protect the integrity of soci- ology as a discipline by safeguarding the interests of those involved or affected by their research through ethical practice.

2. *Relations with and responsibility towards research participants* – Sociologists must ensure that the goal of their research does not impinge on the rights of others. They must safeguard the wellbeing of research participants and obtain their informed consent. The anonymity and privacy of research participants must be respected unless there are 'clear and over-riding' reasons not to do so.

3. *Relations with and responsibilities towards sponsors and/or funders* – Sociologists should ensure that sponsors and/or funders appreciate the obligations that sociologists have to wider society. The relationship between sponsors and researchers must not prevent the research from being as objective as possible.

There are certain problematic issues that arise from any ethical guidelines in research. For example, the issue of informed consent is a central aspect of the guidelines, but there are particular problems with the idea of a fully informed consent being given. For example, it is difficult to argue that it has been given when the researchers are unsure of the total extent of the information that may emerge about participants from the project and so it is impossible to know what is being consented to (see Haverkamp, 2005). In certain situations, consent for female participation in research may be reliant on the prior giving of male permission (by fathers or husbands) and this raises ethical issues of its own (Marshall, 2003). Where deception is an integral part of the research strategy, then consent can be obtained only at the debrief (and not even then if there is to be a follow-up study).

Sociologists should consider the ethical guidelines in all research, although some research may be more controversial and make greater demands on sociologists to exercise their ethical judgement. Research on sexuality requires the researcher to exercise considerable caution, and it is not surprising that systematic research into this area of social life did not occur until relatively recently. Contemporary research has been inspired by the need to understand structural changes within the family and society at large, and to this end, sociologists have become increasingly interested in the study of sex and sexuality. Burke (1994) notes that media coverage on alternative sexualities has grown in recent years, and in the wake of gay liberation there have been an increased number of lesbian and gay studies. Burke undertook a study of lesbian and gay police officers and the difficulties such individuals face if their sexual orientation is known. The following exercise allows you to explore and consider the implications of his work.

Item D

Researching Gay and Lesbian Police Officers

The conservative and discriminatory attitudes held by some sections of the police force – the so-called 'canteen culture' – have long been identified with homophobic sentiment (see Lawson and Heaton, 2009). Along with the military, the police force has been one of the last bastions of acceptable prejudice against gay people and this has had consequences not only for the way the police interact and respond to members of the public who are gay and lesbian, but also for those police officers who are homosexual themselves. While there may be some openly gay police officers, the existence of anti-gay prejudice has contributed to a strategy of remaining invisible. Moreover, anti-police attitudes among the gay community might also encourage gay police men and women to maintain a low profile at work and at play. Those police officers who are open at work about their sexuality may come under particular pressure from non-gay officers looking for any sign of weakness from them.

Exercise 9.8

Read Item D and conduct the following tasks.

1. Consider the difficulties outlined above and the ethical issues detailed earlier, and in pairs or small groups decide:

   (E)   (a) Which research method(s) you would choose for a study of gay/lesbian police officers? Justify your answer.

   (E)   (b) How you might obtain your sample and what difficulties you may face in doing so?

   (E)   (c) Which ethical guidelines would be most applicable to this research?

When a decision is made to proceed with research, sociologists should endeavour to protect the participants as much as possible. This can involve ensuring that they experience no harm or violation during the course of the research, but can also be extended to consider the long-term effects that participation might have. The importance of this is highlighted by Weeks and James (1995). In their book *Eccentrics*, they describe the difficulties involved in selecting and subsequently protecting a sample for their study:

> Having decided to undertake a systematic study of eccentricity, the first challenge was to find the eccentrics. They tend to take themselves seriously, and there was a danger they would not want to be part of a study in which they might fear they would be associated with mental illness or ridiculed. (Ibid., p. 13)

To overcome this difficulty, Weeks and James decided to advertise for participants. Although this posed methodological difficulties, the researchers could be satisfied that those who came forward would be willing participants in the research. Their desire to be ethically sound, however, exposed their study to criticism on the grounds that (1) the self-selecting sample might not be representative (they themselves acknowledged this: '[W]ould there not be something eccentric about any person who answered an advertisement soliciting eccentrics?'), and (2) the sample would be self-defining – that is 'the volunteer would be deciding for himself, at least initially, if he was eccentric' (ibid., p. 13). However they did appear to secure legitimate access to unique individuals perceived to be the embodiment of eccentricity, as the following extract from their book demonstrates:

> Norma Jean Bryant, from western Connecticut, exhibits what might be called global eccentricity: she leads nearly every aspect of her life in a non-conforming way. She believes that it's immoral to throw anything away, so she still owns everything she has ever purchased or been given.
>
> Wherever she goes, Norma Jean pushes around a grocery cart with headlights, loaded with a miscellany of objects from her collection. Among many other hobbies, she plays in a kazoo band. In winter, she wears a fireman's coat. Norma Jean is a great entertainer, but she can't cook very well so she gives what she calls 'canned-food parties'. In summer, she has a Wimbledon party with strawberries (canned, of course) and dresses as a member of the British royal family. (Ibid., p. 19)

In their sympathetic interpretation of Norma Jean's behaviour, Weeks and James demonstrate their ethical responsibility, incorporating respect for the construct system of a research participant. This encourages the reader to value the behaviour as meaningful to Norma Jean and as offering scope to a society constrained by convention:

> At the root of...Norma Jean's nonconformity is a persistent refusal to accept anything as given...to question assumptions that the rest of us take for granted. Norma Jean expressed this state of mind concisely in her statement to us: 'Each of us is born a unique individual...While the results of that sort of extreme non-conformity may be absurd to others, for the eccentric there is a sense of freedom from the constraints of everyday life. The rest of the world believes that there is only one direction to walk, that fireman's coats are for fireman and that a lady should wear a tweed coat in winter; but for eccentrics those are just boring rules, which only exist to be flouted.' (Ibid., p. 20)

Another ethical issue for researchers to consider is the long-term effects that their research might have upon the participants. It is possible for participants to be harmed or otherwise affected during the course of the research but for it only to come to light once the research has finished. One way to have regard to the ethical guidelines on the protection of participants is to conduct a follow-up study on the research group. The value of this can be twofold: it can reveal any harm caused by participating in research generally, and it can reveal any specific harm caused by the research method(s) used. However, despite the obvious value of follow-up studies, it is quite difficult to find examples of the effects of research on participants. Brannen (1993) describes this as a 'neglected topic, largely subject to speculation rather than empirical research'.

Exercise 9.9

Using information in this chapter and elsewhere, form small groups of four to five people and discuss why little attention is paid to studying the effects of research on participants. Present your ideas and feedback to the rest of your class, if possible.

Brannen (1993) has previously conducted a 3-year longitudinal study of mothers returning to work after maternity leave, and in the follow-up research (ibid.) the participants were asked to assess their experience of the research process. Brannen identified three particular aspects of the research process that had had important consequences for the participants: (1) the theoretical framework and research design, (2) the research methods (in her case, interviews, self-completion questionnaires, child development tests and observations) and (3) the study findings.

Brannen describes how the participants had been affected by all stages of the research process, from the theoretical framework to the research methods and the findings themselves. The theoretical framework and design had served to construct the participants as subjects of research in different ways. Methodology was seen to have affected the validity of the data collected. For example, less-structured methods (semistructured interviews) were viewed more positively as they had

> afforded mothers the opportunity to be reflexive about currently salient and immediate concerns, namely returning to work after the birth of the first baby, [and]produced therapeutic pay-offs through the interest and responsiveness of the interviewer, and the interviewee's knowledge that she was part of a wider collectivity. (Ibid., p. 344)

The research findings had a dual impact on the participants. At the individual level the participants had sought to locate themselves in relation to others by comparing their children's development with that of others in the study and with developmental norms. At the group level the participants had become politicized as the project proceeded: through their own experiences and through being sensitized (made more aware) by the research process they had become conscious of the dire straits of British childcare and regarded the research findings as ammunition for social policy change.

Having considered each aspect thoroughly, Brannen concludes that research is least likely to be detrimental to research participants when 'there is a close match between the concerns and characteristics of the researchers and the researched' (ibid., p. 328). This close match is likely to benefit project and participants alike, because the participants will feel valued rather than threatened if the researchers share their interests and thus the researchers will be able to acquire data with a higher degree of validity. The reporting of this can have the positive long-term effect of empowering the research group.

Item E

Researching Shoplifting

For his undergraduate project, a male student decided to research shoplifting. He had seen an interesting programme on TV and thought it would fit in with the crime and deviance topic ('dark figure of crime'). Also, his uncle was a security guard at the local shopping centre and had lots of friends who were store detectives. His uncle could give him some insider information about likely culprits, who is most likely to get caught, what happens to those who get caught – that is, which factors determine who is likely to be prosecuted – and so on.

At the start of his project, the student decided to distribute supposedly anonymous questionnaires to sixth-formers at his former school to see just how widespread shoplifting was among the general population. When preparing the questionnaires he included a secret coding system so that he would know who had completed them. This would enable him to do follow-up interviews later if necessary. He made a note to enter the secret codes onto his computer when he got home, so that he could store each person's data electronically when the questionnaires were returned.

To obtain some extra data, he decided to spend a Saturday doing some observation at the local shopping centre with his uncle. So as not to arouse suspicion, he borrowed a spare uniform. Luckily the uniform fitted him. In fact he looked every inch the part as he paraded around the shopping centre and even got a bit carried away, asking a couple of people if he could see their receipts and turning a blind eye to a brunette who appeared to be slipping some 'passionate plum' lip gloss up her sleeve.

To make his research notes look authentic, he borrowed a few pages of the official incident log book to write down his observations. He also had a quick flick through the records of previous incidents and jotted down some of the information that would provide useful qualitative data to increase the validity of his study.

Exercise 9.10

This exercise requires you to evaluate the consequences of conducting research that fails to follow ethical guidelines. Read Item E and answer the following questions.

1. List as many breaches of ethical guidelines in this research as you can.
2. Compare your answers with those of at least one other sociology student.

3. Suggest how the research could be redesigned to make it more ethically sound.
4. How appropriate do you regard the topic to be for a piece of sociological research? Justify your answer.

Exercise 9.11

The accompanying table summarizes the material covered so far in this chapter on the factors that may affect choice of research method. Copy out the table and fill in the blanks using the sections you have just read to help you.

Choosing a research method – summary of key factors

Factor	Key issues	Applied examples
Theoretical perspective.		
Choice of method can be shaped by theoretical preference, although there has been a contemporary shift towards drawing on diverse perspectives/ methods.	Interactionism has led to the development of alternatives to structuralist methodology Contemporary research from macro and micro perspectives on the increase	C_____ S_____ : 1930s → ecological sociology. 1960 → interactionism. c_____ / t_____ analysis. Surrey University: 3 strands of research: 1. s_____ differentiation. 2. social c_____ . 3. l_____ and interaction.
Practical issues.		
Choice of method is most likely to be determined by a range of practical factors that constrain the researcher.	Topic to be studied Research aim: generalization or in-depth investigation Resources Personal characteristics of researcher Funding	L_____ (1993): sensitive issues. Fuller (1988): f_____ r_____ d_____ G_____ W _____ S_____ (1996)

Padfield and Procter (1996)
i_____ gender effects
O _____ (1981), Langham
(1991).
G _____ (1996), Rhodes
(1994), Tooley (in Budge, 1997).
B_____ (1997), Smithers
(1997)

Ethical issues

The BSA is increasingly affecting the way in which sociologists conduct their research and report their findings.	Self-monitoring issues Responsibility towards those being studied Participant effects	H _____ (1970), Barker (1984). Burke (1994), W_____ and J_____ (1995). B_____ (1993).

Methodological pluralism

Methodological pluralism (or mixed-methods research) is a common solution to the limitations of individual research methods. The approach involves the use of a variety of research methods, ideally both quantitative and qualitative. The aim is to obtain data that is reliable, valid and representative of the group under study, if not the wider population. For example, Brewer and Hunter (2006) argue that by combining the four research methods of fieldwork, surveys, experiments and unobtrusive approaches, the level of validity attained is much higher than if one method is deployed. Hammersley (2008) argues that sociologists should keep a distinction between triangulation and mixed-methods research, as triangulation can be useful where there is not a 'mixed-method' approach, for example, where different sources of qualitative data (observation and personal documents) can also assist the validity of the research.

McNeill (1985) use the term 'triangulation' to describe such an approach, whereby researchers choose a mixture of data sources and research methods in order to present a balanced picture of their topic. He sees the approach as useful to accommodating what he terms the 'four-cornered relationship' between theoretical preferences, choice of topic, practical considerations and choice of research method. By this he means that sociologists' theoretical perspective will guide the choice of topic and the research method adopted. Choice of topic influences research method and *vice versa*. Triangulation could minimize the effect of each individual influence.

The rationale for using more than one research method was initially to overcome the apparent incompatability between quantitative and qualitative approaches, it being held that by including elements of both approaches in a pragmatic way the researcher could get the best of both worlds. Bergman (2008) suggests that the dominant paradigm in research methodology in the 1990s was the view that qualitative and quantitative had such fundamentally different characteristics and philosophies that it would be difficult to find a reason other than pragmatism for practising mixed-methods research. However, he also suggests that the characteristics attributed to each approach were stereotypical and reflected the interests of both qualitative and quantitative researchers, who jealously guarded their own approaches. By rejecting their incompatibility, mixed-methods researchers have deployed a variety of quantitative and qualitative approaches on the grounds that the data generated by both sets of strategies would provide a fuller picture of what was being studied. That is, the strengths of quantitative approaches combined with the strengths of qualitative methods are seen as allowing the exploration of both the objective and the subjective dimensions of any phenomenon (see Erzberger and Kelle, 2003).

Many sociologists use more than one method or source of data in the course of a single piece of research. For example, although Humphreys's (1970) classic study is perhaps remembered for the controversy over his use of participant observation as a research method, he also used unstructured interviews and questionnaires to obtain biographical data on his sample. Similarly, Corrigan (1981) combined a number of methods and types of data in his study of working-class children, using school records, direct observation and interviews. Whether these constitute examples of triangulation is debatable, as the definition does not specify how many methods or types of data must be drawn upon for the approach to be triangulatory. Indeed, Tashakorri and Cresswell (2007) identify studies that pay lip-service to having more than one method (for example, having a few interviews in a predominantly quantitative approach) as 'quasi-mixed studies'. There are also many ways in which the methods can be mixed together, such as a dominant quantitative strategy preceding a qualitative element (or vice versa), or parallel quantitative and qualitative elements in a more equal balance (see Brannen, 2008). Critics of mixed-methods approaches argue that the reality is that quantitative methods dominate in mixed-methods research and that it is really a continuation of positivism except by name (see Giddings, 2006), in which qualitative methods are reduced to an 'after-thought' position.

Barker's (1984) study of a US religious cult is widely regarded as a clear example of methodological pluralism. Barker's research attracted controversy, however, owing in part to the thoroughness with which she conducted the research. During a 6-year research period Barker used in-depth interviews, participant observation and questionnaires and compiled her own personal record of events (her diary) to obtain data on the members of the Unification Church (the Moonies). Her aim was to determine why people joined the cult, what life was like for cult members and how the cult was organized. Barker concluded that membership of the cult was not the result of coercion or manipulation, but served a purpose for the individuals concerned and met certain individual needs.

Although Barker's conclusions were greeted with scepticism and have since been heavily criticized on practical and ethical grounds, she defends her research, arguing that without such a comprehensive approach little would be have been gained. Methodological pluralism enabled Barker to understand the rationale and motives behind the movement and how membership had affected the lives of the members and their families. Before Barker's research little had been known about the cult and public perception had been based on ignorance and prejudice.

Pilcher (1995) has demonstrated the value of combining various methods and types of data to enhance our understanding of social groups and phenomena. Pilcher explored the sociology of age via secondary data drawn from the 1991 census and cross-cultural and historical evidence. Demographic data enabled her to provide an age profile of modern Britain and to speculate about the processes that make up age. She considered the feasibility and consequences of conceptualizing age in chronological, physiological, life course and cohort membership terms, and concluded that 'Age must be understood as a simultaneous combination of these interrelated processes: of biological or physiological ageing; of social or cultural ageing; both of which take place within particular historical contexts' (ibid.). This provides a justification for employing methodological pluralism when attempting to understand the sociology of age. If we regard age as a multifaceted concept, surely it must be studied in these terms, using a range of methods and drawing on varied data.

Pilcher demonstrates the contribution that cross-cultural and historical evidence, analysed comparatively can make to our understanding of age. Such data can be used to show that experiences in childhood, youth and old age vary according to place and time. In turn, this can help to establish the extent to which age and ageing are socially constructed (rather than biologically determined). For example, if comparative research provides evidence that people of similar ages (that is, biological or chronological counterparts/equals) behave or are treated differently in different societies or cultures, this suggests that age identity is at least in part the result of social expectations and pressures. Such comparative data can be combined with demographic secondary data to build up a picture of the key processes involved in growing up and growing older.

Winlow (2001) used participant observation, informal interviews and secondary sources in his study of bouncers and crime in Sunderland which examined changing masculinities among working-class men. As he was part of the community he was studying, Winlow could use his personal contacts to gain access to the doormen he was studying and he took a job as a bouncer himself. Winlow was interested in masculinity and violence in relation to culture of the local community and criminality. The secondary sources such as patterns of crime and previous studies of working-class life allowed him to make comparisons with the past and look at changes in working-class life over time. He also drew upon a range of theoretical approaches such as the sociology of masculinity, subcultural theory, theories of postmodernism and globalization to provide a framework for his practical research.

Allen (2006) refers to mixed-method approaches to investigate whether the often cited gender difference in the 'fear of crime' (with women coming out as more fearful than men) was real or a product of only relying on the analysis of official statistics. In addition to interpreting the British Crime Survey statistics, Allen drew upon other sources of information, including a questionnaire and a subsample of interviewees to test the gender differences in fear of crime. By probing male and female understandings of the intensity of the fear of crime and the risk factors associated with crime, she shows that the differences between men and women are nowhere near as large as would be suggested by looking only at the statistics.

Item F

Being Old

Being old can be great, but nobody ever tells you about some of the hidden pitfalls of getting old. There are so many ways that you have to adjust your lifestyle to deal with the new frailties and uncertainties that come with getting old. You have to take advantage of a toilet whenever you can as it becomes more difficult to hold out if you want to go. You cannot drink as much as when you were young or stay awake to enjoy the night life in the same way. And the noise in public places makes it more difficult to hear what is being said, so you just nod along and hope that this is the right thing to do in response to what people are saying to you.

Exercise 9.12

Pilcher (1995) drew upon demographic, cross-cultural and historical data when conducting her study, but not qualitative data, which could have provided a subjective insight into the process of ageing. This exercise is designed to help you consider the benefits and limitations of using such data when exploring the sociology of age. Read Item F and answer the following questions.

1. What type of data does this account represent?
2. What might Pilcher have gained from including accounts such as the one in Item F in her work?
3. What might be the problems with obtaining this type of data:

   (a) Cross-culturally – that is, from different societies and cultures?
   (b) Historically – that is, from different time periods?

4. What justification might sociologists give for not using data such as the above in their research?

It is becoming increasingly common for researchers to use a range of methods in their research. The above examples have highlighted some of the benefits of methodological pluralism, but inevitably there will also be drawbacks that will deter sociologists from using a plurality (range/variety) of techniques. The following exercise is designed to help you identify both.

Methodological pluralism – an evaluation

Exercise 9.13

1. Using the knowledge you have acquired from the above section (and a research methods textbook if necessary), draw up a table like the one here and summarize the advantages and disadvantages of methodological pluralism. One example of each has been provided to give you a start.
2. Now think about and complete the evaluation section: when and in what circumstances would it be best to use methodological pluralism? Why?

Advantages	Disadvantages
1. A much greater variety of data can be collected.	1. It has cost implications.
2.	2.

Exam focus: structured question

Choosing a research method

This section requires you to apply the knowledge you have acquired in this chapter and practise your exam technique. Work through the questions that follow. If you need help, refer back to the hints offered at the end of Chapters 6 and 7.

Questions

1. What influence does perspective have in shaping a research project?
2. In what circumstances would it be appropriate to adopt a covert participant observation strategy?
3. Identify three problems associated with gaining access to research populations?
4. Evaluate the usefulness of interviews when investigating sensitive topics. (Hint: It may be helpful to look at the section on interviews in Chapter 7, as well as the discussion of Lee's (1993) work on sensitive research earlier in this chapter.)
5. Assess the factors that may affect choice of research method. (Hint: Use the table you completed for Exercise 9.11 to help you structure your ideas.)

Important concepts

theory and practice • choice of method • research aims • bias/characteristics of the researcher • funding • ethics

---

Critical thinking

- Is the researcher's choice of method always influenced by personal and social factors making bias inherent in research?
- Are particular topics of research more likely to be biased than others? Can you give some examples?
- Can sociologists ever divorce themselves from their personal views, attitudes and opinions? Is it desirable to do so in research? Might our personal views act as an ethical consideration in research?

Chapter 10

Sociology and Science

By the end of this chapter you should be able to:

- recognize the rationale behind the scientific method
- understand when and why the scientific method is used
- recognize the limitations of seeing science as associated only with the scientific method
- describe the historical background to the sociology as a science debate
- identify factors and arguments in support of sociology as a science
- identify factors and arguments against sociology as a science
- adopt a position based on your interpretation of the arguments and be able to justify it
- recognize the potential impact of postmodern assumptions about the future of science and the scientific method, positivist methodology and sociological research
- arrive at a balanced judgement about whether science and sociology have a future, and speculate about what this future might hold

INTRODUCTION

Interest in science is widespread in society. Science has long enjoyed high status as an academic discipline owing to its distinguished history of great technological breakthroughs and discoveries about human life and the world in which we live. In recent times, politicians from all the political parties have been keen to endorse the potential of science. There is general recognition that science and scientists hold the key to our future, and if Britain is to keep pace with the rest of the world we must invest in scientific projects and encourage the dissemination of scientific knowledge.

However, Britain's reputation as a nation characterized by discovery and innovation is under threat. Underfunding has forced many science departments to shelve important research projects, and if the popular press is to be believed, only projects that are perceived to have a market value are supported. Those who conduct pure research struggle for funds and receive limited attention, unless a radical discovery is made that affects the way we live our lives. Today, it appears a little ironic that science is suffering a fate similar to sociology, despite the considerable differences in the public's perception of the two disciplines (see Exercise 10.1).

(An)(E)

Exercise 10.1

Think of as many popular ideas as you can that are associated with the words/disciplines 'science' and 'sociology'. List them in separate columns.

1. Mark whether the words/ideas are positive, negative or neutral.
2. Which discipline has most positives/negatives?
3. Why do you think this is?
4. Read your lists again. Identify all ideas/words that could be reinterpreted as positive or negative that were previously the reverse. Explain why.
5. Do you think that science justifies its position as a core subject alongside English and Maths? Why?
6. Do you think it is right that sociology is not included in the National Curriculum? What might be the reasons for its exclusion?

It was the esteem in which science was held in the latter part of the nineteenth century that encouraged sociologists to develop their discipline by adopting the methods of the natural sciences. Science was responsible for many significant discoveries, and this no doubt laid the foundation for future perceptions of the central value of the discipline to our society. To explore the impact that science has had upon the development of sociology, it is useful first to explore a few facts about science.

WHAT IS SCIENCE?

The *Chambers Everyday Paperback Dictionary* defines science as 'knowledge ascertained by observation and experiment, critically tested, systematised, and brought under general principles'. To put it another way, science is a body of knowledge associated with a particular style of research – that is, one characterized by the use of certain methods in specific circumstances and shaped by an underlying rationale. Nonetheless, although many writers have devoted considerable attention to exploring the nature of science, their work, makes it clear that the answer to the question 'What is science?' is far from straightforward.

In seeking to conceptualize science, writers have focused on many factors – the nature of science, the assumptions upon which it is based, the characteristics of science and scientific methodology. It would appear that all of these need to be reviewed to arrive at an understanding of what science actually is.

The nature of science

Lawson (1986) interprets the meaning of science as 'knowledge', but recognizes that it is used in a commonsense way to refer to the natural sciences of chemistry, physics and biology. These disciplines are united by a common aim: they all seek to understand and explain the natural world in a systematic and logical manner with the use of specific techniques and procedures.

Most writers charting the development of science agree that the discipline was developed to provide an alternative form of knowledge to that generated by experience and reason. For example, Cohen and Manion (1994) consider that science was attractive because it offered a radically different approach to experience, involving the construction of a theory that could be tested empirically, rather than based on 'common sense knowing' (ibid., p. 2). It also went beyond inductive and deductive reasoning to offer an approach that combined the induction of an hypothesis from a mass of observed data with the formal and rigorous testing of predated hypotheses.

The historical circumstances in which science developed were influential in determining the nature of the discipline. Although science predated the Enlightenment, it was during that period that academic interest in the potential of science flourished. In the mid eighteenth century science became, 'for the intellectuals of the Enlightenment, the epitome of enlightened reason' (Hamilton, 1992). As noted by Hamilton, science and the Enlightenment were vehicles that together moved human society onwards and upwards to a more enlightened and progressive state. During the nineteenth century science was the domain of wealthy, aristocratic gentlemen who could afford to indulge their interest in the natural world. The dominant paradigm perceived the classification and categorization of the natural world to be of paramount importance so that everything in the natural world had a typology against which new additions could be measured. This is how our current system of science came into being. It is interesting to note that the amateur scientists were the people who weighed human brains and decided that, because women's brains weighed less than men's, women were therefore less intelligent than men. This was also the time when the classification of the human 'races' took place with white Europeans at the top of the hierarchy and black Africans at the bottom. The classification systems developed now seem so obviously and clearly bound to the values and attitudes of the colonial period but at the time this was not even part of their thinking.

Science began to be perceived as an attempt to create knowledge that people could trust, that would be true for all circumstances at all times (Lawson, 1986). The value of this was huge – by knowing something for certain individuals (scientists) could predict the future with some accuracy. Hence, science became a powerful force in society and assumed a new status as a superior form of knowledge.

Science justified this status by claiming that the very nature of the discipline made it unique. This view was espoused by positivists – that is, those who believed that science and only science could provide objective knowledge upon which generalizations could be based. The *raison d'être* for science was problem-solving, and the aim of positivism was to reveal scientific laws on natural and social phenomena that could be used to explain the causes, functioning and consequences of these phenomena. It was possible to reveal such laws through the application of a model approach involving: (1) a certain logical procedure (the traditional scientific or hypothetico-deductive method), (2) the use of specific techniques (the laboratory experiments) and (3) the adoption of a particular position (objectivity).

The assumptions of science

Science employs what Burrell and Morgan (1979) call an 'objectivist' approach to social reality. This conception of the social world involves four underlying assumptions concerning *ontology* (the nature/essence of the social phenomena being investigated), *epistemology* (the bases of knowledge, its nature and forms, how it can be acquired and how it is communicated to other human beings), *human nature* (the relationships between human beings and their environment) and *methodology* (research methods).

In terms of ontology, science favours a realist conception of the social world. Realism assumes that objects have an independent existence and are not dependent on the knower for their existence. Social reality is not the result of individual cognition (thinking), created in one's own mind, but is external to individuals and imposes itself on their consciousness from without.

In terms of epistemology, science advocates a positivist conception of knowledge. This involves the assumption that knowledge is concrete, real and capable of being transmitted in tangible form. The view that knowledge is concrete, objective and tangible requires researchers to adopt an observer role, together with an allegiance to the methods of natural science (Cohen and Manion, 1994).

In terms of human nature, science assumes a determinist position – that is, human beings respond in a mechanistic fashion to their environment. Human beings and their experiences are conditioned by their environment and by circumstances external to them. Determinism applies to factors both within and outside the person. Internal causes (biological determinism) include a state of biological need (for example, hunger or thirst), instinctive energy and genetic endowment. External causes (environmental determinism) include learning experiences and stimuli in the environment. All behaviour thus has a cause and cannot happen any other way.

Malim *et al.* (1992) go on to consider the implications of this approach. Determinists assume that human behaviour is orderly and in accordance with laws, and so is explainable and predictable. A person's current behaviour is the result of what went before it and the cause of what is to come. When you know a person's history and current situation, you can predict what that individual will do next. If you can predict behaviour you can also control it.

In terms of methodology, science advocates an objectivist approach to the social world. Natural phenomena are perceived as concrete, real and external to the individual, and research should therefore be directed at analysing the relationships and patterns between aspects of that world. Scientific investigation emphasizes the need for exploring concepts and identifying and measuring the underlying themes, which may lead to the discovery of universal laws governing the reality that is being observed. Such an approach, characterized by procedures and methods designed to discover general laws, is referred to as 'nomothetic'.

The characteristics of scientific knowledge

Proponents of science and scientific method go to great lengths to point out how scientific knowledge differs from common sense. First, scientific knowledge is based on experience. Unlike common sense, science involves the careful and systematic construction of theory. This is tested empirically, so scientific explanations have a firm basis in fact rather than being mere speculation. In seeking knowledge, scientists endeavour to control for extraneous sources/influences. This ensures that scientific knowledge is pure rather than a product of unexpected and unregulated forces. Any explanation of cause-and-effect relationships offered is a result of rigorous and controlled inquiry.

Second, scientific knowledge is based on reasoning. Modern-day science involves a combination of deductive and inductive reasoning. The former involves the collection of data through a series of formal, logical steps in order to move from a general statement of prediction (hypothesis) to a particular conclusion that supports or refutes the hypothesis. The latter involves the collection of data without preconceived ideas about significance and assuming that any inherent patterns or relationship will emerge and be noted by the researcher. Today, scientific knowledge stems from observations typified by inductive reasoning and the systematic and logical testing of deductive reasoning.

Finally, scientific knowledge is based on research. This research involves a particular methodology being adopted to facilitate the systematic, controlled, empirical and critical investigation of hypothetical propositions about presumed relations among natural phenomena. An essential element of scientific research is its ability to be replicated – that is, repeated under similar conditions so that the results can be verified. This verification makes scientific knowledge reliable – that is, consistent in similar circumstances. Research operates in accordance with the 'principle of parsimony' – that is, all phenomena should be explained in the most economical way possible. Thus, scientific knowledge is characterized by the succinct expression of complex thoughts and ideas. In some forms of science, words have been replaced by symbols that provide scientists with a shared vocabulary that enables them to communicate ideas precisely and efficiently.

The scientific method

Coolican (1994) succinctly summarizes the steps in the scientific method as follows:

1. Observation, gathering and ordering of data.
2. Induction of generalizations, laws.
3. Development of explanatory theories.
4. Deduction of hypotheses to test theories.
5. Testing of the hypotheses.
6. Support or adjustment of theory.

Scientists apply this method through the use of a specific technique – the experiment (see Chapter 7 for a review). This involves the systematic investigation of causal relationships under precisely controlled conditions. In general, experimentation stems from observation and induction and aims to contribute to the development of explanatory theories by enabling scientists to deduce and test hypotheses. Hypothesis-testing provides either evidence to support the explanatory theory or insights that lead to the adjustment of the proposed theory.

Link Exercise 10.1

If you wish to develop your understanding of experimentation, read the section in Chapter 7 on scientific method and conduct the associated activities if you have not done so already.

THE REALITY OF SCIENCE

Despite the widespread support of science, the discipline is not beyond criticism. Challenges to science can be divided into two types: criticism directed at the assumptions upon which science is based, and criticism directed at the practices of scientists, that science does not operate in the way it claims to or in line with commonly held assumptions.

Challenges to the assumptions of science

As noted earlier, science holds a particular conception of social reality. This involves endorsement of four key assumptions with regard to ontology (that is, realism), epistemology (positivism), human nature (determinism) and methodology (nomotheticism). This view of social reality is termed 'objectivist'.

An alternative conception of social reality exists that advocates a 'subjectivist' approach to making sense of the social world. This proposes alternative assumptions with regard to ontology (that is, nominalism), epistemology (antipositivism), human nature (free will) and methodology (ideography).

For subjectivists, social reality is the product of individual consciousness, created by the mind of the individual. Objects of thought are merely words and there is no independently accessible concept encapsulating the meaning of the word. This approach is known as 'nominalism'.

Another challenge to science is posed by the rejection of positivism. Antipositivists claim that it is inappropriate to seek to uncover laws governing relationships between objects, phenomena or people because it denies their independent existence and uniqueness. While it is recognized that there is some value in reducing complex phenomena to simple cause-and-effect relationships, there is danger in taking things out of context and placing them in an artificial, sterile environment. Also, it is assumed that making generalizations dismisses the uniqueness of individuals.

There is also a challenge to scientists' acceptance of determinism. Those who advocate voluntarism imply that there is a danger in dismissing the effect that free will has upon destiny. Although critics would accept that there is little potential for free-will in inanimate objects, they would challenge other tenets of the free-will approach.

Two challenges can be made to the determinist approach. First, it is unwise to assume that precise predictions can be made. Scientists have been forced to build uncertainty factors into their laws, but argue in their defence that it is not the inherent nature of their subject matter but their lack of skill in making precise measurements that makes it difficult for them to make accurate predictions (Malim *et al.*, 1992). Second, if causes for phenomena cannot be found, determinists continue to search for causes rather than assume they do not exist. This is problematic because the search could continue indefinitely, bringing us no closer to understanding social phenomena or developing theories.

Finally, critics of science challenge the appropriateness of nomotheticism as a research methodology. Emphasis on precise measurement, carefully controlled investigations and replicability, and making generalizations rather than specific observations, can mean losing sight of the context in which events occur. Critics insist that experiments conducted in the artificial world of the laboratory are becoming increasingly redundant as a means of studying the natural world, as it is impossible to capture the essence of the natural world in the controlled atmosphere of the laboratory. An example of this is the recent trend in research experiments being conducted in space by astronauts. This highlights both the value of research outside the laboratory and the inability of research scientists to control the precise conditions under which experiments take place.

Challenges to the practice of scientists

Perhaps the biggest criticism of science in recent times concerns how closely scientific research mirrors the image of science. This rhetoric–reality gap has captured the public interest, and newspaper articles have cited examples of scientists appearing to work outside the principles they espouse.

Karl Popper was one of the first to pose a challenge to scientific practice. In *The Logic of Scientific Discovery* (1934), Popper argued that the typical view promoted by scientists about the nature of their discipline was misleading. For example, the principle of verification (seeking evidence to support new hypotheses) is based on the assumption that the accumulation of knowledge allows predictions to be made about the natural world. Popper challenged this, arguing that no theory can ever be fully verified because there is always the possibility that it may be proved wrong at some time in the future.

As a more realistic alternative, Popper advocated the use of falsification, believing that scientists should seek to disprove their theories. No hypothesis could be regarded as true, despite standing up to repeated testing. Instead it could be supported only until refuted in the future. The thinking behind this is simple – in this way weak and inadequate theories can be swiftly eliminated, and only the strongest will survive for future testing and form the basis of temporary advances in scientific knowledge and understanding (Slattery, 1991).

Popper also questioned the assumption that scientific discoveries result from structured observation and rigorous, systematic inquiry. Rather he suggested that discoveries are as likely to come from fluke or unintentional events that affect the research process. He was not alone in suggesting that the work of scientists is not as controlled and precise as they would have us believe. Even in introductory science books, those reviewing the contribution of the great scientists recognize that some discoveries have been unintentional and accidental. For example, Hann (1991) highlights how Galvani discovered current electricity 'almost by accident'.

In *Against Method,* Feyerabend (1975) suggests that modern science has done little to overcome the shortfalls of previous malpractice. When discussing the state of contemporary science he dismisses the sloppy, secretive and unimaginative approach that characterizes research today and advocates a move towards more speculative practices.

Kuhn (1962) challenges the assumption that science is rational, critical and open-minded, arguing that in reality scientists are closed and conservative in their thinking and that their construct system is shaped by the influence of a commonly held set of attitudes and values with regard to what constitutes science. These 'paradigms' are blindly and uncritically applied to the study of the natural world, until such time as they prove unworkable and other paradigms emerge to replace them, presenting a new view of nature and new problems to solve. Far from being open-minded and objective, in Kuhn's view, scientists are heavily committed to the particular paradigm that underpins their field of science, be it physics, chemistry or whatever (Slattery, 1991).

Critics also argue that science is no longer objective because it is at the mercy of social and ideological forces such as funding and politics, as well as what captures the public interest. Such factors help to determine research priorities. Given the crisis facing research departments, scientists may have little choice but to defer to external pressure and conduct research that violates the basic tenets of scientific method. This could have adverse consequences for science as a discipline, as the following exercise demonstrates.

Item A

Do Scientists Cheat?

This is an extremely difficult question to answer because scientists are so secretive. This seems to be a contradiction as the ideal type of science includes openness as one of the key ingredients of the scientific approach, so that results can be verified through replication. Yet, many scientists do not open up their data to others' scrutiny, and this can be for a variety of reasons. First, many scientists work for commercial firms and are required to keep their data private to preserve market advantage. Second, many scientists are in the business of making money from their discoveries and jealously guard their findings. Prestige (not to mention the subsequent promotions and big research grants) in science is gained through the publication of original work in a highly competitive field and the temptation might be to cut corners in order to be the first to publish. This may take the form of ignoring negative results when publishing data, or a more extreme form of cheating, namely just making the data up. Though there have been cases where fraudulent science has been exposed, little replication actually goes on as there is no incentive for scientists to check other people's work rather than publish original material in a field.

Exercise 10.2

Item A highlights some of the implications of malpractice in science. Read the item and answer the following questions.

(E) 1. To what extent to you agree with Item A that making up data is a more extreme form of cheating? Look at both sides of the argument and justify your conclusion.

(An)(E) 2. What difficulties may arise from lumping together promotions, big research grants and prestige as reasons why a scientist might cheat?

(E) 3. Why would Popper's falsification approach limit the type of cheating identified in Item A?

(E) 4. How might Kuhn's 'paradigms' help to explain the unconscious rather than the conscious errors of scientists?

Lawson (1986) also gives credence to the argument that the practices of natural scientists can be fraudulent. For Lawson, the problem is that natural scientists are human beings, usually carry out their work within social organizations and are subject to more or less the same social and economic forces as the members of all organizations. For example, natural scientists are concerned with their own status and career prospects, which may depend on 'successful' publication or achievements. The history of science is littered with premature publication, the discarding of 'inconvenient' results or downright cheating. The direction of research may be determined by the institutions that fund the research; they will certainly influence the questions that natural scientists probe in their research.

Lawson goes on to argue that the institutions of the nation-state fashion the shape of all scientific research, if only through the enormous amount of money that is channelled into the development of weapons. Moreover, the designing of laboratory experiments and the interpretation of results are not objective processes but involve great imagination, human ingenuity, hunches and a good deal of luck. Scientists are members of a scientific community who not only scrutinize the individual's work but also help determine which questions are asked in the first place (see Exercise 10.3).

Lawson echoes a point raised earlier in this chapter – that is, that most scientific work seems not to follow the strict procedures laid down by the positivist model. A number of the natural sciences – for example, astronomy – are not easily conducted in the controlled environment of the laboratory. Also, even in the natural sciences conflicting theories are often put forward by scientists to explain a particular phenomenon. This is because the 'truth' is not always obvious or easily discovered by slavishly following positivist rules.

Exercise 10.3

Read the following scenario and complete the task that accompanies it.

You are an eminent research scientist, appalled by the claims of critics that scientific research is characterized by fraud and cheating. Compose a letter to

The Observer that systematically refutes the allegations made in Item A. Give examples and evidence to support your argument. (Hint: You may need to do additional research for this. You could use your school/college library or access resource materials through IT facilities such as CD-Rom, the internet and so on.)

As shown above, it seems that science and scientific method are not beyond reproach. Criticism has been levelled at the appropriateness of the assumptions upon which science is based and some practices of scientists that do not appear to fit the image of objective, value-free research. The reality of science may be far from the rhetoric. The image of science is linked inextricably to specific characteristics that serve to define what science is. If these characteristics do not exist in practice, does this mean that science itself does not exist or that science is no longer scientific? The debate is complex.

Many scientists and philosophers of science hold today a more pragmatic interpretation that is able to accommodate the selective application of principles historically associated with science. Pohl (1976) gives one such example:

> Most of us hastily and thoughtlessly regard 'science' as a sort of collection of linear accelerators and space vehicles and organic chemistry models. In fact, it is not any of these things; it is only a systematic method of gathering and testing knowledge, involving certain formal procedures; gathering information, forming a hypothesis to explain the information, predicting consequences of the hypothesis and performing an experiment to test the prediction. If you investigate any area of knowledge by this method, you are doing science. If you are using any other method, you are doing something else.

Definitions such as the above open up a new debate – if other disciplines meet the new criteria for science, does this mean they can be regarded as scientific too?

SOCIOLOGY AS A SCIENCE

The Enlightenment

The debate about whether sociology can be considered as a science goes back to the development of the discipline itself. Sociology emerged in the eighteenth century after a period of massive social, cultural and economic change. Academics sought to understand these changes and to make sense of the new world that was emerging. This led to a period in history known as the Enlightenment, 'a time characterised by the development of distinctively modern forms of thought about society and the realm of the social' (Hamilton, 1992, cited in Hall and Gieben, 1992, p. 18). For many, the Enlightenment represented a watershed in human thought about society because it encouraged a new way of thinking marked by the application of reason, experience and experiment to the natural and social world.

In the latter part of the eighteenth century, early sociologists began to study the problems of society to a degree hitherto unknown. Inspired by increased recognition of the value of scientific principles and procedures, they endeavoured to address the study of social structure and change through scientific means. In doing so, they laid the foundation for what became an emergent 'science' of society (see Exercise 10.4).

Item B

Key Ideas of the Enlightenment

1. *Science* – Scientific knowledge and the experimental method was the way to discover useful advances that would benefit humanity.

2. *Reason* – Rationality was the only acceptable way of organizing human knowledge. The development of clear lines of thought that stood separate from any individual's experience was the only way to avoid human error and gain acceptance of ideas by the majority.

3. *Empiricism* – However, reason had to be tempered by experience and ideas had to be supported by the empirical facts established through our sense organs.

4. *Universalism* – Scientific laws could be applied to all similar situations and to all phenomena, including areas previously thought to be outside the realm of science.

5. *Individualism* – The individual was the cornerstone of society and the reason of the individual should not be subjected to higher authorities such as religious bodies. All individuals together, through interacting, created the forms of society.

6. *Progress* – By using reason and science, social conditions were amenable to being improved, with the result that the happiness of individuals in society would increase.

7. *Toleration* – As individuals were fundamentally the same, they were of equal worth regardless of distinction imposed by societies. This was true of all civilizations and not just those of Europe.

8. *Freedom* – There should be limited constraints on individuals in their pursuit of happiness and therefore all feudal and/or religious limits should be removed, as far as was compatible with the happiness of others.

Exercise 10.4

Read Item B and answer the following questions.

1. What conception of reason did the philosophes adopt?
2. Why did the rise of empiricism pose a challenge to religious explanations of phenomena?
3. What scientific method was seen as providing the key to the development of human knowledge ?
4. How were the ideas of science and universalism linked?
5. How did the concept of progress justify the development of a science of society?
6. In what way does individualism appear to contradict universalism?
7. What effect was toleration likely to have on Britain as a nation?
8. What challenge did freedom pose to feudal society?

Two sociologists who drew upon the ideas of the Enlightenment in order to devise a science of society were Saint-Simon and Comte, and the discipline they introduced was positivism.

The rise of positivism – a science of society

A review of the work of the early positivists makes it clear that sociology did not develop independently of science and then seek to be regarded as scientific; rather, scientific thinking provided the inspiration for the development of the discipline. Hence, positivists would argue that sociology is a science because it is based on the principles advocated by the early scientists and shares common assumptions. It is easy to find historical evidence to support this argument as early sociologists took great pains to document the parallels between their new subject and science. Little objection was raised at the time about whether it was appropriate to apply scientific principles and procedures to the study of the social world. It was simply assumed that science was good, science led to progress, science could deliver the answers to life's questions, and science offered more scope than religion for reasoned, empirical explanations of events that could be tested through the application of rigorous, systematic procedures. It was little wonder that early sociologists seeking a conceptual framework for their work embraced science.

The development of positivism, a science of society, has been attributed largely to the Frenchman Auguste Comte (1798–1857). Comte was inspired by the need to make sense of the rapid social change brought about by the industrial, agricultural and political revolutions sweeping across Europe. He suggested that the social world and the natural world could be construed in similar terms, as both had an objective reality that could be studied using the scientific method. As Slattery (1991) notes in his review of Comte's work, what made his perspective unique was his rejection of the metaphysical study of supernatural forces in favour of the observation, categorization and measurement of hard facts, from which could be deduced – by logical reasoning – testable hypotheses, cause-and-effect relationships and, ultimately, laws of causation and evolution that would be comparable to the laws of nature discovered by physicists, chemists and biologists. Comte did not believe there was value in studying feelings and personal constructs as these could not be quantified. Instead the quest should be the discovery of objective, value-free knowledge.

The following exercise is designed to help you appreciate the rationale behind Comte's work and the methodology advocated by him.

(A)

Exercise 10.5

Complete the following passage by selecting the correct words from the list underneath.

Comte's contribution was to initiate _____ as a major form of sociological research and _____ . Having seen in his own time the advances in knowledge achieved by the _____ sciences his overriding aim was to establish the _____ of a comparative 'science of society' which he initially called '_____ ' but later renamed _____ . Comte himself gave various meanings to the term '_____ '. Scientific _____ should concern itself only with what is _____ , useful, certain, precise and constructive, not with _____ , idle, uncertain, vague and _____ or critical questions. The whole emphasis in this new _____ was to be on the positive, on discovering constructive, useful and reliable knowledge as a basis for _____ society. It represented a repudiation of both pre-positive and _____ modes of thought. It was essentially a _____ philosophy, designed to help restore order through scientific _____ and progress, through practical policy. It sought to establish positivism as a _____ . Thereafter, whatever could not be known scientifically could not be known. (Adapted from Slattery, 1991)

Missing words

- foundations • natural • positivism • revolutionary • theorizing
- analysis • conservative • improving • science • sociology
- real • philosophy • social physics • inquiry • destructive

Comte influenced generations of sociologists for a century after the publication of his works. Writers from across the world sought to apply positivist method to the study of the social world in order to contribute to the growing knowledge base of sociology. Among the most notable were Emile Durkheim (1858–1917), with his classic study of suicide, and the structural functionalists of the late 1950s, for example, the American sociologist Talcot Parsons.

Such work formed the basis of much sociological thinking in the first half of the twentieth century. The positivist method, with its emphasis on objective, replicable, controlled, reliable, systematic and standardized data collection, was seen as the key to uncovering the laws that govern human behaviour. While the methodology was adapted over the years to incorporate comparative research, the rationale of positivist research remained – that is, to identify causal relationships between various parts of the social structure, thus providing the basis for generalizations to be made.

Positivism went hand-in-hand with structuralism (see Chapter 3), which suggested that individuals' lives are shaped by social institutions and forces and that individuals have little power over their own destiny. The approach was attractive to positivists because it provided justification for the dismissal of the subjective dimension to the study of the social world. It was this dismissal that became the Achilles' heel of positivism in the 1960s when a newly emerging branch of sociology focused on the role of human consciousness and social interaction in shaping the social world. This approach rejected the claim of positivists that human nature could be studied in the same way as inanimate objects in the natural world, because to do so was to deny the uniqueness of the human spirit and the role of subjective forces in shaping individuals' constructs and action, which in turn shape social reality. This movement, inspired by the writings of symbolic interactionists, phenomenologists and ethnomethodologists, became known as antipositivism.

A challenge to the science of society – the rise of antipositivism

Antipositivism developed through the writing and theorizing of a group of sociologists who were interested in developing an alternative to the conception of social reality that had hitherto dominated sociological thought. Anti-positivists argued that it was wrong to develop a science of society because it was not practical to apply scientific research methods to the study of human beings, and it was not appropriate to assume that parallels could be drawn between the study of the natural world and the study of the social world.

George Herbert Mead (1863–1931) questioned the value of analysing and theorizing about the overall structure of society. He argued that it is more worth while to explore the social worlds that individuals inhabit and how their personal constructs (individual thinking systems) affect their response to this world. For anti-positivists, it is this subconscious interpretation that influences the meaning individuals give to aspects of social life and their response to situations. Social reality is seen to come from within, and if we are to make sense of society we must start with the subjective feelings of individuals and their interpretation of events. This view can be found in the writings of Husserl (1931), Goffman (1959), Garfinkel (1967) and Schutz (Schutz and Luckman, 1973).

Anti-positivists are united in their rejection of the idea that the best way to study society is to adopt the methods of the natural sciences. Rather they view the natural world and the social world as incompatible. Anti-positivists highlight that research in the natural world involves the study of inanimate objects that have no consciousness and are largely influenced by external events. Hence, the natural world is predictable because the only factors that influence it are those imposed from outside. Scientists can engage in the systematic study of the natural world by imposing small changes and studying their impact on objects, matter or chemicals. The conditions under which such 'experiments' are conducted can be strictly controlled to ensure that only the changes imposed by the scientist can be responsible for the subsequent effect. This cause-and-effect relationship can be validated by replicating the experiments under similar conditions using similar methods.

Anti-positivists suggest that if positivist methodology is applied to the study of the social world, it will be found wanting. Husserl exposed the limitations of positivist methodology, claiming that the rational methods of deduction and induction alone are not enough. They cannot accommodate the study of those aspects of human functioning which cannot be directly observed. For this reason, Husserl suggested that intuition should form a part of efforts to analyse and understand all forms of human perception. For Schutz too, rational scientific method offers little scope for increasing our understanding of the social world. He favours a return to philosophy as a route for exploring the commonly shared bases of social order.

For anti-positivists, the social world cannot be studied in the same way as the natural world. First, the social world is made up of human beings with individual motives and the ability to direct their own behaviour. Although some aspects of social life are beyond the control of individuals, anti-positivists argue that it would be wrong to view humans in the same way as the inanimate objects of the natural world. Second, the study of human beings can never be precise. Humans can be studied in a laboratory, but sociologists are not able to control the unobservable aspects of human functioning. Hence at least one aspect of the experiment is beyond the experimenter's control.

Studying human beings in a scientific manner poses further problems. Experimentation raises ethical questions and experimenting on human beings could breach the BSA Code of Ethics (see Chapter 9). Also, returning to the laboratory context, anti-positivists argue that human behaviour should not be studied in isolation from the context in which it normally occurs, as human behaviour does not exist in a vacuum, but is the product of interactions between individuals and social groups. To understand social life fully it is important to study not just human behaviour *per se,* but also the context in which it occurs and the meaning given to it by the 'social actor' – that is, the individual displaying the behaviour. Sociologists do not necessarily have to accept the individual's own explanation of the behaviour being investigated. Instead they may choose to apply their own knowledge and insight to interpret events.

For these reasons, anti-positivists seek to collect valid data to enrich their understanding of peoples' lives and behaviour, and to gain an insight that is as close as possible to real life. Anti-positivists place great emphasis on the in-depth study of individuals in their natural environment and during naturally occurring events in order that the uniqueness of the human spirit can be captured. This might include the use of diaries, letters, novels, observation and so on.

Additional objections to sociology as a science

Anti-positivists are not alone in challenging the assumption that sociology should attempt to adopt the methods of the natural sciences and endeavour to become a science of society. Traditionalists who are keen to preserve the status of science have been determined to prevent it from becoming associated with the younger and more subversive discipline. Working within the traditional definition of science, critics of the positivist movement have condemned sociology as unable to meet the rigid expectations of science.

Sociology cannot be systematic because human behaviour is influenced by the context in which it takes place, and this cannot be controlled. Sociology cannot be replicated because human life is a continuously changing process. It is impossible to freeze life at a certain point in time in order to study and restudy it.

Critics also question the capacity of sociologists to be objective in their study of human behaviour. They point out that sociology is characterized by competing paradigms and perspectives, and suggest that it would be impossible for sociological researchers to divorce their beliefs from their research.

Realism

Realists (see Bhaskar, 1979; Keat and Urry, 1982; Sayer, 1992) offer another dimension to the sociology-as-a-science debate by challenging the traditional objections outlined above. Realists argue that many of the objections of traditionalists are unfair as they are based on the assumption that scientific practice mirrors the definitions historically associated with it. So, sociology is being unfairly judged as unable to match the precise criteria of science, when science itself would struggle to meet the same criteria.

Second, realists claim that far from being objective and value-free in their research, scientists are as prone to bias as the next person. As Kuhn (1962) highlights, science is unified by the acceptance of certain paradigms (ways of thinking) and the desire to uphold them through certain research practices. Scientists also face the pressure of securing funding for research, which may lead them to conduct research that lies outside their chosen field or area of expertise. This may lead to poor-quality research. Some researchers may even be forced to compromise their principles in order to secure lucrative research contracts. It would be difficult to dismiss sociology as unscientific simply because of the existence of bias, particularly if the stronger charge of fraud is levelled at scientists.

Realists also suggest that it is rare for scientists to replicate their research because there is little financial gain to be had from doing so. Although in theory science insists on data being reliable, it is rarely re-tested and is therefore no more reliable than the data obtained from a one-off piece of sociological research.

If realists are to be believed, then several of the objections to sociology as a science are unfounded. Sociology cannot be condemned for not being what science is not either! Sociology and science are more similar than traditionalists would have us believe. For example, they aim to both develop and extend a knowledge base through research. They both apply established procedures and research methods and neither is against the development of innovative methods to push back the boundaries of inquiry. Both seek to improve the human condition through research. And, for both, the purpose of research is to enhance our understanding of the world, be it natural or social.

If we are to establish how scientific each discipline is, we must first consider what 'scientific' constitutes. The old definition that stresses objectivity, system logic, precision, experimentation and replication would have to be applied flexibly to be deemed appropriate today. Realists advocate a pragmatic approach, whereby the definition is broadened to accommodate any research involving the systematic gathering and testing of knowledge, involving certain formal procedures, information gathering, hypotheses and experiments to test predictions.

Open and closed systems of science

Sayer (1992) distinguished between open and closed systems of science. Sciences like physics and chemistry can create closed systems in the laboratory where conditions and variables can be fixed and therefore controlled. Hence predictions can be made reasonably accurately. However, there are also large areas of scientific research which take place within open systems where conditions and variables cannot be controlled. Environmental science, geology, meteorology, oceanography and sociology could be described as open systems where accuracy and prediction can rarely take place with any certainty. Realists would argue that this does not mean these areas are not are not scientific: it is still possible to explain and understand the underlying processes, structures and mechanisms that affect the weather, the formation of rock and oil deposits, and human behaviour. It is just that there is less complete certainty than in the closed system. Hence, according to realists a science of society is possible.

Should sociology aspire to be scientific?

The greater part of this chapter has focused on science as a worthwhile discipline and highlighted how the widespread appreciation of the value of science and scientific discoveries led early sociologists to seek to emulate it. We have considered whether sociology can meet the strict criteria of science. In exploring this, an implicit assumption has been made that science and scientific method is an ideal type of research to which sociologists should aspire.

Anti-positivists have questioned whether it is desirable for sociology to adopt the methods of the natural sciences in a bid to discover general laws governing the functioning of the social world. Positivists are yet to provide a response to the revelations of realists that science is at best a poor imitation of its definition and at worst fraudulent and corrupt. While some may regard as positive the discovery that science is less scientific than it appears because this leaves the way open for sociology to be construed as a science, it does raise the question of whether it is in the interests of sociology to associate itself with a discipline that is regarded by some as fraudulent. Questions have also been raised about whether the assumptions upon which science is based are legitimate. If this is the case, then perhaps sociologists should be cautious about seeking to affirm the 'scientific' status of their discipline.

THE FUTURE OF SOCIOLOGY AND SCIENCE

Postmodernism and science

Postmodernism according to some writers succeeded modernity and called into question many of the assumptions of the modern age (see Chapters 4 and 5). This has implications for the way science is construed and the scientific nature of sociology. As Strinati (1992) notes, postmodernists are sceptical of any absolute, universal and all-embracing claim to knowledge and argue that theories or doctrines that make such claims are increasingly open to criticism, contestation and doubt. As a consequence, postmodernism is sceptical of science because it is based on the assumption that a 'truth' exists that can be expressed in natural laws discovered through scientific research.

Campbell (1996) explores the postmodern attack on science and suggests that its foundation lies in the 'arrogance of modernity'. Campbell argues that both in academic circles and in popular culture there is contempt for the sciences that many find hard to understand. According to Campbell, science is now viewed as the 'vanguard of European exploitation, as discipline ran amok'. He attributes this negativity to scientific involvement in the development of weapons systems, capitalist enterprise and unnatural experimentation.

Campbell argues that science has endured a prolonged attack from Christians, despite the fact that the founders of science were Christian. Science has historically been condemned as arrogant and blinkered. Campbell cites the assumption that modernism equates with rationality as evidence of this, as by implication an assumption is also made that alternative views are irrational.

Disquiet at such arrogance has led to the formation of coherent groups, united in their rejection of science. Campbell identifies two such groups: secular postmodern critics and mystical critics. He sees them as bound together in a common determination to attack traditional science. Secular postmodern critics draw upon the work of Kuhn (1962), who condemned the myths surrounding scientific thinking and practice. For postmodernists, modernist definitions of science are misleading because they claim that science is objective. Objectivity is construed in terms of empiricism (data gathered from our senses) and rationality (reason, logic, defensibility). Postmodernists echo Kuhn's assertion that truth can never be assumed to exist, or to be objectively expressed. Rather, science is merely a social enterprise, and as such is subjective. As Kuhn himself states, 'every individual choice between competing theories depends on a mixture of objective and subjective factors' (ibid.). Such choices are not made independently, but are influenced by the dominant paradigms of the time; thus logic is imposed from without and is relative to history, circumstance and culture.

Campbell (1996) groups the postmodern objections to science into four criticisms, and these provide a succinct summary of the postmodern position:

1. All observations are subjective, including those by scientists. Therefore scientific conclusions are not objective.
2. Although scientists claim to be guided by rationality, rationality itself is guided by dominant theories that are social fabrications.
3. The rules of logic are nothing but socially prescribed ways of thinking.
4. The presuppositions of science are only obviously true of people from the Western culture.

So, for postmodernists, there is no certainty and no global objective truth, just a series of competing, subjective interpretations of events. What exists is an illusion of reality, manufactured by a few powerful Western academics to secure intellectual dominance and cultural subjugation, where non-scientific explanations are dismissed as unworthy. Postmodernists aspire to reverse this trend and demystify science, to show that 'science has no greater authority than any other form of life' (Campbell, 1996) and in doing so to liberate non-Western cultures and alternative forms of knowledge and authority.

Further attack on science comes from the mystical critics Ruby Rucker and Renee Weber (see Campbell, 1996), who argue that scientists are wrong to try to represent our world in terms of abstract, fragmented, theoretical models. Instead, they advocate a holistic approach to understanding phenomena: '[L]et's take our actual thoughts and sensations as the truly fundamental entities' (Rucker, quoted in Campbell, 1996). For mystics, the only appropriate way to approach the study of the natural world is to treat all things as one, a perspective known as monism. As Campbell notes, when such an approach is adopted the source of authority changes to nothing more than personal experience. It is impossible to divorce spiritual energy from physical existence. Thus, the scientist is no more in control of his or her destiny than it is in control of him or her. Any attempt to understand the natural world must acknowledge this complex relationship between researchers and their world.

Campbell (1996) quotes Weber, a postmodern philosopher, to encapsulate this argument:

> Unlike science, which turns to the world outside the seeker, mysticism turns within, to the laws that govern the seeker himself. Science is outer empiricism, mysticism is inner empiricism... for the mystic the inner and outer are reconciled through the hermetic dictum: 'as above, so below...' Both scientist and sage are transformers of energy, involved in the dance of the Shiva. The scientist makes the dense matter dance to produce pure energy, the mystic – master of the subtle matter – dances the dance himself... In the very act of interpreting the universe, we are creating the universe... as we dialogue, the cosmos changes... its idea of itself... it assigns a role to man that was once reserved for the gods.

Campbell highlights the mounting pressure on science to review its assumptions and procedures. Such criticism could be used to inform a reappraisal of the discipline. Whether scientists choose to take on board such criticisms and how they decide to respond may give an interesting indication of how 'arrogant' the discipline actually is.

Implications for the future of science/scientific research

It appears from the above that there is little future for scientific research in the postmodern world, but this is misleading. For a start, postmodern criticisms are levelled at traditional science. This chapter has noted that science is being forced to move away from traditional theory and practice in seeking to understand the contemporary world. A distinction is now being drawn in academic circles between traditional or 'hard' science and a more fluid conception of events, where deterministic and absolute 'metanarratives' (see Chapter 4) are replaced by more contingent and probabilistic claims to truth (Strinati, 1992). There is recognition that scientific practice today may not reflect the rigid definitions that characterized it earlier in history. There is more acceptance of the uncertainty and unpredictability of the world and a greater desire to undertake speculative research beyond the confines of laboratory based hypothesis testing.

Science also appears to have shed some of its exclusivity over research and invited contributions from those who in previous times might have been regarded as unworthy or eccentric. The increased involvement of the general public in scientific ventures and collaboration between traditional scientists and professionals from alternative disciplines (astronomy, astrology, philosophy and so on) has been evident in recent years. There is little doubt that developments in information technology have made science and scientific discovery more accessible to the masses. Interactive technology and autonomous computer systems have changed the nature of scientific practice and redefined the role of the scientist.

Today there is more scope for exploration through simulation rather than experimentation. Defenders of science would cite this as an example of how science has sought to seize new opportunities in order to broaden the scope of inquiry while maintaining the control, system and rigor associated with experimentation. Computer programs now facilitate the testing of a large number of hypotheses simultaneously and reduce the likelihood that vital discoveries will be missed by linear inquiry. By adopting such technology, scientists have been able to repel some of the postmodernist attack. They are adapting their methods to the postmodern world and seeking to redefine knowledge in the light of the global revolution in information technology. Such efforts formed the basis of a series of papers presented at a 1987 conference in Santa Barbara – 'Towards a Postmodern World' – where several leading scientists attempted to redefine their disciplines in postmodern terms.

Although the postmodern attack on science has gathered momentum in the 1990s, it would be wrong to assume that simply because science is perceived as 'under attack' its death is inevitable. Historically, science has endured many attacks by religious leaders keen to dismiss the threat it has posed to religious authority.

Also, if we consider the social context in which the debate occurs, science is still regarded as a high-status discipline in the Western world, and is perceived as far more productive and useful to society than the radical disciplines that seek to erode its foundations. It seems unlikely that science could be usurped by sociology and the abstract theorizing of a group of social philosophers. It is more likely that science will not even need to defend itself from attack. Its contributions to the modern world speak for it, and those who benefit from science are not likely to allow their interests to be jeopardized by the cynical allegations of academics.

Postmodernism, however, is vulnerable to attack. Many of the ideas that form the basis of the movement are without empirical foundation and practical application. Given that information in the global market is judged in terms of its market value, it is unlikely that postmodernism will be feted as a new intellectual revolution, set to transform the nature of the social or natural world. Instead it will attract the kind of ridicule and stigma associated with anything that poses a challenge to the established social order. Criticism of postmodernism has already been voiced in academic circles, as highlighted in Chapter 4. It would not be surprising if this movement gained momentum and postmodernists found themselves under attack from those they seek to condemn.

The impact of postmodernism on positivist methodology

Acceptance of postmodernism would presumably lead to the rejection of positivism and positivist methodology. Positivism identifies with traditional science and emulates traditional scientific methods, so if the postmodernists are to be believed, positivism is as worthless as science. Early sociology was based on the assumption that social laws could be discovered if scientific methodology was employed. The fact that social laws do not exist could be used both to attack and to defend positivism. Positivism could be rejected as worthless because it is based on a flawed assumption, or it could be liberated by the fact that a universal truth does not exist. For years, positivism has been attracting criticism for its limited success in uncovering general laws that could be used to explain how human functioning is governed. Positivists have had to endure comparison with the natural sciences, and have been found wanting. Now it appears that the 'discoveries' of the natural sciences are less revered. Thus, positivism can no longer be judged harshly relative to science. Instead, it can claim that it has been unable to discover laws because none exist.

However, to level this argument would lead to dissonance (internal contradiction) within the discipline because it would be based on the assumption that a universal truth exists that can be discovered by scientific means, while at the same time claiming that such a truth does not exist. The only way that positivism could free itself from such dissonance, short of blindly persisting to claim that a universal truth does exist (thus flying in the face of postmodernism), would be to reinvent itself by adopting a different conception of social reality. In doing so, it could cease to be 'positivism'.

Positivists could go the way of the natural scientists and try to incorporate postmodern thinking into their practice. This would involve a move away from the beliefs associated with traditional science and towards acceptance of a more subjective reality, based on a variety of interconnected interpretations of phenomena. In doing so, positivism would move closer to its polar extreme – that is, antipositivism.

Alternatively, positivists could choose to fly in the face of postmodernism and continue to apply their established methods in a bid to prove that the truth is 'out there' and can be objectively established, or they could try to disprove the claims of postmodernists. In doing so, they could gain some support for their cause by drawing on the knowledge and technology of the postmodern age.

The implications of postmodernism for the future of sociology and sociological research

Postmodernism is seen as having something to offer sociology, particularly with regard to its rejection of the metanarrative. Postmodernism offers sociology an escape from the internal fragmentation that has characterized it over the years. By rejecting global explanations and the existence of an overarching truth, postmodernism offers sociology an opportunity to allow competing perspectives to exist side by side and possibly contribute to a contemporary synthesis.

For Ritzer (2008), postmodernism stands for four things that are highly relevant to the move towards the new synthesis within sociology. First, there is the rejection of the earlier search for a single grand and synthetic theory. Second, there is the acceptance of a range of narrower synthetic efforts. Third, there is the dissolving of boundaries between disciplines and the idea that the new syntheses can include ideas drawn from a range of different disciplines. Fourth there is the demystification of theoretical rhetoric, allowing sociologists to borrow freely from one another in the creation of synthetic theories. The following exercise enables you to explore one of these issues in greater detail.

Item C

Postmodernism

Postmodernists reject the idea of a grand narrative or a metanarrative. It is in the rejection of these ideas that we encounter one of the most important postmodernists, Jean-Francois Lyotard. Lyotard (1984) begins by identifying modern (scientific) knowledge with the kind of single grand synthesis (or 'meta-discourse') we have associated with the work of theorists like Marx and Parsons. The kinds of grand narratives he associates with modern science include 'the dialectics of Spirit, the hermeneutics of meaning, the emancipation of the rational or working subject, or the creation of wealth' (Lyotard, 1984: xxiii).

If modern knowledge is identified in Lyotard's view with metanarratives, then postmodern knowledge involves a rejection of such grand narratives...In fact, postmodern social theory becomes a celebration of a range of different theoretical perspectives; 'Postmodern knowledge is not simply a tool of authorities; it redefines our sensitivity to differences and reinforces our ability to tolerate the incommensurable' (Lyotard, 1984: xxv). In these terms, sociology has moved beyond the modern period, into the postmodern period, in its search for a range of more specific syntheses...

While Lyotard rejects the grand narrative in general, Baudrillard rejects the idea of a grand narrative in sociology. For one thing, Baudrillard rejects the whole idea of the social. For another, this leads to a rejection of the meta-narrative of sociology that is associated with modernity...

Thus, postmodern social theory stands for the rejection of meta-narratives in general and of grand narratives within sociology in particular.

(*Source*: G. Ritzer, *Modern Sociological Theory*, 7th edn. New York: McGraw-Hill, 2008)

Exercise 10.6

Read Item C and answer the following questions.

Ⓐ 1. Whose views are cited in Item C as important in influencing the impact of postmodernism on sociology?

Ⓐ 2. What did the individual in the answer to question 1 reject, and on what grounds?

Ⓐ 3. What effect did this have on the way in which sociology was construed?

Postmodernism could also be seen as offering scope for a reappraisal of sociological research. The most obvious effect of postmodernism is the rejection of the positivist method, leaving the way clear for anti-positivist methodology to flourish. However, rejection of all but anti-positivist methodology is unlikely. Postmodernism advocates an eclectic approach to conceptualizing the social world, and presumably this extends to the way in which the social world is studied. Methodological pluralism is not a new theme in sociology, but traditional attempts have focused more on using the technique as a means to mask or compensate for the limitations of complementary methodology. Postmodern sociological research may be uniquely characterized by the application of an array of diverse methodologies to capture and synthesize the plethora of localized narratives that are assumed to typify the discipline in the twenty-first century.

However, it is worth reiterating that postmodernism is not beyond reproach, and it is possible that as the anti-postmodernist movement gains momentum, researchers will return to methods that are regarded as central to the development of sociology as a discipline. Indeed, postmodern social theory has been criticized as being ideological and only able to critique other approaches while offering nothing substantive in their place. In particular, by engaging in the 'playful' exploration of a wide range of ideas, postmodernists are accused of having little empirical support for their own 'metanarrative' of the 'end of modernity'. As a result, they often ignore what other sociologists see as the key social, political and environmental dilemmas facing the world (see Ritzer, 2008).

Exam focus: structured questions

The structured questions below are designed to test your understanding of and ability to apply the material covered in this chapter. If you need help, refer back to the hints given at the end of Chapters 6 and 7.

Questions

1. Who was responsible for introducing the term 'positivism' to sociology?
2. With which branch of sociology is symbolic interactionism associated?
3. Identify two assumptions associated with positivism.
4. What methods do symbolic interactionists adopt to develop an understanding of social life?
5. Select two basic tenets of the Enlightenment and provide a critique of them as might be offered by symbolic interactionists and Marxists.
6. Assess whether sociology could and/or should be construed as scientific.

(Hint: The last question raises two issues: (a) is it possible – that is practical/feasible – for sociology to be seen as a science, and (b) it is desirable? To answer effectively, you need systematically to explore (a) the established arguments about the nature of science – its features/characteristics; whether sociology could match this; the traditional objections of scientists and the counter-arguments – that is, realism; and (b) the ongoing philosophical debate about whether sociology should aspire to be seen as scientific, even if it could meet scientific criteria. Positivists would say yes – why? Anti-positivists would say no – why? Conclude by considering the impact that postmodern thinking – for example, the decline of the metanarrative and so on – has had upon the status of science in society and the implications this might have for the debate about sociology as a science.)

Important concepts

The Enlightenment • positivism/antipositivism • realism • scientificity • ontology • epistemology

Critical thinking

- Has science ever changed or does it follow the methods it always has done?
- Has postmodernism provided us with the final challenge to the positivist view of sociology and positivist methodology?
- Provide a critique of postmodernist thinking from a sociological perspective.

References

Abbott, P. and Wallace, C. (1997) *An Introduction to Sociology: Feminist Perspectives*, 2nd edn. (London: Routledge).

Abercrombie, N., Hill, S. and Turner, B. S. (1984) *The Penguin Dictionary of Sociology* (London: Penguin).

Acton, T. A. (1994) 'Modernisation, Moral Panics and the Gypsies', *Sociology Review* 4(1).

Allen, J. (2006) *Worry about Crime in England and Wales: Findings from the 2003/04 and 2004/05 British Crime Survey*, Home Office Online Report 15/06. www.homeoffice.gov.uk/rds/pdfs06/rdsolr1506.pdf

Anderson, M. (1971) *Sociology of the Family* (Harmondsworth: Penguin).

Archer, M. (1988) *Culture and Agency* (Cambridge University Press).

Atkinson, J. M. (1971) 'Societal Reactions to Suicide: The Role of Coroners' Definitions', in S. Cohen (ed.) *Images of Deviance* (Harmondsworth: Penguin).

Atkinson, K. (1995) *Behind the Scenes at the Museum* (Ealing: Black Swan).

Ball, S. J. (2000) 'Performativity and Fragmentation in "Postmodern Schooling"', in J. Carter (ed.) *Postmodernity and Fragmentation of Welfare* (London: Routledge).

Banyard, P. and Hayes, N. (1994) *Psychology: Theory and Application* (London: Chapman & Hall).

Baracco, L. (2006) 'Globalisation', *Sociology Review* 16(2).

Bardwick (1992) in R. Gross, *Psychology: The Science of Mind and Behaviour* (London: Hodder & Stoughton).

Barker, E. (1984) *The Making of a Moonie: Choice or Brainwashing?* (Oxford: Blackwell).

Barnard, N. (1997) 'Most Research is "Waste of Time"', *Times Educational Supplement*, September.

Barrett, M. (1980) *Women's Oppression Today* (London: Verso).

Bassey, M. (1998) 'Fuzzy Generalisation and Professional Discourse' *Research Intelligence*, 63.

Baudrillard, J. (1983) *Simulations* (New York: Semiotext).

Baudrillard, J. (1988) *The Ecstasy of Communication – Semiotext(e)* (New York: Autonomedia).

Beck, U. (1992) *Risk Society: Towards a New Modernity* (London: Sage).

Bell, D. (1987) 'The World and the United States in 2013', *Daedalus* 116(3).

Berger, P. and Luckmann, T. (1967) *The Social Construction of Reality* (Garden City, NY: Anchor).

Bergman, M. M. 'The Straw Men of the Qualitative–Quantitative Divide and their Influence on Mixed Methods Research', in M. M. Bergman (ed.) *Advances in Mixed Methods Research* (London: Sage).

Bernard, J. (1982) *The Future of Marriage* (New Haven, CT: Yale University Press).

Bernard, T. (1983) *The Consensus Conflict Debate: Form and Content in Sociological Theories* (New York: Columbia University Press).

Berry, M. and Philo, G. (2006) *Israel and Palestine: Competing Histories* (London: Pluto).

Best, L. (1993) 'Dragons, Dinner Ladies and Ferrets: Sex Roles in Children's Books', *Sociology Review* 2(3).

Best, S., Griffiths, J. and Hope, T. (2000) *Active Sociology* (Harlow: Longman).

Bhaskar, R. (1979) *The Possibility of Naturalism* (Brighton: Harvester).

Billig, M. (1990) 'Collective Memory, Ideology and the British Royal Family', in D. Middleton and D. Edward (eds) *Collective Remembering* (London: Sage).

Billig, M. (1997) *Arguing and Thinking: A Rhetorical Approach to Social Psychology* (Cambridge University Press).

Black, N. *et al.* (1984) *Health and Disease: A Reader* (Milton Keynes: Open University Press).

Blandon, J., Gregg, P. and Machin, S. (2005) 'Intergenerational Mobility in Europe and North America', Report, Centre for Economic Performance, London School of Economics, at: cep.lse.ac.uk/about/news/IntergenerationalMobility.pdf (last accessed 7 July 2009).

Blank, G., McCartney, J. L. and Brent, E. E. (1989) *New Technology in Sociology: Practical Applications in Research and Work* (New Brunswick, NJ: Transaction).

Bloxham, A. (2008) 'Lap-Dancing Clubs to be Reclassified as Sex Show Venues under Government Crackdown', *Daily Telegraph*, 19 June.

Blumer, H. (1954/1969) 'What is Wrong with Social Theory?', in H. Blumer *Symbolic Interaction* (Englewood Cliffs, NJ: Prentice-Hall).

Bonilla-Silva, E. (2003) *Racism without Racists: Color-Blind Racism and the Persistence of Racial Inequality in the United States* (Lanham, MD: Rowman & Littlefield).

Boronski, T. (1987) *The Sociology of Knowledge* (London: Longman).

Bourdieu, P. (1984) *Distinction: A Social Critique of the Judgement of Taste* (Cambridge, MA: Harvard University Press).

Bozic, N. (1997) 'Language and Discourse: Promoting Effective Interaction between SENCOs and E.P.s', unpublished MEd (Ed Psych) thesis, University of Birmingham.

Brannen, J. (1993) 'The Effects of Research on Participants: Findings From A Study of Mothers and Employment', *Sociological Review* 41(2).

Brannen, J. (2008) 'The Practice of a Mixed Methods Research Strategy', in M. M. Bergman (ed.) *Advances in Mixed Methods Research* (London: Sage).

Brewer, J. and Hunter, A. (2006) *Multimethod Research: A Synthesis of Styles* (Newbury Park, CA: Sage).

Brown, M. K. *et al.* (2003) *Whitewashing Race: The Myth of a Color-Blind Society* (Berkeley: University of California Press).

Brown, P. (1996) 'Modernism, Postmodernism and Sociological Theory: A Beginner's Guide', *Sociology Review* 5(3).

Brown, R. (1990) 'Rhetoric, Textuality and the Postmodern Turn in Sociological Theory', *Sociological Theory* 8(2).

Bruner, J. (1966) *Towards a Theory of Instruction* (Boston, MA: Harvard University Press).

Budge, D. (1997) 'Bias Fears as Right-winger Heads Inquiry', *The Times Educational Supplement*, September.

Burke, M. (1994) 'Homosexuality as Deviance: The Case of the Gay Police Officer', *British Journal of Criminology* 34(2).

Burrell, G. and Morgan, G. (1979) *Sociological Paradigms and Organisational Analysis* (London: Heinemann).

Butler, C. (1995) 'Religion and Gender: Young Muslim Women in Britain', *Sociology Review* 4(3).

Callinicos, A. (1989) *Against Postmodernism: A Marxist Critique* (Cambridge: Polity).

Calvey, D. (2000) 'Getting on the Door and Staying There: A Covert Participation Observational Study of Bouncers', in G. Lee-Treweek and S. Linkogle (eds) *Danger in the Field: Risk and Ethics in Social Research* (London: Routledge).

Campbell, L. (1996) *The Post Modern Method: Science* (Xenos Christian Fellowship) www.crossrds.org/webmaster@office.xenos.org

Chambliss, D. F. (2005) 'Frame Analysis', in G. Ritzer (ed.) *Encyclopedia of Social Theory* (Thousand Oaks, CA: Sage).

Cherrington, R. (1993) 'Drugs: A Comparative View', *Sociology Review* 3(1).

Chignell, H. and Abbott, D. (1995) 'An Interview with Anthony Giddens', *Sociology Review* 5(2).

Christopher, F. S. (2001) *To Dance the Dance: A Symbolic Interactional Exploration of Premarital Sexuality* (Mahwah, NJ: Erlbaum).

Clarke, J. (1996) 'Feminism Revisited', *Sociology Review* 6(2).

Clarke, J. and Layder, D. (1994) 'Let's Get Real: The Realist Approach to Sociology', *Sociology Review* 4(2).

Clegg, S. (1992) 'Modern and Postmodern Organisations', *Sociology Review* 1(4).

Cohen, L. and Manion, L. (1994) *Research Methods in Education*, 3rd edn. (London: Routledge).

Connell, R. W. (2000) *The Men and the Boys* (Sydney: Allen & Unwin).

Connolly, P. (2006) 'Young Boys, Masculinities and Schooling', *Sociology Review* 15(3).

Coolican, H. (1994) *Research Methods and Statistics in Psychology* (London: Hodder & Stoughton).

Corrigan, P. (1981) *Schooling the Smash Street Kids* (London: Macmillan).

Craib, I. (1984) *Modern Social Theory from Parsons to Harbermas* (Brighton: Wheatsheaf).

Craib, I. (1994) 'Going to Pieces or Getting It Together?: Giddens and the Sociology of Self', *Sociology Review* 4(2).

Crawford, C. (2005) 'Actor Network Theory in G. Ritzer (ed.) *Encyclopedia of Social Theory* (Thousand Oaks, CA: Sage).

Culley, L. (2008) 'Focus Groups and ethnic minorities', *Sociology Review* 18(1).

Dahrendorf, R. (1959) *Class and Class Conflict in Industrial Society* (Stanford University Press).

Darder, A. and Torres, R. D. (2004) *After Race: Racism after Multiculturalism* (New York University Press).

De Vaus, D. (1986) *Surveys in Social Research* (London: Allen & Unwin).

Delgado, R. and Stefancic, J. (2001) *Critical Race Theory: An Introduction* (New York University Press).

Dennison, B. and Kirk, R. (1990) *Do, Review, Learn, Apply: A Simple Guide to Experiential Learning* (Oxford: Blackwell).

Denscombe, M. (1991) 'Part-time and Flexible Working Patterns', *Sociology Update* (Leicester: Olympus).

Dobash, R. P. and Dobash, R. E. (1980) *Violence Against Wives: A Case Against the Patriarchy* (London: Open Books).

Douglas, J. and Johnson, J. (1977) *Existential Sociology* (Cambridge: Cambridge University Press).

Douglas, J. D. (1967) *The Social Meanings of Suicide* (Princeton University Press).

Douglas, J. W. B. (1964) *The Home and the School* (London: MacGibbon & Kee).

Duncombe, J. and Marsden, D. (1995) 'Women's Triple Shift: Paid Employment, Domestic Labour and Emotion Work', *Sociology Review* 4(4).

Durkheim, E. (1893/1894) *The Division of Labour in Society* (New York: Free Press).

Durkheim, E. (1895/1964) *The Rules of Sociological Method* (New York: Free Press).

Durkheim, E. (1897/1951) *Suicide* (New York: Free Press).

Durkheim, E. (1912/1965) *The Elementary Forms of Religious Life* (New York: Free Press).

Durkheim, E. (1973) *Moral Education: A Study in the Theory and Application of the Sociology of Education* (New York: Free Press).

Dyson, S. (1995) 'Research Roundup: Research Diaries and the Research Process', *Sociology Review* 4(3).

Economic and Social Research Council (ESRC) (2005) *Society Today*, at: www.esrcsocietytoday.ac.uk/ESRCInfoCentre/index.aspx (last accessed 6 July 2009).

EOC (2005) *Sex and Power*. Manchester.

Erzberger, C. and Kelle, U. (2003) 'Making Inferences in Mixed Methods: The Rules of Integration', in A. Tashakkori and C. Teddlie (eds) *Handbook of Mixed Methods in Social and Behavioral Research* (Thousand Oaks, CA: Sage).

Evans, K. (1997) 'Men's Towns: Women and the Urban Environment', *Sociology Review* 6(3).

Fay, M. (2007) 'Mobile Subjects, Mobile Methods: Doing Virtual Ethnography in a Feminist Online Network', *Forum: Qualitiative Social Research* 8(3).

Feyerabend, P. (1975) *Against Method* (London: New Left Books).

Firestone, S. (1974) *The Dialectic of Sex: The Case for Feminist Revolution* (New York: Morrow).

Flanagan, C. (1994) *Psychology A Level: Letts Revise Guide*. London: Letts.

Fontes, T. and O'Mahony, M. (2008) 'In-depth Interviewing by Instant Messaging '*Social Research Update University of Surrey* (53). Online: sru.soc.surrey.ac.uk/ SRU53.pdf (last accessed 30 April 2009).

Foucault, M. (1965) *Madness and Civilization: A History of Insanity in the Age of Reason* (New York: Vintage).

Foucault, M. (1979) *Discipline and Punish: The Birth of the Prison* (New York: Vintage).

Francis, B. (2000) 'The Gendered Subject: Students' Subject Preferences and Discussions of Gender and Ability', *Oxford Review of Education* 26(4).

Friedman, M. (1980) *Free to Choose* (London: Secker & Warburg).

Friedman, T. (2000) *The Lexus and the Olive Tree*. New York: Anchor.

Fukuyama, F. (1992) *The End of History and the Last Man* (Harmondsworth: Penguin).

Fuller, M. (1988) 'Fieldwork in Forbidden Research Terrains: The US State and the Case of Cuba', *American Sociologist* 19(2).

Furlong, A. and Cartmel, F. (1997) *Young People and Social Change: Individualization and Risk in Late Modernity* (Buckingham: Open University Press).

Gajjala, R. (1997) Cyberethnography, at: www.pitt.educ/-gajjala/define.html (last accessed 12 August 2003).

Gallie, D. (1978) *In Search of the New Working Class* (Cambridge: Cambridge University Press).

Garfinkel, H. (1967) *Studies in Ethnomethodology* (Englewood Cliffs, NJ: Prentice Hall).

Gauntlett, D. (2007) *Creative Explorations: New Approaches to Identities and Audiences* (London: Routledge).

Gerth, H. and Wright Mills, C. (eds) (1958) *From Max Weber* (New York: Oxford University Press).

Giddens, A. (1984) *The Constitution of Society* (Cambridge: Polity).

Giddens, A. (1987) *The Nation-State and Violence* (Berkeley: University of California Press).

Giddens, A. (1990) *The Consequences of Modernity* (Cambridge: Polity).

Giddens, A. (1991) *Modernity and Self-identity* (Cambridge: Polity).

Giddens, A. (1992) *The Transformation of Intimacy: Sexuality, Love and Eroticism in Modern Societies* (Cambridge: Polity).

Giddens, A. (1994) *Beyond Left and Right: The Future of Radical Politics* (Cambridge: Polity).

Giddens, A. (1995) in H. Chignell and D. Abbott, 'An Interview with Anthony Giddens', *Sociology Review* 5(2).

Giddens, A. (1999) 'Risk and Responsibility', *Modern Law Review* 62(1).

Giddens, A. (2003) *Runaway World: How Globalisation Is Shaping Our Lives*, 2nd edn. (London: Routledge).

Giddings, L. S. (2006) 'Mixed Methods Research: Positivism Dressed in Drag?', *Journal of Research in Nursing* 11(3).

Giffney, N. (2004) 'Denormatizing Queer Theory: More than (Simply) Gay and Lesbian Studies', *Feminist Theory* 5(1).

Gilmore, D. D. (1990) *Manhood in the Making: Cultural Concepts of Masculinity* (New Haven, CT: Yale University Press).

Gilpin, R. (1987) *The Political Economy of International Relations* (Princeton University Press).

Goffman, E. *(1979) Gender Advertisements* (New York: Harper & Row).

Goffman, E. (1959) *Presentation of Self in Everyday Life* (Garden City, NY: Anchor).

Goffman, E. (1961) *Asylums* (Harmondsworth: Penguin).

Goffman, E. (1961) *Strategic Interaction* (Oxford: Blackwell).

Goldthorpe, J., Lockwood, D., Bechhofer, F. and Platt, J. (1969) *The Affluent Worker and the Class Structure* (Cambridge: Cambridge University Press).

Goode, W. J. (1963) *World Revolution and Family Patterns* (New York: Free Press).

Gouldner, A. W. (1973) 'Anti-Minotaur: The Myth of a Value-Free Sociology', in *For Sociology* (Harmondsworth: Penguin).

Graham, H. (1984) *Women, Health and Family* (Brighton: Wheatsheaf).

Gramsci, A. (1917/1977) 'The Revolution against Capital', in Q. Hoare (ed.) *Antonio Gramsci: Selections from Political Writings (1910–1920)* (New York: International Publishers).

Gramsci, A. (1932/1975) *Letters from Prison: Antonio Gramsci*, ed. Lynne Lawner (New York: Harper Colophon).

Griffiths, M. (1996) 'Research Roundup: Observing the Social World of Fruit Machine Playing', *Sociology Review* 6(1).

Gross, R. (1992) *Psychology: The Science of Mind and Behaviour* (London: Hodder & Stoughton).

Habermas, J. (1970) *Toward a Rational Society* (Boston, MA: Beacon).

Habermas, J. (1979) *Communication and the Evolution of Society* (Boston, MA: Beacon).

Habermas, J. (1984) *The Theory of Communicative Action, vol. 1: Reason and the Rationalization of Society* (Boston, MA: Beacon).

Habermas, J. (1987) *The Theory of Communicative Action, vol. 2: Lifeworld and System: A Critique of Functionalist Reason* (Boston, MA: Beacon).

Hall, S. and Gieben, B. (1992) *Formations of Modernity* (Cambridge: Polity).

Hamilton, P. (1992) 'The Enlightenment and the Birth of Social Science', in S. Hall and B. Gieben (eds) *Formations of Modernity* (Cambridge: Polity).

Hammersley, M. (1992) 'Introducing Ethnography', *Sociology Review* 2(2).

Hammersley, M. (2008) 'Troubles with Triangulation', in M. M. Bergman (ed.) *Advances in Mixed Methods Research* (London: Sage).

Hamshire, J. (1994) 'Two Worlds Collide', *Daily Mail* (London) 16 March.

Hann, J. (1991) *Eyewitness Science Guides – How Science Works* (London: Dorling Kindersley).

Haralambos, M. and Holborn, M. (2004) *Sociology: Themes and Perspectives*, 6th edn. (London: Collins).

Harper, D. (1998) 'An Argument for Visual Sociology', in J. Prosser (ed.) *Image-Based Research: A Sourcebook for Qualitative Researchers* (London: Falmer).

Harvey, D. (2005) *The New Imperialism* (Oxford: Oxford University Press).

Harvey, L. (1990) *Critical Social Research* (London: Allen & Unwin).

Haverkamp, B. E. (2005) 'Ethical Perspectives on Qualitative Research in Applied Psychology', *Journal of Counseling Psychology* 52(2).

Hayes, N. (1991) 'Social Identity, Social Representations and Organisational Culture', doctoral thesis (University of Huddersfield).

Hekman, S. (1983) *Weber, the Ideal Type, and Contemporary Social Theory* (Notre Dame, IN: University of Notre Dame Press).

Hillyard, S. (2007) 'Is Image Everything? Visual Methods in Rural Sociology', *Sociology Review* 16(4).

Hine, C. (2005) 'Internet Research and the Sociology of Cyber-Social-Scientific Knowledge', *Information Society* 21(4).

Hitchcock, G. and Hughes, D. (1995) *Research and the Teacher: A Qualitative Introduction to School-Based Research* (London: Routledge).

Hobbs, D. and Dunningham, C. (1998) 'Glocal Organised Crime: Context and Pretext', in V. Ruggerio, N. South and I. Taylor (eds) *The New European Criminology* (London: Sage).

Humphreys, L. (1970) *Tearoom Trade* (London: Duckworth).

Humphreys, L. (1975) *Tearoom Trade: Impersonal Sex in Public Places* (New Brunswick, NJ: Aldine).

Husserl, E. (1931) *Ideas* (London: Allen & Unwin).

Irvine, J., Miles, I. and Evans, J. (eds) (1979) *Demystifying Social Statistics* (London: Pluto).

Jameson, F. (1984) 'Postmodernism, or the Cultural Logic of Late Capitalism', *New Left Review* 146.

Jameson, F. (1991) *Post Modernism or the Cultural Logic of Late Capitalism* (London: Verso).

Jankowski, N. W. *et al.* (2004) 'The Internet and Communication Studies', in H. Nissenbaum and M. E. Price (eds) *Academy and the Internet* (New York: Peter Lang).

Jones, P. (1993) 'Structuralism and Post Structuralism', in *Resources For Sociology: The Best of Social Science Teacher*. Manchester: Association for the Teaching of the Social Sciences (ATSS).

Jordan, B. (1989) 'Universal Welfare Provision Creates A Dependent Population: The Case Against', *Social Studies Review* 5(2).

Kaiser, K. (1972) 'Transnational Relations as a Threat to the Democratic Process', in R. Keohane and J. Nye (eds) (1972) *Transnational Relations and World Politics* (Boston, MA: Harvard University Press).

Keat, R. and Urry, J. (1975) *Social Theory as Science* (London: Longman).

Keat, R. and Urry, J. (1982) *Social Theory as Science* 2nd edn. (London: Routledge & Kegan Paul).

Kelly, L. (1988) *Surviving Sexual Violence* (Cambridge: Polity).

Kelly, P. (1999) 'Wild and Tame Zones: Regulating the Transitions of Youth at Risk', *Journal of Youth Studies* 2(3).

Kinsey, A., Pomeroy, W. and Martin, C. E. (1948) *Sexual Behavior in the Human Male* (Philadelphia: Saunders).

Kinsey, A., Pomeroy, W., Martin, C. E. and Gebhard, P. H. (1953) *Sexual Behavior in the Human Female* (Philadelphia: Saunders).

Kirby, M. (1999) *Stratification and Differentiation* (Basingstoke: Palgrave Macmillan).

Knorr-Cetina, K. D. (2007) 'Postsocial', in *The Blackwell Encyclopedia of Sociology* (Oxford: Blackwell).

Knowles, C. and Sweetman, P. (2004) *Picturing the Social Landscape: Visual Methods and the Sociological Imagination* (London: Routledge).

Kuhn, T. (1962) *The Structure of Scientific Revolutions* (Chicago University Press).

Laclau, E. and Mouffe, C. (1985) *Hegemony and Socialist Strategy: Towards a Radical Democratic Politics* (London: Verso).

Lambevski, S. A. (1999) 'Suck My Nation: Masculinity, Ethnicity and the Politics of Homo-sex', *Sexualities* 2(4).

Langham, S. (1991) 'Research Roundup: Women in the Force – A Series of Glass Ceilings', *Social Studies Review* 6(5).

Law, J. and Hetherington, K. (2002) 'Materialities, Spatialities, Globalities', in M. J. Dear and S. Flusty (eds) *The Spaces of Postmodernity: Readings in Human Geography* (Oxford: Blackwell).

Lawson, T. (1986) 'In the Shadow of Science', *Social Studies Review* 2(2).

Lawson, T. (1993) 'I.T. Graphics Packages and Coursework', *Sociology Review* 3(2).

Lawson, T. and Garrod, J. (2009) *A–Z Sociology Handbook* (London: Hodder & Stoughton).

Lawson, T. and Heaton, T. (2010) *Crime and Deviance (Skills-Based Sociology)* (Basingstoke: Palgrave Macmillan).

Lawson, T., Brown, A. and Heaton, T. (2010) *Education and Training* (Basingstoke: Palgrave).

Layder, D. (1990) *The Realist Image in Social Science* (Basingstoke: Macmillan).

Layder, D. (1993) *New Strategies in Social Research* (London: Polity).

Leach, M. (1994) 'The Politics of Masculinity: An Overview of Contemporary Theories', *Social Alternatives* 12(4).

Lee, R. (1993) *Doing Research on Sensitive Topics* (London: Sage).

Lee, R. (1995) *IT for Social Scientists* (London: UCL Press).

Lee, R. and Renzetti, C. (1990) *Researching Sensitive Topics* (London: Sage).

Lefebvre, H. (1968) *The Sociology of Marx* (New York: Vintage).

Lenhart, A., Madden, M., Macgill, A. R. and Smith, A. (2007) *Teens and Social Media* (Washington, DC: Pew Internet and American Life Project).

Levi-Strauss, C. (1967) *Structural Anthropology* (Garden City, NY: Anchor).

Livesey, C. and Lawson, T. (2005) *AS Sociology for AQA* (London: Hodder Arnold).

Lobban, G. (1974) 'Data Report on British Reading Schemes', *Times Educational Supplement*, 1 March.

Lyon, D. (2000) *Jesus in Disneyland: Religion in Postmodern Times* (Cambridge: Polity).

Lyotard, J. F. (1984) *The Post-Modern Condition* (Minneapolis: University of Minnesota Press).

Mac an Ghaill, M. (1992) 'Teachers' Work: Curriculum Restructuring, Culture, Power and Comprehensive Schooling', *British Journal of Sociology of Education*, 13(2).

Mac an Ghaill, M. (1994) *The Making of Men: Masculinities, Sexualities and Schooling* (Buckingham: Open University Press).

Maccoby, E. and Jacklin, C. (1974) *The Psychology of Sex Differences* (Stanford University Press).

Macionis, J. J. and Plummer, K. (2005) *Sociology: A Global Introduction* (Harlow: Pearson).

Malim, T., A. Birch and Wadeley, A. (1992) *Perspectives in Psychology* (Basingstoke: Macmillan).

Marcuse, H. (1964) *One Dimensional Man* (Boston, MA: Beacon).

Marshall, P. L. (2003) 'Human Subjects Protections, Institutional Review Boards and Cultural Anthropological Research', *Anthropological Quarterly* 76(2).

Marsland, D. (1989) 'Universal Welfare Provision Creates a Dependent Population. The Case For', *Social Studies Review* 5(2).

Martin, J., and Roberts, C. (1984) *Women and Employment: A Lifetime Perspective* (London: Department of Employment).

Marx, K. (1852/1970) 'The Eighteenth Brumaire of Louis Bonaparte', in R. C. Tucker (ed.) *The Marx–Engels Reader* (New York: Norton).

Marx, K. (1857–1858/1964) *Pre-Capitalist Economic Formations*, ed. E. J. Hobsbawm (New York: International Publishers).

Marx, K. (1857–1858/1974) *The Grundrisse: Foundations of the Critique of Political Economy* (New York: Random House).

Marx, K. (1867/1967) *Capital: A Critique of Political Economy, vol. 1* (New York: International Publishers).

Marx, K. (1932/1964) *The Economic and Philosophic Manuscripts of 1844*, ed. Struik, D. J. (New York: International Publishers).

Marx, K. (1894/1974) *Capital, vol. 3* (London: Lawrence & Wishart).

Marx, K. and Engels, F. (1845/1956) *The Holy Family* (Moscow: Foreign Languages Publishing House).

Matsuda, M., Lawrence, C. R., Delgado, R. and Crenshaw, K. (2003) *Words that Wound: Critical Race Theory, Assaultive Speech and the First Amendment* (Boulder, CO: Westview).

McGrew, A. (1992) 'A Global Society?', in S. Hall, D. Held and T. McGrew *Modernity and Its Futures* (Cambridge: Polity/Open University).

McKee, L. and O'Brien, M. (1983) 'Interviewing Men: Taking Gender Seriously', in: E. Gamarnikow, D. Morgan, J. Purvis and D. Taylorson (eds) *The Public and the Private* (London: Heinemann).

McNeill, P. (1985) *Research Methods* (London: Tavistock).

McRobbie, A. (1989) Comment on 'Young Motherhood', *Guardian*, 5 September.

McRobbie, A. (1996) 'More!: New Sexualities in Girls' and Women's Magazines', in J. Curran, D. Morley and V. Walkerdine (eds) *Cultural Studies and Communications* (London: Arnold).

McRobbie, A. (2008) *The Aftermath of Feminism: Gender, Culture and Social Change* (London: Sage).

Mead, G. H. (1934) *Mind, Self and Society: From the Standpoint of the Social Behaviorist* (University of Chicago Press).

Mead, M. (1935) *Sex and Temperament in Three Primitive Societies* (New York: Dell).

Messerschmidt, J. W. (1995) 'Managing to Kill: Masculinities and the Space Shuttle Challenger Explosion', *Masculinities* 3(4).

Mies, M. (1986) *Patriarchy and Accumulation on a World Scale: Women in the International Division of Labour* (London: Zed).

Milgram, S. (1974) 'Obedience', cited in Gross, R. (1992) *Psychology: The Science of Mind and Behaviour* (London: Hodder & Stoughton).

Mills, C. W. (1959) *The Sociological Imagination* (Oxford University Press).

Mitter, S. (1986) *Common Fate, Common Bond: Women in the Global Economy* (London: Pluto).

Modelski, G. (1972) *The Principles of World Politics* (New York: Free Press).

Moore, S. (1988) *Investigating Deviance* (London: Unwin Hyman).

Morgan, D. (1998) *The Focus Group Guidebook. Book 1. The Focus Group Kit* (Thousand Oaks, CA: Sage).

Morris (1993) cited by D. Abbott, in 'Family Conjugal Roles and the Labour Market', *Sociology Review* 4(1).

Morris, B. (2003) 'At the Michigan Womyn's Music Festival', *The Gay and Lesbian Review Worldwide* 10(5).

Morrison, D. (1994) 'From the Falklands to the Gulf – Doing Sociology and Reporting War', *Sociology Review* 3(3).

Mouzelis, N. (1992) 'Existing Socialism: Is It Marx's Fault?', *Sociology Review* 2(2).

New, C. (1994) 'Structuration Theory Revisited – Some Reflections on Agency', in *Resources for Sociology: The Best of Social Science Teacher*. Manchester: Association for the Teaching of the Social Sciences (ATSS).

Oakley, A, (1979) Becoming a Mother (Oxford: Martin Robertson).

Oakley, A. (1974) *The Sociology of Housework* (Oxford: Martin Robertson).

Oakley, A. (1980) *Women Confined* (Oxford: Martin Robertson).

Oakley, A. (1981) *From Here to Maternity* (Harmondsworth: Penguin).

Oakley, A. (2005) 'Gender, Women and Science', *Sociology Review* 15(2).

Oakley, Ann (2005) *The Ann Oakley Reader: Gender, Women and Social Science* (Bristol: Policy).

O'Brien, M. and Jones, D. (1996) 'Revisiting Family and Kinship', *Sociology Review* 5(3).

Organization for Security and Cooperation in Europe (OSCE) (1992) Helsinki Document: The Challenges of Change, chapter 6, para. 35, at: www.osce.org/documents/mcs/1992/07/4046_en.pdf (last accessed 13 July 2009).

Padfield, M. and Procter, I. (1996) 'The Effect of Interviewer's Gender on the Interviewing Process: A Comparative Enquiry', *Sociology* 30(2).

Parker, A. and Lyle, S. (2005) 'Chavs and Metrosexuals: New Men, Masculinities and Popular Culture', *Sociology Review* 15(1).

Parsons, T. (1937) *The Structure of Social Action* (New York: McGraw-Hill).

Parsons, T. (1951) *The Social System* (New York: Free Press).

Parsons, T. (1959) 'The Social Structure of the Family', in R. N. Ashen (ed.) *The Family: Its Functions and Destiny* (New York: Harper & Row).

Pascall, G. (1995) 'Women on Top? Women's Careers in the 1990s', *Sociology Review* 4(3).

Paterson, E. (1984) 'Food Work: Maids in a Hospital Kitchen', in N. Black *et al.* (eds) *Health and Disease: A Reader* (Milton Keynes: Open University Press).

Patrick, J. (1981) *A Glasgow Gang Observed* (London: Eyre Methuen).

Pawson, R. (1989) 'Methodology', in M. Haralambos (ed.) *Developments in Sociology*, vol. 5 (Ormskirk: Causeway).

Pawson, R. (1995) 'Methods of Content/Document/Media Analysis', in M. Haralambos (ed.) *Developments in Sociology*, vol. 11 (Ormskirk: Causeway).

Payne, G., Williams, M. and Chamberlain, S. (2004) 'Methodological Pluralism in British Sociology', *Sociology* 38(1).

Perlmutter, H. V. (1991) 'On the Rocky Road to the First Global Civilisation', *Human Relations* 44(9).

Philo, G. (1990) *Seeing and Believing* (London: Routledge).

Philo, G. and Berry, M. (2004) *Bad News from Israel* (London: Pluto).

Philo, G. and Miller, D. (2002) 'Circuits of Communication and Power: Recent Developments in Media Sociology', in M. Holborn (ed.) *Developments in Sociology* (Ormskirk: Causeway).

Phoenix, A. (1988) 'The Afro-Caribbean Myth', *New Society*, 4 March.

Piaget, J. (1973) *The Child's Conception of the World* (London: Paladin).

Pilcher, J. (1993) ' "I'm Not a Feminist, But...": Understanding Feminism', *Sociology Review* 3(2).

Pilcher, J. (1995) 'Growing Up and Growing Older: The Sociology of Age', *Sociology Review* 5(1).

Pink, S. (2001) *Doing Visual Ethnography* (London: Sage).

Piontek, T. (2006) *Queering Gay and Lesbian Studies* (Urbana: University of Illinois Press).

Pitts, M. and Phillips, K. (eds) (1991) *The Psychology of Health* (London: Routledge).

Platt, J. (1993) 'Case Studies: Their Uses and Limits', *Sociology Review* 2(3).

Plummer, K. (1975) Sexual Stigma: An Interactionist Account (London: Routledge).

Plummer, K. (1981) *The Making of the Modern Homosexual* (London: Hutchinson).

Plummer, K. (1983) *Documents of Life: An Introduction to the Problems and Literature of a Humanistic Method* (London: Allen & Unwin).

Plummer, K. (1992) *Modern Homosexualities: Fragments of Lesbian and Gay Experience* (London: Routledge).

Plummer, K. (1995) *Telling Sexual Stories: Power, Change and Social Worlds* (London: Routledge).

Plummer, K. (2001) *Documents of Life 2* (London: Sage).

Pohl, F. (1976) *In the Problem Pit* (London: Corgi).

Popper, K. (1934) *The Logic of Scientific Discovery* (London: Hutchinson).

Reiner, R. (2000) *The Politics of the Police* (Oxford University Press).

Rhodes, P. (1994) 'Race-of-Interviewer Effects: A Brief Comment', *Sociology* 28(2).

Ritzer, G. (1992) *Sociological Theory* (New York: McGraw-Hill).

Ritzer, G. (2008) *Modern Sociological Theory* (New York: McGraw-Hill).

Roberts, H. (1991) *Doing Feminist Research* (London: Routledge).

Robertson, R. (1991) 'The Globalisation Paradigm', in D. G. Bromley (ed.) *Religion and the Social Order* (London: JAI).

Robins, K. (1997) 'What Is Globalisation?', *Sociology Review* 6(3).

Rose, D. and Gershuny, J. (1995) 'Social Surveys and Social Change', *Sociology Review* 4(4).

Rose, G. (2001) *Visual Methodologies: An Introduction to the Interpretation of Visual Materials* (London: Sage).

Rosenau, J. (1990) *Turbulence in World Politics* (Brighton: Harvester Wheatsheaf).

Rosenthal, R. and Jacobson, L. (1968) *Pygmalion in the Classroom* (New York: Holt, Rinehart & Winston).

Rubin, G. (1989) 'Thinking Sex: Notes for a Radical Theory of the Politics of Sexuality', in C. Vance (ed.) *Pleasure and Danger: Exploring Female Sexuality* (London: Pandora).

Rybas, N. and Gajjala, R. (2007) 'Developing Cyberethnographic Research Methods by Understanding Digitally Mediated Identities', *Forum: Qualitative Social Research* 8(3).

Sayer, R. A. (1992) *Method in Social Science: A Realist Approach* (London: Routledge).

Schlager, M. S. *et al.* (2009) 'Analyzing Online Teacher Networks: Cyber Networks Require Cyber Research Tools', *Journal of Teacher Education* 60(1).

Schutz, A. and Luckmann, T. (1973) *The Structure of the Life-World* (Evanston, IL: Northwestern University Press).

Scott, J. (1992) 'Key Thinkers: Anthony Giddens', *Sociology Review* 1(3).

Sedgewick, E. (1990) *Epistemology of the Closet* (Berkeley: University of California Press).

Seidman, S. and Alexander, J. (2001) *The New Social Theory Reader* (New York: Routledge).

Senior, M. (1996) 'Health, Illness and Postmodernism', *Sociology Review* 6(1).

Shakespeare, T. (2006) *Disability Rights and Wrongs* (London: Routledge).

Shaw, M. and Mitzen, P. (2007) 'Photography and Sociology', *Sociology Review* 16(4).

Sheehy, G. (1974) *Passages: Predictable Crises in Adult Life* (New York: Bantam).

Sieber, J. E. and Stanley, B. (1988) 'Ethical and Professional Dimensions of Socially Sensitive Research', *American Psychologist* 43(1).

Sim, A. (1994) 'Did You See "Witness"? The Myth of Amish Separatism', *Sociology Review* 3(3).

Simpson, M. (2007) 'Metrosexual Writings', at: www.marksimpson.com/pages/metrosexual.html (last accessed 7 July 2009).

Sklair, L. (1991) *Sociology of the Global System* (Brighton: Harvester Wheatsheaf).

Sklair, L. (1993) 'Going Global: Competing Models of Globalisation', *Sociology Review* 3(2).

Sklair, L. (2003) 'Sociology of the Global System', in F. Lechner and J. Boli (eds.) *The Globalization Reader* (Oxford: Blackwell).

Slattery, M. (1991) *Key Ideas in Sociology* (London: Macmillan).

Sloboda, J. (1985) *The Musical Mind: The Cognitive Psychology of Music* (Oxford: Clarendon Press).

Smith D. and Thomas, L. (1996) 'Jobs for Women Hit Record Level', *Sunday Times*, February.

Smith, D. (2005) *Institutional Ethnography: A Sociology for People* (Oxford: AltaMira).

Smith, D. E. (1990) *The Conceptual Practices of Power* (Toronto University Press).

Snow, D. (2007) 'Frame', in G. Ritzer (ed.) *The Blackwell Encyclopedia of Sociology* (Oxford: Blackwell).

Spybey, T. (1998) 'Globalisation or Imperialism?', *Sociology Review* 7(3).

Stainton-Rogers, W. (1991) *Explaining Health and Illness* (London: Harvester Wheatsheaf).

Stanley, L. and Wise, S. (1990) 'Method, Methodology and Epistemology in Feminist Research Processes', in L. Stanley (ed.) *Feminist Praxis: Research, Theory and Epistemology in Feminist Sociology* (London: Taylor & Francis).

Stein, A. and Plummer, K. (1994) ' "I Can't Even Think Straight": "Queer" Theory and the Missing Revolution in Sociology', *Sociological Theory* 12(2).

Stephenson, G. M. (1981) 'Intergroup Bargaining and Negotiation', in J. C. Turner and H. Giles (eds) *Intergroup Behaviour* (Oxford: Blackwell).

Stockman, N., Bonney, N. and Xuewen, S. (1992) 'Women's Work in China, Japan and Britain', *Sociology Review* 2(1).

Strinati, D. (1992) 'Postmodernism and Popular Culture', *Sociology Review* 1(4).

Sugrue, B. and Taylor, C. (1996) 'From Marx to Man. City', *Sociology Review* 6(1).

Sullivan. N. (2003) *A Critical Introduction to Queer Theory* (New York University Press).

Swale, J. (2006) Meet the 'NEETS': Media Accounts of the Underclass Debate', *Sociology Review* 15(3).

Sweetman, P. (2000) 'Anchoring the (Postmodern) Self? Body Modification, Fashion and Identity', in M. Featherstone (ed.) *Body Modification* (London: Sage).

Sweetman, P. and Knowles, C. (eds.) (2004) *Picturing the Social Landscape: Visual Methods and the Sociological Imagination* (London: Routledge).

Swingewood, A. (2000) *A Short History of Sociological Thought*, 3rd edn. (New York: St Martin's Press).

Tashakkori, A. and Cresswell, J. W. (2007) 'The New Era of Mixed Methods', *Journal of Mixed Methods Research* 1(1).

Tattersall, M. (1997) 'From Punk to Pastiche: Are Oasis Postmodernists?', *Sociology Review* 6(3).

Taylor, I. (1994) 'The Gun Club: Men, Firearms and the New Economic Order', *Sociology Review* 3(4).

Taylor, S. (1982) *Durkheim and the Study of Suicide* (Basingstoke: Macmillan).

Taylor, S. (1989) *Suicide* (London: Longman).

Taylor, S. (1990) 'Beyond Durkheim: Sociology and Suicide', *Social Studies Review* 6(2).

Thibaut, J. and Kelley, H. (1959) *The Social Psychology of Groups* (New York: Wiley).

Thompson, K. (1992) 'Social Pluralism and Postmodernity', in S. Hall, D. Held and T. McGrew *Modernity and Its Futures* (Cambridge: Polity/Open University).

Thompson, K. (2007) 'Radical Theory and 9/11', *Sociology Review* 16(3).

Toynbee, P. (2008) 'Signs of Progress at Last, but Profound Inequality Remains', *Guardian* 4 November.

Trowler P. (1991) *Investigating the Media* (London: Collins).

Turkle, S. (1996) *Life on the Screen: Identity in the Age of the Internet* (London: Weidenfeld & Nicholson).

Turner, J. and Maryanski, A. (1979) *Functionalism* (Menlo Park, CA: Benjamin/Cummings).

Urry, J. (2003) 'Social Networks, Travel and Talk', *British Journal of Sociology* 54(2).

Van den Haag (1975) *Punishing Criminals* (New York: Basic Books).

Varadarajan, T. (1996) 'How Children Instinctively Know the Laws of Language', *Times* 21 February.

Vygotsky, L. (1962) *Thought and Language* (Cambridge, MA: MIT Press).

Wagg, S. (1992) 'I Blame The Parents: Childhood and Politics in Modern Britain', *Sociology Review* 1(4).

Walby, S. (1988) 'Gender, Politics and Social Theory', *Sociology* 22.

Walby, S. (1994) 'Post-Postmodernism? Theorising Gender', *The Polity Reader in Social Theory* (Cambridge: Polity).

Wallerstein, I. (1984) 'Patterns and Perspectives of the Capitalist World-Economy', in *The Politics of the World-Economy* (Cambridge: Cambridge University Press).

Wallerstein, I. (1991) 'The Lessons of the 1980s', *Geopolitics and Geoculture* (Cambridge: Cambridge University Press).

Walster, E., Walster, G. and Bercheid, E. (1978) *Equity: Theory and Research* (Boston, MA: Allyn & Bacon).

Ward, K. J. (1999) 'The Cyber-Ethnographic (Re)Construction of Two Feminist Online Communities', *Sociological Research Online* 4.

Ward, T. (1997) 'A Three Way Split? The 30–30–40 Thesis', *Sociology Review* 6(3).

Warde, A. (1989) 'The Future of Work', *Social Studies Review* 5(1).

Warren, C. A. B. (1988) *Gender Issues in Field Research* (Newbury Park, CA: Sage).

Weber, M. (1903–1917/1949) *The Methodology of the Social Sciences*, ed. E. Shils and H. Finch (New York: Free Press).

Weber, M. (1904–1905/1958) *The Protestant Ethic and the Spirit of Capitalism* (New York: Scribner's).

Weber, M. (1921/1968) *Economy and Society* (Totowa, NJ: Bedminster).

Weber, M. (1927/1981) *General Economic History* (New Brunswick, NJ: Transaction).

Weeks, D. and James, J. (1995) *Eccentrics: A Study of Sanity and Strangeness* (New York: Kodansha).

Wellman, B. and Haythornthwaite, C. (eds) (2002) *The Internet in Everyday Life* (Oxford: Blackwell).

Werbner, P. (1992) 'Social Networks and the Gift Economy Among British Pakistanis', *Sociology Review* 1(3).

Westwood, S. (1984) *All Day, Every Day: Factory and Family in the Making of Women's Lives* (London: Pluto).

Whorf, B. L. (1941) 'The Relation of Habitual Thought and Behavior to Language', in L. Spier (ed.) *Language Culture and Personality* (Provo: University of Utah Press).

Whyte, W. F. (1993) *Street Corner Society: The Social Structure of an Italian Slum* (University of Chicago Press).

Wilkinson, H. (1994) *No Turning Back: Generations and the Genderquake* (London: Demos).

Williams, J. (1995) 'In Focus: Single Parents', *Sociology Review* 4(4).

Williams, J., Dunning, E. and Murphy, P. (1984) *Hooligans Abroad: The Behaviour and Control of English Fans in Continental Europe* (London: Routledge).

Willis, P. (1977) *Learning to Labour* (Farnborough: Saxon House).

Willmott, P. (1987) *Friendship Networks and Social Support* (London: Policy Studies Institute).

Wilson, J. Q. (1977) *Thinking About Crime* (New York: Random House).

Winlow, S. (2001) *Badfellas: Crime, Tradition and New Masculinities* (Oxford: Berg).

Winnett, R. (2005) 'Meet the NEETS', *Sunday Times* 27 March.

Wood, E. M. (1986) *The Retreat from Class: A New 'True' Socialism* (London: Verso).

Young, M. and Willmott, P. (1961) *Family and Kinship in East London* (Harmondsworth: Penguin).

Young, M. and Willmott, P. (1975) *The Symmetrical Family* (Harmondsworth: Penguin).

Index

Access 265
Achievement 40
Act 49
Action 8, 41, 42, 43, 51, 60, 95, 160,
    165ff, 167, 170f, 173, 203, 288, 291,
    326, 376
Actor-network theory 174
Actors 40, 49ff, 52, 107, 171, 174, 193,
    267, 378
Adaptation 38, 57
Advertising 51, 134, 179, 181, 275, 280,
    301, 302
Age 62, 70, 81, 150, 205, 276, 300, 328,
    336, 343, 345, 355f
Agency 169, 172, 199, 204
Agenda-setting 276
Alienation 9, 10, 12, 18, 125
Allocation function 40
Al-Qaeda 14f, 31
Altruistic suicide 111
Animal rights 30
Anomic suicide 111
Anomie 125
Anonymity 290, 347
Anorexia 200f
Anti-feminist backlash 142, 144
Anti-positivism 80, 84, 110ff, 123, 177,
    217, 221, 231, 245, 247, 251, 254, 256,
    267, 291, 298, 367, 376, 377ff
Anti-structuralism 160, 161ff
Architecture 177, 180
Art 15, 177, 179, 180
Artificiality 241, 245, 262, 368
Attitudes 34, 74, 97, 273, 285, 300, 343,
    364, 369
Attrition rate 296
Audience 276
Authority 29, 47, 74, 135, 170, 260, 383
Autobiography 297, 298
Automation 12
Autonomy 37, 201f

Behaviour 4, 29, 39, 41, 50, 51, 53, 58, 60,
    74, 96, 106, 112, 115, 125, 244, 283,
    291, 296, 301, 327, 365, 376, 378
Behaviourism 49
Beliefs 74, 97, 170, 305, 323, 343
Bias 4, 20, 216, 227, 276, 277, 284, 287,
    323, 329, 344
Bifurcated world 197
Biography 299
Biological explanations 149, 291, 356, 365
Black feminism 63, 77ff, 143
Black women 66
Body 149, 302
Boundaries 135, 143, 155, 178, 188, 196,
    247, 287, 386
Bourgeoisie 11, 13, 15, 16, 17, 18
Breaching experiments 58
Built environment 100f, 180
Bureaucracy 47, 164, 176

Capital 11
Capitalism 8f, 10ff, 14, 15, 16, 17f, 31,
    63f, 70, 76, 109, 125, 138,
    151, 272
Capitalist economies 11, 125, 176 191f
Capitalist world economy 196
Case studies 115, 271ff
Causality 44f
Cause-and-effect 218, 244, 334, 365, 367,
    375, 377
Change see Social change
Charismatic authority 47
Chavs 62, 130
Childcare 66, 141, 143
Chilling 331
Choice 119, 123, 170, 171, 178, 301
Choice of method 237, 262, 265,
    272, Ch. 9 passim
Church attendance 333
Circuit of communication 277
Citizenship 345
Class consciousness 14, 19

Class dealignment   46
Closed questions   251, 253
Codes   20, 51
Coercion   34, 162
Cohesion   39, 43, 92
Cohort studies   246, 247
Collective conscience   35, 125, 202
Colonialism   31, 192, 364
Commodities   10
Commodity fetishism   18
Commonsense knowledge   86, 97, 363, 365
Communication   27, 189, 203
Communism   13, 15, 16, 18f
Community   13, 190, 205, 285, 286f, 301, 338, 357
Community of fate   195
Comparative method   239, 270, 272, 289ff, 304, 320, 335, 357
Confidentiality   346
Conflict   7ff, 39, 41, 51, 165, 196
Conflict groups   29, 31
Conflict theory   28ff, 96, 99
Conformity   129
Confounding effect   242
Connotative code   276, 277
Consciousness   3, 9, 15, 20, 39, 53f, 57, 63, 367, 376
Consensus   7, 28, 34ff, 42, 331
Consensus theory   28, 32, 34ff
Consent   19
Conservative Party   34
Constraints   8, 51, 88, 104, 121, 165, 170, 171, 173, 323, 331, 350
Consumerism   13, 178, 193, 194, 280
Consumption   9, 13, 125, 176f, 181, 307
Contemporary Left   118, 119ff
Content analysis   218, 275, 276ff, 302, 311
Contingency   441, 43
Contradiction   11, 192
Control   214, 238, 241
Control group   242
Convenience sampling   227
Convergence theory   292
Conversation analysis   97, 300, 327
Correlations   218
Cosmopolitanism   see Global cosmopolitan culture
Covert observation   261, 265, 284, 345f
Creativity   9, 19
Credit crunch   11, 128
Crime   51, 119, 122, 126f, 130, 131, 150, 273, 282, 291, 327, 352, 357
Crisis of profitability   13
Critical race theory   118, 151f
Critical reflexivity   80
Critical theory   24ff, 99, 135, 285

Cross-cultural research   289, 290f, 293, 356, 358
Cross-sectional surveys   246, 289, 293
Crowd analysis   300
Cultural system   42
Culture   14, 24, 27, 32, 44, 65, 91, 93, 124, 149, 155, 174, 176, 180, 183, 186, 189, 193, 209, 211, 286, 287, 301, 332, 342
Culture industry   24, 25
Culture of dependency   127, 131
Culture of poverty   129
Culture of simulation   180
Customs   39
Cyberethnography   285ff, 288

Data   208, Ch. 6 *passim*
Data protection   331
Death of the subject   133f, 139, 233
Decentralization   15, 18
Decolonialism   152
Deconstruction   133, 233, 281
Deductive reasoning   363, 366, 377
Demand characteristics   245, 261
Democracy   15, 16, 34, 176, 339
Demographic data   356, 358
Demystification   382, 386
Denotative code   276, 277
Dependence   74, 127, 143
Dependent variable   238, 241, 243
Deprivation   127
Deserving poor   128
Desirability effect   254, 261
Determinism   23, 169, 171, 365, 367, 368
Deviance   119, 126, 150, 273, 291, 352
Dialectic   8, 17, 23, 27, 387
Diaries   86, 220, 273, 275, 297, 378
Difference   78, 135, 143, 218
Differentiation   328
Digital technology   301
Direct democracy   15, 16
Disability   277, 300
Disability theory   118, 156ff
Disciplinary society   162
Discipline   302
Discourse   90, 132, 136, 138, 139, 152, 154, 162ff, 299, 328
Discourse analysis   97
Discrimination   57, 74, 76, 125, 142, 143, 151, 157
Disorganized capitalism   145, 178
Dissonance   385
Diversity   121, 134, 143, 182
Division of labour   35
Divorce   129, 232
Documentary analysis   86, 275f, 283, 297ff, 311, 320
Domestic labour   64, 75, 293

Domestic role   70
Dominant groups   7, 28, 303
Dominant ideas/discourse   19, 90, 300, 355
Dominant paradigm   363
Dominant value system   42
Domination   23, 24, 28, 61ff, 77f, 102, 142, 285
Double burden   143
Dramaturgy   50
Dualism   171
Duality of structure   170ff
Dysfunction   43

Ecological validity   241, 244
Economic determinism   19, 23, 24, 73, 92
Economic globalisation   181, 190, 299
Economic power   15f, 196
Economy   91, 92, 95, 119, 124, 126, 152, 176, 185, 196
Education   23, 24, 36f, 40, 42, 77f, 90, 136, 140, 143, 149, 152, 154, 164, 172, 177, 183, 243f, 294, 307, 310f
Educational attainment   4, 232, 294
Effort bargaining   201
Egoistic suicide   111
Electronic interviews   287
Electronic questionnaires   287
Elites   16
Emancipation   17, 27, 62f, 68, 78
Embourgeoisement   273
Emotion work   64, 75f
Emotions   212
Empathy   217f, 260, 263, 297
Empirical evidence   86, 132f, 140, 272, 350, 363, 365
Empiricism   138, 373, 374, 382
Employment   65, 71, 72, 232, 257, 328
Empowerment   345, 351
Encoding   20, 337
Enlightenment   48, 175, 363, 372f
Environment   42, 47, 49, 97, 157, 365
Episodic characterization   85, 106
Epistemology   86f, 139, 140, 364, 367
Equality   61, 76, 141
Equality of opportunity   40f, 76
Equilibrium   38
Equity theory   202
Ethical obligations   346f
Ethics   240, 250, 255, 261, 267, 285, 288, 290, 323, 324, 329, 333, 345ff, 356, 378
Ethnic groups   4, 7, 143, 147, 149, 299, 305
Ethnicity   62, 70, 81, 125, 145, 149, 150, 205, 209, 276, 300, 328, 335f
Ethnography   50, 107, 154, 282ff, 288, 298
Ethnomethodology   57ff, 87, 96, 376

Ethnonationalism   152
Everyday life   2, 126, 139, 170, 204, 285
Evidence   84, 85f
Evolutionary view   84, 104ff, 247
Examinations   4, 41
Exchange value   10
Existentialism   163, 165
Experimental group   242
Experimenter expectancy   245
Experiments   58, 214, 224, 238ff, 354, 362, 366, 373, 377, 378
Exploitation   11, 13, 63, 66, 75, 77, 125, 148

Face-to-face questionnaires   248
Factor analysis   300
Facts   8
False consciousness   14, 15, 77
False culture   24
Falsification   369, 371
Falsity   86
Familial ideology   64
Family   13, 40, 42, 63f, 69, 91, 93, 112, 120f, 130f, 149, 151, 152, 154, 181, 205, 248, 293, 335
Family structure   121
Family values   131, 144
Fatalistic suicide   111
Feelings   14, 377
Female employment   74
Femininity   149, 151, 303
Feminism   7, 30, 61ff, 104, 135, 153, 179, 255, 284f, 297, 298, 303, 336
Fetishism   10
Field experiments   241
Fieldwork   354
Film   301
Focus groups   273, 301, 305f
Forbidden research terrains   331
Fordism   177, 183
Formal interviews   217, 255
Fragmentation   9, 13, 34, 48, 134, 136, 138, 145, 182, 196, 303, 306, 382, 386
Frame of understanding   51
Frankfurt School   24
Free market economy   18, 34, 93f
Free response questions   see Open-ended questions
Free will   169, 171, 367, 368
Freedom   35, 62, 374
Friendship   338
Functional prerequisites   91
Functionalism   34, 43, 48, 86, 87, 95, 327
Functions   3, 17, 38f, 40, 42, 88, 91
Funding   288, 306, 324, 330, 331, 333, 337, 338ff, 379

Gays   30, 147, 149, 154, 273, 285, 347f
Gender   51, 61ff, 125, 138 141ff, 145f, 152, 205, 232, 257, 277, 290, 300, 302, 310f, 328, 335, 343, 345, 357
Genderquake   142
Generalization   93, 133f, 146, 209f, 213, 216, 224, 233, 244, 245, 247, 248, 249, 253, 255, 272, 273, 274f, 333, 366, 368
Gestures   49
Global communications   285, 307
Global cosmopolitan culture   194, 299
Globalization   31f, 125, 146, 160, 184, 188ff, 246f, 270, 291, 299, 301, 357
Glocalization   192
Goal attainment   38
Goals   29, 46, 347
Governance   189
Grand theory   5
Great Depression   11
Gross Domestic Product   11f
Group effect   254
Group interviews   see Focus groups
Groups   see Social groups

Health   136, 140, 177, 207, 232, 245, 305
Hegemonic masculinity   149
Hegemony   19f, 213, 276
Here-and-now analysis   84, 106ff
Hermeneutics   387
Heterosexism   77
Heterosexuality   153
Heuristic tool   45
Hierarchies   70, 107, 191
Hierarchies of sex   154
High culture   137
High modernity   185
Higher education   142
Historical materialism   24
Holism   382
Homophobia   151, 348
Homosexuality   153, 262, 277, 331
Housework   80, 141, 285
Housing   152, 232
Human nature   364
Human rights   157, 196
Hyperlink analyses   287
Hypermasculinity   150
Hypotheses   5, 110f, 115, 213, 214, 239, 241, 265, 266, 281, 283f, 288, 293, 311, 343, 363, 366f, 369, 372, 375, 384
Hypothetico-deductive method   110, 364

'I'   50, 200
Ideal speech situation   28
Ideal type   35, 44f, 47
Ideas   19
Identity   3, 9, 32, 70, 97f, 108, 151, 152, 155, 163, 181, 190, 209, 233, 299, 303, 304, 343, 356
Ideography   367
Ideology   4, 15, 18, 19, 20, 23, 27, 32, 33, 43, 63f, 68, 73, 124f, 132, 138, 142, 157, 177, 193, 302, 368
Images   276
Imperialism   31, 77, 152
Incarceration   51
Independent variable   238, 241, 243
In-depth interviews   326, 356
Individuals   9f, 14, 29, 40f, 49ff, 85, 95, 96, 119, 124, 166, 174, 182, 202, 205, 247, 289, 301, 373, 377
Inductive reasoning   363, 366, 377
Industrial society   88, 191
Industrialization   72, 102, 292
Inequality   15f, 17, 19, 31, 142f, 146
Inferential statistics   218
Informal interviews   217, 256, 273, 357
Information and communication technology   5, 104, 183, 194, 218, 246, 293, 306ff, 311, 340, 384
Informed consent   331, 347
Insight   274, 294, 300, 326, 333, 337, 345, 346, 378
Institution   see Social Institutions
Integration   39, 79, 112
Intelligence   49
Interaction   4, 37, 97, 106, 109, 124, 245, 285, 301, 376
Interactionism   41, 50, 58, 99, 326, 353
Interest groups   29, 31
Internalization   36, 41, 262
Internet   285, 301, 306
Interpretation   7, 44ff
Interpretive sociology   49ff, 87, 133, 203, 239, 288, 291, 297
Intersubjectivity   52
Interview schedule   215
Interview transcripts   218, 260, 274
Interviews   73, 80, 86, 100, 210, 211, 214, 218, 250, 251, 254ff, 283, 286, 294, 296, 300, 303, 305, 335f, 337f, 345, 351f, 355
Intimacy   75, 199, 201f
Intuition   377

Journals   275, 311
Justice   61, 63

Kinship   90
Knowledge   17, 27, 28, 48, 54f, 58, 70, 79,
    86, 125, 132ff, 139, 146, 161ff, 176,
    189, 228, 231, 233f, 281, 285, 299, 329,
    336, 339, 342, 361, 362, 364, 369, 372,
    381, 386

Labelling   51, 119, 149, 262, 331
Laboratory experiments   214, 238, 239f,
    261, 364, 368, 371
Labour   9, 10, 17
Labour market   73, 74, 77, 142, 153, 292
Labour Party   34
Labour power   12, 13
Labour process   9
Laddettes   147
Laddism   62, 148
Language   53, 88f, 97, 132, 139, 152, 157,
    161ff, 166f, 168, 208, 305, 328, 342
Late capitalism   184
Late modern society   201, 301
Latency   39
Law   15, 35, 62, 90, 152, 169, 331
Legislation   76, 345
Legitimation   27, 29, 55, 57, 64, 151
Letters   297, 298f, 378
Liberal feminism   63, 73ff, 104
Life histories/stories   271, 289, 297, 298f,
    300
Lifestyle   205, 252, 304
Life-world   53f
Living standards   11, 13
Local   189
Location   70
Lone-parent families   121, 129, 130, 230
Longitudinal studies   246, 289, 294ff, 350

Macro analysis   33, 38, 41, 44, 47f, 50, 57,
    62, 66, 73, 93, 99, 119, 220, 246, 247,
    291, 319, 326, 353
Malestream knowledge   77, 78f
Manual workers   34, 273
Mapping exercises   287
Marginalization   57, 70, 129, 147, 155,
    203, 331
Market forces   340
Marriage   74, 205
Marxism   7, 8ff, 23, 48, 86, 92, 95, 135,
    146, 147, 184, 327
Marxist feminism   63ff, 151
Masculinity   62, 148ff, 285, 303, 357
Mass culture   26, 179
Mass media   16, 20f, 39, 46, 74, 76, 130,
    134, 136, 141, 147, 149, 180f, 182, 193,
    203, 213, 230, 275, 279, 303,
    343, 347

Mass production   9, 176, 177
McDonaldization   31
'Me'   50, 200
Meaning   7, 44ff, 97, 99f, 106, 133, 267,
    303, 326, 387
Means of production   13, 16, 23
Mechanistic solidarity   35
Media   see Mass media
Mediation   40, 152
Medical model   156
Men   7, 20, 61ff, 101f, 145, 153, 213, 297,
    302, 335f, 347f, 357, 363
Metanarratives   48, 133ff, 139, 145, 180,
    233f, 298, 301, 383, 386, 388
Methodological pluralism   223, 258, 279,
    288, 323, 354, 388
Methodology   5f, 110, 113, 124, Chs 6,
    7, 8, 9 *passim*
Metrosexuals   62, 148
Micro analysis   33, 37, 41, 44, 45, 47f, 57,
    62, 99, 119, 221, 246, 247, 255, 301,
    319, 326, 353
Middle class   20, 73, 150, 213
Mixed-methods approaches   354ff
Mobility   189, 291, 294f
Model   4, 120, 123, 166
Modernization   55
Modernism   48, 84, 85ff, 132f, 139ff, 145,
    233, 382
Modernity   132, 160, 175ff, 300, 373, 381
Monarchy   3, 186f
Monism   383
Monogamy   63
Moral panics   55f, 289
Morality   35, 36, 63, 129, 203, 323, 333
Motivation   119, 203, 301, 378
Mysticism   382f

Narratives   139, 162, 273, 303, 388
Nationalism   192
Nation-states   176, 187, 190f, 195, 198,
    247, 371
Natural experiments   243
Natural sciences   85, 124, 174, 362,
    381, 385
Natural world   115, 363, 375, 377f, 383
NEETs   130
Neo-colonialism   152
Neo-conservatism   178
Neofunctionalism   41, 43
Neo-Marxism   7, 19ff, 184
Nesting   77
Networks   174, 175, 197, 273, 285
New global culture   197
New imperialism   31, 192
New international division of labour   188
New man   148

New modernity   204
New Religious Movements   31
New Right   2, 118, 127ff
New Social Movements   30, 46f
New technology   275, 278, 291
New Times   184
New tribe   130
News values   20
Newspapers   275
Nominalism   367
Nomothetic approach   365, 367, 368
Non-participant observation   210, 261, 342f
Non-random sampling   226f
Norms   29, 35, 38, 39, 58, 149, 153, 267, 291, 305
Novels   378

Objective knowledge   162ff, 233, 239
Objective social class   291
Objectivity   45, 61, 86, 111, 115, 132f, 140, 216, 255, 260, 284, 288, 343, 345, 355, 364f, 372, 376, 379, 382
Observation   50, 60, 86, 126, 218, 250, 251, 261ff, 283, 286, 326, 343, 351, 354, 355, 362, 366, 369, 375, 378
Official statistics   86, 112, 115, 232, 275, 283, 326
Old people   7, 206, 277, 357
Old social movements   31
Oligarchy   16, 17
One-dimensional culture   24f
One-parent families   see Lone-parent families
Ontological security   170, 205
Ontology   364, 367
Open-ended questions   217, 251, 253, 254
Opportunity sampling   248
Oral history   218, 297, 299
Organic solidarity   35
Organizations   8, 29, 47, 136
Overt observation   261, 284

Paradigm   355, 369, 371, 379
Parity of esteem   76
Participant observation   107, 261, 271, 273, 342, 355, 356, 357
Partisan dealignment   46f
Party   46
PASW   312ff
Pathology   36, 130
Patriarchy   63, 66ff, 76, 138, 142, 145
Patrilineal descent   63
Patterns   4, 41, 53, 58, 74, 103, 152, 170, 209, 244, 245, 247, 289, 292, 295, 338
Perceptions   14
Personal characteristics   342ff

Personal documents   220, 275, 354, 356
Personality system   42
Perspectives   4, 48, 62, 84f, 323, 327, 329, 379
Phenomenology   52ff, 96, 115, 147, 229, 234, 327, 376
Philosophy   15, 86, 88, 124
Photographs   220, 301, 302
Pluralism   15, 17, 18
Polarization   94
Policing   20, 105, 284, 328, 337, 347
Political apathy   15, 16
Politics   15, 90, 124, 126, 176, 186, 232
Polysemic   303
Popular culture   10, 134, 136, 150, 180f, 279, 299
Population   209, 213, 216, 224, 225f, 247, 248, 253
Positivism   84, 110ff, 123f, 133, 216, 217, 228, 231, 239, 247, 254, 260, 272, 288, 291, 298, 327, Ch. 10 *passim*
Postal questionnaires   248, 250
Postfeminism   118, 141ff
Postfordism   178
Post-industrial society   191
Post-international politics   191
Post-Marxism   19, 34, 151
Postmodernism   2, 10, 48, 81, 84, 85ff, 118, 132ff, 145, 160, 161, 165ff, 233f, 279, 284, 298, 299, 303, 307ff, 357, 361, 381ff, 383ff
Postsocial   175
Poststructuralism   132, 151, 160, 161ff, 284, 301
Poverty   31, 94, 127, 131, 226f, 232
Power   7, 14, 15, 17, 27, 28, 29, 41, 43, 46, 51, 61ff, 107, 124f, 138, 144, 149, 151, 152, 154, 162ff, 170, 173, 191, 197, 202, 231, 239, 300, 302, 303
Powerlessness   74, 80, 162, 172
Practical factors   256, 267, 323, 324, 328, 330ff
Practical intelligence   53
Pragmatism   49
Pre-coded responses   250, 253
Predictability   365, 368, 377, 384
Pre-industrial society   88
Prejudice   57, 74, 345
Primary methods/data   86, 212, 218f, 245, 279, 326
Primitive society   9, 35, 36
Principle of parsimony   366
Privacy   218, 261, 347
Private ownership   18, 125, 128
Private sphere   71, 74, 102, 143, 147
Privatization   164, 177
Production process   9, 12f

Productivity   9
Profit   10, 11f, 13, 196
Progress   373
Proletariat   11, 13, 15, 18, 19, 24
Protocol analysis   300
Public sphere   71, 74, 102, 147
Purposive sampling   305

Q-methodology   300
Qualitative methods/data   50, 80, 86, 217,
    221f, 245, 247, 266f, 270, 271, 275f,
    283, 287, 288, 296, 300ff, 328, 337ff,
    354f
Quantitative methods/data   86, 220, 246f,
    254, 266f, 270, 271, 275f, 283, 287,
    288, 296, 310, 328, 333, 337ff, 354f
Quasi-groups   29f
Queer theory   118, 152ff
Questionnaires   5, 86, 210, 214, 218, 221,
    222, 247, 248ff, 258, 260, 283, 294,
    296, 303, 305, 351f, 355, 356
Questions   73, 102, 248ff, 251, 259
Quota sampling   226, 248, 249f

Race   70, 145f, 151f, 328, 345, 364
Racism   70, 74, 77, 138, 143, 145, 151f
Radical feminism   63, 66ff, 147, 153
Radical modernity   184
Random sampling   225, 248, 249f, 275
Rape   144, 148, 153
Rapport   260, 336, 337
Rationalization   25, 47, 164
Rationality   20, 25, 28, 176, 177, 369, 373,
    378, 382
Rational-legal authority   47
Real world   2f, 89, 228, 241
Realism   115, 118, 123ff, 196, 216, 217,
    301, 364, 367, 379f
Recession   11f, 31, 57
Recipes   53
Reflexivity   50, 51, 57, 146, 170, 182, 200,
    202, 205, 301, 306
Regularities   4
Regulation   36, 331
Reification   11, 18, 37, 55, 57, 98
Relations of ruling   147
Relationships   see Social relationships
Relativism   86, 133, 140f, 162, 233, 332
Reliability   209f, 213, 215, 220, 221, Ch. 7
    passim, 288, 290, 295, 298, 376, 379
Religion   15, 36, 62, 90, 112, 124, 126,
    152, 172, 176, 181, 194, 234, 257, 333
Replication   209f, 215, 220, 221, 239, 242,
    255, 279, 306, 310, 366, 368, 376, 377,
    379
Representations   3, 284, 286, 299

Representativeness   213f, 216, 227, 255,
    258, 265, 272, 274, 290, 295, 296, 298,
    306
Reproduction   12, 24, 92, 169f, 200
Research   34, 58, 110, 138, Chs 6, 7, 8, 9
    passim
Research aim   333ff
Research log/diary   261, 266, 278ff, 311
Reserve army of labour   64
Resistance   13, 191
Resources   169f, 337
Response rate   254
Reverse colonialism   194
Revolution   8, 13, 15, 18, 19, 23, 27, 68
Rights   62
Risk society   160, 189, 204ff
Rituals   35, 39
Role   3, 8, 12, 38, 39, 40f, 65, 92, 95, 96,
    142, 149, 191, 202, 290, 302, 310f
Role model   148, 149
Role performance   39
Role strain   107
Routines   4, 169
Rules   34, 44, 52, 58, 60, 99, 152, 163,
    166f, 169, 327
Ruling class   15, 20, 23, 27, 43, 147
Runaway world   197

Sample frame   224
Sample size   224f
Sampling   208, 213, 214, 216, 218, 220,
    223ff, 248, 253, 274, 286, 290, 293, 349
Scapegoating   56, 131, 144
Schema   51, 53
Science   8, 60, 68, 110, 113, 114, 126, 140,
    176, 177, 204, 238, 299, 326, Ch. 10
    passim
Scientific malpractice   370f
Scientific method   37, 45, 48, 50, 80, 113,
    115, 214, 238, 244, 299, 306, Ch. 10
    passim
Secondary methods/data   86, 212, 219f,
    246, 247, 275, 279, 294, 326, 328, 356,
    357
Secular postmodernism   382
Selection function   41
Self   49f, 160, 199ff, 202, 204, 216, 286f,
    301
Self-ethnography   343
Self-realization   202
Self-selecting samples   227, 248, 349
Semiology   26, 174, 276, 277, 302
Semi-structured interviews   215, 256, 286,
    335f, 351
Semi-structured questionnaires   248, 251,
    253
Sensitive topics   331f

Separatism   69, 79
Sexism   74, 76, 79, 151, 310f
Sexual division of labour   74, 151
Sexual preference   70
Sexuality   62, 150, 152, 154, 205, 277, 347f
Signifier   25, 145, 276
Signs   180, 276, 280
Skills   41, 342
Snowball sampling   227, 248
Social action   7, 41, 44ff, 57, 84, 96ff, 106f, 325
Social authoritarianism   129
Social capital   287
Social change   8, 17, 19, 27, 28, 29, 33, 35, 38, 45, 51, 77, 88, 95, 104, 133, 182, 247, 303, 328
Social class   7, 13, 34, 45f, 62, 64, 70, 81, 125, 129, 145f, 147, 150, 152, 181, 184, 204, 205, 276, 300, 328
Social construction   53, 86, 98, 139, 151, 155, 231f, 233, 291, 301f, 356
Social control   39, 67
Social engineering   104
Social exchange   202
Social fabrications   382
Social fact   35, 37, 113, 162, 208, 209, 220, 221, 228ff, 247, 282, 327
Social groups   4, 28, 289, 295, 378
Social honour   45
Social institutions   3, 38, 55, 105, 123, 125, 152, 376
Social model of disability   157
Social networking technology   286
Social order   28, 35, 38, 40, 41, 385
Social policy   4, 76, 94, 127f, 140, 232, 245, 351
Social problem   56, 131, 133, 139, 232, 244
Social relationships   3, 8, 12ff, 17, 27, 36, 47, 201
Social science   341
Social solidarity   35f
Social stability   33, 36, 92, 181
Social structure   7, 8f, 10ff, 15f, 17, 19, 27, 29, 34, 36, 38, 47, 49, 51, 55, 85, 91, 105, 123, 133, 160, 163, 165ff, 199, 204, 373, 377
Social surveys   218, 234f, 245ff, 275, 326, 338, 354
Social system   40, 42, 91, 95, 171
Social world   44, 49ff, 52, 58, 85, 93, 97, 106, 115, 132, 139, 162, 182, 283, 342, 375, 377f, 381, 385
Socialization   36, 39, 40, 41, 74, 92, 149
Socialism   18, 23, 184
Socialist feminism   63, 70ff

Society   3, 34, 40f, 42, 49ff, 86, 119, 124, 133, 160, 166, 195, 198, 199ff, 204, 205
Sociogram   297
Sociological imagination   124f, 306
Sociology as a science Ch. 10 *passim*
Space   99f, 101f, 137, 180
Specialization   9, 12
Sport   193
Stabilization   40
Standardization   214f, 256, 260, 338, 376
State   16, 20, 46, 128, 129, 136, 147, 177, 183, 191, 198, 331
Statistical significance   218, 246
Statistics   4, 86, 140, 218, 220f, 228, 231, 233, 251, 271, 281, 306, 310ff, 312ff, 327, 357
Status   45f, 70, 107, 149, 150, 239, 371
Stereotyping   57, 131, 148f, 157, 264, 277, 345, 355
Stigma   51
Stratification   42, 45f, 154, 291
Stratified sampling   226f, 248
Street crime   129
Structural functionalism   28, 33, 34, 38ff, 43, 45, 57, 90, 96, 99, 376
Structuralism   84, 87ff, 105, 119, 164, 291, 319, 325, 326f, 353, 376
Structuration theory   99, 160, 165ff, 203, 301
Structure   *see* Social structure
Structured interview   245f, 255
Structured questionnaire   245, 248, 250, 326
Style   137, 177, 183, 280
Subject   162, 287
Subjective social class   291
Subjectivity   61, 115, 163, 216, 217f, 260, 263, 267, 282, 288, 323, 329, 355, 367, 376, 382
Subordinate groups   7, 62ff
Subordinate masculinity   149
Subordination   62, 63, 69, 107, 151, 153
Suicide   36, 37, 110ff, 291, 327, 376
Suicide rate   113
Superstructure   15
Surplus capital   10
Surveys   *see* Social surveys
Symbolic annihilation   74
Symbolic interactionism   42, 44, 48ff, 87, 96, 199, 200, 376
Symbols   40, 52, 366
System maintenance   15, 38f, 40, 169
Systematic sampling   225

Talent   41
Tapes   218

Technocratic thinking   25
Technology   177, 191, 195, 205
Technology of disciplinary power   163
Television   301
Terrorism   14, 31
Texts   135, 138, 276, 302
Thematic analysis   300
Theoretical considerations   324ff
Theories of sexuality   118, 152ff
Theory Chs   1, 2, 3, 4, 5 *passim*
Third-phase capitalism   184
Third-wave feminism   77
Time   137, 247, 289, 304, 337f
Toleration   374
Topic of study   330ff
Total institutions   51
Trade unions   30, 46, 144, 181
Tradition   39, 186, 301
Traditional authority   47
Tragedy/charity model   156
Transgression   150
Transnational capitalist class   193
Transnational corporations   188, 191f, 193, 196
Transnational movements   191
Trends   209, 245, 247, 295, 338
Triad of disadvantage   77
Triangulation   223, 258, 278f, 354f
Triple shift   75
Truth   86, 141, 211, 233f, 239, 262, 279, 285, 299, 371, 381, 382
Typifications   53
Typology   363

Unanticipated consequences   171
Uncertainty   368
Underachievement   4, 129
Underclass   129, 130
Undeserving poor   128
Unemployment   14, 73, 129, 232
Universal laws   4, 115, 244, 364, 366, 367, 373, 381
Universal welfare provision   129, 131
Universes of meaning   231, 233

Unobtrusive methods   354
Unstructured interviews   218, 246, 355
Unstructured questionnaires   248, 251, 326
Use value   10
Utopia   28

Validity   132, 211ff, 217f, 221, 233, 238, Ch.7 *passim*, 274f, 286, 288, 290, 295, 305, 345, 352, 354, 378
Value consensus   40, 43
Value-freedom   45, 115, 132, 216, 229, 244, 260, 323, 339, 345, 372, 379
Values   8, 14, 28, 31, 34, 35, 38, 39, 42, 44f, 115, 170, 267, 285, 300, 328, 364, 369
Variables   295, 310ff, 312ff
Verification   209, 366, 369
Verstehen   44f, 47, 99f
Videos   275, 283, 301
Violence   67, 141, 151, 153, 337, 357
Virtual communities   286
Virtual culture   285
Visual culture   303
Visual methodologies   301
Voluntarism   42

War on terror   14
Wealth   13, 125
Weberianism   48, 87, 133
Welfare   65, 127, 131, 140, 232
Welfare state   128, 129, 177, 183
White males   125
White women   73
Wild zones   205
Women   7, 24, 61ff, 101f, 145, 153, 277, 293, 297, 302, 328, 335f, 338, 347f, 357, 363
Work   53, 57, 141f, 149, 150, 155, 205, 335
Working class   4, 17, 24, 27, 34, 63, 130, 150, 248, 277, 357
World society   195, 198
World-systems theory   190

Young people   7, 206, 277

Titles in the
Skills-Based Sociology *series*

978-0-333-68763-5   978-0-230-21782-9   978-0-230-21781-2

*Designed to cover the key concepts, issues and
contemporary debates in Sociology*

978-0-333-96889-5   978-0-230-21792-8

To order visit www.palgrave.com